THE MAKING
OF THE
ANGLICAN CHURCH
WORLDWIDE

THE MAKING
OF THE
ANGLICAN CHURCH
WORLDWIDE

W. M. Jacob

*In thanksgiving for the work of
Lincoln Theological College 1874–1996
and for its staff and students who have served
the Anglican Communion as
archbishops, bishops, priests, deacons and lay people.*

First published in Great Britain 1997
Society for Promoting Christian Knowledge
Holy Trinity Church
Marylebone Road
London NW1 4DU

British Library Cataloguing-in-Publication Data

A catalogue record of this book is available from
the British Library

ISBN 0-281-05043-0

Typeset by
Pioneer Associates, Perthshire, Scotland
Printed in Great Britain by
Arrowsmiths Ltd, Bristol

Contents

Abbreviations

CMS	Church Missionary Society
JEH	*Journal of Ecclesiastical History*
Prayer Book	Book of Common Prayer 1662
SCH	*Studies in Church History*
SPCK	Society for Promoting Christian Knowledge
SPG	Society for the Propagation of the Gospel in Foreign Parts

Countries, towns and churches are normally referred to by the names which contemporaries would have used, e.g. Ceylon rather than Sri Lanka. Hence also

PECUSA	Protestant Episcopal Church of the United States of America

Unless otherwise specified the place of publication of all books cited is London.

Preface

The Anglican Communion has received little attention from historians in England or elsewhere. The standard histories of Christianity in England in the nineteenth and twentieth centuries make few, if any, references to the overseas episcopate, the Lambeth Conferences, or to the Anglican Communion. This book sets out to remedy this omission. Its aim is to help anyone who is interested in Anglicanism and the Anglican Communion to know more about how Anglicanism evolved into a world-wide Communion, and how and why it has the form and structures it has. It is a history, not a theology, of the Anglican Communion. It is an account of the reform of the Church in the British Isles in the sixteenth century, and of how that reformed, episcopal Church spread overseas, through the colonization of parts of North America, Australia and New Zealand, and of how it was planted in Africa and Asia and elsewhere by missionaries. By providing an outline of the spread of Anglicanism across the world, it is hoped to provide theologians with raw material for considering further the nature of Anglicanism, and its contribution to understandings of the nature of the Church, and of ministry and authority in the Church.

It is hoped that a clearer understanding of the past will help people to do better theology in the present and the future. Too many churches in the late twentieth century limit their concern with the past to popular myths about the glories or disasters of the past, and fail to be aware that many of these myths are themselves theological or apologetic constructs which require careful re-examination to prevent them from misdirecting contemporary theology.

The resources used in writing this book have been drawn from libraries, and in particular from the library of Lincoln Theological College, which has illustrated the immense resources that a well-maintained theological college library offers the Church for theological and historical research. Caroline Dicker, the College Librarian has been of great assistance in seeking and finding material for me, and I have also called upon the assistance of the staff at the CMS Library at Partnership House, and of Lambeth Palace Library.

The impulse for writing this book came from an invitation from the Ming Hua College and Religious Education Resource Centre of the Anglican diocese of Hong Kong to give a series of lectures on the development of Anglicanism. I am grateful to the people who attended the lectures and who asked questions which prompted me to follow up new ideas and helped me to view Anglicanism from a less English perspective. I am grateful to the Bishop of Hong Kong, the Right Reverend Peter Kwong and his clergy who gave me much time and generous hospitality, and to the Reverend Lysta Leung, the vicar of St Peter's Church, North Point, who organized my visit. The bishops of the Church of England inadvertently provided me with a considerably lighter workload during the academic year 1995–1996, which made it possible for me to write this book during that year. Dr Nigel Yates and Canon Rex Davies, the Sub Dean of Lincoln Cathedral, and formerly of the staff of the World Council of Churches, read an earlier draft of the book, and I am grateful for their helpful and perceptive comments, which have considerably improved the book.

This book is dedicated to the memory of Lincoln Theological College because, as my research has progressed, I have become increasingly aware of how significant a contribution people who have been associated with the College have made to the Anglican Communion. Three of the originators of the College, Francis Massingberd, Christopher Wordsworth and E.W. Benson were promoters of the idea of a Lambeth Conference, and the latter two lived to play significant parts in successive Conferences. Two former Wardens went on to be bishops in overseas dioceses, and played significant parts in the development of the Communion, and many members of the teaching staff and students have worked in the Communion. Alas, the tradition of training for ordination at Lincoln has now ended.

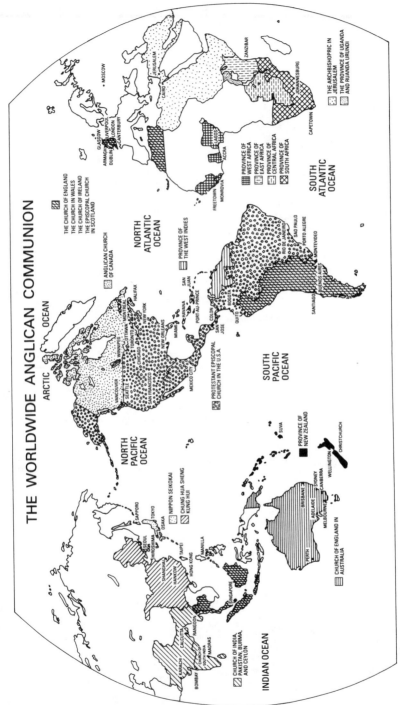

Introduction

The aim of this book is to describe the development of the Anglican Communion from its origins in the Reformation in the British Isles until 1960. The sixteenth-century Reformation is taken as the starting point because that was the point at which the Church in England separated from the Roman jurisdiction. It then assumed a distinctive form as a national, reformed church standing in the historic succession of the universal Church, reformed 'according to the model of the primitive Church'. It maintained the episcopal succession and the three orders of ministry and an ordered liturgy, and doctrines consonant with holy Scripture and the Ecumenical Councils. 1960 is taken as the end point, because it is the end of an important phase in the life of the Communion, in which the Communion achieved its present form as a multi-national and multi-racial association of episcopal churches in communion with the see of Canterbury. By 1960 it was clear that in the Anglican churches in Africa and Asia local leaders were assuming authority and that 'Anglican' could mean something more than 'English' or 'European'. Also during the 1960s the Communion began to develop more institutions to enable it to respond in a world of more rapid communication and new developments in the lives of the churches, for example ecumenical dialogue with the Roman Catholic Church, and the admission of women to holy orders.

This book is not intended to be an account of Anglican theology, or of the distinctiveness of Anglican thought or method. Many books have been written on these subjects in the past twenty years, and while this book may be seen as complementary, it should not be seen as one of them. No book that I am aware of has attempted to trace the evolution of the institutions of the Anglican Communion, which is what this book does. In

so far as institutions and structures influence thought, this book
may throw light on why Anglican thought and self-understanding
takes the forms it has, and so it may contribute to the discussion
of the nature of Anglicanism.

It is the contention of this book that the traditional threefold
ministry is the most distinctive institution of Anglicanism, and
so this book will be much preoccupied with bishops, and with
the establishment of Anglican dioceses around the world.
However, a distinctive feature of the English Reformation was
that it was a lay initiative, as well as a clerical initiative. Godly
princes, who saw themselves as successors to the kings of Israel
and to Constantine, believed that they had a God-given duty to
supervise and govern the Church, in order to ensure that bishops might properly undertake their spiritual duties, and on any
major decisions about the Church, godly princes associated with
themselves representatives of God's faithful people in Parliament.
Anglicanism has never been about unfettered episcopacy.

The story of Anglicanism is not therefore merely an account
of burgeoning numbers of bishops in communion with the
archbishop of Canterbury, nor a series of episcopal decisions, as
a result of which new dioceses and provinces have been created.
Nor, as is sometimes implied, is Anglicanism merely an aspect
of Englishness, that English people have transplanted wherever
they have settled, and which has been imposed as part of
colonial rule. Within the Anglican Communion bishops have
seldom acted entirely on their own, except, as in Scotland in the
eighteenth century, in emergency situations where persecution
might prevent more general consultations with the clergy and
the people. From its very beginnings Anglicanism has been
more than merely English; it took root in Wales, it took partial
root in Scotland in a modified form, and it took partial root in
Ireland. The examples of Scotland and Ireland in the sixteenth
and seventeenth centuries were important models for the
development of Anglicanism overseas in the eighteenth and
nineteenth centuries. The Episcopal Church in Scotland demonstrated that Anglicanism did not need to be identified with the
State in order to be able to survive. The example of Ireland
reminded Anglican strategists in the nineteenth century that,
for the Church in its Anglican form to flourish, it needed to be
identified with the local context, using the local language, and
recruiting its clergy locally.

The English reformers believed that they were purifying the Church of error and that they were identifying the Church with its roots. Their study of Scripture and the early Church convinced them that the decision-making processes of the Church should not merely be in the hands of the successors of the apostles, the bishops, but that representatives of the clergy should also be involved, and that representatives of the people of God too had a part to play. Because of the communitarian nature of the English State in the sixteenth century the representatives of the people of God insisted on signifying their approval of changes in the Church through the Crown-in-Parliament. In the Anglican dispensation the people of God, through the crown and their representatives in Parliament have always thus had an involvement in and a veto over decisions in the life of the Church.

In any organic and living institution there is development and change. As the social and political context has changed the Church has needed to adjust. This can be a painful process and there are likely to be tensions in an institution like the Church which includes people who believe that change should be viewed with caution and that all risks should be carefully weighed before any alterations are made, and also people who believe that radical review and dynamic reaction is of the essence of Christian discipleship. The development of the Anglican Communion is an account of how these tensions have been managed as the Anglican polity has been carried across the British Isles and across the world. Anglican churches are not centralized structures, so the spread of Anglicanism has not been systematic, it has been largely spontaneous and has been as much at the initiative of lay people as bishops and clergy. As we will see, where Anglicans travelled and settled, they took clergy with them. Part of the history of Anglicanism therefore is an account of the spread of British settlers and traders in North America, India, Australasia and South Africa. But part also is an account of missionary endeavours by small numbers of dedicated and determined people, fired by the conviction of the need to preach the gospel to those who had not had the opportunity to hear it, in order to free them from the slavery of sin and the sin of slavery, particularly in Africa and Asia, and of creating church structures appropriate to these contexts.

The Church, and least of all its Anglican manifestation, is not like a carefully pruned shrub, growing evenly and tidily on every side. Growth has been sporadic and untidy. There have been significant disagreements about how growth might be encouraged, or whether encouragement was necessary, and especially about the place of bishops in the life of the Church, and the institutions necessary to order and regulate a church, and about the relationships between dioceses and provinces.

Anglicans were living and working for 180 years in North America before they received direct episcopal ministrations. It took a constitutional revolt before the issue was settled that Anglican bishops did not require the lay element in their appointment to be through the Crown-in-Parliament, but by election by representatives of the laity, along with the clergy of a diocese, who, together with the bishop, took responsibility for ordering the life of the Church. Although this essentially congregationalist element, which was an adjustment to a new political and social context in the newly independent United States, was achieved in the late eighteenth century, it took another hundred years for such a pattern to begin to become acceptable in dioceses and provinces which remained under British rule.

This study will show that Anglicans have been very ambivalent in their attitudes to bishops and to the involvement of representatives of clergy and laity in the government of the Church. Surprisingly for an episcopal Church, bishops do not seem to have been viewed with much enthusiasm by the parishes they were sent to minister to in British North America, India, Australasia, South Africa and Europe. Where clergy and congregations were established they were not necessarily pleased to have their freedom restrained, or their links with 'the mother country' broken, by the creation of a new local diocese. As Anglican congregations in the United States, Australia and South Africa became used to paying for their church and their clergy they became resistant to the interference of a bishop for whom they suspected, they would also end up paying. Governors of colonies also resented the fact that bishops had often been allocated part of what had previously been their jurisdiction for recruiting, instituting and disciplining clergy.

Missionary societies had a significant involvement in supporting the spread of Anglicanism and they too found it difficult to adjust to the presence of bishops in their spheres of influence, claiming to license and direct the work of missionaries whom the societies had recruited and were paying, and whom the societies had previously directed. Apart from such practical matters there could also be major theological differences between bishops and missionary societies about the nature and ordering of the Church. Although there was considerable common ground between many of the traditional High Churchmen among the bishops and some of the missionary societies, there could be considerable tensions between some bishops, including evangelical bishops, and the evangelical missionary societies.

In fact many of the tensions that characterized the Church in England in the nineteenth century, were played out, in some cases more dramatically, in the overseas dioceses. Churchmanship is an obvious example. Evangelical missionaries and rather old-fashioned congregations were deeply suspicious of the most modest liturgical or theological innovations of bishops or new clergy. They suspected that the clericalism and 'professionalism' that characterized many Anglican bishops and priests from the 1840s onwards were precursors of attempts to pervert their church to Roman Catholicism, which in some of the Australian colonies, for example, they saw flourishing around them. The tensions between Church and State were passed onto the overseas Church, particularly as successive British governments, recognizing the growing denominational pluralism in England, Wales and Ireland as well as in most of the colonies, withdrew from making grants to support bishops and clergy in the colonies, while more slowly relinquishing authority to establish dioceses and appoint bishops. The tensions between Anglicans and nonconformists were also imposed on overseas dioceses, as nonconformist Members of Parliament joined with Anglican evangelicals to oppose legislation to grant autonomy to dioceses and to allow them to establish synodical forms of government. Anglican evangelicals were motivated by fears that such initiatives would reduce the restraining hand of the Crown-in-Parliament on the Church, and would allow Romanizing clergy and bishops to seduce good Anglican lay people into the clutches of the scarlet woman in Rome. Nonconformists, while sharing the Anglican evangelicals' fears, suspected that Anglicans might manage to achieve the benefits of disestablishment overseas, while retaining the privileges of establishment.

Anglican traditional High Churchmen and Tractarians,

viewing the same events from a different perspective, wished to free the Church from what they saw as the shackles of the State, so that bishops might assert their authority as successors of the apostles to exercise authority in the Church, but in consultation with the clergy and laity. They wished to establish representative forms of government within their dioceses and to create provinces independent of, but in communion with, the arch-bishop of Canterbury, which also had representative forms of government, and to secure procedures for discipline within the dioceses and provinces independent of secular, and especially British, courts. As British governments distanced themselves from the Church (even to the extent of disestablishing the Church of Ireland), it was thought entirely wrong that British courts should be able to intervene in matters of doctrine and the discipline of the clergy in England, let alone in South Africa. As the Church of England struggled to establish its identity as a denomination, rather than the national Church, during the nineteenth and twentieth centuries, so were the overseas dioceses involved with this.

This tension between Church and State, as we will see, has been formative for the Anglican Communion and has contributed to the informal nature of the Communion. The complex relation-ship between the Church and State in England has made it impossible for the English Church to submit itself to any higher body, and thus has ensured that the meetings of Anglican bishops in Lambeth Conferences have been merely consultative processes without any legislative authority. While the American Church and some other provinces have viewed the complex relationship between the Church of England and the State with suspicion, the limitations which this link with the State has placed on the English Church may have been beneficial to the Communion, in preventing the English Church from absolutely dominating the Communion to the even greater exclusion of Americans and others.

The final tension has been that between mission and colonial expansion. The non-established form of Anglicanism in Scotland and the United States has ensured that Anglicanism has always had an independence of merely British rule. In fact Anglican missionaries have, as we will see, often preceded British rule, for example in West Africa, Madagascar and East Africa, and

Anglican missionaries have often been well aware of the risks of identifying Christian mission with colonial rule by Europeans. All the Anglican missionary societies were concerned to establish indigenous churches and developed, as we will see, various strategies to achieve this. However, as we will also see, that process was much slowed down in the last years of the nineteenth and early years of the twentieth century by the rise of British imperialism alongside a new rigorism in evangelicalism, both of which tended to reject indigenous customs and practices as primitive or corrupt, and to identify European ways with Christianity and civilization. As a result, particularly in Africa, there was a reluctance to give leadership in churches to Africans, with the consequence that many breakaway churches were formed. Only in the years after the Second World War did Archbishop Fisher take the initiative to force independence on European-dominated Anglican churches in Africa and elsewhere, so that they would have to develop their own national and regional identities in the process of taking responsibility, within the context of the support and fellowship of the Anglican Communion, for their own lives and mission.

In writing this account of the development of Anglicanism as a world Church not every diocese and province and its particular development has been described. To focus the argument certain areas and events have been selected either because they established important precedents that were followed elsewhere, or because they provide significant illustrations of what was happening. The scope of this study has also been determined by the available sources, which have been limited to published histories of dioceses and provinces and studies of missionary societies, and to the biographies of bishops and others who have played a significant role in the development of the Anglican Communion. It is hoped that this study at least provides a framework for understanding the development of the Anglican Communion. However, much more work needs to be done which will offer new interpretations and explanations in an area which, so far as I am aware has been greatly neglected.

Bishop Hensley Henson of Durham described the 'Organization of the Anglican Communion' as a 'subject of portentous dullness'. Perhaps this explains that a need noted by Bishop Stephen Neill in the introduction to his *Anglicanism* in 1958 that there was no general book dealing with the expansion of the Anglican Church in the English-speaking world, still exists nearly forty years later.[1] I hope that this study rises above Henson's comment and meets the need noted by Neill.

CHAPTER 1

The Reformation in the British Isles

The Anglican Communion by its very name creates a misapprehension about its nature. A communion it most certainly is. The Lambeth Conference in 1930 described it as:

> A fellowship, within the one Holy Catholic and Apostolic Church, of those duly constituted dioceses, provinces, or regional Churches in communion with the see of Canterbury, which have the following characteristics in common:
>
> a. They uphold and propagate the Catholic and Apostolic faith and order as they are generally set forth in the Book of Common Prayer as authorized in their several Churches;
>
> b. They are particular or national churches, and, as such, promote within each of their territories a national expression of Christian faith and worship; and
>
> c. They are bound together not by a central legislative and executive authority, but by mutual loyalty sustained through the common counsel of the Bishops in conference.[1]

While its origins may be in the Reformation in sixteenth-century England, it has never been entirely English. A guiding principle among those engaged in the reform of the Church in England was that they were reforming the Church according to the principles of the Church in its pristine youth, during the first four centuries of its existence, before the 'Church of Jerusalem, Alexandria, and Antioch . . . erred [as] also the church of Rome hath erred, not only in their living and manner of Ceremonies, but also in matters of Faith' (Article XIX). The English reformers saw themselves as both reacting against the failure of the 'conciliar movement' in the late medieval Church, and continuing the movement. This movement in the late thirteenth and fourteenth centuries had arisen over the resistance of French kings to papal intervention in their kingdom, and also from the advancement of the ideas of the independence of the State in the temporal sphere, and the insistence on speaking of the Church as the whole body of believers, not merely a clerical institution. So in Article XXI it was stated that 'General Councils may not be gathered together without the commandment and will of Princes. And when they be gathered together... they may err, and sometimes have erred, even in things pertaining unto God.' They also believed that 'Every particular or national Church hath authority to ordain, change and abolish ceremonies or rites of the Church ordained by man's authority, so that all things be done to edify' (Article XXXIV).

The English reformers were committed to an ideal of a catholic, reformed and national church which should exist in relation to, and communion with, other national churches, and even with the bishop of Rome. They looked to the early centuries of the Church, and saw themselves not as creating a new church but as purging the Church of errors that had crept in, and saw the English Church as in succession to the 'primitive Church', and especially the British Church, which predated the mission of Augustine to Kent.

However, while the Anglican Communion is in many ways quintessentially English, it was more than English, for at root it was about establishing reformed, catholic, national churches, and the English, with varying success, encouraged the idea in Wales, Scotland and Ireland, and these traditions of reformed catholicism have contributed in a variety of ways to the development of what has become known as the Anglican Communion.

Although Henry VIII's urgent need for a male heir in the 1520s triggered the events which led to the denial of the jurisdiction of the pope over the Church in England in the 1530s, this was part of a long-standing tension over the nature of papal jurisdiction over the English and other churches. Throughout the medieval period there had been frequent clashes between secular rulers and popes over questions of jurisdiction; however with the emergence of more powerful nation states in the late middle ages, for example in Spain, France and Sweden, as well as England, kings were in a more powerful position to assert their own jurisdiction against the pope. The new Tudor dynasty in England, with its emphasis on strong and efficient central government, and its conscious identification with early British traditions, for example in Henry VII naming his eldest son and heir, Arthur, was in a particularly strong position to do this. While papal support and approval might be valuable, English kings were confident in disputing papal claims to exercise legal jurisdiction in England, and even the confirmation of the election of bishops. The pope's temporal authority could be questioned without inevitably casting doubt on his spiritual primacy as bishop of the apostolic see of Rome.

THE ENGLISH REFORMATION

One of the strongest factors influencing the reform of the English Church was the assertion of the authority of the English crown in relation to the Church. While Henry VIII, under whom the English Reformation began, obviously emphasized particular theological views in relation to diplomatic considerations, he also read and wrote theology. In spite of his many shortcomings he was a devout Christian and took seriously his high calling of kingship, believing himself to be divinely appointed to that office. He suspected that the Church, especially as manifested in Cardinal Wolsey's pretensions, was encroaching on his own God-given royal authority and dignity. As a devout man, he came to see the failure of his marriage to Catherine of Aragon, who, in her youth, had been married to his deceased brother, to produce a male heir, as a visitation of divine anger for having offended against a divine commandment in Leviticus 20.21. The sin would also be visited upon his kingdom, for if he died with no obvious male heir, there was every likelihood of a return to the anarchy from which his father had rescued the nation a generation before.

The pope, by granting a dispensation to permit him to marry his deceased brother's wife, appeared to have brought about this sorry state of affairs, and so, in Henry's view, he must rectify it by annulling the marriage, which Henry had come to believe was an abomination to God, and absolving the king from the sin, so releasing him to contract another marriage which would be blessed by God, and thus produce a male heir. The pope, on the advice of most of the canon lawyers of Europe, who quoted Deuteronomy 25.5 against Henry's case, hesitated, and then under additional pressure from Catherine's nephew, the Holy Roman Emperor Charles V, who had sacked Rome in 1527 and taken the pope prisoner, denied the king his annulment. The

king then began to be confirmed in his suspicion that the pretensions of the pope to mediate God's justice throughout the
Church might not be valid, and that the pope might not have
divine authority to overrule Scripture. He came to see the papacy
as standing in the way of God's condemnation of his sin, and of
his desire to repent of its evil and to exercise the authority given
him by God to rule his kingdom. He was convinced that he was
the Lord's anointed, recognized, in happier times, by the pope
himself, as Defender of the Faith. He must therefore defend his
people against the presumptions of the pope and his agents, the
bishops and clergy who supported the pope.

The traditional sabre rattling which English kings had often
used against the pope, of calling Parliament, in which public
criticisms of the clergy could be orchestrated, and the sorry state
of the Church, at the mercy of these hireling shepherds, might
be exhibited, failed to move the pope. Nor did the customary
next step of pressurizing the holy father by passing anti-clerical
legislation, the implementation of which was dependent on the
royal pleasure.

However, a new idea began to emerge from the summer of
1531, which suggested that in truth the pope could be ignored,
and the matter could be settled in England, on royal authority.
This radical suggestion emerged from the New Learning, which
had taken root in the universities, promoting the study of Greek,
in addition to Latin and also Hebrew, had opened up the Bible,
and the Greek Fathers and the Eastern Church to English theologians. It was claimed that anciently, reserved causes arising in
metropolitan provinces could be finally decided in the pro-vince,
and that imperial authority left a king without superiors on
earth, and therefore outside anyone's jurisdiction. This was
derived from an awareness of the role that the first Christian
emperor, Constantine, had played in the Church in the fourth
century, and which emperors had continued to exercise in the
Eastern Church. It was pointed out that Constantine's mother was
a British princess, and that he had been proclaimed emperor in
Britain, and misty legends were recalled that the origins of the
English kingdom lay with Constantine. As the 1530s advanced
and pressure on the papacy failed to bear fruit, and Henry
became more desperate for a male heir, help was sought from
more radical advisers, such as Thomas Cromwell and Thomas
Cranmer, and their arguments came to the fore.

Parliament was nervous of going too far in the campaign against the papacy. It was necessary for Cromwell to work hard to orchestrate awareness of alleged clerical malpractices to arouse the House of Commons to complain to the convocation of Canterbury, in the Supplication Against the Ordinaries, about the bishops' alleged cruel treatment of heretics, and of the right of convocation to make laws contrary to the statute law, and without royal assent or the assent of lay subjects. Convocation, which was in fact busy passing modest reforming canons, dismissed the complaints of the House of Commons, and appealed to the king to protect the Church's liberties. The king claimed to be affronted at the easy dismissal of the complaints of his loyal subjects, and responded by demanding that in future canons should only be made with royal assent, and that all existing canons should be scrutinized by a commission, half of whose members should be Members of Parliament, and the other half clergy, and then confirmed by the king. The convocation, fearing new demands by the House of Commons, accepted the king's demands, and surrendered the legislative independence of convocation.

Meanwhile, a propaganda campaign was underway, organized by Thomas Cromwell, using printed pamphlets, to promote the arguments for believing that the king had never been properly married to Catherine, and that ecclesiastically England was not dependent on Rome. Whether the king's advisers doubted that they could persuade the convocation to support a bill annulling the king's marriage, or whether they intended to assert the authority of Parliament over the Church, is unclear, but in any event, it was Parliament they turned to with a bill which claimed to be a development of anti-papal legislation of the fourteenth century. In the preamble to the bill a concept was set out that 'this realm of England [is] an empire', ruled by a supreme king under God, owing obedience to one supreme head in matters temporal and spiritual, and thus abolishing appeals to any foreign tribunal in testamentary, matrimonial, or spiritual cases, and establishing national tribunals to hear such cases. The House of Commons, with some hesitation, passed the bill, and although in practice the bill only affected a limited aspect of Church life, it established a theological and legal basis for the separation of the English Church from Rome. Archbishop Cranmer now tried the issue of the king's marriage to Catherine of Aragon, and pronounced it unlawful, and the king's recent marriage to Anne Boleyn lawful, and the pope, a few months later, excommunicated the king.

The English Church was thus separated from the Roman Church. It was not a particularly popular move. A propaganda campaign was required to attempt to convince the English that this constitutional revolution would not bring the wrath of God upon the nation. It was pointed out that the divorce was legal, and that providence continued to smile upon the land – the Queen was pregnant, there had been a good harvest, God had not visited the cattle or people with plague and had not raised up other nations to punish England. The king himself seems to have taken consolation from the example of the Old Testament hero-king, David and his matrimonial irregularities – for an illuminated Psalter made for him in the late 1530s depicted the king as David in five of its miniatures. The 1534 session of Parliament was orchestrated to follow up the consequences of this constitutional revolution, with a series of Acts including the Act for the Submission of the Clergy, which confirmed the convocation's surrender of their legislative independence, and placed ultimate spiritual authority in lay hands in the High Court of Delegates, thereby amending and strengthening the Act of Appeals. Later in the year both convocations accepted resolutions stating that the bishop of Rome had no greater jurisdiction in England than any other bishop. In a further meeting of Parliament in November 1534 the Act of Supremacy was passed, which recognized the king's status as supreme head of the Church of England, with spiritual authority, including the right of visitation, and of disciplining the clergy and correcting preachers, of supervising canon law and doctrine, and of trying heretics, thus giving the king quasi-episcopal powers. In January 1535 Henry appointed Thomas Cromwell his vicegerent in spiritual matters.

In a brief span the English Church was brought brutally under royal control. However, because Parliament had been used to executing the king's will, no subsequent changes could be made without the consent of Parliament. Thomas Cromwell, with the support of Cranmer, had laid the foundations of a unitary realm, reformed in body and soul under the protection of the law, and ruled by the king-in-Parliament. This was to provide the framework for English Christianity and Anglicanism for the next centuries. However, they failed to persuade the king of a need for a radical reform of the Church's theology.

This sense of a national, reformed, catholic Church focused the nature of the Church of England, rather than any theological confession of faith, or particular liturgical expression. The principles of subsequent reformation were set out on this basis; for example, the principles upon which the first Book of Common Prayer of 1549 were based were spelled out in the order calling in the old service books, and in the Act of Uniformity for the first revision. These documents indicate that the Prayer Book was intended to be 'grounded upon the Holy Scriptures', 'agreeable to the order of the primitive Church', designed to be unifying to the realm and for the edification of the people. Unlike many of the continental reformers, the English reformers did not take the view that something must have biblical precedent to be included in the liturgy or in the ordering of the Church. The English reformers saw the period of the 'primitive Church' as normative. The 'primitive Church' provided a model for interpreting Scripture and a norm for doctrine, discipline and worship.

Although Cranmer did not have any early liturgies available to him, he went through the early sources that he could discover, for example sermons and catechetical instructions and letters of the patristic period that were then in print, and made lists in his common-place books of the details he could glean about the liturgy of the early Church. On this basis he devised a book that brought together all the services in one book, which, along with the Bible, would provide all the necessary texts for worship for the whole Church, and which would be within the financial reach of every parish, and of many individuals, in a 'language understanded of the people'. It was assumed that the rites of the liturgy would be subject to revision or modernization, for it was noted that they 'may be altered and changed, and are therefore not to be esteemed equal to God's law'. Nor was it thought that this order would be suitable for other nations, for '. . . in these our doings we condemn no other nations, nor prescribe any thing but to our own people only: We think it convenient that every country should use Ceremonies as they shall think best to the setting forth of God's honour and glory, and to the reducing of the people to a most perfect and godly living without error or superstition . . .'.[2]

In *A Defence of the True and Catholic Doctrine of the Sacrament of the Body and Blood of our Saviour Christ: with a Confutation of Sundry Errors concerning the Same, Grounded and Established upon God's Holy Word, and Approved by the Consent of the Most Antient Doctors of the Church* in 1550, Cranmer gave a clear statement of the basic characteristics of the theology of the Church of England. It should base itself upon Scripture, next in the teachings of the Fathers of the early Church and in its doctors, and finally in reason and experience.

The liturgy for the reformed Church was set out in the Book of Common Prayer, which was contained in an appendix to the Act of Uniformity of 1549, passed by Parliament in the reign of Henry's son, Edward VI. This was a major constitutional innovation. Previous attempts to define faith had been made by the supreme head of the Church with Parliament authorizing the penalties to enforce the definitions. This was an Act of Parliament, indicating that the supremacy in the Church was to be found in the king-in-Parliament, thus giving representative lay people a say in the liturgy and doctrine of the Church, as well as the organization of the Church. The more obviously radically reformed Prayer Book of 1552 was passed in the same way.

By the death of Edward VI in 1553 the constitutional revolution brought about by Cromwell nearly twenty years before was firmly established. The original changes had been brought about in the first half of the 1530s, gradually and almost imperceptibly. Only when they were in place did Cromwell attempt more radical and open changes, especially the dissolution of the monasteries. That, too, could be made palatable by the hope that there might be some financial advantage in it for everyone. Doctrinal change was more difficult and encountered greater resistance, and it was seen that more Protestant changes were countered by more conservative reactions.

Both Henry's and Edward's governments were ruthless in their treatment of bishops. Henry forced Bishop Holbeach to exchange lands with which the diocese of Lincoln was endowed to an extent that it was estimated that the income of the bishop was reduced by half. The long-term plan of Edward's governments seems to have been to make bishops salaried officials. Elizabeth, however, wished to preserve the authority of the bishops in order to be able to use them to maintain her authority, particularly in the provinces, and to stabilize her government. While the English Church reaffirmed episcopal supervision, it was made clear to bishops that the Crown-in-Parliament monitored their activities, to ensure that they exercised their stewardship of the Lord's flock appropriately, as primitive and spiritual bishops, and did not become worldly prelates.

The Church of England, like the early Church, never attempted to set out its beliefs beyond its liturgy. The Thirty-Nine Articles merely provided basic guidelines and more especially pointed out errors. The English reformers did not set out to make changes in the substance of the Christian faith. Their aim was to recover and preserve the truth once and for all delivered to the saints, and to set that forth in the Church's liturgy. It was recognized that this expression might change in accordance with the conditions and needs of the people of God. It was therefore a Church which involved the people of God in the ordering of the tradition.

The English Reformation emphasized the role of the people of God in the Church, and their responsibility for accepting the ordering and disciplining of the Church. The representatives of the people of God assembled in Parliament recognized the King's imperial authority over the Church in the Act of Supremacy, and authorized the liturgies of 1549 and 1552. Queen Mary, when she wished to restore the temporal authority of the pope in England, had to secure the consent of Parliament, and after her early death, Elizabeth's supremacy was restored 'by the authority of this present Parliament'. In this instance it was done by the faithful laity against the wishes of all of the bishops in the House of Lords, and without consulting the clergy in convocation. Parliament also restored the reformed liturgy (though with modest but significant changes, to make it acceptable to as many people as possible) against the wishes of the bishops and the convocation.

The Elizabethan Settlement was based on the Edwardian model, and on the tradition forged by Cranmer and Henry VIII between 1534 and 1547. The English Church was an aspect of the autonomous nation, ruled by the same head and government. It was not a very logical settlement, because the tension between the royal and episcopal authority was never far below the surface. However, it was a practical settlement. Given reasonable common sense, it worked, because it was not exclusively dependent upon doctrinal commitment.

A wave of propaganda during Elizabeth's reign helped to reorientate the self-understanding of the English Church. Archbishop Parker, in his *De Antiquatate Britannicae* claimed that the British Church had been planted by Joseph of Arimathea or St Paul. In his view this church had anciently been independent of the papacy, and had its own tradition of martyrs and ministerial succession. The English Church of which he was primate was not therefore a new church, but a reformed and purified part of the one Church of Christ. Perhaps most important for popularizing these views was John Foxe's *Book of Martyrs*. He aimed to portray the religious changes in England during the previous thirty years as a renewal of the 'antient Church of Christ'. The Roman Church was depicted as decadent and degenerate, and the English Church was shown to be primitive and pure. Foxe described a struggle between Christ and anti-Christ, with Elizabeth as a second Deborah, raised up by God to rescue the nation from anti-Christ and to restore the rule of Christ, in which 'popery' represented innovation and Protestantism the true Church. He strongly emphasized the role of the monarchy. The Elizabethan printers skilfully brought this before the English people, illustrating the book with woodcuts to wean them away from the Catholic view of history. The dominant themes of Foxe's history was that England was a nation elected by God to restore his Church. It gave the Reformation form and meaning for contemporaries, and helped to make sense of and to create a framework for their experiences. Foxe depicted Constantine as a kind of Englishman, son of a British princess, and proclaimed in England at York.

John Jewel, bishop of Salisbury, set out in his *Apology of the Church of England*, which was published in 1561 and translated into English in 1564 by Lady Ann Bacon, to explain the refusal of the Privy Council to receive an emissary from the pope at the Council of Trent, which had been called to reform the dioceses of the Western Church that continued in communion with Rome, with an invitation to send representatives to submit the cause of the English Reformation to Rome. He also wished to defend the English government and bishops from the charge of promoting lawlessness and irreligion by dividing the Church. The English government wished to develop the argument that it was the Roman Church, not the Church of England, that was schismatic, heretical, divisive and immoral. Their chief protagonist was Jewel, who used the New Learning to provide an opportunity and means to probe into the period of the early Church, and to recover the Scriptures from their medieval interpreters. The *Apology* and Jewel's substantially expanded *Defence of the Apology of the Church of England* published in 1568 were intended to explain the position of the English Church in relation to the Council of Trent, and to the world, to show that the Scriptures and the Fathers supported the English who had left the Roman Church with just cause and had 'returned to the apostles and old catholic fathers'. Jewel's aim was first, to present the truth, and thus to refute rumours and lies spread against the English Church; and second, to demonstrate the manifold errors of the papists, which prevented the English from sending representatives to Trent.

Jewel considered that the monarch had a God-given duty to act in the sphere of ecclesiastical jurisdiction (although not in the sphere of doctrine). He repeatedly compared the powers of the English crown with the powers Constantine had exercised, as well as drawing on examples of godly monarchs in the Old Testament. He claimed that while in doctrinal matters the clergy retained their independence, a godly prince had a moral right to supervise the reformation of the Church in his own dominions, and that subjects had a duty to obey a godly prince, but not an ungodly prince. Jewel saw Parliament as representing the whole Christian commonwealth, both clerical and lay.

Jewel defended the apparent divisions in the English Church, showing that their unity greatly outweighed their diversity, and referring to the diversity in the New Testament and the early Church, and the serious divisions in the Roman Church in the Middle Ages. He argued that truth was of far greater importance than unity. He argued that the Roman Church had departed from the ancient Church, and he discredited Trent as a true council, for being subservient to the pope, and asserted the right of princes, quoting the Old Testament and the early Church, to govern religion in their own realms, pointing out that the first four General Councils were called by civil magistrates, who themselves took part in the discussions. He also pointed out that popes had allowed both Henry VII and Henry VIII to nominate bishops for English sees at will and to translate bishops from see to see. For Jewel the catholicity of the Church of England lay not in the sucession of bishops, but in the succession of true doctrine.

A generation later Richard Hooker built on Jewel's arguments, in his apology for the Church of England against Presbyterians, *The Laws of Ecclesiastical Polity*, the first four books of which were published in 1593. He maintained that Church and State were two inseparable aspects of one commonwealth. The monarch's authority, limited by law and custom, in his view, would reflect the spirituality of the people as a whole. Hooker held that the crown protected the Church in order that it should be free to govern itself, but that as membership of Church and State were coextensive, Parliament had the right to legislate in ecclesiastical matters. Parliament, with convocation, represented the whole Christian commonwealth, and could therefore make laws for the Church. Hooker did not think that to ascribe apostolic descent for bishops implied that episcopacy was of dominical institution. It would seem for Hooker that episcopacy, by reason of its historical tradition from the apostolic age to his own had demonstrated its divine authority. However, this was very different from claiming that it was the exclusive form of ministry prescribed by Scripture. When bishops were not available, Hooker believed that the Church had power to create a ministry *de novo*. Hooker's assessment of the ministries of foreign churches was in line with these principles.

Both Jewel's and Hooker's works mark the *via media* of the Church of England: Catholic in that it believed itself to contain all the essentials of the Church of the early centuries, reformed in that it felt obliged to rid itself of some of the doctrinal and practical innovations that had accrued to the Church in the Middle Ages. Jewel and Hooker agreed that the bishops' specific function was to order and elect ministers. This view was also taken by Archbishop Whitgift of Canterbury who, whilst espousing Calvinist theology reacted firmly against the more radical Calvinists' view that bishops and priests should be dispensed with in favour of a single order of ministers. Royal supremacy, they believed, was derived from Scripture, and episcopacy proved itself of divine origin by its continuance from apostolic times. Later in Elizabeth's reign the presbyterian claim that its form of polity alone was prescribed in Scripture forced Anglicans to seek evidence for episcopacy in Scripture.

In practice, churchmen raised to the episcopate during Elizabeth's reign showed a determination in reminding the Supreme Governor of the limits of her authority and influence in the Church, and of their allegiance, in the final resort, to a higher power. Archbishop Parker protested successfully against Elizabeth's reluctance to order the removal of images from churches, and to accept married clergy. Bancroft, preaching at Paul's Cross in February 1589, emphasized the existence of bishops, priests and deacons in apostolic times, and then implied the divine appointment of bishops over against the royal supremacy. When lay authority over bishops was recognized, it was in terms of the authority of the crown, not the Crown-in-Parliament, to appoint bishops.

Part of its real continuity with the primitive Church was the Church of England's continuity of the ordering of the Church in the holy orders of its deacons, priests and bishops, and a requirement that ministers of the Church should receive episcopal ordination or consecration to maintain that continuity. Next to their advocacy of the godly prince, the Anglican reformers were at pains to restore godly bishops to the Church in contradistinction to the 'corrupt prelacy' which they held had existed in the late Middle Ages, and against which they had revolted. Reformed bishops were required to be 'pastors, labourers, watchmen'. Elizabethan churchmen understood bishops to derive their authority from God as well as mediately through the Supreme Governor, who nominated them for election by their cathedral chapters, and issued a mandate for their consecration; but they never precisely defined the relationship between these powers. Basically a bishop made known his authority through his faith and works, and it was widely held that orders conferred by godly presbyters in Geneva might be more sound than those conferred by ungodly bishops using the Roman ordinal. While it was generally held that in an established church there should be an ordered episcopal succession, in churches such as in Denmark, where the Roman authorities had neglected to consecrate bishops before the Reformation, and after the Reformation superintendents were appointed by the crown to exercise the role of bishops, or in countries where bishops had declined to take part in the reform of the church and had therefore been excluded from the church, or when a church was under persecution, and it was not possible to elect a bishop recognized by the State, it was agreed that the validity of the orders of that church should not be questioned. The preface to the Ordinal in the Prayer Book left open the acceptance of non-episcopally ordained ministers until it was revised in 1662, and as we will see, until the mid-nineteenth century, Anglicans accepted the ministrations as missionaries of Danish and German Lutheran pastors who had not been episcopally ordained, provided they used Anglican liturgies.

In the seventeenth century in England, there was a renewed emphasis on episcopacy as an apostolic institution and of bishops as channels of sacramental grace, but this was not seen as necessarily denying the validity of the orders and authority of other reformed churches. Bishop Bramhall of Derry argued that the Lutheran churches possessed the reality of episcopacy, even though they had abandoned the traditional name. Archbishop Laud also subscribed to this view.

It is these features that are characteristic of what later came to be called Anglicanism – a national church reformed according to the principles discerned in the New Testament and the early Church, in which authority is seen as vested in the people of God, represented by a godly ruler and a representative assembly of godly people, and a faithful and godly ministry standing in the succession of the bishops of the primitive Church. Beyond this it was not thought that it required further definition. These characteristics were to be looked for and encouraged in other churches.[3]

THE REFORMATION IN WALES

Although Wales was legally assimilated into England in 1536 when an Act of Parliament divided it up into counties on the English model, and gave it representatives in the English Parliament, Wales remained a distinctive nation, if for no other reason than that the Welsh language survived. The reformed Church therefore took seriously the need to teach and preach and conduct the liturgy in a language 'understanded of the people'. In 1542 Bishop Bulkeley of Bangor ordered the clergy and schoolmasters of his diocese to give religious instruction in Welsh. Before 1543 part of Tyndale's English New Testament had been translated into Welsh, and manuscripts of Welsh translations of Cranmer's English Litany and Order of Communion were in circulation in Wales. In 1546 Sir John Price of Brecon published the first Welsh printed book, which was a primer containing the Creed, the Lord's Prayer, and the Ten Commandments and other items in Welsh.

The new English Prayer Book issued in 1549 was as incomprehensible to most Welsh people as Latin had been. But in 1551 William Salusbury, a layman, published a Welsh translation of the Epistles and Gospels in the Prayer Book, which formed a first step towards a Welsh translation of the whole Bible and the Prayer Book. Under Elizabeth there was a determined attempt to make the reformed Church accessible to the people of Wales. Thirteen of the fourteen bishops appointed to Welsh dioceses during Elizabeth's reign were Welsh, and most of them lived in their dioceses. In 1563 a private Act of Parliament required the four Welsh bishops and the bishop of Hereford to be responsible for issuing a Welsh translation of the Bible and the Prayer Book by 1567. These translations were to be required to be used in all public services conducted in those places where the language normally used by the parishioners was Welsh. By 1567 the task was completed by Richard Davies, bishop of St David's and William Salusbury, and the books were published. Unfortunately it was quickly apparent that Salusbury's Welsh was very Latinized, and it was not very easy for the average Welsh parish priest to use, nor was it probably very accessible to the average Welsh-speaker, because of the significant differences between the Welsh spoken in North Wales and that spoken in the South. In 1588, with Whitgift's encouragement, William Morgan, the vicar of Llanrhaedr ym Mochnant, completed a new and more acceptable translation of the Bible into Welsh, and in 1597 he also completed a new Welsh translation of the Prayer Book.

In the preface to his translation of the New Testament, Bishop Davies had argued that the Reformation in Wales was a return to the Church of the early days of British Christianity, before it was corrupted with Romanism by Augustine of Canterbury. His aim was to refute the accusation that the Reformation was an English imposition, and to identify the reformed Church with age-old notions of Welsh nationalism. This worked to a very considerable extent, for William Morgan's translation of the Bible became an important focus for the

Welsh language and for national identity, and, despite a slow start, until the late eighteenth century at least, Anglicanism flourished in Wales.[4]

THE SCOTTISH REFORMATION

Although they were independent kingdoms, there were also close links between the English and Scottish reformers. It must have been no small consolation to the English reformers that when a reform movement began in Scotland in the 1560s, there was considerable common ground with the English Church, especially with regard to the notion of a reformed episcopate.

Many of the leading reformers in both countries were well-known to each other, and had shared common experiences of exile. John Knox, John Spottiswood and William Harlow had all served in England. The Scottish Reformation was carried through by the pro-English party in Scotland, with English help. In 1560 the Scottish diocesan organization survived the first phase of the Reformation and the bishops of Galloway, Orkney and Caithness, identified with the reforms. Although they and those commissioned in other dioceses were described as 'super-intendents', they seem to have identified themselves as bishops, and to have claimed it as an order of divine institution. In 1571, at the Convention of Leith, bishops were firmly identified as superintendents of dioceses and identity was claimed with the 'Kirk of England'. It was agreed that bishops should be nominated by the crown and were to be instituted by the laying on of hands by existing bishops. There was in fact a significant convergence between the Church of England and the Church of Scotland in the early 1570s, with the Scots frequently using the English Prayer Book.

During the century and a half following the Reformation there was a protracted struggle for control of the Scottish Church. By 1574 new ideas were coming from Geneva and England, that questioned episcopacy (in England as well as in Scotland). Presbyterianism, which held that there was only one order of ministry in the Church, and that a godly prince had no role in the Church, except as a member, was introduced into Scotland in 1574 by Andrew Melville, who became principal of Glasgow University, where he was succeeded by a disciple when he moved to St Andrews. The principal of Aberdeen University was also a friend of Melville's, so within a few years most of the men training to be ministers in the Church of Scotland came under the influence of divines committed to a Presbyterian programme. In England, with a strong royal government and a strong episcopate, such views were confined to a minority. In Scotland, with a weak crown during the minority of James VI, the Presbyterian system proved attractive to the clergy, for Melville had attacked the wealth of the bishops, and suggested that it should be confiscated in order to augment parochial endowments, which were often very small. He also campaigned for the return to the clergy of all endowments and rights which had been alienated from the Church to lay people. In 1578 the General Assembly of the clergy of the Church of Scotland voted to elect no more bishops thereafter. In spite of this the government continued to appoint bishops and most of the bishops continued to exercise their episcopal functions, and in 1584 the Black Acts reaffirmed the authority of the bishops, and restated the authority of the crown and Parliament over the Church, and forbade convocations of ministers to meet without the king's consent.

However, from the early 1580s presbyteries in towns, notably Edinburgh and Stirling, began to usurp the power of bishops, and in 1586 the Black Acts were modified to allow for the continuance of presbyteries, and affirmed the rights of synods and the General Assembly to deal with ecclesiastical causes, while still retaining the office of bishop. During the remainder of the sixteenth century the presbyteries continued to increase in number and gradually to usurp the duties of bishops. Nevertheless, ministers continued to be appointed to episcopal titles by James VI and from 1600, as bishops, they had the right to sit in the Scottish Parliament and to represent the clergy there. In most places bishops were part of the Presbyterian polity, and tended to become permanent moderators of presbyteries and synods.[5]

That the Church of England saw itself in close relationship with the Church of Scotland is demonstrated by the Bidding Prayer prescribed in the English Canons of 1604, which exhorted the people to pray for 'Christ's holy, catholic Church . . . and especially for the Churches of England, Scotland and Ireland', without any difference or inequality being implied between these three branches of the Church. In 1606 James achieved an agreement at the General Assembly at Linlithgow, that bishops should be permanent moderators of synods.

In 1610 three Scottish bishops, in order to reintegrate the Scottish bishops into the episcopal succession, were sent to England to be consecrated by Bishops Abbot, Andrewes and Montagu. Significantly neither of the English archbishops took part in the consecrations, in order to avoid any impression that the English archbishops were claiming jurisdiction over the Church in Scotland. Meanwhile, although the General Assembly continued to be the highest authority in Church affairs, the combination of the newly consecrated bishops and presbyteries seems to have worked satisfactorily.

Charles I's policy of using his claim to royal supremacy to further Anglicanize the Scottish Church in the 1630s without consultation with the Scottish Parliament or the General Assembly, alienated Scottish churchmen, and caused a revival of Presbyterianism, and bishops were abolished in the Church of Scotland. After the Restoration of the monarchy in 1660 episcopacy was again restored to the Church of Scotland as well as to the Church of England. However, because the Scots were held to have deliberately abandoned episcopacy, it was considered that the ministry of the Church needed to be authenticated again by integration into the unbroken English episcopal succession, and four Scottish divines were sent to England to be consecrated as bishops. On their return they consecrated six other bishops to fill the remaining Scottish dioceses. They also followed the traditional Scottish custom and immediately constituted kirk sessions, and returned to the earlier mixture of episcopacy and Presbyterianism. However, in 1689 the Scottish bishops all refused to swear allegiance to William III, on the grounds that they could not break the oath of allegiance they had already taken to James VII who was still alive. Despite what seems to have been William's intention to retain a comprehension of Presbyterianism and episcopacy, the General Assembly voted that only ministers who had subscribed to the Westminster Confession and the Presbyterian form of government should be permitted to retain their livings. Episcopalians were thus excluded from the established Church of Scotland.[6]

The exclusion was brought about by an active minority in the Assembly, with the reluctant support of the crown, who suspected the loyalty of any who would not forswear their loyalty to James VII. It has been estimated that when the Scottish Parliament, following the General Assembly, imposed Presbyterianism on the Church in 1690 more than half of the clergy were disaffected to Presbyterianism. Throughout the seventeenth century the Stuart kings had seemed intent on imposing bishops on the Scottish Church. Episcopalianism was often portrayed as the religion of royalty and the aristocracy. Because in fact the bishops did often have the support of the nobility and many of the lairds, they were often able to retain their parochial charges, until well into the eighteenth century. However, in the early eighteenth century Episcopalianism was not merely the monopoly of the aristocracy and the gentry. It appears still to have retained general support from the population north of the Tay, where half of the population of the country lived, and many south of the Tay also shared this view. Archbishop Tenison of Canterbury supported the Episcopalians, and protested on their behalf against their exclusion from public life in Scotland. He was one of the commissioners appointed in 1705 to draw up the Act of Union between England and Scotland, and in the English parliamentary debates prior to the passage of the Act in 1707, he managed to give the impression of disparaging the Presbyterian establishment in Scotland, and caused considerable offence. Thus when he urged toleration for the Episcopalians in order to prevent them from aligning themselves with those working for the return of the Stuart Pretender, he was unsuccessful. A Toleration Act for Scotland was, however, passed in 1712, based on Tenison's proposals.[7]

In 1705 the Scottish bishops had resumed the consecration of bishops to replace those who had died since 1690, but without title or jurisdiction of a diocese, but as members of an episcopal 'college', so as not to infringe the right of the Stuart Pretender to nominate bishops to dioceses. Many episcopal clergy and laity did in fact remain loyal to the Stuarts, and supported the 1715 Rebellion, which attracted punitive legislation against them by the British Parliament which imposed six months' imprisonment on ministers who omitted the State prayers, and the closure of their chapels for a similar period.

Its allegiance to an exiled king had an important impact on the Episcopal Church. In the 1720s there was a movement among a minority of the bishops to elect bishops to specific dioceses without a royal mandate, which was opposed by a majority of the bishops. The bishops, pressing for the re-establishment of a diocesan episcopate, began to question the place of royal authority in the Church. In 1731 the bishops established a concordat, to which they could all subscribe, agreeing only to consecrate bishops to whose election they could all assent, that bishops elected by presbyters might only be consecrated by a mandate from the primus of the Church, and that the bishops should elect the primus. Districts corresponding to the former dioceses were then allocated to the bishops. In 1743 the Scottish bishops held a synod and made canons without the licence of the Stuart Pretender. None of the bishops supported the 1745 Rebellion, and only two clergy took part in it. After the collapse of the Stuart cause in 1746 the bishops were confirmed in the wisdom of the initiative they had taken twenty years before in looking to the apostolic succession for their authority, rather than to their adherence to what had been regarded as the legitimate line of British kings. Also during the 1740s they began to develop their own Communion Office which was eventually approved for use in 1764.

Despite the minimal involvement of the bishops and clergy in the 1745 Rebellion, punitive action was taken against the Episcopal Church by the British Parliament, for Episcopalian lay people formed the backbone of the Jacobite army. An Act of 1748 banned all clergy ordained by Scottish bishops from officiating at public worship, and chapels were closed. This legislation was fairly actively enforced for the next ten years. The English bishops opposed the legislation in the House of Lords, about twenty of them voting against it at the committee stage.

During the 1780s there were a number of attempts to secure the repeal of the penal laws against the Scottish Episcopalians. In 1788 after the death of Charles Edward Stuart, and his brother's disqualification from the line of succession, by virtue of being a cardinal of the Roman Church, thus owing allegiance to the head of a foreign state, five of the six Scottish bishops and nearly all the clergy and the vast majority of the laity were prepared to use the State prayers, including the names of George III and his family. Subsequently, in April 1789, three of the Scottish bishops visited London to plead for the repeal of the penal laws. Scots Members of Parliament introduced a bill for the repeal, which passed the House of Commons, but was shelved by the House of Lords without a decision, and with only three English bishops present. The English bishops may have avoided assisting their Scottish colleagues because they feared that a repeal of the penal laws for Scotland would fuel attempts in England to secure a repeal of the Test and Corporation Acts, which in theory excluded dissenters from the established Church from holding civic office in England and from entrance at Oxford and from taking degrees at Cambridge universities. In 1792 an Act was passed releasing the Scottish episcopal clergy from any penalties under the penal laws, providing they subscribed to the Thirty-Nine Articles of the Church of England to demonstrate their doctrinal orthodoxy, and to ensure their political soundness, they were also required to swear an oath of abjuration of the Pretender. The Act also inhibited the Scottish clergy from serving any cures in England and Wales, thus putting them on the same footing as the American episcopal clergy.

The primus of the Scottish Church, Bishop Skinner of Aberdeen, persuaded the clergy of his diocese to adopt the Thirty-Nine Articles as a statement of their own beliefs, and also required all ordination candidates to subscribe to them. The other Scottish bishops followed suit, at a convocation of bishops and clergy in 1804. Close links developed between English High Churchmen and the Scottish Church and its bishops during the early nineteenth century. Episcopalians were symbolically accepted back into the fold of British respectability when George IV received the six Scottish bishops at Holyroodhouse on his visit to Edinburgh in 1827. However, it was not until 1840 that an Act was passed which recognized the dioceses of the Scottish bishops and confirmed the validity of the orders they conferred.

The blight cast by the identification of the Scottish bishops and many of their clergy and laity with the Stuart claimants to the British throne was long-lasting and deeply damaging to the Scottish episcopal cause. It also presented a major dilemma for the English bishops. Following the Act of Union with Scotland in 1707 they, having sworn oaths of allegiance to the reigning British sovereign at their consecrations, had great difficulty in offering support and encouragement to bishops and clergy who gave their allegiance to a rival claimant to the throne, who was also a Roman Catholic, and who was thus barred by an Act of the British Parliament from succeeding to the British throne. Although the English bishops did oppose the severity of the penal laws introduced in 1748, it is less obvious why they were so reticent in their support for the Scottish Church after 1788. The most likely explanation seems to be that already noted, that they were increasingly nervous about the security of the establishment in England, after the rise of more militant dissenting groups in England in the last quarter of the eighteenth century. If they had supported recognition for the Episcopal Church in Scotland, consistency would have required them to support the granting of recognition to the dissenting churches in England, thus undermining the traditional Anglican understanding of identity between Church and State.[8]

THE REFORMATION IN IRELAND

In Ireland the situation was different again from England, Wales and Scotland. Ireland, like Wales was ruled by the English crown, and also like Wales, it had only been partially colonized by the English, and it had its own language and distinctive culture. As in all the Western European countries, in Ireland too, there was a movement for reform and change in the Church in the early sixteenth century, and there was a recognition of the need to carry out reforms in ecclesiastical systems. A group of moderate reformers were advising the English crown about needs for change in the Irish Church, and under Henry VIII it seemed that there was a good chance the Irish Church might be reformed according to the English model. There was a group of Irish reformers, drawn from the old 'Englishry', who wished for Irish churchmen to be appointed to Irish bishoprics, and who advocated a Hibernian character for the reform of the Irish Church, by developing an Irish ancestry for it. They wished to identify the reforms with a supposed independent Irish Church, existing before the time of St Malachy, and founded by St Patrick.

However, such people were alienated by the more radical English reformers and were pushed aside when, in the 1530s, Thomas Cromwell was given responsibility for ecclesiastical affairs, and more radical English reformers were appointed to posts in the nomination of the crown in Ireland. These radical reformers became more prominent under Edward VI, and under Elizabeth the more moderate reformers, in frustration and anger at being excluded from power, began to move into alliance with the supporters of the Counter-Reformation.

Although bishops from both the Henrician and Marian periods found it possible to remain in office, the Anglican reformation of the Irish Church became associated with, and increasingly tainted by, external authority. Ireland lacked a 'godly prince' with the ability to mould the Church and society to his (or her) will. The English government was distracted under Elizabeth by attempts at the military conquest of the Gaelic areas of Ireland, which had never previously been seriously brought under the rule of the crown. The Irish Reformation legislation of 1560 was designed not to create a new church, but to reform the Church, and where the government's writ did not run, which was in three quarters of the dioceses, no attempt was made to substitute a reformed hierarchy. Some of the bishops, notably the archbishop of Tuam, took the oath of supremacy, but continued to use the old liturgy. However, the majority of the bishops were not required to take the oath of allegiance nor to subscribe to the Act of Supremacy.

The crown seems in fact to have paid little attention to the need to assist the Reformation to take root in Ireland, by the provision of godly ministers to teach about the reformed faith, and for publications in a language 'understanded of the people'. In 1573 the government did order three hundred catechisms to be printed in Irish but no attempt was made to provide godly preachers of the word in Irish, or even in English. The incomes of Irish bishops and parish priests had always been lower than in England, and during the Reformation period they were further impoverished by the depredations of the crown. Also many of the better endowments were lost to the Church as a result of the dissolution of religious houses, and came into the hands of lay people who were apathetic or actively hostile to the Anglican reform of the Church, and therefore only paid the lowest incomes to clergy to minister in the parishes.

Although a half of the livings in the diocese of Kildare to the west of Dublin were in the gift of the crown, all of them were granted on long leases to lay people who enjoyed the use and the income of the property, and the right to appoint an incumbent without any stipulation as to the level of salary. Another quarter of the livings were in the gift of the bishop, but they had been similarly alienated by previous bishops. The remaining quarter were in the full possession of lay people. Even in a diocese within the 'Pale' which was well-settled by the English, the bishop could not appoint clergy, or influence their conditions of service, to ensure that preaching ministers were appointed to parishes. The ability of the Church to manage its own affairs, to advance its interests, and to perform its minimal functions was thus subverted by the influence of interests which ran counter not just to the Reformation, but to ecclesiastical autonomy. Beyond the 'Pale', neither the Church nor the State possessed the organization to achieve the reform of the clergy, let alone the conformity of the laity. The parish system had never been more than nominal in most of Ireland. Once the monastic houses had been abolished, there were few pastoral structures for the reformed Church to relate to, and through which to influence communities. The English government took little interest in the religious convictions of those appointed to Irish bishoprics, and paid more attention to co-operating with or placating local interests, than to implanting the reformed faith in Ireland.

In England modest though the return of monastic and chantry endowments was to the Church, it did provide at least some endowments for four additional bishoprics, and for additional foundations in the universities and for grammar schools for the education of clergy and the sons of lay people in the doctrine, discipline and worship of the reformed Church, and also associated some cathedral canonries with attempts to encourage godly and learned ministers. Had even some of the money similarly wrested by the crown from the Irish Church been utilized in the endowment of colleges, schools and a university, and for preachers and canonries and lectureships in towns, men might have been attracted to the ministry of the Church of Ireland in sufficient numbers to provide the Church with the leadership necessary to plant the reformed Church firmly in Irish soil.

In the second generation of the Irish Reformation, learned clergy did begin to be appointed to Irish livings, but they tended to stand apart from Irish life, and to form a separated minority. Trinity College, Dublin, which was founded in the 1590s, was planned and nurtured by a group of Cambridge theologians of doubtfully orthodox persuasion, whose interest lay in the

formation of a puritan clergy. Although the College was founded to encourage the study of Irish, and although the Queen
donated a fount of Gaelic type in 1570, there were few Irish
speakers among the reformed clergy, and the first Irish translation of the New Testament was not printed until 1602. Irish was
despised by the majority of the reformed clergy as a barbarous
language of a backward people, and it was argued that as most
literate Irish were bilingual, it was unnecessary to teach or
preach in Irish. The reformed clergy tended to confine their
ministry to those who were already Protestant. They identified
the elect of God with the elite of the English Elizabethan
colonists, who were separated out from the Irish, and identified
the Roman Church with anti-Christ, its adherents being regarded
as the reprobate, and beyond redemption.

By 1615 it was reckoned that there were eight hundred or so
Protestant clergy to serve 2,492 parishes in Ireland. The paucity
of ministers, and particularly of preaching ministers, meant that
in many parts of Ireland the Church of Ireland simply lacked an
effective presence. Only in the dioceses of Dublin and Meath
did the Church of Ireland have the resources to establish the
reforms. For the rest, the Irish were largely left to their own
devices, and the alienated old English gentry were free to
support recusant clergy. Similarly the merchants of the ports,
which in Ireland did not look to trade with Protestant northern
Europe, like the merchants of England and Scotland, but to the
Catholic Iberian peninsula, were influenced by their Spanish
trading partners to engage with the new initiatives of the
Counter-Reformation, rather than the Protestant Reformation.

Although in the seventeenth century better episcopal
appointments were made in Ireland, and the Irish Church established its independence of the Church of England, the Church
continued to be impoverished, and there was still no real effort
made to convert Roman Catholics to the reformed faith. The
Church also lacked the capacity to expand into Ulster to minister
to the Scots settlers, who brought their own Presbyterian ministers with them. In the 1670s there was an attempt to revitalize
Trinity College as a nursery for Irish-speaking Church of Ireland
clergy, and Robert Boyle devised a scheme for revising and
reprinting the Irish New Testament and for printing William
Bedell's translation of the Old Testament into Irish, which had
originally been made in the 1630s. However, after James II's

attempts to use Ireland as a stepping stone to reclaim his throne, the use of English, rather than Irish, in education and worship was emphasized, in an attempt to unite the English and Irish populations of Ireland. In spite of attempts by Archbishop King of Dublin to encourage Irish-speaking clergy, and the use of Irish for preaching and worship, and an unsuccessful attempt by the SPCK to promote education in Irish – even Roman Catholics tended to see Irish as a subversive language – little attempt was made to plant the reformed faith of Anglicans into the hearts and minds of the great majority of Irish people.[9]

By the beginning of the eighteenth century Anglicanism had established itself as more than the Church of England. It had transcended the English language and was flourishing in Welsh-speaking Wales. In Scotland it had demonstrated a capacity to adapt to a changing polity, until bishops were excluded from the Church of Scotland. Thereafter the Episcopal Church showed that Anglicanism could survive without the support of the crown and the civil government. However, the tendency in the Scottish Episcopal Church in the eighteenth and early nineteenth centuries to become the church of the gentry and the aristocracy (it was estimated in 1843 that 86 per cent of the titled nobility, and perhaps two thirds of the landowning classes were Episcopalians),[10] perhaps demonstrated the risk of becoming a minority church identified with the governing classes. The failure to appoint Welsh-speaking bishops to the Welsh dioceses during most of the eighteenth and much of the nineteenth centuries may have contributed to the apparent alienation of much of the Welsh population from the established Church by the mid-nineteenth century. Ireland in particular illustrates the need to provide the Bible and the liturgy in the vernacular, and of locally-based preaching ministers. Although in Ireland it would seem that by the early nineteenth century the Church of Ireland had acquired a significant popular support, it is clear that the coercive power of the State was insufficient to impose Anglicanism.

For Anglicanism to flourish, a number of ingredients were necessary, including a combination of pastoral bishops and godly ministers and lay people inspired by the Scriptures and visions of the 'primitive' Church, with its emphasis on the due succession of bishops, and an ordered and regular ministry, adapted to the circumstances of the country in which it found itself, and preaching the faith of the Church in the language of the people. It was this model of a church which was transplanted, as we will see, from the British Isles to North America and around the world.

CHAPTER 2

The Church of England Overseas
1570–1780

In an age when spiritual welfare was regarded as important as physical welfare, when people travelled they expected to include in the party a physician for their souls as well as for their bodies. As every parish required the services of a minister of the established Church, so every mobile community, in the form of a party of travellers or merchants, required a chaplain. When sixteenth- or seventeenth-century English people (or Dutch, Portuguese, Spanish or French people, for that matter) travelled they expected to be accompanied by a chaplain.

This was most important if a long sea-journey was involved. In most people's minds the sea was a frightening element. It was from the chaos of the waters that God had claimed dry land. To travel on the sea was to venture into the realms of chaos. In small sailing ships, storms must have been very frightening. People's letters and diaries, for example John Wesley's description of crossing the Atlantic in his *Journal* show how frightened people were of storms, and saw them as part of the elemental battle between God and the forces of evil. The newly discovered lands, especially in North America, were interpreted by many travellers and settlers in biblical terms as a 'promised land' given by God, which needed to be reclaimed from heathen ways. In such stark situations, where people were on the borderlands of theology as well as geography, a chaplain's presence, if at all possible, was essential to call down the blessing of God on the enterprise, as well as to rebuke sinners, in order to avert divine wrath. It was important for people, wherever they were, to be instructed and edified, and to have the events of their daily lives reviewed in the light of God's word by the preaching of sermons. They needed to receive the sacraments, and, when they were ill or dying, they needed the comfort of the presence of a priest to pray with them, and, if they wished, to absolve them, as provided for in the Prayer Book office for the visitation of the sick, to administer the holy communion to them, and to commend their souls to God's mercy.

It is not therefore surprising that, when in the last quarter of the sixteenth century, the English began to explore across the Atlantic, they were accompanied on their expeditions by chaplains. In the late 1570s Henry Frobisher, in his search for a north-west passage, was accompanied by a chaplain, as was Sir Francis Drake when he circumnavigated the earth.[1]

From 1603 the East India Company appointed chaplains for its ships on their voyages to the Far East and India, 'that prayers be said every morning and evening in every ship, and the whole company called thereunto with diligent eyes, that none be wanting; so that all may with reverence and humility pray unto Almighty God to bless and preserve them from all dangers on this long and tedious voyage'.[2] The Levant Company, established in London to develop trade in the Middle East in the early seventeenth century, appointed chaplains at its factories or stations at Constantinople from 1611, Aleppo from 1624, and Smyrna from 1635.[3] Where the English travelled, they took their reformed practice of the Christain faith and liturgy with them.

When they settled in new territories, they organized themselves as they had been organized at home. When Newfoundland was established as a colony of the English crown in 1578 Sir Humphrey Gilbert, in his patent, was required to establish a form of government, '. . . so always that the sayd statutes, lawes and ordinances may be as neer as conveniently mayd agreeable to the forme of the lawes and policy of England; and also that they be not against the true Christian faith or religion now professed in the church of England . . .'.

In the sixteenth century it was generally agreed that 'There is not any man of the Church of England but the same man is also a member of the commonwealth; nor any man a member of the commonwealth which is not also of the Church of England.' It was also thought that there might be great land masses as yet unexplored '. . . reserved by God to be reduced unto Christian civility by the English nation'.[4]

In the 'factories' in the Far East and the Middle East, as well as in the embassy chapels in Europe, Anglican chaplains only served for relatively short periods before returning to England, and those to whom they ministered, the merchants and ambassadors and their employees and servants, also usually expected to return to England fairly regularly, or at least to retire to England. In the North American colonies the situation was different. There people went to settle for the rest of their lives. Many were looking for a new life in a new world. Some were looking to establish a new order, apart from the restrictions imposed on them by the English government and Parliament and the established Church and the parochial system, and to establish a separate religious system. It was separatists from the Church of England who began to colonize New England in the early seventeenth century, and who established forms of government and the church which excluded bishops. Not all the new colonies established in North America, however, were inspired by a wish to be separate and independent. The charter granted by James I in 1606 to the Virginia Company to exploit and develop a new colony on the east coast of North America, included an evangelistic purpose. The hope was expressed that '... so noble work may by the Providence of Almighty God, hereafter tend to the glory of his Divine Majesty, in propagating of Christian Religion to such people as yet live in darkness and miserable ignorance of the true knowledge and worship of God and may in time bring the infidels and savages (living in those parts) to human civility, and, to a settled and quiet government...'.[5] For the furtherance of this purpose, a chaplain, chosen on the advice of the archbishop of Canterbury, accompanied the first group of settlers to Virginia.

Understandably, unless they were attempting to create an alternative society, settlers wished to model their new life on their old, and to establish in the new territory institutions and arrangements which had worked at home. Thus parishes, which were the basis of civil and church life in England, were exported to Virginia. If clergy were supported by glebe and tithe in England, so they should be in North America. It therefore became customary to make grants of land to clergy, upon which they might build a parsonage house, and which they might cultivate to support themselves and their families. By 1619 Virginia had been divided up into parishes, and by 1630 there were vestries, electing churchwardens in each parish.[6] When governors were appointed to the colonies they had delegated to them, to exercise on behalf of the crown, jurisdiction over the temporal concerns of the Church – to present and institute clergy to parishes, and to grant marriage licences and the probate of wills.

In view of the tensions within the Church of England in the 1630s, as Charles I and Archbishop Laud attempted to impose a more rigorous episcopal jurisdiction on the Church, it is not surprising that some thought was given to the supervision and accountability of members of the English Church, both clergy and laity, who had settled overseas, either as traders or as colonists. Thus in 1634, probably at the initiative of Laud, an order of the Privy Council was issued which extended the jurisdiction of the bishop of London to 'English congregations gathering abroad and to the clergy ministering to them'. However, this was only an interim measure, for it was thought that where settlements had become established and the Church was flourishing, the presence of a bishop would be necessary for the well-being of the Church, so that young people could be confirmed, churches consecrated for worship, and church-yards consecrated for the burial of the dead, and so that congregations could produce their own deacons and priests for ordination. His existing vast diocese made it impossible to expect a bishop of London to visit North America, and it was equally impossible for confirmation candidates to travel to London. Although ordination candidates, in due course often graduates of the colleges at Cambridge, Massachusetts, New Haven, New York and Williamsburg, ventured across the Atlantic for ordination, a number died in the attempt, by shipwreck or drowning.

From the 1630s there were moves to extend the episcopate to English settlements overseas. In 1638 Archbishop Laud drew up a scheme to provide a bishop for the New England colonies, in order to establish episcopal discipline over the independent congregations that had grown up there. However, his plans came to nothing because of the outbreak of war with Scotland, which contributed to Laud's own loss of authority, and even-tual arrest and execution, and the abolition, by Parliament, of episcopacy in the Church of England. Peter Heylyn, Laud's biographer, reported that Laud had 'hoped that there would be a Church of England in all courts of Christendom, in the chief cities of the Turk . . . in all our factories and plantations, in every known part of the world, by which it might be as diffused and catholic as the Church of Rome'.[7]

After the Restoration of the crown and of episcopacy in the Church of England in 1660, further attempts were made to extend the episcopate to North America. Dr Alexander Murray was nominated to be appointed bishop of Virginia, and letters patent were granted by the crown for his consecration.[8] However, nothing happened, probably because no provision was made for the endowment of the bishopric, which had probably been promised from the profits of the customs on goods imported into Virginia, to provide a stipend for a bishop. In 1672 Archbishop Sheldon of Canterbury prepared a proposal for the establishment of a bishopric in Jamestown, of which nothing came.[9]

Henry Compton, when he was appointed bishop of London in 1675, recognized the difficulties in administering and supervising the life of the Church in the colonies from London. Each colony was independent, with its own governor and constitution and traditions, and had to be dealt with separately and independently. The difficulties were exacerbated by distance; it could easily take six months to obtain a reply to a letter to the colonies because of the length and uncertainty of the sea journey. He also however, recognizing that the achievement of a bishopric overseas might be a long-term project, began to activate his own authority over the Church overseas. He secured the agreement of the governors of the East India Company and of the Admiralty Board that they would only accept as chaplains clergy who held his licence.[10] In order to clarify his authority over the colonies, Compton persuaded the Lords of Trade and Plantations, who supervised the colonies on behalf of the Privy Council, to insert an order into their instructions to all colonial governors, 'That . . . our will and pleasure is that no minister be preferred by you to any ecclesiastical Benefice in that our Colony without a certificate from the Bishop of London of his being conformable to the Doctrine of the Church of England', and that the Prayer Book should be used for all services.[11] Compton secured himself membership of the Privy Council Board of the Lords of Trade and Plantations to enable him to promote the work of the Church in the colonies and in 1680 secured an order from the Privy Council requiring that every clergyman in the colonies should be a member of the vestry meeting in his parish and should not be excluded from the vestry meeting by the parishioners.[12]

Compton was convinced that in order for the Church to flourish in the American colonies the co-operation of the governor of each colony was essential. He also believed that more clergy were required, and that the clergy needed to be supervised, in the absence of a bishop, by a commissary in every colony. He was concerned too for the material well-being of the clergy in the North American colonies. To this end he established the custom of paying chaplains a £20 royal bounty when they took up missionary work overseas, and sought endowments for American parishes including securing a handsome endowment of land for Holy Trinity, New York.[13] In recruiting able clergy for the colonies Compton turned to the episcopal clergy in Scotland to supplement the supply from England and Wales.

To further the supervision of the clergy Compton appointed commissaries to act on his behalf in the colonies. He began appointing commissaries in 1685 when he appointed a commissary for Barbados and in 1689 appointed James Blair, a Scots episcopalian, as his commissary in Virginia, where he served until 1743. The role of a commissary was difficult. His authority depended on the support he received from the far-distant bishop of London, and also on the current standing of the bishop of London with the royal court and the government, who advised the crown on the appointment of governors to the colonies. The governor's attitude to a commissary was all-important, for a governor could either support and enhance his authority, or undermine and destroy it. It was very easy for a governor and a commissary to be rivals for power and to quarrel.

The willingness of congregations and clergy to accept the authority of a commissary was also an important factor. If they had got on for many years without any local manifestation of a bishop's authority they might not be very enthusiastic about the arrival of a commissary. Perhaps most important of all was the character of the commissary and his manner of establishing authority on behalf of the bishop. Blair had some success in establishing a good relationship with the governor of Virginia when he arrived, and in 1694 he secured a seat on the legislative council of the colony. He was also instrumental in founding, with the governor, William and Mary College. However, although

Blair established his, and therefore the bishop's, authority over the clergy of Virginia, he failed to establish his authority over the laity, and the pattern of supervision of the souls of parishioners through visitations and the ecclesiastical courts that, in England, continued for much of the eighteenth century, was not established in the American colonies.

On the whole, the policy of appointing commissaries for the colonies did not fulfil Compton's hopes. It was difficult to recruit able men because the role lacked prestige and any independent stipend or income from fees, or any customary or legal framework, such as an English archdeacon had, within which to operate. A commissary's authority depended on his own capacity to negotiate and achieve respect and authority. Compton discovered that after Thomas Bray ceased to be commissary for Maryland, because of the governor's opposition, it was impossible to appoint another commissary for the colony. Compton became convinced that the only satisfactory resolution to the difficulties of the ecclesiastical administration of the colonies was to have a bishop in the colonies. He thought that a suffragan would be the best solution, being less threatening to governors and colonists than a full diocesan bishop.[14]

The first commissary appointed by Compton to Maryland, Thomas Bray was probably the most influential and significant of the commissaries. He was a man of ability, enthusiasm and initiative and did careful research about the situation in Maryland before visiting the colony for three months in 1699. He was shocked by the shortage of clergy and by their poverty, and he sought ways of raising funds for the Church in the colonies.[15] His original intention was to establish a 'congregation for the propagation of the faith' under the direction of the bishop of London, modelled on the papal *Congregatio de Propaganda Fide* which had been established in 1622. However, on his return to London, he became involved with three laymen in setting up a private society, with the original purpose of converting Quakers to Anglicanism, but with the more general purpose of encouraging the provision of literature and education to promote Christian knowledge. The result was the Society for Promoting Christian Knowledge (SPCK), which was intended to support work in England and the colonies.

The SPCK was a private society, a ginger group, and after his visit to Maryland, Bray believed that a more substantial and official body was required to provide spiritual provision in the North American colonies and in the East, where English trade and settlements were expanding. He therefore renewed negotiations for a royal charter for a Society for the Propagation of the Gospel in Foreign Parts (SPG), which was eventually granted in 1701. This new Society was not an official organ of the Church of England, which because of its complex interdependent relationship with the crown, arising from the English Reformation settlement, had no capacity to create such a body. However, it was as near as the circumstances of the time would permit an official body of the Church of England. Its charter laid down that the archbishops of Canterbury and York, the bishops of London and Ely, the deans of Westminster and St Paul's, the archdeacon of London and the Regius and Lady Margaret Professors of Divinity in the Universities of Oxford and Cambridge should be *ex officio* members of the governing body. Thus although the Society was not a creation of the bishops, it was under the direction of some of the Church's most senior bishops and theologians. The archbishop of Canterbury was not *ex officio* president of the society (until a new charter was granted in 1882), but he was annually elected president. He normally chaired the Society's monthly committee meetings, and, in his absence the bishop of London took the chair, and a significant number of bishops always attended committee meetings.[16]

In its first report in 1704 the Society noted that earnest addresses had been received 'from divers parts of the Continent and Islands adjacent for a Suffragan to visit the several Churches, to ordain some, confirm others, and bless all'. In the same year the Society stated a case to the law officers of the crown for reviving the suffragan sees of Colchester, Dover, Nottingham and Hull, established under an Act of 1534 for the creation of suffragan sees, for the service of the Church in foreign parts. Inquiries were also made whether the archbishops and bishops would be liable to any penalties under statutory or ecclesiastical laws if they were to consecrate bishops for foreign parts to act solely as commissaries of the bishop of London. It was further inquired whether under an Act of Edward VI for the election of bishops, the crown might not appoint new suffragans for foreign parts within the royal dominions. The Society was firmly of the view that bishops were 'necessary in ye Christian Church' and as part of the divine law and will for the Church. Bray pointed to the example of the Roman Church in sending bishops *ad partis infidelium*. Archbisop Tenison, as president of the Society was entrusted with the negotiations with the law officers of the crown.

The Society also pointed to a desire for bishops in the North American colonies, for in 1705 fourteen missionaries, meeting at Burlington in New Jersey, had petitioned for the appointment of a bishop. After nothing had come of the explorations with the law officers, Tenison was again requested in 1707 to lay the proposal before the Queen herself. She directed that a plan be submitted to her to effect the proposal. Again, nothing happened, and in 1710 the committee, chaired by Tenison, resolved

1. The design of propagating the Gospel in foreign parts chiefly concerns the conversion of the heathen, and this must be placed first.
2. Itinerant ministers to preach the Gospel should therefore be sent amongst the six Indian Nations.
3. That a stop be put to sending any new Missionaries among Christians except to such places where Ministers shall be dead or removed, unless it may consist with the funds of the Society to prosecute both designs. [They noted] their just Apprehension that the good design of this Society cannot be well carryed out for want of a Bishop to Govern the clergy in the plantations; and that they are of opinion that the French King's early sending a Bishop to Canada or Quebec has been one great successful cause of propagating Popish error among Indians of those parts.[17]

Further representations were made to the Queen by Tenison, and in 1711 Archbishop Sharp of York prepared a proposal for a bishop for the colonies, to be submitted to convocation. However, he did not put his proposal, because the bishop of London, whose jurisdiction would be most affected, was unable to be at the meeting planning the agenda.

The SPG's optimism that a bishopric would be established to provide episcopal oversight in North America is demonstrated by their opening negotiations to buy a site for a house for a bishop in Burlington, New Jersey in 1711 which were brought to a successful conclusion at a cost of £610 in 1713. Meanwhile in 1712, an attempt was made to break the frustration of dealing with the crown law officers and the Queen's ministers. On the motion of Lord Clarendon, the Society drafted a parliamentary bill to establish bishoprics and bishops in North America. This attempt was frustrated by the dissolution of Parliament on the death of Queen Anne in August 1714.[18]

George I's accession provoked a new round of activity by the SPG. A petition was prepared and put before the king for bishoprics to be established in Barbados, Jamaica, Burlington, New Jersey and Williamsburg, Virginia. It was recommended that endowments should be provided to allow the mainland bishops a stipend of £1,000 a year, and the island bishops £1,500 a year.[19] The petition seems to have been ignored, perhaps because of the outbreak of the Rebellion in Scotland and northern England, and also because of doubts about the loyalty to the Hanoverian Succession of the English clergy. Some clergy, including senior clergy, were known Stuart sympathizers, and many more were suspected, probably justly, of disaffection towards the new king. It is perhaps not surprising if the new king and his ministers were at that stage unwilling to risk the appointment of people to prominent positions in the colonies whose loyalty might prove to be doubtful. The idea, however, was not abandoned by senior Whig bishops, for when Tenison died in 1717, he left £1,000 to the SPG to be applied in equal portions to the

> Settlement of Protestant Bishops, one for the Continent, Another for the Isles in North America . . . until such lawful Appointment and Consecrations are compleated, I am very sensible (as many of my Brethren of that Society also am) that as there has not hitherto been, not withstanding much importunity and many Promises to the Contrary; so there never will or can be any Regular Church discipline in those Parts, or any Confirmation or due Ordination, or any setting apart in Ecclesiastical Manner; or any preventing or abating of Factions and Divisions which have been and are very rife; no Ecclesiastical legal Discipline or Correction of Scandalous Manners either in the Clergy or Laity, or Synodical Assemblies as may be a proper Means to regulate Ecclesiastical Proceedings.

He laid down that until bishops were appointed in America the interest on the £1,000 should be devoted to helping infirm missionaries who were forced to return to England.[20] He also left some of his library to the proposed college in Barbados[21] for which in 1710 Christopher Coddrington, a fellow of All Souls' College, Oxford had left to the SPG two plantations in Barbados on which 300 'negroes were always to be kept' to pay for 'Professors and Scholars' to study medicine and divinity.[22]

Compton's successor as bishop of London, Edmund Gibson, was unwilling to issue licences for places where they carried no legal authority, for example in the English chaplaincies in Europe, and so he ceased to license chaplains to congregations in Europe and the Middle East.[23] In 1724 he submitted a memorandum to Lord Townshend, the secretary of state, seeking to clarify the bishop of London's authority, and seeking its confirmation by the Privy Council. After lengthy consultation with the law officers, an order in Council was granted in October 1726 empowering the bishop of London to exercise jurisdiction in the colonies – in the visitation of churches, the citation of all priests and deacons to inquire into their morals and conduct, and to correct and punish offences by suspension and excommunication. He was also authorized to appoint commissaries, removable at pleasure, who should exercise delegated jurisdiction. A right of appeal was allowed from their decisions to the Privy Council.

On the death of George I nine months later, the commission issued to Gibson lapsed, and he had to begin the lengthy process again. A new commission was issued on 29 April 1728. However, although clear authority over the clergy was established, episcopal authority over lay people was excluded. Gibson proceeded to appoint commissaries in the various colonies, and to draw up an elaborate plan for regulating the legal procedures to be followed in the trials of irregular or immoral clergy. The commissaries were also required to undertake annual visitations, and to send reports on the state of church buildings and the clergy to the bishop.[24]

Gibson's success in attempting to legitimate his authority in the colonies was very limited. No copy of the commission granted to him in 1728 was sent to the colonial governors, and some of them ignored Gibson's claim to authority, and declined to support his commissaries. Lord Baltimore, for example, as proprietor of Maryland, claimed absolute authority in matters ecclesiastical. In the 1730s he appointed two clergy whom it was claimed had been 'driven from Virginia for immorality'. Gibson and Baltimore quarrelled over this, and Baltimore seems to have deliberately appointed clergy whom Gibson had declined to license.[25] The commissary in Maryland resigned in despair in 1734, and was never replaced. In Carolina the commissary did hold annual visitations for the clergy and called a convention when business required it. But even there the weakness of the commissary's position was demonstrated when he began proceedings against George Whitefield for preaching in a dissenting meeting house and conducting services without using the forms prescribed by the Prayer Book. Whitefield ignored the sentence of suspension, and the commissary dare not excommunicate him, and in 1749 the commissary resigned. The commissaries in Jamaica and Barbados also found themselves opposed by the clergy and resisted by local lawyers. Not even the requirement that all clergy should be licensed by the bishop carried much weight, for vestries seem to have employed clergy at will, and seldom presented them to a governor for induction.[26]

Between 1701 and 1786 the SPG sent out 309 missionaries to North America.[27] However, a supply of priests was not really enough to sustain the links between parishes and congregations in the colonies and the Church in England. If the Anglican congregations in the colonies were to flourish and to take seriously mission amongst the native Americans, as successive bishops had noted, they needed the stimulus of local management and leadership, which could not be provided by the few commissaries.

Gibson was well aware that what was really needed was a bishop living in North America. However, initially he feared that any scheme for a bishop in the colonies might be set back by a report he had received in August 1724 from his commissary in Maryland, that 'Mr Talbot, late minister of Burlington ... had returned from England two years ago in Episcopal Orders', and of Dr Welton, who had arrived 'about six weeks ago' and had secured a church in Philadelphia. Welton was well-known to Gibson as a London incumbent who was notorious for his Jacobite sympathies and anti-government activities, and now also appeared to have been consecrated, like Talbot, by one of the bishops claiming succession from the bishops who had been excluded from office when they failed to take the oaths of allegiance to William and Mary when James II was deposed. The commissary feared that these two clergy 'would poison the people of the province', since people 'would rather take Confirmation from them than have none at all'. He reported that although the people in Maryland had no regard for them, in Philadelphia much disturbance had been caused. He reported that 'Mr Talbot had convened all the clergy to meet him, put on his robes, and demanded episcopal obedience from them', but the governor had intervened, and ordered the church to be closed. Gibson reported this to the government, and the law officers of the crown issued writs to the two clergy, requiring them to return to England, which Welton obeyed, while Talbot promised to be of good behaviour, and not to attempt to exercise an episcopal ministry, if he were permitted to remain.[28] The government and Gibson were understandably nervous about this, for only two years before Francis Atterbury, the bishop of Rochester, had been exiled for his part in a Jacobite plot to restore the Stuart monarchy.[29]

Subsequently, and perhaps to counteract this, Gibson proposed plans for two suffragan bishops, one for 'the Islands' and one for 'the Mainland'. He invited the clergy of Maryland to nominate one of their number to be consecrated as a bishop. They nominated a Mr Colebatch, who was described as a 'Whig and ye best of ministers', but the Maryland courts granted a writ of *ne exeat* against him, and he was prevented from sailing for England.[30] Gibson was much attacked during the outburst of anti-clericalism in England in the 1730s for his attempts to establish bishops in the North American colonies.[31]

In spite of all these setbacks, however, money continued to be contributed to pay for bishops for the colonies. In 1728 an anonymous benefactor donated £1,000, and in 1741 Dugald Campbell and Lady Elizabeth Hastings each gave £200 to the fund the SPG had set up following Tenison's bequest. In 1745 Governor Wentworth of New Hampshire offered the SPG some tracts of land for the support of a bishop, and Bishops Maddocks of Worcester and Pearce of Bangor consulted the government on behalf of the Society and were surprised to discover the duke of Newcastle, the secretary of state, willing to consider this proposal. He agreed to ask Archbishop Potter to draw up a plan for one or more bishops for the colonies. Potter consulted Gibson, and they began to move in the matter. Although in due course a plan was presented by Potter and the other bishops to Newcastle, on behalf of the Society, nothing more was heard of it, even after Potter sent the duke a reminder in March 1746. The government had probably been diverted by the 1745 Rebellion. In 1749 it was suggested at a meeting of the SPG that a new approach should be made to the government with Wentworth's scheme, but Potter's successor, Archbishop Herring deflected the suggestion saying it was 'not a proper time'.[32]

When the real threat of a Stuart restoration had receded after the Battle of Culloden in 1746, it might have been expected that the government would look more enthusiastically on a proposal for the establishment of bishoprics in the colonies. Thomas Sherlock, on taking up office as bishop of London in 1748 had been shocked by the level of work and expense Gibson had undertaken in the ecclesiastical administration of the North American colonies. He suggested that it was inappropriate that all the business should be the responsibility of the bishop of London alone. Nor did he think that the jurisdiction was being exercised effectively. Robert Jenney, Gibson's commissary in Pennsylvania had complained to him that 'the Laity laughed at [his commission] and the clergy seem to despise it'. The commission did not even give a commissary power to admonish or suspend erring clergy.[33] Sherlock therefore saw little point in applying to the Privy Council for a new commission to exercise ecclesiastical jurisdiction in the North American colonies. Instead he suggested that the American jurisdiction should be divided up amongst the English bishops, and also that suffragans might be appointed to live and work in the colonies to achieve a more effective episcopal oversight of them. He was ambitious to resolve the problem of the spiritual supervision of the colonies and claimed that he would regard it as 'the glory of my life, if I c'd be the instrument . . . of putting the Church abroad upon a true and primitive foot'.[34]

Subsequently in February 1749, Sherlock waited upon the king and 'laid before him the state of Religion in the Plantations and the Necessity there was of having a Bishop' and he obtained the king's permission to apply to his ministers with his proposal to resolve the matter. After frequent delays and postponements he 'waited upon the King again and had his leave to acquaint his Ministers that it was his Majesty's Pleasure that they should take the Affair into their Consideration'. This resulted in a barren meeting at Newcastle House, following which Sherlock drew up a paper in which he pointed out that Gibson's commission, obtained in 1728, had been defective, confining his authority to the clergy.[35] As a result he had no authority over churchwardens and other laity, or even over counterfeit clergy; nor could he hear appeals from his commissaries' decisions; for appeal lay only to the officers of state in England. Sherlock went on to point out that American Anglicans were being deprived of confirmation and ordination, and that there was a risk that the Moravian bishops, who had been permitted to minister in the colonies in 1736, might intervene by conducting ordinations of Anglican candidates. He answered the objection that there was opposition to bishops in the colonies by pointing out that bishops would not be forced upon the New England colonies where there were very few Anglican congregations or clergy; and that it was not intended that the bishops should have civil powers or that consistory courts should be introduced to America: the bishops' functions being limited to confirmation, ordination and the superintendence of the clergy, nor would they be maintained out of taxes in the colonies, nor by the crown, but by granting them other preferment, and by means of endowments.[36]

The king referred Sherlock's paper to the Privy Council. Again nothing happened, but Archbishop Herring, in mid-April commended to the attention of the Lord Chancellor, Lord Hardwicke, the possibility of creating bishops without civil powers for the colonies.[37] Meanwhile Sherlock was sounding out opinion in the colonies through an agent, and discovered that there was apprehension that the appointment of bishops would infringe the privileges and freedoms of the colonists, and the rights of the proprietors of proprietorial colonies. The government, apparently fearing the arousal of party passions in the Church, and of attracting the enmity of dissenters, tried to prevent Sherlock from bringing his paper to the Privy Council. The duke of Newcastle firmly indicated his opposition to the proposal. However, Sherlock was determined to put it to the Privy Council, and submitted his paper to a meeting in April 1750, at which consideration of it was postponed until after the king's forthcoming visit to Hanover.[38]

Sherlock attempted to rally support for his proposals through a general meeting of the SPG from which the archbishop of Canterbury was absent. The Society agreed to print 2,000 copies of Sherlock's proposals, and to send a letter to the governors of the American colonies to consult them about 'the utility of Episcopacy unoffensively settled in their several colonies'. Sherlock was asked to draft the letter, which it was agreed should be put to another meeting of the Society the following Friday. Archbishop Herring, as president of the SPG, received a copy of Sherlock's proposal, and immediately forwarded it to Lord Hardwicke, and arranged to meet Lord Hardwicke and the Lord President of the Council. They agreed that the bishop of London's action in bringing his proposal before the SPG, while it was still before the king in Council, was 'an improper and irregular Step', and they sent one of the clerks of the Council to acquaint the bishop with their opinion. When the Society met the following Friday, Sherlock explained to members what had happened, and stated that it had always been his custom 'never to engage in anything contrary to the Opinion of those noble Persons who the king entrusted with the Affairs of the Publick'. He thus withdrew his proposals from the Society's consideration.[39]

Horatio Walpole, the auditor general of the plantations' revenues, set out the ministry's views on the matter in a subsequent letter to Sherlock, which had probably been the basis of the resistance of successive governments since the beginning of the century. He pointed out that there was no evidence that the colonial governors wanted bishops in their territories, they were quite happy with the commissaries. The creation of bishoprics would also arouse the opposition of dissenters both in England and in America. This would arouse the High Church party to agitate against the government, as it had during Queen Anne's reign, and the Low Church party would attack the bishops for attempting to increase ecclesiastical power, as a result Parliament would divide into Church factions on the question, and the Church might be fatally damaged by the intervention of anti-Church factions, and government might be rendered impossible. The government were successful in suppressing Sherlock's proposals, for, when the king returned from Hanover, the proposals never reappeared for discussion at the Privy Council.

Sherlock was not deterred. In November 1750 he was still pushing the project, and Herring suspected that most of the bishops would support him. It would seem that Bishop Butler of Durham had also drawn up a paper proposing that 'spiritual bishops' might be sent to the colonies without offence.[40]

However, by December, Sherlock was diverted to a new approach of attempting to persuade the king to accept his nomination of a suffragan, and to issue a commission to consecrate a bishop for the West Indies. He proposed to the duke of Newcastle that one of the canonries of St Paul's cathedral should be annexed to a suffragan bishop of the diocese of London, authorized to work in the colonies. After a second letter to remind him, Newcastle replied that 'the king was not pleased to approve the proposal', and pointed out, 'The appointment of Bishops in the West Indies is a great and national issue: [and] has long been under the deliberation of great and wise Men heretofore and was by them laid aside: and ought not to be resumed for personal considerations: or at all looked upon in that light.' Sherlock replied to this snub pointing out that it was not a personal matter but 'a scheme for the public Service to enable not only myself but every bishop of London to execute with some tolerable degree of care the Extensive commission he is to have in his Majesty's foreign dominions'. However, Newcastle was immovable.[41]

News of this attempt to secure bishops for America led to much opposition from English dissenters, which confirmed the government in their desire to let the matter drop.

Sherlock's next ploy was to commence a policy of inaction, by which he hoped to force the hands of the government. He pointed out that the powers given to Gibson under the commission issued in 1728 were personal to Gibson, and so confirmed no powers upon him to appoint commissaries for the American colonies. He also refused to take out a new commission to give him legal authority to exercise ecclesiastical jurisdiction in the colonies, and gave the least attention possible to American affairs. He saw himself as taking a stand once and for all for the appointment of bishops to the North American colonies by refusing to accept a commission of doubtful legal authority and by perpetuating a system which was intrinsically incapable of caring for the spiritual needs of the American colonists.[42] In writing to Horatio Walpole, in 1751, Sherlock pointed out that, in his view, the spiritual care of the colonies was 'improperly lodged [in the bishop of London]: for a Bishop to live at one end of the world and his Church at another, must make the office very uncomfortable to the Bishop, and in a great measure useless to his people'.[43] Sherlock thus allowed a general anarchy to fall upon the Anglican Church in America, in order to force the hand of the government. However, he failed to provoke the government, which declined to reconsider the matter, and he was reduced to consenting to exercise spiritual oversight of the American colonies; but he only agreed to do it provisionally and did not agree to apply for another commission.

The very negative attitude towards ecclesiastical jurisdiction in the North American colonies of a government, led by good churchmen such as the duke of Newcastle, Henry Pelham and Lord Hardwicke, requires some explanation. Probably their view was accurately represented in Horatio Walpole's letter to Sherlock. They believed that the High Church party was still 'so numerous and warm and ready to lay hold of any occasion to inflame the nation, that any alteration in ye form or doctrine of ye Church of England would be . . . a dangerous attempt as productive of greater troubles than ye good expected from it would compensate'.[44] None of them ever denied the desirability of a colonial episcopate on purely ecclesiastical grounds. The duke of Bedford appears to have privately approved it, as did the earl of Halifax at a later date.

The bishops seem to have generally acquiesced to the government view, in spite of their own belief that episcopacy was pastorally essential, for they never contradicted it. They too feared the repercussions of political controversy about the Church. They were aware that the domestic political repercussions from an untimely agitation about the affair might be as damaging to the Church as to the State. That was why Sherlock's plan to air his paper at the SPG meeting was thought so unwise by both ministers and the bishops, and why the bishops never publicly challenged successive governments on the matter.[45] However much reform might be needed in the Church, the bishops saw it as too dangerous to restir the disputes that had broken out in Queen Anne's reign, and which might allow the Church's enemies to have their say in Parliament, and even to tack an anti-church clause on to a church bill. It was only bishops of London, who were weighed down with the considerable burden of correspondence about ecclesiastical matters in North America, in addition to their responsibilities for London and the counties of Middlesex, Hertfordshire and Essex, who were willing to push for an improvement of the pastoral oversight of the Church in the American colonies.

When Sherlock died in 1761 his successor, Thomas Secker continued to press the matter. He pointed out to Horatio Walpole that, 'I believe there never is or was a Bishop of the church of England from the Revolution [1688] to this present day, that hath not desired the establishment of Bishoprics in our Colonies ... And many more, of the greatest eminence might be named who were and are zealous for it ... nor have the lay part of [the committee of the SPG] ever refused to concur in them'.[46] He went on to point out to Walpole that, by being excluded from confirmation Anglicans in North America were 'prohibited from the exercise of one part of their religion'. Secker also noted that Lord Halifax, then President of the Board of Trade was 'very earnest for Bishops in America'. In 1762 William Smith, a leading American clergyman visited London to present a petition in favour of unifying the Anglican Church in the colonies by means of the appointment of bishops. Secker supported this, and urged the secretary of state to propose the petition to the Privy Council.[47]

However, by the early 1760s there had begun to be close links between the Independents in New England and in England. Both were deeply opposed to the appointment of bishops to the colonies, and they were very suspicious of the intentions of the English clergy. In 1763 Secker doubted that the government would 'dare to meddle with what will certainly raise opposition'. In 1771 when a further petition was sent from the Anglican clergy of New York and New Jersey to the secretary of state for the American department requesting the appointment of bishops in the colonies, the agents in London of the New England Independents immediately and successfully lobbied against it.[48]

In addition, in the 1760s a new political problem had emerged which made governments equally reluctant to permit legislation or royal letters patent to be granted for the creation of bishoprics in the North American colonies. There was a growing mood of independence in the colonies, and it was feared that while the creation of bishoprics might offend dissenting non-Anglicans in New England, the bishops themselves might become foci of opposition and independence in other colonies. Once appointed, a bishop would be less easily controlled than a governor. Unless a bishop were seeking further preferment to an English diocese, he need feel no particular loyalty to a

British government. The Irish precedent suggested that it might be exceptional for bishops to be translated to English sees. Secker, writing in 1766, noted that after the furore over the Stamp Act it would not be possible to introduce a bishop into America, because such an action would be suspected of trying to assert greater government control over the colonies. It was not thought that George III's suggestion that a bishopric should be created in Quebec, where there was already a Roman Catholic bishop, and there were few Protestant dissenters, with jurisdiction over all of North America, was realistic.[49]

Separated by the North Atlantic, Anglicans, over time, developed differently in North America from England. By the 1760s some areas of the colonies had been settled for several generations, and no longer saw themselves as dependent upon London and England for ideas, or even for higher education. Although the SPG recruited English candidates for parishes in the colonies, colleges had been established at Cambridge, Massachusetts, New Haven, New York and Williamsburg, Virginia, where local ordination candidates could be educated and, even though they had to travel to London for ordination, their socialization and education was colonial American and not English. The contacts of the American clergy with the Church of England were relatively few and remote. They had little experience of bishops and of episcopal supervision at firsthand, and no experience of diocesan administration, with its regular round of archdeacons' and bishops' visitations, and the work of their courts.

Although, as we have noted, the parish system, with churchwardens and vestry meetings, had been transplanted into the colonies in the seventeenth century, it had developed in its own way. Most significantly, parishes were expected to support their own clergy. A parish was expected to provide a church, a parsonage house, some glebe, and to contribute towards the stipend. Although the SPG was normally willing to provide a contribution of £50 a year for a number of years and a 'parcel of books' to provide a basic library for an incumbent, the parishioners were expected in the end to provide all the stipend for the incumbent. The SPG acting on behalf of the English bishops, and more especially the bishop of London, provided invaluable support for the expanding work of the ministry of the Church in the American colonies, but its long-term aim was that colonial parishes should become financially self-supporting. By 1759 the Society felt the parishes in Carolina were sufficiently well-established to no longer need their grants. However, by the outbreak of the American War of Independence in 1776 the Society was still supporting seventy-seven missionaries in the colonies which declared independence.[50]

In the majority of the colonies, the Anglican laity, having committed themselves to housing and paying their incumbent, expected to appoint him themselves. In the majority of New England parishes either the laity elected the incumbent themselves, or the churchwardens, acting on behalf of the vestry, chose the incumbent. Even where the parish was dependent on the SPG for a grant to pay the incumbent, they merely reported their choice of incumbent to the Society, with the expectation that the grant would be continued. When a priest could not be obtained, for there was a shortage of priests, a lay reader would be appointed. In Pennsylvania the laity meeting in vestry nominated their rectors, and in Virginia vestries had also secured the right to elect their incumbents and had effectively taken charge of all ecclesiastical affairs. In Carolina the vestries elected their incumbents, and by 1766 the Church in South Carolina being financially self-supporting, and with probably half the legislature Anglicans, the Church there felt confidently independent of London. Only in Maryland did the laity not appoint the parish priests, where, under the founding charter, Lord Baltimore, the proprietor, appointed parish priests.

While English parishes in the eighteenth century were in no way dominated or controlled by their clergy, and in some cases they too elected their own incumbents or made grants to supplement their stipends, no English parishes had such control of their incumbents, as did the colonial parishes. Parishioners appointed the incumbent, and because they paid him they could also dismiss him at will. Although Anglicanism seems to have been increasing in numbers in the colonies, especially in New England after 1760, part of the increase was derived from converts from Presbyterianism and Independency, who again emphasized the role of lay people in managing the affairs of the parish and the acceptability of a lay reader to conduct worship and undertake pastoral care, if an ordained minister could not be procured.

In many ways Anglicanism in North America was developing

along congregationalist lines. In each colony the particular constitution and attitude of the legislature led to different relationships between the Anglican Church and the government of the colony, varying from the establishment of the Church in Maryland and Virginia, where in 1771 at least 130 of the 230 or so Anglican clergy in North America were to be found, to the minority position of the Church in some of the New England colonies. There was no unifying factor between the congregations of each colony, nor was there any unifying factor between the congregations within each colony. They all separately looked to the far-distant bishop of London for their authority, and as since 1748 he had appointed no more commissaries, there was no local manifestation of the bishop's authority in any of the colonies. There were no formal requirements for clergy and churchwardens to meet regularly at an archdeacon's visitation in order to worship together and to hear the archdeacon's charge, or more infrequently, to be summoned to the bishop's visitation to hear his charge and report on the condition of their parishes and to present candidates for confirmation. Nor were there the triennial or so visits to parishes by archdeacons to inspect the fabric of the parish churches. Eighteenth-century English bishops may have spent half their year sitting in the House of Lords in London, but they still carefully supervised their dioceses, and were potent symbols of unity for their dioceses. As successive bishops of London acknowledged, they were unable to meet this need in the various American colonies.

What the American clergy and laity had never had, on the whole they did not miss; nor did they want a local episcopate. In the early years of the century there may have been some wish among colonists for a bishop among them, but, with a growing sense of independence from London, this had largely disappeared. In Maryland in the 1760s there was no enthusiasm for bishops, for they were associated with interference by the British government. In Virginia, too, Anglican laymen were opposed to the usurpation of their authority by an Anglican bishop. In this most Anglican of the colonies the determined dominance of the laity, and their resistance to external interference is most striking. The enthusiasm of Bishop Secker and others for the establishment of bishoprics in the colonies was regarded with great suspicion by the colonists, including devout Anglican lay people. It was feared that bishops would be forced upon unwilling colonial legislatures, and through their influence the liberties and gains that the dissenting congregations, many of which in New England traced their origins to groups who in the early seventeenth century had fled from England to escape episcopal interference, would be snatched away. The argument that the appointment of bishops would link the colonies more closely with the mother country was not one that appealed to the colonists; it only heightened their alarm about interference with their liberties and separate development.

The anxiety was exacerbated by the agitation over the Stamp Act in 1765, which intensified resistance to the introduction of bishops to the colonies, for it was argued that if Parliament could fix a tax without reference to the colonial assemblies, it could also establish the Church throughout the colonies, and could impose bishops upon them. Proposals to establish bishops were seen as a further attempt at royal encroachment. Churchmen who had successfully defended the rights of their vestries against the interference of commissioners, royal governors, colonial legislatures and zealous clergymen, were not willing to condone any proposals for an ecclesiastical officer whose claim to authority might well produce the most serious challenge yet to local autonomy in church government.

However, not everyone saw episcopacy as a threat. Some of the converts from Independency in New England were attracted by the idea of an episcopally governed Church. In the 1760s a group of New England clergy, mostly converts or sons of converts from Independency, organized a convention to promote the idea of a 'purely spiritual episcopacy' deriving its authority from the Church of England, not from the British government. They suggested that bishops in North America should be 'primitive bishops' exercising the authority of the sacraments that the bishops in the early Church had exercised, confirming, ordaining and overseeing the clergy, but not holding the jurisdiction that, over time, had accrued to English bishops, such as granting probate of wills, issuing marriage licences, supervising the spiritual lives and morality of the laity through their courts, above all, not sitting in the legislature and taking part in civil government with the rank and accoutrements of a peer. The advocates of this form of episcopacy included two New York parish priests, Samuel Seabury and Charles Inglis who, in due course, would have the opportunity to try out their ideas about episcopacy.

The public expression of such ideas aroused considerable opposition among both presbyterians and Independents in New York, who jointly organized annual conferences from 1766 until the outbreak of the War of Independence to counter these ideas. They claimed that a 'spiritual episcopate' would be used as a Trojan horse by the British government to gain authority in moral and spiritual matters over the colonists. They added fuel to the argument by suggesting that tithes might be introduced into the colonies. Most significantly for their case, however, they pointed out that the Anglicans themselves in the colonies were not united over the desire for bishops.

Apart from this group of clergy from New York and some parts of New England, where in any case Anglicans were in a minority, there seems to have been little enthusiasm among clergy or laity for bishops. Insistence upon local ecclesiastial autonomy was uniformly evident, and resistance to hierarchical control was universal. In Maryland the legislature went so far as to express the view that bishops were unnecessary and that the laity should have greater power to supervise the clergy. People were generally happy with the way things were. The controversy aroused by the proposals to introduce episcopacy to the colonies played a considerable part in the growing resentment against Britain, and in the intensification of the revolutionary spirit.

Average American Anglicans probably did not see themselves as radicals, but as moderates or conservatives who wished to maintain the long-standing *status quo* in the colonies. It was the English bishops, possibly supported by the British government, who were taking the radical action. In the southern colonies the majority of both the laity and the clergy supported the struggle against the British for the independence of the colonies. In the northern colonies, where Anglicans were in the minority and parishes needed more support from the SPG, both financially and in the form of English clergy, the majority of Anglicans opposed independence. When the leaders of the colonies asserted their independence from Britain two thirds of the fifty-five signatories of the Declaration of Independence were Anglicans. The Declaration and the subsequent War, however were to have a dramatic impact on the Anglican Church in the new United States.

All Anglicans were faced with moral and practical dilemmas. At their ordinations clergy had been required to take an oath of loyalty to the king. The Declaration of Independence now required them to break that oath. They had also undertaken to use the Book of Common Prayer which required them to pray publicly twice daily for the king. Congregations therefore would know precisely where their incumbent stood, and might react accordingly. In Virginia and Maryland the legislatures in 1776 passed Acts requiring the clergy to omit the prayers for the king from the liturgy, and in some states vestries overruled clergy who insisted on praying for the king. It has been estimated that of the 250 or so Anglican clergy in America in 1776, a third supported independence, while a third were committed loyalists to the British crown. During the course of the War the number of Anglican clergy dropped by nearly a half. Some were English SPG missionaries who returned to England and some of the New England clergy with their parishioners moved north to the loyalist colonies of Nova Scotia and New Brunswick. Also there were no replacements for the clergy who died. Even if it had been possible to travel to England, any ordinand would have had to show his disloyalty to his new nation by taking an oath of allegiance to a foreign ruler, and English bishops were bound, by law, to extract such an oath before a man was ordained.

Practically too the clergy suffered. Those who received a grant from the SPG to supplement their income lost it. In the six states where the Church was established the legislatures abolished the establishment, and clergy lost any financial support they might have received from the taxes levied by the government. Strong popular prejudices against Britain were easily focused upon Anglican churches because of their ties with the Church of England. Seven years of war inflicted significant damage on many Anglican church buildings, which were often the most prominent buildings in a settlement. No other religious body suffered so extensively or severely during the War.[51]

The Declaration of Independence, and the subsequent War was disastrous for the Anglican Church in the new United States. It had no centralized leadership; it had lost public financial support and loyalty; and it had lost nearly half its clergy and had no obvious means of replacing them without radically changing its nature. To thoughtful Anglicans it became clear that to survive as a distinctive church in the post-war era, they would have to reorganize their Church structure, accept a new status and achieve their identity under drastically altered conditions from those they had known in the past. How they did this would have important precedents for the development of a world-wide Anglican communion. This will be the subject of the next chapter.

CHAPTER 3

The Origins of the Overseas Episcopate

In 1780 Anglican dioceses were confined to the British Isles, by 1840 there were thirty-seven Anglican dioceses outside Britain. In spite of the intense lobbying of bishops of London from 1660 to 1776 no overseas bishopric had been established to meet the needs for episcopal sacraments of the significant numbers of Anglicans living in North America. However, after 1776 the situation changed rapidly, for successive British governments began to see some advantage in creating overseas bishoprics, as part of a policy for the long-term settlement of overseas territories under the much firmer control of the British government than had been the case with the former American colonies. Additionally a new concern for mission among native peoples, stimulated by both the evangelical revival, through the Church Missionary Society (CMS), and the High Church revival, focused in the re-invigoration of the SPG, created a need for the supervision of missionaries. The encouragement of migration to the colonies from the 1820s onwards created a need for clergy to minister to the migrants, and to create institutions that would reflect life at home. For a time, both the government and the English bishops had a common interest in promoting an overseas episcopate.

NORTH AMERICA

The first moves for an overseas episcopate did not come from England, but from the Anglican citizens of the new United States.[1] As we have seen, their predicament was great. How could they continue to be an episcopal Church if their bishops were citizens of a foreign country, and, to be ordained, their clergy had to swear an oath of allegiance to a foreign ruler, thus making them traitors to their own country?

In 1776 Granville Sharpe, an Anglican layman, had published

two tracts, *The Law of Retribution* and *Congregational Courts* which set out to show the importance of episcopacy as being, according to a maxim of English Common Law, 'the strength of the Republic'. The publication of the tracts 'had the extraordinary effect of convincing a very large body of Dissenters and Presbyterians, as well as Churchmen in America of the propriety of establishing Episcopacy among themselves in the United States; so that even during the war a motion had been made in the Congress for that purpose'.[2] Benjamin Franklin and other leaders of the new republic had their prejudices against the institution of episcopacy removed after reading this.

Subsequently, in the summer of 1782 William White, the rector of Christ and St Peter's Church in Philadelphia, published *The Case of the Protestant Episcopal Church in the USA Considered*. He contended that the former ties binding the Anglicans in America were broken, and that 'their future continuance can be provided for only by voluntary associations for union and good government'. In essence this implied that, in his view, each episcopal parish was independent and free to participate in any plan for organization it wished, at either state or national levels. The basic tenet of White's plan was that the organization of the Church should be built from the parish upwards, not from a diocese downwards. This proposal expressed the American revolutionary idea that in a free government, the people's interest and good government are identical, and that the best way to ensure this is to allow the people a maximum say in the formation and opinion of government. White argued that what was good for the formation of the state and national governments was equally valid for the development of an ecclesiastical government.

In order to provide a forum where the problems and solutions involved in reorganizing the Church could be discussed, White advocated a convention, composed of clergy and laity elected from the local parishes, to decide matters in respect of religion. This was not in fact an entirely new idea, for it had been customary for the clergy in each colony to meet together in conventions to discuss matters of common interest, as the need arose. The SPG, in its instructions issued to the clergy it sent to work in the American colonies, had recommended them to 'keep up a brotherly correspondence' with their fellow clergy, by meeting together from time to time, in the absence of episcopal leadership, for 'mutual advice and assistance'. White proposed, however, that the conventions should include lay people and that there should be no designated differentiation between the power of the clergy and that of the laity in the convention. Both groups, he proposed, should meet in one body and vote together on all issues. Neither should have the power of veto. This assembly should exercise the authority to elect a 'superior order of ministers'. White was thus applying the concepts of natural rights, and a contractual theory of government to the practical problem of reorganizing the Anglican Church in the United States. In principle he was proposing that each Anglican had a basic right to participate in the development of his Church's government, and this right could be expressed through the parish delegate elected to the state convention. On all these points White's suggestions were carbon copies of ideas that had been developed and used in the preparation of the several state constitutions, and the Articles of Confederation. Bishops in White's proposal were to be introduced into the Church in America as the presiding ministers of the Church, but he recommended that after their election, they should still continue to function as parish clergy.

Because of the impossibility of obtaining episcopal consecration for these superior ministers while hostilities continued between Britain and the United States, White favoured a presbyteral pattern of ordination by three priests, as an emergency measure in order to maintain the number of clergy required to minister in the parishes during the War. He cited Cranmer, Whitgift and Hooker, in support of this emergency plan. Charles Inglis, rector of Holy Trinity, New York, opposed this departure from regular episcopal order, even in the current emergency. However, in general, White's plan met with approval from both clergy and laity in the American Church.

In 1783 an Anglican convention met in Maryland comprising only clergy. They affirmed the necessity of the three orders of the Church and required that all ministers should be episcopally ordained, and that ministers had the right to meet and order the liturgy and organization of the Church. They also elected one of their number, William Smith, rector of St Paul's parish Chestertown, Maryland, and formerly provost of the college in Philadelphia, as their bishop, and drew up a testimonial on his behalf to the bishop of London requesting him to arrange for

Smith's consecration. However, at a subsequent meeting of a Maryland convention, lay representatives who were present, but meeting separately from the clergy, proposed four additional articles to be included in the constitution of the Church. First, that any clergyman ordained in any foreign State should be forbidden to take any oath or obligation to any foreign power, civil or ecclesiastical. Second, a bishop's authority was defined as merely the right to ordain and confirm and to serve as president of ecclesiastical meetings. Third, while the training, examination and recommendation of clergy should be the responsibility of the clergy, the acceptance of a minister in a parish should be reserved exclusively to the people of the parish who maintained him. Fourth, it was ruled that every parish should be entitled to representation by one clergyman and one lay person at all future conventions. They recommended that change in any of these rules should be by a two-thirds majority of the convention. The clergy accepted these four additional articles. This effectively nullified Smith's election. The proposals that a bishop should be consecrated by the bishop of London, and that the clergy might have a veto in the convention were also excluded.

Conventions followed in other states. The convention for Pennsylvania in Philadelphia in 1784 affirmed the place of the laity in the Church's decision-making. A convention of clergy and laity in Massachusetts affirmed the decisions which they had received from the Pennsylvania convention. The Virginia convention, which met in 1785, was dominated by lay people, and they and the conventions in the other states where they were subsequently called, gave priority to the reorganization of the Church, rather than to the provision of bishops. The people who led in the reorganization of the Church in their states were, for the most part, committed to the realization of principles of representative government in church polity. By arranging their church government within the acceptable ideological and practical methods of the time they were hoping to rebuild their Church in a form acceptable to their compatriots, and to remove much of the stigma that had fallen upon it for deriving its authority from Britain, which had been exacerbated by the actions of the Anglican loyalists, who had opposed and resisted the establishment of the republic, and in some cases migrated to Nova Scotia.

Significantly, the two leading Methodists in the United States,

Thomas Coke and Francis Asbury, who were both Anglican clergy, met two representatives of the Episcopal convention during the 'Christmas Conference' of the American Methodist Church in 1784. It was at this conference that the American Methodists established their independence of British Methodism. The delegates recognized that the two groups shared the same liturgy, Articles and discipline, and it was suggested that some sort of merger or working relationship might be worked out for the two groups in America. However, in the end the negotiations failed; it was claimed by one of the Episcopal delegates, John Andrews, because the Episcopalians felt that the Methodists were bound to claim that 'Mr Wesley be the first link in the chain upon which their church is suspended'. However, the new American Methodist Church also, like the emerging Episcopal Church bore the marks of American liberty in its foundations, which were not viewed sympathetically by John Wesley himself. However, the American Anglican-Methodist clergy did ordain Coke and Asbury as their bishops, as White had suggested might be a way for the continuing Anglicans to obtain episcopal government for their own church.[3]

A notably different approach to developing new authority patterns in the Church was taken in Connecticut, where in March 1783 the clergy met secretly and decided that the first priority in the development of the Church was to obtain a bishop to guide the Church. They believed that episcopacy was an ordinance of Christ, and that lay people should not be involved in decisions about the faith, order and practice of the Church. They feared that unless they acted quickly and decisively the Anglican Church in the United States would reorganize itself on a basis of state and national conventions, without bishops. The Connecticut clergy acted quickly to head off this possibility, and in April 1783, called a meeting of Anglican clergy in New York to draw up a letter requesting the archbishop of York (Canterbury being vacant following the death of Archbishop Cornwallis on March 19th) to consecrate a bishop for America. Their choice was Samuel Seabury, a refugee Anglican priest in New York, who had been an enthusiastic supporter of bishops in the 1760s, and had been loyal to Britain during the War of Independence.

Seabury arrived in England on 7 July 1783, with the request from the clergy at the New York meeting for his consecration, and a plea for funds to support him if the laity refused to provide funds for a bishop. He reported back to Connecticut that the English bishops had declined to consecrate him because they did not wish to appear to be interfering in the affairs of an independent State, and also because there was no financial provision for his support, and because he did not have the support of the laity of his proposed diocese. He was requested to obtain a statement from the state's legislative assembly assuring the English bishops that a bishop consecrated by them would be accepted without controversy in Connecticut. The bishops also thought that an Enabling Act of the British Parliament would be required to permit them to consecrate a bishop without requiring him to take the oath of allegiance to the king. Although Robert Lowth, the bishop of London had taken a step in this direction when in August 1784 he introduced a bill permitting bishops to ordain subjects of foreign countries deacon and priest without requiring the oath, which was passed, no mention was made of the consecration of a bishop.

Probably the most important factor weighing against Seabury was the unwillingness of the British government to allow anything to be done that might unnecessarily antagonize the government of the new United States. In September 1784 Seabury turned to the Scottish bishops. They had already been approached in 1782 by George Berkeley, a prebendary of Canterbury and son of Bishop Berkeley, the distinguished philosopher, who had wished to establish a college in the American colonies. Berkeley's plan was to send a bishop, consecrated by the Scottish bishops, to forestall White's proposal for a presbyteral consecration of a bishop. Berkeley had failed to convince the Scottish bishops to take part in this, but he was instrumental in persuading them to consecrate Seabury.[4] They agreed to consecrate him at their next meeting, in November 1784. Seabury seems to have been unaware that his consecration by the Scottish bishops would not be acceptable to the English bishops, for the bishops of the Scottish Episcopal Church were still proscribed under the Penal Laws passed following the 1745 Rebellion. At his consecration the Scottish bishops required Seabury to affirm that bishops exercised their office 'independent of all lay persons' and to declare that the Anglican Church in Connecticut and the Scottish Episcopal Church were in full communion, and to undertake to try to introduce the communion office, approved by the Scottish bishops in 1764, into any American Prayer Book that might be produced.

News of the Connecticut initiative did not leak into the other states until May 1784. When it did, a meeting was called in New York in October 1784, which was attended by sixteen clergy and eleven lay people representing the conventions of seven states, the Anglican congregations in Massachusetts and Rhode Island having rejected the invitation to send representatives. At this meeting a draft constitution was approved for a general convention comprising state representatives of clergy and laity meeting together, but voting by houses, which would keep as close as possible in liturgy and doctrine to the Church of England, with a bishop in every state, who would *ex officio* be a member of the general convention. This meeting in effect adopted the strategy set out in White's *Case*. It had met publicly, after all the churches had been notified and invited to send lay as well as clerical representatives, who had deliberated together. It had decided that a national legislative body should be established and the question of episcopacy or executive authority had been considered subsequently. This convention adopted the name 'The Protestant Episcopal Church'.

On his return in 1785, Seabury summoned a convention of the clergy of Connecticut. At this meeting he criticized the 1784 general convention. He also ordained three deacons for Connecticut parishes and one for a Maryland parish, and he subsequently ordained eight more deacons for parishes in other states. He also administered confirmation in other New England states, thus ensuring that his influence, and possibly his ideas, would not be confined to Connecticut.

Connecticut did not send any representatives to the 1785 general convention, for it would have been difficult not to include Seabury himself among the representatives, and he declined to attend lest he should not be elected chairman, and as a bishop, would have to accept the chairmanship of someone who was not a bishop. The convention, at Philadelphia, was attended by sixteen clergy and twenty-six lay people from seven states, and was dominated by clergy and laity who were aggressively loyal to the principles of the republic. The draft constitution that they drew up made no concessions to Seabury's views. Lay representatives were insisted upon, and the activities of bishops were to be restricted to their own states unless they were otherwise requested. It was also recommended that a bishop might be suspended from office by his state convention. It was agreed that a request should be drafted to be sent to the English bishops to ask them to consecrate as bishops priests who had been elected by their state conventions and recommended by the general convention. It was also agreed that the state conventions might proceed to elect candidates for consecration as bishops, after having secured the approval of their states' legislatures for this.

By the next general convention in 1786 the New York, Pennsylvania, and Virginia conventions had elected candidates for consecration as bishops. The Pennsylvania convention had even agreed to assume responsibility for the expenses of the bishop-elect. However, the Virginia convention had elected their candidate by a majority of only one, with a quarter of the members abstaining, and the general convention felt unable to confirm his candidature. The request to the archbishop of Canterbury to consecrate the two candidates was agreed and John Adams, the United States minister in London was asked to present the request to the archbishop, with the assurance that any consecration would not be regarded as an interference in the affairs of the American states.

A second general convention was called in 1786 to receive the archbishop's reply. He expressed himself positively, and asked to receive a copy of the constitution of the American Church, and a copy of their proposed Prayer Book, in order to discuss them with his fellow bishops. In October 1786 a third general convention was called, at which it was reported that the archbishop had secured an Act of Parliament to authorize the English bishops to consecrate 'persons who are subjects or citizens of countries outside his Majesty's dominions' without requiring them to take the oath of allegiance. It was also reported that the English bishops had commented favourably on the constitution, apart from the position it gave to bishops. In their consideration of the American Prayer Book they had suggested the reinstatement of the Nicene and Athanasian creeds. The convention agreed the reinstatement of the Nicene creed in the communion office, but courteously declined to increase the prestige of bishops in the constitution. The two candidates for consecration, William White, rector of Christ's and St Peter's Church Philadelphia, and Samuel Prevost, rector of Holy Trinity New York, both of whom had been strong supporters of independence, sailed for England in November 1786, and were consecrated by the archbishop of Canterbury in Lambeth Palace chapel in February 1787, being presented to the archbishop by John Adams, the United States minister in London.

Meanwhile, in February 1787, the Connecticut clergy met in convention and elected (at the third attempt) a priest to present to the Scottish bishops for consecration as a coadjutor to Seabury. However, John Skinner, the primus of the Scottish Episcopal Church, declined to consecrate him, and referred Seabury to the two new American bishops. They, however, declined Seabury's invitation to meet him.

After 150 years of frustrated attempts, there were now bishops in North America, but their place in this predominantly congregational development of Anglicanism, was not yet clear. Seabury was much disliked because of his aggressive loyalism to Britain during the War of Independence. His resistance to lay involvement in the government of the Church, and his seeking consecration without reference to the Church in other states, by the Scottish bishops whose constitutional relationship with the English bishops raised difficulties about establishing a new relationship with the Church of England, had also alienated him from many American Anglicans. Even in Connecticut there were clergy who were hostile to what was considered his high-handed manner. Also, in spite of Granville's tracts and White's *Case*, the long-standing opposition to bishops continued and was fuelled by reports of Seabury's actions among Anglican congregations and clergy in Maryland, Virginia and South Carolina, with the result that the state conventions continued to be unwilling to elect a bishop. In May 1788 the Maryland state convention had set up two committees, each consisting of five clergy and five lay people to supervise the churches on the east and the west shores of the Chesapeake respectively. The committees were empowered to examine ordination candidates. The convention also agreed to elect its president annually. The Maryland Anglicans were effectively adopting a presbyterian church polity.

However, a rapprochement was being established with Seabury. His consecration was made more acceptable to the

English bishops by the Scottish bishops' acceptance of George III as the legitimate ruler of Great Britain, after the death of Charles Edward Stuart in 1788. At the general convention in Philadelphia in 1789 three clergy who had been ordained by Seabury were accepted as representatives of their states. The convention also made concessions to Seabury by agreeing to amend its constitution to allow a state to be represented by either clerical or lay representatives, and agreed that the bishops should constitute a house of revision to approve Acts of the general convention. It was provided, however, that if the bishops rejected an Act, it could still be passed by a two-thirds majority of the convention.

At a subsequent general convention, in September 1789, nine states were represented and Seabury attended as one of the representatives from Connecticut. The Connecticut clergy requested a revision to the constitution, to allow bishops to originate Acts in the convention and to negate any Act, unless it was supported by four-fifths of the representatives. This revision was approved with the proviso that bishops must indicate their approval in writing within three days. It was also agreed to ask the English bishops' opinion on the wisdom of the three American bishops consecrating a fourth bishop. The Prayer Book was revised, and the Scottish prayer of consecration was included in the communion service, but 'minister' was substituted for 'priest' in the rubrics throughout the book, except at the absolution, to allow deacons and readers to officiate in the absence of priests; it was also agreed that the sign of the cross might be omitted in the rite of baptism, at the request of the parents of a child, and to omit the proper preface for Trinity Sunday, and references to private confession in the exhortation in the communion service and in the visitation of the sick, and to abridge the Benedictus at morning prayer and to omit the Magnificat and the Nunc Dimittis at evening prayer.[5] In 1790 the English bishops consecrated a bishop elected by the convention in Virginia, and in 1792 the four American bishops consecrated a bishop elected by the Maryland convention, after which the American Church had enough bishops of its own to maintain its own episcopate.

After a very shaky period following the War of Independence, Anglicanism continued to develop in the United States as the Protestant Episcopal Church. American Anglicans managed to draw on the resources of early Christian practice, and on current political models in revolutionary America to develop a pattern of episcopal government for their Church which ensured a distinctive voice for the laity, who in effect gave authority to those they elected as bishops, and provided the funds to support the clergy and bishops. It was also due to the political skills of William White, and his integrity, that a working relationship was achieved between the disparate theological positions and attitudes in the Anglican congregations in the various states, and between the states; as well as between the Protestant Episcopal Church and the Church of England.

As a result of the War the Episcopal Church had lost many adherents, and suffered from lack of direction and internal divisions in the post-war period. By 1800 it had only 12,000 or so communicants and it continued to be a minority church, in terms of numbers, in the United States. However, a framework had been created which would permit the Church to grow, and which would be highly influential in the development of other overseas dioceses in the future.

The loss of the colonies on the Eastern seaboard of North America led to a major review of the British government's colonial policy, including the attitude to the creation of bishoprics overseas in the surviving colonies. However, no other colonies were largely the creation of migrants seeking refuge and separation from the established Church of England, so nowhere else was there likely to be quite such resistance to the introduction of bishops in a colony, or such nervousness on the part of British governments to reactions to such initiatives among English dissenters. The new colonial policy emphasized more effective central control of colonies, and a closer assimilation of colonial institutions to their English counterparts. The Church of England was seen as a partner with the British government in developing this relationship, and as an agency for cementing the loyalty of the settlers in the surviving North American colonies. The strong elements of religious dissent in the former colonies were thought to have stimulated radical political opinions, though, as we have seen, many Anglicans supported the move to independence. It was therefore thought that the legal establishment of the Church of England in the remaining colonies in British North America would inhibit the growth of dissent and the risk of radical political movements. In Nova

Scotia it was thought that most of the loyalist migrants from the United States, who nearly doubled the population, were Anglicans, and it was expected that they would wish for an Anglican establishment.

Also towards the end of the eighteenth century there was a renewed emphasis in political and theological thought on the idea of the single Christian commonwealth. Edmund Burke reiterated Hooker's doctrine in which Church and State or clergy and laity, comprised the two parts of the Christian commonwealth. For Burke, in a Christian commonwealth, the Church and the State were one and the same thing, being different integral parts of the same whole. For the Church had always been divided into two parts, the clergy and the laity; of which the laity were as much an integral part, and had as many duties and privileges as the clergy. In Burke's opinion, in the rule, order and government of the Church, the laity also should have their share.[6] In the light of such views it is not surprising to find successive British Tory governments providing support for the Church in the colonies, as well as in England.

From the 1740s the SPG had, at the request of the Board of Trade and Plantations, recruited missionaries to work amongst the relatively few migrants in Nova Scotia. When the provincial legislature had been established in 1758, at its first meeting, it had established the Church of England, but had also provided for religious freedom for Protestant dissenters. Following the beginning of the influx of New Englanders after 1759, including many Independents, the privileges of the Anglican Church were curtailed by the legislature; town meetings replaced vestries as disseminators of public charity, and the right to perform marriages was also given to other churches.[7]

After the acquisition of Canada by Britain at the end of the Seven Years' War, and the migration from the former American colonies during and after the American War of Independence, Nova Scotia became much more important to the British government. Refugee clergy, especially those from New York, lobbied for the creation of a bishopric in Nova Scotia. The SPG and the English bishops also supported the proposal. It was pointed out that there was unlikely to be any local opposition to the idea. However, after the end of the American War, it was thought amongst some American diplomats in London, and by some pro-American elements in the British government that the establishment of an Anglican bishop in Nova Scotia might offend the United States' government, and lead to a suspicion that the British were trying to poach Episcopalians into the surviving British colonies. However, after 1787, when the Episcopal Church had its own bishops, it was conversely feared that the colonists might recruit American republican clergy to minister in their parishes, and send their sons to be educated at American colleges, with the result that the colony might be subverted from British rule.

In May 1786 the archbishop of Canterbury and the bishop of London memorialized the British government, pointing out that without a bishop, the Church of England was at a great disadvantage to the numerous Presbyterians, Independents, Lutherans, Roman Catholics and other religious groups who had settled in Nova Scotia, and that the SPG missionaries needed the guidance of a bishop. The government, with its new policy of supporting the establishment of British institutions in the colonies, accepted the proposal, and set up a committee of the Privy Council to recommend how to implement it. It was agreed that a bishopric should be established in order to supervise the clergy, and to institute and license them, and to confirm the laity. The bishop would be subordinate to the archbishop of Canterbury, but appeals from the bishop's decisions would be to the Court of Chancery. The right of presentation to livings and to grant marriage licences and probate of wills was to remain with the lieutenant governor of the colony. The creation of the bishopric would not therefore interfere with any pre-existing legal powers. The bishop was to be regarded as a partner with the lieutenant governor in the civil government of the colony. The bishop was to be paid by a government grant, and from the income from a grant made by the SPG from the funds originally donated for the establishment of bishops in the American colonies.[8]

The diocese was to be established and the bishop appointed by the issue of royal letters patent, a method which seems to have been adopted from the Church of Ireland, where bishops were not even nominally elected by their cathedral chapters, as in the Church of England, but were appointed by royal letters patent issued by the crown.[9] A bishop thus received authority through a direct grant from the crown. It was a method that depended on the assumption that the temporal organ used for giving spiritual authority was itself an organ of the Church as well as of the State.

It was agreed that the person chosen as bishop should be someone with experience of the colonies and a loyalist. There was a modest campaign by the clergy in Nova Scotia and New Brunswick, which had been separated from Nova Scotia in 1784, and where also the Church had been established by the first legislative assembly meeting in 1786, for them to have a part in the selection of the new bishop. However, the appointment was made, without reference to them, by the crown. The man chosen was Charles Inglis. He was of Irish descent, and had been an SPG missionary and latterly, rector of Holy Trinity New York. He had been a loyalist in the War of Independence, and was a close associate of Seabury, and the New England High Churchmen. He was deeply conservative, and much attached to English institutions and ways of doing things. He was also suspicious of dissenters, and tended to associate dissent from the established Church with disloyalty to the British State.

When Inglis arrived in Nova Scotia as bishop, after his consecration in London, it was to a diocese that had about a dozen clergy, who increased to fifteen by 1790 and to nineteen by 1800, supported by a British government grant, distributed by the SPG, and supplemented by a grant from the SPG's own funds. In 1787 the SPG also secured a grant from the government of £2,000, and an additional grant in 1788 of £1,000 to build churches in new settlements in Nova Scotia. By 1795 eleven new churches had been built, largely out of these funds. When the colony had been first surveyed in 1785 grants of 600 acres of land had been made to support the church in each settlement, and 400 acres for a school. In 1788 the Nova Scotia legislature granted £400 to rent buildings for a grammar school in Halifax, and to pay a master. In 1789 the legislature voted a further £500 to purchase land for the grammar school and a college, and provided a perpetual grant of £400 a year. In 1792 the British government granted £1,000 towards building the college, and it was granted a royal charter and another £1,000 in 1802. All this looked very promising for the establishment of a new diocese, with the strong support of the British government and the local legislature, and the Church of England through the SPG, whose entire energies and resources were now concentrated on the remaining British North American colonies.

Inglis, whose major experience had been in urbane New York, was ill-prepared for the frontier life of Nova Scotia. His desire to promote the pattern of English society in the colonies made him unwilling to adapt his attitudes and the liturgy of the Church of England to the needs and peculiarities of a situation in Nova Scotia which differed greatly from either England or New York. He had assumed that the majority of the inhabitants of the colony would be Anglicans, but although the population had roughly doubled in the 1780s, as a result of the migration from the United States, probably well under half the migrants were Anglicans. Inglis was disappointed to find Methodist and revivalist preachers active in the colony, as well as a substantial presence of Independents, Presbyterians, Lutherans and Roman Catholics. He was also dismayed by the lukewarmness of most Anglicans, and the lack of energy of the few Anglican clergy.

The task facing him was formidable. The few clergy were not enthusiastic about the presence of a bishop to supervise their activities. More clergy were needed, but the SPG had little success in recruiting clergy from England, perhaps because of the relatively poor pay on offer and the remoteness of the colony. Some clergy were recruited from the United States, but they too were not used to a bishop on hand. The parishes were vast, and usually contained a number of settlements, visiting which, involved difficult journeys over mountainous terrain. Only a few clergy were prepared to visit the more far-flung settlements in their parishes. If they did, and it involved being absent on a Sunday, they were likely to run into opposition from the few wealthy people in the major settlement where the church was usually sited, who expected to have the incumbent present every Sunday. Although each parish had been provided with a grant of land to support the church and the incumbent, the land had often been lost. There was no central authority to oversee the land granted, the land had seldom been surveyed to establish its boundaries, and deeds were not issued. If it could be proved that land had been lost, the lieutenant governor was willing to replace it, but usually with poorer land. In any case, most missionaries had neither the skill nor the funds to clear the land and farm it themselves, and there was little market for rented land.

The grants made by the government through the SPG to support the clergy encouraged the independence of the clergy from their congregations, and the grants to pay the clergy and the grants to build churches gave the laity no vested interest in the Church, and may have sapped their will to raise money themselves for the benefit of the Church. It was noted that where new churches were built with the money from the government grants, they were quickly allowed to fall into disrepair. In any case, in most settlements the inhabitants were very poor, and probably had little money to give to support the Church. Also, in most settlements Anglicans were in a minority. The Anglicans were amongst the better-off settlers, and the preponderance of Anglicans among the governing class, and their support of the established Church, through grants from the legislature, did not endear their church to poor settlers. Often a wealthy and vociferous minority in a parish could be very conservative in their outlook, and hostile to adaptations to the liturgy to suit local circumstances, and might be highly critical of the clergy. Such people often formed the majority in a vestry, and expected to be consulted in the appointment of an incumbent.

The bishop, therefore, had considerable difficulty in establishing a good working relationship with both the clergy and the laity and achieving their respect, especially where there were so many conflicting interests between maintaining the *status quo* and initiating missionary work. The bishop also had to establish a working relationship with the civil authorities, and especially the lieutenant governor and the legislature. Although Inglis was offered a seat in the legislature he did not take it up until 1809, and then only attended infrequently. The lieutenant governor, who until Inglis's arrival had exercised authority in ecclesiastical matters on behalf of the crown, was also reluctant to surrender any of his authority to a bishop, and Inglis had to seek the support of the archbishop of Canterbury in his difficulties with the governor.

More surprisingly, Inglis found that he had a difficult relationship with the SPG. Clergy supported by the SPG, continued to refer to their paymaster, rather than to adapt to new ways and refer their questions and difficulties to the bishop. Because of the vastness of the diocese and the difficulty of the terrain the clergy had little sense of being part of a diocese. Nor were matters helped by the secretary of the SPG, William Morrice, who did not refer the clergy back to the bishop, and seems to have acted as though the bishop did not exist. Although the Society's reports spoke very flatteringly about Inglis and his work in the new diocese, in practice the secretary ignored him. The secretary tended to appoint missionaries to the diocese without consulting the bishop. The bishop's local knowledge was not sought, and often when he made proposals or requests to the Society, they were ignored. Morrice tended to imply that the bishop should carry out the Society's orders and wishes. It would seem that the secretary resented the restraint placed upon his authority by the presence of the bishop in the colony. Again Inglis turned to the archbishop of Canterbury for support, and he, as chairman of the Society's committee, intervened on behalf of Inglis. Inglis's willingness to consult the archbishop, and the archbishop's careful and supportive advice were invaluable in the establishment of episcopal authority in the new diocese.[10]

Given the difficulties he faced, and the vast area of his diocese, even after Quebec was created a separate diocese in 1793, it is perhaps understandable that Inglis seems to have spent most of his time on his country estate, not even visiting Halifax many times between 1795 and 1809. Even his foundation of King's College in Halifax did not flourish. It was granted a further endowment of 26,000 acres by the government in 1813, but there were only nine students in the College, and there was great difficulty in recruiting staff. There were probably not enough potential Anglican students in the colony to make a college feasible, and its strict Anglicanism deterred Presbyterians and others from sending their sons there.

It was probably a mistake to have recruited as bishop someone who, though he had worked in the colonies for most of his life, had had a very different experience from the colony to which he was sent as bishop. He also lacked experience of working with other people and winning their support, or had not learned this skill while rector of Holy Trinity, New York. He similarly lacked experience of the English Church, and was utterly dependent on the archbishop of Canterbury, who fortunately proved very supportive. A bishop with more knowledge of the Church of England, and with a wider network of support might have been more able to challenge the obstructiveness of the secretary of the SPG, and might have had more people to encourage him to develop a new model of episcopal oversight in a missionary context.

Government support for the established Church in the colonies continued to be substantial. No doubt the anxiety in Britain caused by the French Revolution and the encouragement it gave to protests by radicals against the Church and traditional authority structures in the State, prompted positive funding for a church regarded as a bulwark of order, in an attempt to attract people to its services and away from dissenting meeting houses, where they might be led astray by radical political sermons. Canada, as a former French colony, where there were still many French settlers, was obviously an important area in which to establish the Anglican Church.

In 1791, the British Parliament passed the Constitutional Act for Canada which divided Canada into Upper and Lower Canada (Ontario and Quebec), and also authorized the government to allocate lands for the support and maintenance of Protestant clergy and to erect parsonage houses for them. Presentation to parishes in the provinces was to be a crown prerogative. The land reserved for the maintenance of the clergy was to represent one-seventh of the land grant in the provinces. In 1793 the diocese of Quebec was formed and grants were paid from the government's 'army extraordinaries' fund for the maintenance of the bishop of Quebec, and the beneficed clergy in Lower Canada. Jacob Mountain, the vicar of St Andrew's Norwich, who was appointed bishop of Quebec, also found that he had a difficult relationship with successive governors. He was thwarted in most of his attempted initiatives and forced to fight every inch of the way in establishing his authority.[11]

During the early years of the nineteenth century the SPG was revitalized by a group of High Church laymen and clergy, known as the Hackney Phalanx, some of the lay members of which were City merchants living in the then pleasant rural suburb of Hackney, and the rector of Hackney, Archdeacon Watson, being a leading member of the group. The Phalanx also included among their associates a number of bishops, including Archbishop Manners-Sutton of Canterbury. They had close links with a number of leading politicians, one of their associates, the earl of Liverpool, becoming Prime Minister in 1812.[12]

The Hackney Phalanx were a dynamic part of the English High Church tradition who upheld the doctrine of the apostolic succession of the bishops, which had been regularly restated in theological publications throughout the eighteenth century, notably in Steven's *Nature and Constitution of the Christian Church* in 1773 and Jones of Nayland's *Essay in the Church* in 1780, and more recently in J.J. Watson's *Divine Commission and Perpetuity of the Christian Priesthood* published in 1816. They followed the lead of the seventeenth-century theologians known as the Caroline Divines, in seeing catholicism not as implying a dogmatic centre of unity embodying the universal Church, as Roman Catholic controversialists asserted, but as a federation of separate territorial entities, each upholding certain notes or 'fundamentals' of catholic order and apostolic order. They did not claim that the Church of England was itself that universal Church as the Church of Rome professed to be, but rather saw the Church of England as a branch of that universal Church. In their view the Church of England's claim to be a true branch of the universal Church stood or fell by its preservation of apostolic order through the succession of bishops. The claim of other branches to true catholicism rested on the same basis. They insisted that the unity of the Church did not entail the dependence of one branch of the Church upon another, but rather a coexistence on an equal basis.[13]

Possibly as a result of the close links between the associates of the Phalanx, the committee members of the SPG and leading members of the government, from 1814 a government grant was paid to the Society in aid of the salaries of clergy in British North America. Out of this grant SPG made grants to the bishop of Nova Scotia, and the archdeacons in Nova Scotia, New Brunswick and Newfoundland and King's College, Halifax, and towards the stipends of the clergy in Upper and Lower Canada, Nova Scotia, New Brunswick, Newfoundland and Prince Edward Island. To show some modest even-handedness, very small grants were also made by the British government towards the stipends of the Church of Scotland ministers in Halifax and St John. In effect the government grant provided each clergyman with a stipend of £150 a year, to which the SPG added a further £50 a year, and encouraged each parish to provide a church and a parsonage house.[14] In order to increase its fundraising capacity, and to raise the consciousness of the Church of England to the work of the Church overseas, from 1819 the Society began to encourage the establishment of SPG 'parochial associations' and also the setting up of diocesan committees.[15]

The Hackney Phalanx were also involved in the revitalization of the SPCK, as well as the SPG. In 1810 a special committee was set up to organize local committees with the sanction of, and under the supervision of, the relevant diocesan bishops.[16] Part of the result of this was the SPCK's encouragement of the development of education in the British North American colonies. Many of the Hackney Phalanx members of the SPCK committee were also involved in the establishment of the National Society for Promoting the Education of the Poor in the Principles of the Established Church which aimed to assist in the establishment of a school to teach reading, writing and 'reckoning', and the Church catechism in every parish in England. From 1816 the SPCK supported schools using the 'Madras system' (which was also recommended for use by the National Society in England) in Nova Scotia and then subsequently in New Brunswick. From this time onwards schools were a prime area of interest for the SPCK in all its overseas spheres of influence.[17]

From 1819, as a result of the economic depression in England following the end of the Napoleonic Wars, there was a rapid increase of migration into Canada, and the very limited episcopal supervision provided by the two vast dioceses of Nova Scotia and Quebec, was grossly inadequate, especially as Inglis's successor enjoyed poor health, and spent most of his time in London, leaving Inglis's son, as archdeacon, to administer the diocese. This, however, was not tackled until the next phase of the development of the Communion, which will be discussed in the next chapter.

In the early 1820s the SPG began to press the British government to make provision for a bishopric in the West Indies. From at least the late eighteenth century chaplains in Barbados had been encouraged to include negroes in their pastoral ministrations, as well as white settlers. The SPG had set an example on its Codrington estates in providing better physical conditions for black slaves, providing medical care, reducing the working hours, and providing educational opportunities, and a chaplain, John Pinder, who subsequently became principal of Codrington College and then of Wells Theological College, who introduced Sunday schools on the plantations.

The SPG's lobbying coincided with the desire of the British government to find ways of implementing a policy of ameliorating the conditions of slaves, and it turned to the Church for assistance. In the Canning Resolution in 1823 the government required religious instruction to be offered to slaves, with Parliament making provision for an adequate number of clergy and teachers, under episcopal oversight, Sunday markets were also to be abolished, laws were to be passed enabling a slave to give testimony, if he could produce a certificate from a religious instructor to show that he understood the nature of an oath, marriage of slaves was to be encouraged, and mothers with a number of legitimate children were to be exempted from field labour, control was to be exercised over punishment, with proper records of whipping exceeding three lashes being required, and savings banks were to be established to enable slaves to save money to purchase their freedom.

However, the various West Indian colonial legislatures refused to adopt the proposed reforms. In the face of the ensuing uproar, violence and riots in the West Indian colonies, Canning announced that the government had decided to strengthen the Church in the West Indies, by the establishment of two dioceses, and that the Exchequer would provide a grant for the cost, £10,000 a year, to each, to support a bishop, an archdeacon, and six other clergy. This demonstrated the importance the government attached to the role of the Church in assisting in implementing the policy of ameliorating the condition of slaves. In both dioceses the new bishops had some difficulty in establishing themselves among both the clergy and the laity.

William Hart Coleridge, who was appointed the first bishop of Barbados, had previously been secretary of the SPCK, and was a member of the Hackney Phalanx. He was determined to establish the authority of the bishop. The government grant enabled him to ensure that clergy were adequately paid independently of the parish vestries, so that the clergy would not be influenced by their parishioners' views about slavery. He also wrested from the vestries their responsibility for maintaining church buildings, and ensured that all ecclesiastical jurisdiction was vested in the bishop, and not in the governor, and that all power to appoint to livings should be vested in him and that all clergy, including missionaries paid by the SPG, should be licensed by the bishop. In all his initiatives he was supported by the British government, who required the governor to consult him about the appointment of clergy.[18]

The new bishop of Jamaica encountered a problem that was to feature in many dioceses. He had to relate to two Anglican missionary societies rather than one. In 1799 a group of English Anglican evangelical laity and clergy had established a new missionary society to supplement SPG's work among the settlers in British North America, by undertaking missionary work among the indigenous inhabitants of Africa and Asia. As the SPCK had had difficulties a century before in recruiting missionaries to work in India, so did the new CMS, and they adopted a similar solution, of employing German Lutheran pastors who had been ordained in Germany as missionaries. By extension of their work amongst Africans in Africa, in 1815 the CMS had opened a school for former African slaves in Antigua, and because of a lack of English Anglican teachers, they had employed Moravian and Methodist teachers. When Antigua became part of the diocese of Jamaica, the CMS asked the new bishop to license the teachers. However, he insisted that he would only accept Anglicans as teachers, with the result that the school was closed, and it was claimed that 2,000 children ceased to be taught.

In the 1830s there was a major dispute between the bishop of Jamaica and the CMS. The secretary of the CMS wanted the bishop to merely ordain and license their missionaries to work in his diocese, whilst the Society would have the authority to appoint a missionary to a particular location, to receive reports from him and to supervise his work, and to move him or dismiss him. This was unacceptable to the bishop. The Society tried hard to persuade the archbishop of Canterbury to intervene in their support, but he declined.[19]

In the late 1820s the traditional solidarity between Church and State in England was beginning to break down. Although they may have seemed obstructive, ministers of successive governments of all political complexions in eighteenth-century England did have the best interests of the established Church at heart, and worked to protect the Church, and to advance its cause whenever they considered it possible. It had proved much easier to do this in the 1790s and the early nineteenth century, with the generally conservative reaction to the French Revolution and the succeeding wars. However, in the 1820s it became clear to ministers that dissent from the established Church in England would need to be more adequately accommodated, if for no other reason than to protect the Church and traditional institutions from more radical attacks. So in 1828 the Test and Corporation Acts, which had in theory excluded nonconformists from civic life in England, were repealed, and in 1829 the Emancipation Act granted similar freedom of worship and participation in civic life to Roman Catholics. Against this background of growing denominational pluralism in England, it was clear that it could no longer be anticipated that the British government would continue to make grants for exclusively Anglican purposes, whether in England or the colonies.

It was not surprising that the long-standing government policy of supporting the Anglican Church in the colonies should come under fire from a new generation of radical and liberal Whig MPs in the House of Commons. They believed that Anglicans, like members of other denominations, should provide the funds to finance their own clergy and ministers. Even those who were Anglicans and believed in an established Church thought that the Anglican reliance on government grants was debilitating for the Church and that it would be reinvigorated by going out to seek its own funding. In 1830 a Whig government came into office committed to a programme of financial stringency and tax reduction. The grants paid to the SPG to provide incomes for the bishops and clergy in the Canadian colonies, were an obvious target. In spite of the establishment of the bishoprics in British North America, Anglicanism had not made much headway there. It was estimated that, at best, Anglicans only comprised 20 per cent of the population in Nova Scotia and New Brunswick, and probably 3.5 per cent of the population in Lower Canada.

The original intention had been to transfer the costs of the grants to the colonial legislatures in the various colonies. However, this had not proved feasible, for most legislatures did not have sufficient surplus revenue to take on this burden without increasing taxation, and in view of the minority position of Anglicans in the colonies, it would be unlikely that the members of the legislative assemblies would be willing to vote for taxes to provide grants to support Anglican clergy. In 1831 the British government informed the SPG that although the grant for supporting Anglican clergy in Canada would be continued for that year, it would be withdrawn over the following four years, except that grants would be still payable to support clergy then in office until they moved or died.[20] This was the beginning of the end of the policy inaugurated by the British government after the American War of Independence. British colonial policy had come full circle. The maintenance of a privileged Church in British North America, previously regarded as the bulwark of colonial loyalty to the imperial connection was now seen as a dangerous solvent of Canadian allegiance, and as unhealthy for the Church. After 1830 the Anglican Church could no longer look to the government for support in providing episcopal supervision for its congregations in the colonies and elsewhere.

There were two responses to this amongst Canadian Anglicans. The first was a discussion of the possibility of establishing self-government for the Church, on the lines of the Episcopal Church in the United States. The second, which was adopted, was to seek additional funding from the SPG, which, with the encouragement of local financial support, would enable the Anglicans to weather the storm. This worked, for the supporters of the SPG in particular, rose to the challenge. In 1839, when Newfoundland was constituted a separate diocese, carved out of Nova Scotia, and including Bermuda, which had been added to Nova Scotia in 1825, the SPG gave generous financial support for the establishment of the diocese, granting £500 a year to the bishop's salary, and £200 a year to each of the clergy. In the same year, however, when the impossibly unwieldy diocese of Quebec was divided to form the diocese of Toronto, the new diocese was able to be self-supporting. By 1846, when the number of clergy in Newfoundland had increased from eight to twenty-seven, the bishop reduced the SPG contribution to £100 per man and required the congregations to find the other £100, in order to double the number of clergy.[21]

THE ANGLICAN CHURCH IN INDIA

The expansion of the Anglican episcopate in the East took a different form from the pattern in North America and the West Indies. This is partly accounted for by the different pattern of expansion of British influence in the two spheres. In North America and the West Indies the British went as settlers or refugees. They seem to have had little interest in the indigenous inhabitants – in trading with them for profit, or in working with them, or even in converting them to Christianity.

In the East in general, and in India in particular, the situation was different. In India British adventurers encountered a densely populated country with highly developed and sophisticated societies. India could not be regarded as a vacant space to be filled. The British initially went to India as traders, to obtain products that were scarce or unobtainable in Western Europe, and which would thus fetch a high price on the home market. They did not go to carve out new territories to settle permanently. They established trading stations and colonies of merchants who would normally, if they lived long enough and made enough money, expect to retire to Britain. In the course of time, in the interests of trade, and to increase and stabilize supplies, the British East India Company, which had by royal charter, a monopoly of trade with India and the East Indies, began to become involved in the civil administration of some of the areas where it traded, initially as advisers to Indian rulers, and subsequently, in some areas, replacing Indian rulers.

As we have seen, traders and travellers took chaplains with them to provide for their spiritual welfare. In 1694 Humphrey Prideaux, subsequently dean of Norwich, set out proposals for 'the propagation of Christianity in the East Indies'. He maintained 'that the existing evils and deficiencies cannot be otherwise remedied than by setting Bishops and Seminaries in these countries, where Ministers may be bred and ordained on the spot'.[22] A very modest step in this direction was made when the royal charter granted to the East India Company in 1698 required the governors to maintain a minister, approved by the bishop of London, in every garrison and factory, and to provide a place of worship. This provision was intended mainly for the employees of the Company, and their dependants. Daily prayers were held on the Company's estates. However, the chaplains were also required to learn Portuguese and the local languages, 'so as to enable them to instruct the natives in the Protestant religion'. Already in 1694 the Company had had the Prayer Book translated into Portuguese, at its own expense, and printed at Oxford and sent to its factories.[23]

The Company's factories in Madras, Calcutta and Bombay became flourishing English enclaves in India, and provision was made for their spiritual welfare by building a church in each of the settlements as well as employing a chaplain in each. The needs of the children of the poor employees of the Company were met by the generosity of individuals. In 1715 a charity school was established in Madras to teach 'poor Protestant children' the Prayer Book catechism, and reading, writing and 'reckoning'. A similar charity school was established in Calcutta in 1734. The employees of the Company did not encourage chaplains to undertake missionary work for fear that they might offend the Indians upon whose goodwill they were dependent for trade.[24]

The SPG also declined to send missionaries to India because in their view the East India Company's charter gave the Company responsibility for proclaiming the gospel in India. In 1728, however, their sister society, the SPCK began to support a mission to work among Indians in Madras. The initiative for this had come from the Danish Mission which had been founded at the Danish trading station at Tranquebar by Frederick IV of Denmark in 1708. There had already been contacts between the Society and the Danish Church through the King's uncle, Prince Georg of Denmark, Queen Anne's husband, whose chaplain was an associate of the founders of the Society. The Society published an account of the progress of the Mission in 1713. Earlier, in 1710, the SPCK had sent a printing press to Tranquebar; the ship transporting it being captured by a French privateer and the Society having to contribute to the ransom, the gold that was sent with the press to support the missionaries was also stolen, and the printer who was sent out went with the press committed suicide off the Cape of Good Hope, but the press eventually got there safely and was set up. In 1714 the Gospels and the Acts of the Apostles were translated into Tamil and published. The Danish Mission recruited most of its missionaries from the University of Halle in Saxony, which was very influential in disseminating pietist spirituality and theology, and with which the SPCK also had links. The Society sent an annual cargo of money and goods to the Danish Mission, the East India Company providing them with free freight and also free passages to outgoing and returning missionaries.

The SPCK originally intended to establish its own mission but was unable to persuade any English clergyman to go to India, so in 1716 it resolved to support the Danish mission, in order not to 'mingle together in the mission field workers of different beliefs in Christian doctrine and government', and the Society paid the salary of one of the missionaries. In 1726 the secretary of the SPCK negotiated with the directors of the Company for the Danish missionaries to preach in the territories ruled by the Company. Then in 1728 the Society resolved to support its own mission in Madras. Because of the continuing lack of any English clergyman willing to go to India as a missionary, the Society sent two German Lutherans recommended by Augustus Hermann Francke, professor of divinity at Halle, who was a corresponding member of the Society. Although the Society provided the funds for the mission, and the missionaries reported to the Society, because of the distance at which they were working, the missionaries were largely independent. The Society did, however, try to enforce the use of the Prayer Book, translated into Tamil, for the mission's worship. There was some questioning of the propriety of an Anglican society employing Lutheran clergy to undertake an Anglican mission.[25] However, the view of the Caroline Divines was accepted that although Danish and German Lutheran orders were not perfect, in that they lacked the episcopal regimen, they did adhere to the fundamental principles of the gospel, and though it was regretted that they had abandoned episcopacy, it had been unavoidable in the circumstances of the sixteenth century.[26]

By the middle of the century the Bible had also been trans-lated into Tamil and Hindi. However, the SPCK mission was never other than a very small-scale exercise, and its connections with the Society were always tenuous. The Society had no real means of enforcing its requirements on the missionaries, and had no means of disciplining recalcitrant missionaries. The mis-sionaries also found it hard to work together and when a major dispute broke out, it was resolved by sending two of them to Cuddalore to establish a new mission, also supported by the Society.[27]

In the late 1780s, the evangelical revival which had emerged in the Church of England a generation or so earlier, again with some influence from Halle, began to impinge on the Anglican chaplaincies in India. In 1786 David Brown, who had followed one of the classic routes of evangelical influence in the later eighteenth century, being educated at Hull Grammar School, where Joseph Milner, a noted evangelical clergyman was the master, and Magdalene College, Cambridge, which was a centre of evangelical influence, was appointed a chaplain by the Company.[28] He had also been influenced by Charles Simeon, fellow of King's College, Cambridge, and vicar of Holy Trinity,

Cambridge, who by his preaching and example was a major attraction to many prospective ordination candidates. Simeon subsequently came to have a special interest in India and in recruiting chaplains, and began to recruit missionaries to work there. Brown began his work in India as superintendent of the orphan house at Madras, but subsequently became garrison chaplain in Calcutta. There he became an important influence on Charles Grant, an official of the Company. Grant, on his return to England, subsequently became a director of the Company, and settled in Clapham, then a village from which it was easy to commute to the City or Westminster. There his neighbours included William Wilberforce, MP for Hull, who had also been greatly influenced by the evangelical movement, and was part of the Hull evangelical network, and Zachary Macauley, Henry Thornton, Granville Sharp and John Venn, the evangelical rector of Clapham, all of whom were in touch with Simeon in Cambridge. All of these had played an important part in the foundation of the CMS, and subsequently strongly influenced the development of Anglicanism in India.[29]

Grant was able to recommend good evangelical clergy, on the advice of Simeon, to the Company for appointment as chaplains in the company's settlements, and from the early years of the nineteenth century the CMS was attempting to recruit missionaries in England to work among Indians, and particularly encouraged its missionaries to learn Indian languages. By 1808 Henry Martyn had translated the Bible into Urdu.

However, the CMS were severely hampered in their missionary work by two factors. First, the great difficulty they had in recruiting missionaries. Although the network of evangelical clergy was circulated, none of them could suggest anyone as a suitable missionary. Like the SPCK a century before, they had to resort to recruiting German Lutherans. By the late eighteenth century the University of Halle had ceased to be a recruiting ground for missionaries, but after 1817 a seminary was opened at Basle as a thank offering for the delivery of Germany from Napoleon, with Blumhardt, a good friend of the CMS, as principal. This became a major recruiting ground for missionaries for India. However, the employment of German Lutherans as Anglican missionaries posed problems of language, as well as theology, liturgy and church order. Second, the directors of the East India Company were not enthusiastic about missionary work among Indians. They believed that they had a duty 'to protect the native inhabitants in the free and undisturbed profession of their religious opinions, and to take care that they are neither harassed nor irritated by any premature or over-zealous attempts to convert them to Christianity'. The Company feared that aggressive Christian evangelism might lead to communal tensions, or even strife within its territories, which would be detrimental to good government. Communal tension and conflict might also be detrimental to the Company's trading activities, and might endanger the lives of its servants, Indian and European.[30]

In 1808, Charles Buchanan, one of Simeon's protégés, returned from India to London, and published a pamphlet proposing an episcopal establishment for the British colonial empire, with bishops for India, South Africa, the West Indies and New South Wales, who would, as soon as possible, ordain a native clergy, and direct the work of missionaries. He suggested that they should initially be financed by the missionary societies, but, in due course, be paid for by the local churches. He envisaged the pastoral care of colonists as their primary duty. Buchanan's pamphlet seems to have been little noticed at the time of its publication.[31]

However, in 1811, William Wilberforce sent a *Prospectus of an Ecclesiatical Establishment for the Indian Church* based upon Buchanan's proposals, to the British government and to the East India Committee of the SPCK. In 1812, the Prime Minister, Lord Liverpool, an associate of the High Church Hackney Phalanx, responded by offering to include a clause in the new East India Company bill to provide for a seminary in each Indian presidency to train Indians for the ministry, to permit missionaries to be licensed to work in India, and to establish a bishopric in India, divided into three archdeaconries. In spite of strong opposition in the House of Commons fanned by some Directors of the Company opposed to mission work, the clause embodying these principles was passed, on the understanding that the ecclesiastical establishment was intended primarily to provide for the spiritual welfare of English people serving in India. The salaries of the bishop and the archdeacons, fixed at £5,000 and £2,000 a year respectively in order to cover all their expenses of office, were to be paid out of the local revenues.

The bishop and the archdeacons were to be appointed by the crown.[32]

Wilberforce and his evangelical associates among the directors of the Company recognized that it would be unwise to press for an evangelical clergyman to be appointed as the first bishop of Calcutta. The first bishop, Thomas Middleton, had been closely involved with the SPCK, and was a close friend of Joshua Watson and the members of the Hackney Phalanx. He was appointed under letters patent, issued by the crown, which provided that he should 'perform all the . . . functions peculiar and appropriate to the office of a Bishop within the limits of the said see, and not elsewhere . . . according to the Ecclesiastical Laws of our Realm of England . . . '. He was to be subordinate to the arch-bishop of Canterbury. The letters patent were to turn out to be very unsatisfactory, for they left undefined the relationship between the governor general and the bishop, and made no reference to missionary work. However, the situation was unprecedented, and it would have been impossible in London to have envisaged the Indian context and how events might develop.

Middleton was interested in, and well informed about, India. He believed that an indigenous ordained ministry should be trained and ordained as soon as possible, and that the teaching in the training should be in local languages, and that there should be research and teaching about Hindu culture. His reception in Calcutta was cool. While the governor general, Lord Hastings, was prepared to allow the bishop to appoint the chaplains paid by the Company to their stations, rather than make the appointments himself, the court of directors of the Company objected, and insisted that all appointments should be by strict seniority, which left the bishop with little authority over the chaplains. Also, while the advocate-general of Bengal encouraged the bishop to set up a consistory court, as provided for by the letters patent, for the discipline of the clergy, the advocate-general of Madras held that to set up a consistory court would be illegal. As a result, the provision for consistory courts in India was stillborn.

Some help was forthcoming from his former associates in England. In May 1818 the SPG agreed to direct its attention East as well as to the West Indies and British North America.

They noted that the Society had delayed the commencement of its work in India, until the establishment of a bishopric and the subsequent extension of his jurisdiction to Ceylon in 1817 had furnished the means of placing their missionaries under proper direction and control. Joshua Watson was very active in mobilizing the SPG in Middleton's support. At his instance, Lord Liverpool had advised the Prince Regent to grant a royal letter authorizing a collection in all churches in England on the Society's behalf, which raised nearly £50,000 for their work in India. The diocesan and parochial committees which had been set up stimulated the Society's income from subscriptions from an average of £400 a year between 1780 and 1819 to £1,300 in 1820 and to £51,000 in 1855.[33]

The Society asked Middleton about ways in which they might help him, and he suggested the foundation of a college in the neighbourhood of Calcutta to train Indians as 'preachers, catechists, and school masters to teach English, Hindus, and Muslims, to translate the Scriptures, Liturgy, and Moral and Religious Tracts' and to receive missionaries and train them for mission work. The proposal received glowing commendation from Lord Liverpool, the Prime Minister, and the site was given by Lord Hastings, the governor general. The SPG placed £5,000 at the bishop's disposal for the college. The SPCK and the CMS also each gave £5,000 for the project and the British and Foreign Bible Society gave £200 towards Bible translations into vernacular languages. The SPCK referred all matters relating to its missionaries in South India to the bishop, as part of its continuing policy of placing responsibility in the hands of people on the spot.

Middleton had formed a good opinion of the CMS, and the draft statutes of Bishop's College show that he wished it to be used by them for training their missionaries. However, the SPG objected to the proposal that another missionary society might endow scholarships there and nominate for them in perpetuity, and so the good will of the CMS was offended. In general Middleton's relations with the CMS were no easier than his relations with the East India Company. Those who paid for clergy expected to appoint and control them, and did not expect to have to defer or refer to a bishop. Initially Middleton doubted whether he could license missionaries to work amongst Indians, for mission work had not been included in his letters patent. He also believed that because he did not license CMS missionaries, he could not permit them to preach in the cathedral in Calcutta, or any other church built with government or Company money for the use of English people. The secretary of CMS neglected to tell Middleton that counsel's opinion, which the Society had sought, was that the bishop of Calcutta's authority over all Anglican clergy in India was the same as an English bishop's authority would be in England. When the bishop did ascertain that he could license missionary clergy, he was still reluctant to do so, even though he was willing to turn a blind eye to their unlicensed state if they worked among English people, for fear of giving the Company an excuse for not sending chaplains to India.

Ordination was also a problem for Middleton. He did not think that his letters patent permitted him to ordain people as missionaries, nor did he think that he could ordain German missionaries, without requiring them to take the oaths of allegiance and supremacy to the king. Nor did he think that he was authorized to ordain any Indians until his authority was clarified and confirmed, which could only be achieved by further legislation in the British Parliament. He was doubtful that the two Indians that the CMS wished him to ordain on the recommendation of their missionaries could be deemed to be British subjects. He much regretted this caution, which he felt he must exercise, and regarded himself as 'labouring in chains'. In 1819 the problem was partially resolved by the passage of an Act of Parliament which enabled the archbishops of Canterbury and York and the bishop of London to ordain men specifically for the colonies and foreign possessions of the United Kingdom. It became customary for German recruits from Basle to go over to London as laymen and after a year or two's study at the new CMS missionary college in Islington, to be ordained by the bishop of London for work in India. Meanwhile, for the German missionaries already working in India, whom the CMS wished to be ordained, they turned, as was customary, to the senior Lutheran missionary in holy orders, and asked him to join with other Lutheran missionaries in ordaining them. Middleton died in 1822, before most of these problems had been resolved.[34]

Middleton was succeeded, after a long delay because of the distance from England and the long sea-journeys involved, by

Reginald Heber, whose legal position was somewhat easier than Middleton's had been. In 1823 an Act of Parliament was passed authorizing the bishop of Calcutta to ordain Indians, provided they lived in British territories and took an oath of allegiance to the king. Heber's letters patent also clarified some of the legal difficulties that Middleton had faced, but added Australia and New Zealand to the already vast diocese. Heber took legal advice before leaving London, and ascertained that any missionaries within his diocese were as much under his authority as chaplains appointed by the Company, and required his licence. Heber also took seriously the need to learn as much as possible about India, and learned Hindi, and with the approval of the governor general, travelled widely, including to areas not under British rule, but where there were substantial English populations. Heber, like Middleton before him, was a traditional High Churchman, and a close friend of Joshua Watson, and associated with the Hackney Phalanx.

In 1825 Heber ordained the two Indians who had been previously ordained by the German Lutheran missionaries in 1819, and also a German Lutheran missionary. He explained his action in reordaining them in classical Anglican terms as, 'You suppose that I generally admit ordination by Presbyters without a Bishop to be valid. I do not admit this. All I said is that when a Christian nation has, by force of circumstances, lost its apostolical succession of Bishops, the continuance of Ministry being a thing absolutely needful and essential, those good men are not to be censured who perpetrated it by the best means in their power.'[35] On these grounds he considered that ordinations performed in the churches of Denmark and Sweden where the succession of bishops had been maintained were valid and regular, while those by Danish and German Lutherans, in whose churches the succession of bishops had not been maintained, were valid, but needed to be regularized by episcopal ordination, if it was available.

Heber inherited some of Middleton's problems. The CMS had set up a corresponding committee in Calcutta in 1807, and Bishop Middleton had set up a Calcutta committee of the SPG in 1818. Although the SPG, like the SPCK, were clear that they provided the money and the missionaries for the bishop to direct the work of the missionaries, the local committees, for example in Madras, wished the money to be paid to them, so that they could distribute it to the missionaries and nominate missionaries to particular stations. This desire of the local committee to take on what the Society and the bishop saw as the bishop's responsibility, caused tension with the Society, and the bishop and the missionaries, who did not want to receive their salaries through the local committees.

In Calcutta the local CMS committee objected to Heber's licensing of all the CMS missionaries. In the licence Heber stated his authority to decide where a missionary should be stationed, and his authority to revoke the licence, but the local CMS committee wished to appoint where missionaries should serve, and to be able to dismiss them, without reference to the bishop. Heber managed to charm the committee into accepting his authority, whilst agreeing to consult them about appointments. Heber also discovered that Bishop's College had not been the success that Middleton had hoped for. The site had proved unsatisfactory, more money was needed to endow it, and by 1825 there were only eight students.

Heber died suddenly in the midst of his labours, at the age of forty-two.[36] He was succeeded, at lengthy intervals, by two bishops who also died shortly after taking up office. These short episcopates illustrate very well the hazardous nature of service in the Indian climate for Englishmen, and perhaps offer one explanation for the difficulty of recruiting missionaries from amongst the English clergy.

After seventeen years of non-evangelical bishops, the President of the Board of Control for India who had the nomination to the crown of the next bishop of Calcutta, was Charles Grant, eldest son of the Charles Grant who had assisted in the establishment of the diocese. He too was an evangelical, and was determined to appoint a good evangelical to Calcutta. It was not, however, easy to find anyone prepared to take the risk of going to India. Daniel Wilson, the distinguished evangelical vicar of Islington volunteered, and survived for twenty-six years.

It might have been expected that after the East India Company Act of 1833 divided the diocese of Calcutta into three, creating two new dioceses, Bombay and Madras, and designating the bishop of Calcutta as metropolitan, and with a bishop who had for long been a CMS supporter, and was a close friend of Josiah Pratt, the Society's secretary, that the bishop's task would be more manageable. His sphere of activity was much smaller, and as an evangelical working in partnership with an evangelical missionary society, and with a predominantly evangelical clergy, the bishop's relations with his clergy, and the local committee of the CMS, and the secretary and the London committee, should have been ideal. Wilson was in fact, on his arrival in India, invited to become president of the local CMS committee in Calcutta.

Wilson, however, had strong church principles. He was well-read in patristic theology, and had a high view of the apostolic succession of the ministry, and of the authority and duties of a bishop. He followed in the tradition of Middleton and Heber in wishing to regularize the position of missionaries in his diocese by licensing them. A three-cornered quarrel developed between the local CMS committees in Calcutta and Madras, which were elected by all the local subscribers to the Society, and usually included leading local figures, and the London committee of the Society, and the bishop, over the authority of the bishop over missionaries. The Society saw themselves in a position analogous to patrons of English parishes, presenting a priest to a bishop for induction to a parish. Wilson pointed out that a missionary was more like a curate appointed and paid by an incumbent, but licensed by a bishop to a particular parish. The Society feared that the bishop's analogy would interfere with its claim to locate its missionaries where it pleased. The corresponding committee compounded matters by refusing to allow the bishop to receive information about the missionaries and their work as of right, which he deemed necessary for his supervision of their work.

Eventually Wilson's friends in the CMS in London worked out an agreement in 1836, which established four ground rules for the relationship between the bishop (and subsequently other bishops) and the Society. First, the bishop expressed, by granting or withholding his licence, in which the sphere of the missionary's work was noted, his approbation, or otherwise, of the sphere of work. Second, the bishop superintended missionaries in the same way as other clergy in the execution of their duties. Third, the bishop was to receive from those (i.e. the London committee) who still stood in the relation of lay patrons to the missionaries, 'such communication respecting his ecclesiastical duties as may enable the Bishop to discharge that paternal superintendence to the best advantage'. Fourth, if the bishop or the archdeacon were, at the request of the Society, to become an officer of the corresponding committee, he would receive all confidential material on all topics which the bishop or the archdeacon officially neither could wish nor properly ask to receive.[37]

The local CMS committee in Calcutta fell into dispute with Wilson over two further issues. First, the local committee were suspicious of what they regarded as the High Church doctrines taught by the Bishop's College, and in 1835, proposed establishing a 'head seminary' in Calcutta to educate CMS missionaries. Despite their theological differences, Wilson liked and respected the principal of the College, and objected to the establishment of a new seminary, even though the proposal was supported by the London committee, who did not appreciate what a small pool there was from which to recruit students for one, let alone two colleges. Although the project did not succeed, the Society maintained its prejudice against the College, and declined to appoint candidates for their scholarships there. Sadly, their suspicions were partially fulfilled when in 1841 the SPG appointed a member of staff with strong Tractarian sympathies. They had originally approached Henry Manning for the post, but he had declined.[38] Wilson disliked the new member of the staff and laid a complaint against him which the SPG failed to uphold, and Wilson withdrew from any involvement with the College. Second, the local committee, as representatives of local opinion, set themselves the responsibility of recommending, or more especially not recommending, candidates for ordination. Wilson resented this, and ordained three candidates whom the committee had not recommended. When, in addition to this, the corresponding committee discovered the agreement that the London committee had arrived at with Wilson the previous year, some of them resigned, and the London committee took the opportunity to appoint a new committee, as they had appointed a new committee in Madras in 1833, with nine members chosen by them, and a missionary sent out for the purpose from London to act as the secretary.

In 1839 Wilson resolved the question of Lutheran orders, by securing an agreement with the German Lutheran missionaries employed by the CMS that they would only administer the sacraments to Indian congregations in their charge, and that they would only use the Prayer Book. In addition they agreed to observe the Anglican custom of reserving confirmation and ordination to the bishop. It was agreed that, in future, all Lutheran missionaries employed by the Society would be required to receive Anglican orders. Thus Wilson, though an evangelical, followed the traditional Anglican line taken by Heber.

There could also be significant tensions between missionaries and the CMS. Once they were established in India, missionaries sometimes felt very unhappy about their salaries and their terms of service in comparison with the chaplains appointed by the East India Company. There were also problems about the expectations by missionaries of European standards of accommodation and living. However, it was pointed out to missionaries that they needed to remember, that was provided for them was comparative luxury and wealth in comparison with what Indian catechists and teachers were provided with.

On the one hand Wilson had to resist the encroachment of the CMS on his episcopal authority, on the other hand he had to try to establish his authority in relation to the administration in India. The governor general was prepared to consult Wilson about church matters and the appointment of chaplains, but then made his own decisions, which were not always what Wilson would have wished. He was also in the invidious position of having no resources with which to meet what he saw as the spiritual needs of his diocese. The East India Company would only provide chaplains where its servants were based, and the missionary societies would only provide missionaries to work with Indians. Wilson and his predecessors, as a result of their travels in India, were well aware of large colonies of English people and Anglo-Indians not in the employment of the Company, and not living within its sphere of influence, who required pastoral care. His power and authority between the Company and the government, on the one hand, and a determinedly independent voluntary society on the other hand, was very limited.[39]

Because of the expansion in the Church establishment in India to comprise three bishops and archdeacons by the mid-1830s, it would be very easy to exaggerate the expansion of Anglicanism and the scale of missionary activity. The great difficulty in recruiting Anglican clergy to work in India, and the very limited funds available to the CMS and the SPG meant that there were relatively few missionaries working in India under Anglican auspices. In fact between 1789 and 1858, only 559 Christian missionaries of any denomination served in India.[40]

THE ORIGINS OF THE ANGLICAN CHURCH IN AUSTRALASIA

In Heber's letters patent, on his appointment to Calcutta, in 1824, Australia and New Zealand were added to the territory of his diocese, and an archdeaconry of New South Wales was created as part of the diocese, with the archdeacon appointed and funded by the crown.

New South Wales had been established as a penal colony in 1788. At the insistence of William Wilberforce and Henry Thornton in Parliament, a chaplain, Richard Johnson, was appointed by the government, who also paid his salary, to the first penal fleet to the colony. He was appointed on the nomination of Wilberforce, having been educated at the evangelical stronghold of Magdalene College, Cambridge, and having been curate to Henry Foster, who was one of the founders of the evangelical Eclectic Society, and subsequently of the CMS. The SPCK, at the suggestion of the archbishop of Canterbury, made up a consignment of Bibles, psalters and catechisms, and an assortment of tracts for the chaplain to take with him and distribute among the convicts. In 1790 the SPG agreed to make an annual grant of £40 for the salaries of four Anglican school masters for the colony. In 1800 Johnson returned to England, because of his health, and was succeeded by Samuel Marsden, who had gone out to New South Wales as the assistant chaplain in 1794. Marsden was a protégé of the evangelical Elland Clerical Society, who had sent him, when he was twenty-four, to Hull Grammar School to study under Milner, and from thence to Magdalene College, Cambridge. He was sent out to New South Wales at Simeon's recommendation, where he was not very successful, because he agreed to become a magistrate, which did not endear him to the convicts. By 1819 there were four Anglican chaplains (and two Methodist ministers) in New South Wales. In 1819 there was a government inquiry following numerous complaints about the unsatisfactory state of the administration in the colony. Following the publication of the report in 1823, a further report was made recommending the strengthening of the established Church in Australia, using the Canadian model

of extensive land endowments and a regular ecclesiastical establishment with a school system, under an archdeacon. The secretary of state for the colonies, implemented this and the new
archdeaconry of New South Wales in the diocese of Calcutta
was established by royal letters patent in 1825. In 1819 an
Ecclesiastical Board had been attached to the Colonial Office to
advise on and control the supply of clergy for the colonies, with
Archdeacon Anthony Hammond, a strong supporter of the
SPG as its principal officer. By 1823 there were nine chaplains
in New South Wales, and between 1824 and 1829 another seven
arrived.

On a visit to London in 1807–9 Marsden had sought the
CMS's support for missionary work in New South Wales, and
the Society encouraged the formation of a local committee in
Sydney, and a subsequent plan for a mission to the native
Aboriginals, but withdrew its support when the mission proved
unsuccessful. In 1825 the SPCK made a substantial grant to the
new archdeacon, and SPCK auxiliary committees were formed
in Sydney and in Van Diemen's Land.

In 1829 W. G. Broughton, who was a close friend of Joshua
Watson and of the Hackney Phalanx, and a protégé of the duke
of Wellington, was appointed by the crown to the archdeaconry
of New South Wales. He put a strong case that the English
people and Church had a duty to support the colonial Church
beyond meeting the stipend of the archdeacon. However, this
was the wrong moment to be arguing such a case, as we have
seen in Canada. The formation of a Whig government in 1830
signalled a change in political attitudes to the established
Church. Government money was no longer likely to be forthcoming for one particular church and Broughton was going
to be unlucky on this front. The SPG, however, accepted his
challenge to assist in making provision for the spiritual needs of
English migrants to Australia, when the attempt to endow the
Church with a seventh of the colony's surveyed land, which was
bitterly opposed by landowners, nonconformists and Roman
Catholics, was abandoned by the government in 1829, and in
1831 made him a grant of £1,000 for his work, and in 1835–6
the SPCK joined in by making two grants of £1,000 each.

By the Church Act 1836, the New South Wales legislature
granted a subsidy to provide for the support of religion and
education on terms which would not discriminate between the

various Christian bodies then working in the colony. This followed the policy now being pursued by the British government in allocating grants to the National Society for Promoting the Education of the Poor in the Principles of the Established Church, and the nonconformist British and Foreign Schools Society, in proportion to the number of schools they provided and supported. Although the legislation was a defeat for Broughton, it did improve the position of the Anglican Church, as well as other churches. The Act provided for grants to match private donations to build churches and houses for clergy, and also provided for a stipend for clergy where a congregation numbered a hundred or more people. However, it did nothing to help small struggling congregations. Although as a result of the Act, the Church of England lost its established status in the colony, it did well out of the Act, within three years the number of Anglican clergy virtually doubled to thirty-five and by 1847 there were sixty-four clergy, and numerous churches were built.

In addition to this, the SPG agreed to recruit clergy to work in the colony, and to provide a grant of £150 each to assist with their passage to Australia and re-establishment there, and a gratuity of £50 a year each for five years to give the congregations time to organize themselves to support their own clergy. Between 1835 and 1855 the SPG granted a total of £110,000 for work in Australia. The SPG, and to a lesser extent, the SPCK primed the pump of government aid, and increased the incentive for local fund-raising, which it was hoped would enable the Anglican Church in Australia to be self-supporting. Broughton was enormously encouraged by this support from England for he had great difficulty raising funds in Australia.

In 1836 the diocese of Calcutta was divided further, and a diocese of Australia, based on Sydney, was created by letters patent, and Broughton was appointed bishop with a salary, provided by the British government, of £2,000 a year, which was also intended to meet all his considerable expenses of office. Broughton, like the other pioneering colonial bishops experienced great difficulty establishing the role of bishop over against the governor and the Colonial Office, and the clergy and the laity. As in other colonies, there were always tensions between governors and the bishop over power and precedence. There could be frequent clashes of personality and policy between a governor and a bishop. In New South Wales key

issues were schools and Roman Catholics. Broughton, as a traditional High Churchman, expected the governor's support in
providing funds for church schools, and for maintaining the
precedence of the established Church in the face of increasing
Irish Roman Catholic immigration and a thrusting and energetic
Roman Catholic bishop. However, this was not something that
could be relied on, especially after 1830, when the long Tory/
High Church monopoly of political power in Britain came to
an end. Broughton feared that governors appointed by Whig
colonial secretaries had an eye on reducing expenditure, rather
than supporting the established Church. He fought hard to
maintain the traditional position of the Church, but he came to
see the disadvantages of the establishment, and the vulnerability
of the Church to the vagaries of government policy, and the
personal enthusiasm or prejudice of ministers. He came
increasingly to the view that the Church needed to be independent of the State.[41]

On his visit to England in 1807–9 Marsden had persuaded
the CMS to undertake a mission to New Zealand. They agreed
to his suggestion that the missionaries should comprise a carpenter, a smith and a twine spinner. However, it was 1814 before
Marsden was able to arrange for his missionaries, to whom a
teacher had been added, to go on to New Zealand from Sydney.
Having got them established, he left them to their own devices.
In 1818 the CMS recruited a clergyman to join them, but
Marsden decided that he should begin a new settlement in a
new place. The earliest missionaries mastered the Maori language, and one of them contributed to the first publication
about the Maori language. However, they lacked much in the
way of leadership abilities, and had difficulties working with
each other, and incurred disapproval because they engaged in
trading with the Maoris (including trading in guns).

In 1823 the CMS recruited a clergyman, Henry Williams,
who had some leadership potential, for work in New Zealand,
and thereafter they began to recruit and keep more people, and
in 1825 the Society set up a local committee in Sydney to supervise the New Zealand mission. By the late 1830s there were four
clergy and twenty-two lay catechists working in New Zealand.
There were, however, tensions between the clergy, who saw
themselves as superintending, and the lay catechists, who had
often had much longer experience of the country. There was

also a dispute between the missionaries and the London committee of the Society over the extent of land purchases made from the Maoris by the missionaries for their families.

In 1838–9 the CMS asked Bishop Broughton of Australia to visit New Zealand on their behalf. In his report to the CMS he recommended that more ordained missionaries should be recruited, and that some of the lay catechists might be ordained. In the light of this the CMS London committee asked the bishop of London to endorse their proposal for a bishop in New Zealand. The reports of an expected influx of English emigrants to New Zealand encouraged both the bishop and the existing missionaries to support the proposal. In March 1840 a New Zealand Church Society was formed in London to promote the idea, which was supported by the bishop of London and the archbishop of Canterbury, and the secretary of state for the colonies, Lord John Russell, was reported to be sympathetic. In 1840 by the Treaty of Waitangi, which was translated into Maori for the benefit of the Maoris by one of the missionaries, Henry Williams, New Zealand became a British colony, and the scene was set for the creation of a new colonial bishopric, supported by the CMS.[42]

By 1840, in addition to the bishops of the Protestant Episcopal Church in the USA, there were ten overseas Anglican bishops. Apart from the new bishoprics founded in India, which were set up by Acts of the British Parliament, the dioceses in British colonies had been established under letters patent issued by the crown, and were funded by government grants to pay the bishops' salaries and expenses. The real objection to the use of letters patent for the appointment of bishops was not so much the method of appointment, as the inadequate jurisdiction which they might confer. They worked well enough in Ireland, where there was a church with long-standing institutions, to which the letters patent related, but they were less satisfactory when they were required to minutely specify a bishop's authority and jurisdiction for a new situation and his relationship with the secular authorities. Thus they gave a bishop no authority to call synods or to make rules for the Church, for the institutions to achieve these already existed in Ireland. Further, after 1842, the letters patent issued to new bishops omitted the power of holding an ecclesiastical court, which meant that the bishops so appointed could only discipline clergy by revoking their licences, or through the civil courts of a colony. However, letters patent did have the advantage during this interim period, of allowing bishops to develop representative synodical systems appropriate to their contexts.

Bishoprics were established, as we have seen, as part of the policy pursued by a succession of British governments of mostly conservative views, from 1787 to 1830, of maintaining close links between the colonies and the mother country by the establishment and support of English institutions in the colonies. As has been shown in relation to Canada, after 1830, with the formation of a Whig government and the recognition of denominational pluralism in England, British governments, whether Whig or Tory, liberal or conservative, believed that their dependence on the electoral support and goodwill of nonconformists was too important to risk alienating them by giving grants to support the established Church whether in England or the colonies. After 1840 there would be no new government grants to support Anglican bishops, and apart from India, there was a continuing withdrawal of existing grants, which as we will see in the next chapter, posed new questions for Anglicans about the support of their Church in overseas territories.

CHAPTER 4

The Beginnings of an
Anglican Communion 1840–1860

The 1830s were a highly significant decade for the Church of England, and ultimately for the Anglican Communion. As we have already seen, the old hegemony between Church and State in England was changing. The traditional view of the State as the protector of, and provider for, the Church became less tenable, though we will see that many influential churchmen, clerical and lay, continued to espouse it, in a modified form, for the rest of the century. However, from the 1830s successive British governments, whether Tory or Whig, recognized and provided for denominational pluralism in England. Most Whig politicians did not think that this should preclude the government from taking a special interest in the established Church's affairs and even legislating on behalf of the Church of England, especially if this assisted the Church or churches to act as agents for the moral and religious education of the nation, as well as saving souls. Many churchmen, however, especially the more conservative, regarded the intervention of a government and legislature which, since the repeal of the Test and Corporation Acts in 1827 and the passage of the Roman Catholic Emancipation Act in 1828 was no longer exclusively Anglican in its composition, and might include those who did not conform to the established Church, as an act of sacrilege. In their view Parliament and the government had abdicated responsibility for the Church by surrendering membership of Parliament and occupancy of civic offices to non-Anglicans.

From the 1830s there was a tendency towards a division of opinion about authority in the Church. Evangelicals and Broad Churchmen tended to continue to look to the State to protect and provide for the Church. They tended to see the lay people of the Church, broadly represented in Parliament, as having a responsibility for ensuring that the gospel was preached and a Christian life was led throughout all the British dominions. High Churchmen of all schools of thought, in reaction against the changes in the British political constitution during the 1830s, began to look askance at the close link between Church and State, as we have already seen Bishop Broughton doing in Australia. They ceased to view it as a partnership, as High Churchmen of previous generations had regarded it, in which the State had a duty to ensure that the national Church was enabled to proclaim the gospel. Instead, they began to see the State as attempting to achieve a domination over and control of the Church. Thus they saw the Irish Church Temporalities Bill in 1833 as an intrusion by the State into the affairs of the Church, even though they might agree that what it was intending to do, to reduce the number of bishops in Ireland by amalgamating some sees, so as to improve the incomes of the remaining bishops, was in itself admirable. In their view the Church should put its own house in order, and should be released by the State to do this, under the bishops.

It was not just the group of younger, more extreme High Churchmen dominated by J.H. Newman and concentrated in Oxford, who proclaimed the Church of England to be part of the one Catholic Church, as though no one had ever thought of it before, who were suspicious of the continuing role of the State in the life of the Church. The group included more traditional High Churchmen, such as Samuel Wilberforce, who had forsaken the evangelical ways of his father. In 1838, in writing of the missionary expansion of the Church, Wilberforce had commented,

> The great object . . . we now ought to aim at in our missionary exertions is to give them a much more Church character than we have done – to send out the Church, and not merely instructions about religion. This is the way in which in primitive times the world was converted; and if episcopacy, a native clergy, a visible communion, due celebration of the Sacraments, Confirmation, &, &c – if these things be really important, then how can we expect full success, till we send out missionary bishops, i.e. bishops and a missionary clergy as a visible Church.[1]

The ten overseas bishops and the Episcopal Church in the USA had caught the imaginations of English Churchpeople. Bishop Heber's *Memoirs and Correspondence*, edited by his widow on her return from India, was in its fourth edition within three years of his death.[2] Samuel Wilberforce in 1837 published the *Journals* of Henry Martyn, the evangelical chaplain of the East India Company who had undertaken pioneering missionary work in India in the early years of the century.[3] In 1823 Henry Hobart, the bishop of New York, had visited England for his health, and was introduced to Joshua Watson and other members of the Hackney Phalanx, and also to Newman. Watson remained in touch with Hobart for the rest of his life. In 1839 Walter Hook, the leading High Churchman who was vicar of Holy Trinity, Coventry, met John Inglis, the bishop of Nova Scotia at Watson's house and established a strong friendship with him. When Hobart's disciple, Bishop Doane of New Jersey, visited England in 1841, he similarly received a warm welcome, and was invited by Walter Hook, now vicar of Leeds, to preach at the consecration of the new parish church in Leeds. He also invited the bishop of Ross, Moray and Argyll to attend as a bishop. Hook was keen throughout his life to promote knowledge in England about the American and Scottish churches. In 1838 he wrote 'A Preface Containing a History of the Church in America' for John McVicar's *Life of Bishop Hobart*. In 1839 Henry Caswall, an English priest who had worked in the United States, published *America and the American Church*. Wilberforce himself wrote *A History of the Protestant Episcopal Church in America* published in 1844, and in 1846 Edward Waylen, who also had worked in the United States published his *Ecclesiastical Reminiscences* about the United States.[4] There was thus a considerable amount of information available in England about the American Church.

Hook, Newman and Pusey, however, viewed the American Church with some anxiety. Apart from Bishop Doane, they had not been impressed by the American clergy they had met in England, and they feared that the American Church was likely to split over disagreements about baptismal regeneration, the Anglicans in the western states taking an extreme Protestant position and the New York clergy following a traditional High Church line. In response to this Newman had wanted to send two or three English clergy to New York to reinforce the traditional High Churchmen, but he failed to find anyone willing to go. Hook had proposed sending sound books instead of men, having discovered that there were very few editions of any of the Church Fathers in the library of the General Theological Seminary in New York, and he started a subscription to send a complete set of the Fathers to the Seminary. He suspected that the Americans were '. . . too apt to consider that if they maintain the one doctrine of Episcopacy . . . nothing more is required'.[5]

For thirty or forty years after 1787 there had been little contact between the American and the English churches. The Act of 1787 permitting the consecration of bishops without requiring them to take the oath of allegiance to the British crown had also debarred American bishops and clergy from exercising their orders in England. In any case, for a significant part of the period Britain and the United States had been either at war, or in a relationship of armed neutrality. In addition to Hobart's visit in 1823, and continuing contacts with members of the Hackney Phalanx, Bishop Chase of Illinois had also visited England to raise funds for a seminary on the Ohio frontier, and had become acquainted with English evangelicals. In the 1830s and 40s there had been a steady stream of American clergy visiting England.[6]

At the general convention in 1838 the House of Bishops took the initial steps to regularize relations between the Anglican churches. A committee was appointed to report on measures for 'obtaining the requisite securities in reference to the passing of Clergymen to and from countries in which are Protestant Episcopal Churches, for the purpose of settlement'. A committee of three bishops recommended that a formal letter be sent to the archbishops of Canterbury and Armagh, the primus of the Scottish Episcopal Church and the bishops of the Protestant churches in the West Indies, Canada and Nova Scotia. Favourable replies were received to this initiative, and a canon was passed at the next convention to regulate the reception of foreign clergy into the American Church. Perhaps in response to this, Archbishop Howley introduced a bill into the House of Lords to permit clergymen of the American and Scottish churches to officiate, on occasion, in England. Bishop Hopkins of Vermont and Bishop Russell of Glasgow had both lobbied Howley about this in 1838. The bill was passed in 1840, and so formal inter-communion was established among the churches.[7] This interaction with and knowledge of the American Church was an important influence in the development of the Anglican Communion.

In the research for his book about the American Church Wilberforce had reported to Newman in 1837 that he had discovered that in 1835 the PECUSA had ordained two missionary bishops for Missouri and Indiana, to meet the spiritual needs of the people migrating westwards.[8] It was no doubt this that prompted him to think about the spiritual needs of the English people who were migrating in increasing numbers in the 1830s to Canada, Australia, New Zealand and South Africa. Bishop Wilberforce suggested that the Act which had permitted the American bishops to be consecrated without taking the oath of allegiance to the crown would permit the consecration of bishops to lead missions beyond the boundaries of the British Empire. Wilberforce wished the CMS, of which he was a member, to place greater emphasis on the 'Church in its name and to see episcopacy as a central feature of its mission, with bishops heading missionary work, rather than being introduced at a later date'.[9] It was perhaps under this influence that the CMS supported the idea of bishops for New Zealand and for Sierra Leone, and were willing to make an annual grant to pay the bishops' salaries. The government was not yet sufficiently secularized not to support church work and offered a parliamentary grant to pay the other half of the salaries. Indeed, surprisingly, in 1844 the government provided a grant to pay a bishop of Colombo for Ceylon. Successive governments continued the grant made since 1824 to pay the bishops of Jamaica and Barbados until 1868 when the grants were discontinued, and the colonial legislatures were instructed to follow suit and to withdraw their grants. The legislature in Barbados refused to withdraw its grant for the support of the bishop and the clergy, and continued to vote for the grant.[10]

In the early 1840s the CMS seems to have become much more willing to co-operate with bishops and the Church. Perhaps the presence of Henry Venn, a clergyman descended from a long line of clergy as secretary, and one of the controlling influences in the Society, rather than a layman, Dandeson Coates, was an important factor. In 1841, at the invitation of Bishop

Blomfield of London, the Society agreed that in any future disagreement with a colonial bishop, the dispute should be referred to the archbishops of the United Church of England and Ireland, and that their decision should be binding on the Society.[11] In 1841 the Society agreed to make the archbishop of Canterbury *ex officio* their vice-patron. There were even suggestions that the CMS and the SPG should amalgamate. However, this was an unfortunate moment for a rapprochement between the Society and episcopacy, for the more radical High Church followers of Newman, the Tractarians from Oxford, began to criticize the CMS (and the SPG and the SPCK, for that matter) for not being more 'Church', by which they meant under the influence of the bishops, whom they also criticized for not sufficiently exercising their apostolic authority to guide the Church into the ways in which the Tractarians wished it to go. Whilst the CMS might be persuaded to accommodate itself to the existing bishops, the evangelical laymen and clergy who constituted the committee of the Society did not believe that it was either scriptural, nor part of the Anglican tradition for bishops to direct the Church, even with the assistance of lay people. Bishops, they suspected, were being encouraged to usurp the role of the Crown-in-Parliament in the government of the Church, and that they feared, was aping the renewed emphasis on the papacy in the Roman Catholic Church, and might even be a movement by a fifth column within the Church of England to subvert (pervert, they might say) the Church to Rome.

The view of the CMS and most evangelical Anglicans, articulated by Venn, was that colonial churches themselves should give rise to an indigenous episcopate, and that episcopacy should grow from a local church, and should not be its precursor. Venn therefore disagreed with the policy that had begun in the American Church of establishing missionary bishoprics, and which was being encouraged and promoted in England by the traditional High Church bishops and the SPG. Venn and most evangelicals, and many Broad Churchmen, believed that bishops should only be sent by the crown to work in places within the crown's dominions. Venn saw episcopacy as an expression of godly order within the Church, not as fundamental to the Church. For Venn the ecclesiastical framework should be derived from and subordinate to the primary work of evangelism within the Church. The bishop was, in his view, a keystone of the local church, not as for High Churchmen, the foundation upon which a church was built.[12]

1841 saw two important developments in the provision for overseas bishoprics. The first was less important in the short-term, but has attracted more attention from historians, because it was strongly attacked by Newman and his followers. In 1841 the king of Prussia, Frederick William IV, proposed to the British government the establishment of a Protestant bishopric in Jerusalem. His motives were mixed. Prussia wished to promote its commercial and colonial interests in the Middle East, as well as Protestant unity in Prussia, by introducing bishops into the recently united Protestant Church in Prussia. The proposal appealed to the British government, and especially to Lord Palmerston, the foreign secretary, as a means of strengthening British interests in the Middle East, and of counterbalancing the influences of the Orthodox and Roman Catholic churches, which were suspected of aiding the interests of Russia and France. The scheme was enthusiastically supported by traditional High Churchmen, such as Howley, Blomfield, Wilberforce, Hook and Gladstone, as a unique opportunity to assert the Church of England's claim and vocation to be a standard or model of catholicity. Blomfield saw it as 'eminently calculated to advance the boundaries of Christ's Church'. Archdeacon Edward Churton, an associate of the Hackney Phalanx, said that the Church of England had a 'duty to give an Episcopate to all communities of Christians which may seek it, if their belief is orthodox'.[13] The evangelicals welcomed it as the beginning of the fulfilment of apocalyptic prophecy of the restoration of a Christian Palestine; and Broad Churchmen saw it as an affirmation of the idea of the national Church in Prussia.

The Foreigners Consecration Act Amendment Bill, to amend the Act permitting the consecration of the American bishops in 1787, was passed in October 1841. It extended the authority of the archbishops of Canterbury and York to consecrate foreigners to the office of bishop in the Church. Such persons might be excused taking the oaths of allegiance and supremacy, no royal licence was required for their election, and no royal mandate under the great seal was needed for their confirmation and consecration. A bishop so consecrated might exercise spiritual jurisdiction over the ministers of the United Church of England

and Ireland, and over such Protestant congregations as might wish to place themselves under his authority. No person, however, could be so consecrated until the archbishop had applied for and been granted a royal licence, and no person so consecrated, nor anyone he admitted to orders could exercise a spiritual office in England. The British and Prussian crowns were to nominate alternatively to the bishopric, but the archbishop of Canterbury was always to have an absolute veto over the Prussian nominee. The British and Prussian crowns each subscribed £15,000 capital to endow the bishopric to provide a salary for the bishop and funds to enable him to administer the diocese.

Pusey, among the Tractarians leaders, was optimistic about the scheme, but Newman attacked it, alleging that Archbishop Howley had done all he could to 'unchurch' the Church of England. He sent the bishop of Oxford a public protest, claiming 'Lutheranism and Calvinism are heresies, repugnant to Scripture . . . and anathematised by east as well as west'. Gladstone afterwards thought that the Jerusalem bishopric lost Newman to the Church of England.[14] It is highly likely that the implications of this attack on the Lutheran Church, with which the CMS had worked so closely in India and Sierra Leone did much to raise suspicions among the CMS committee about Tractarianism, and any whom they might judge to be tainted by it.

Then, in April 1840, Bishop Blomfield of London, realizing that, following the parliamentary debates over the Canadian Clergy Reserves Act, new government funding for the Church in the colonies was unlikely, had written to the archbishop of Canterbury:

> The time appears to me to have arrived at which a great effort is required on the part of the Church of England to impart the full benefits of her apostolical government and discipline, as well as of her doctrine and ordinances, to those distant parts of the British Empire where, if the Christian religion is expressed at all, it is left to depend for its continuance, under the blessing of its Divine Head, upon the energies of individual piety and zeal, without being enshrined in the sanctuary of a rightly-constituted Church, the only sure and trustworthy instrument of its perpetuation and sufficiency.[15]

He went on to argue that it was the manifest duty of the government of a Christian State 'that Government being part of the Church Catholic' to equip the Church with 'its worldly means and appliances'. He suggested, however, that there seemed little hope of securing provision for new dioceses out of State revenues, as the propriety of the State supporting the Church was 'openly called into question by a large proportion of the members of one branch of our legislature'. He proposed that if the State refused to act, it was the duty of the Church itself 'to take the work in hand, and do that which in no case may be left undone'.

In response to this letter Howley called a public meeting. In his letter of invitation to the meeting he noted 'the defective provision hitherto made for planting the Church in the distant dependencies of the British Empire [and desired] that an effort be made to extend to them the full benefit of its apostolic government and discipline', and recommended 'commencing a fund for the endowment of additional Bishoprics in the Colonies'. The subsequent meeting was attended by 'all the Bishops within reach of London, many lay peers, and many hundreds of the most distinguished of the clergy and lay members of the Church'. At the meeting Howley pointed out that a church without a bishop could hardly be called episcopal, and that 'a body without a head is impotent'. He summed up by saying, 'This is no Question of episcopacy, but whether a church being episcopal can prosper without a Bishop'. Blomfield stated the points he had made in his letter to Howley, and urged action on the Church, as the State had neglected its duty. Mr Justice Coleridge spoke in support of the archbishop, as did Archdeacon Henry Manning of Chichester, and Gladstone, who had recently been under-secretary of state for the colonies, moved a formal motion that a fund should be set up to collect money to endow more bishoprics in the colonies. He also agreed to be the first treasurer of the Fund, an office which he held until his death in 1898. The Revd Ernest Hawkins, the secretary of the SPG, who was to become the first secretary of the Fund, announced that £80,000 had already been given or promised, if the Fund were established. The archbishop of Armagh moved a vote of thanks. The meeting went on to resolve that

> a Fund be raised towards providing for the Endowment of Bishoprics in such of the foreign possessions of Great Britain

as shall be determined by the Archbishops and Bishops of the United Church of England and Ireland, that their lordships be requested to undertake the charge and application of the Fund, and to name a Treasurer or treasurers, and such other officers as may be required for conducting the necessary details.[16]

This marked a highly significant new stage in the attitude of the English bishops to their responsibility for the overseas Church. In the past, as we have seen, bishops had expressed their concern for the provision of bishops for the Church overseas by privately lobbying governments for funds and for royal letters patent for the establishment of dioceses and for the support and consecration of bishops. The only time a bishop had previously been involved in a semi-public attempt to bring pressure for the appointment of a bishop had been when Sherlock had attempted to rally support for the appointment of a bishop for the North American colonies in 1751, and he had been sharply rebuked for interfering in the government's business by the then archbishop and the secretary of state. Here was a meeting called by the archbishop of Canterbury to put pressure on the government, and with the knowledge that it might fail, to call for funds to endow new bishoprics. Clearly from the bishops' point of view, there had been a change of perception of the nature of the relationship between the Church and the State.

On 1 June 1841 the archbishops and bishops met to implement the resolutions passed at the earlier meeting. They appointed a steering committee of four archbishops and five bishops of the United Church of England and Ireland, and appointed four treasurers and a secretary. They resolved that, 'in no case shall we proceed without the concurrence of Her Majesty's government' and decided that the first six bishoprics to be endowed should be New Zealand, Valetta (later to be Gibraltar), New Brunswick, the Cape of Good Hope (later to be Cape Town), Van Diemen's Land (later to be Hobart) and Ceylon. They issued an appeal for donations, either earmarked for a particular diocese, or for the general purposes of the Fund. In the appeal they listed an additional seven areas where they hoped new dioceses might be set up. They formed themselves into subcommittees to prepare and to circulate information about each proposed new diocese. In the advertisement for a diocese for Van Diemen's Land they noted that 'the history of our North American settlements may teach us the wisdom of anticipating the evil of a colony growing in strength and in ignorance of the benefits of efficient Church government'.[17]

When the bishops were later criticized for sending bishops rather than missionaries to the colonies, they pointed out that their strategy had worked, for, in colonies to which bishops had been sent, the numbers of clergy had doubled or trebled. They would not normally sanction the establishment of a diocese until an endowment had been secured sufficient to ensure the permanence of the appointment, although in some cases they approved a bishop being paid for a strictly limited term of years by one of the missionary societies, if there was adequate guarantee that in the meantime a proper endowment could be provided. The Colonial Office similarly insisted that a permanent endowment should be available before letters patent were granted for the creation of a diocese and the appointment of a bishop. The episcopal committee which managed the Fund became effectively a steering group responsible for the creation of new dioceses, and negotiated, when necessary, with the government on these matters, for example, to persuade the government to make some financial provision for a bishopric in Ceylon, and for interim funding arrangements when, eventually, in 1868 the British government withdrew its annual grant to pay the bishops and their establishments in the two original dioceses in the West Indies.

The Colonial Bishoprics Fund was very closely linked to the SPG through its secretary, Ernest Hawkins. Subsequently the secretaryships were held in tandem. Unfortunately that meant that because the Fund only had a very small permanent staff, in order to reduce overheads, it was always under the shadow of the Society. In its first years large sums of money were raised for the Fund. By 1849, £133,000 had been raised and expended in providing endowments for new bishoprics. Most of the money had been raised as large individual benefactions. The SPG and the SPCK were the largest contributors. During the hundred years from 1841 to 1941 the SPG contributed £134,500 of the £900,000 the Fund received during the period, and the SPCK contributed a further £85,822, so two missionary societies, from their own resources arising from their own fund-raising, contributed well over 20 per cent of the total sum. The CMS also contributed to the Fund in its early days. Baroness Angela Burdett-Coutts was the principal individual benefactor, giving over £35,000 to endow the dioceses of Cape Town and Adelaide, and to assist towards the endowments of bishops in Sierra Leone and Brisbane. A 'brother and sister' gave £10,000 to endow the diocese of Victoria (Hong Kong) in 1854. When the Fund was initiated, the archbishop of Canterbury gave £1,500 and the archbishop of York and the bishop of London gave £1,000 each, and the University of Oxford gave £2,000.[18]

Not much was done, after the initial meeting, to boost funds and to encourage continuing donations. By 1853 funds were at a low ebb, and a second public meeting was called. The speakers included, in addition to the archbishop of Canterbury and the bishop of London, the colonial secretary, the earl of Chichester (who was also a committee member of the CMS, and a former colonial secretary), the duke of Newcastle, and the bishops of Cape Town and Quebec, who were in London for the SPG jubilee celebrations. The meeting was greatly inspired by the presence of a bishop supported by the Fund, and agreed to appeal for £45,000, and passed a resolution for the establishment of new dioceses in Africa, Canada, and Australia. Donations to the Fund were greatly stimulated by this.[19] However, after the death of Blomfield, who had been the driving force behind the Fund, its activities were muted, and no attempt was made to turn it into an important fund-raising agency or pressure group for developing new overseas dioceses. As we will see, it continued to make important financial contributions to the development of the Anglican Communion, but it might have been used more creatively. Part of the limitation of its work must have been that the committee consisted entirely of English and Irish bishops who were also preoccupied with other matters, and the secretariat was shared with the SPG, which may have made for economy, but probably detracted from energy being put into the Fund. It might have been very different if Joshua Watson had been younger, or had had a successor with the time, energy and his ability on the committee. However, the Fund did make a very important contribution towards the development of Anglicanism overseas. By 1872 it had provided funds to wholly or partially endow thirty new dioceses.

Funds might be raised to pay bishops in new dioceses, ministers might even be persuaded to advise the crown to authorize the archbishop to consecrate new bishops, but, as we will see, there continued to be major tensions between government ministers and bishops, and between bishops and clergy and laity in their new dioceses. There were also new tensions about the ways in which an Anglican diocese might be governed, as a new relationship between the Church and the State emerged when colonies became self-governing, as well as the continuing tensions between bishops and the missionary societies.

A complex example is provided by the diocese of Gibraltar, founded in 1842, and endowed by the Colonial Bishoprics Fund. Here as in some other dioceses, some of the clergy were chaplains appointed by the British government, in this instance by the Foreign Office, rather than the Colonial Office, while others were appointed by missionary societies. The bishop of London had been in the anomalous position, as nominally the ordinary of Anglican congregations in Europe, of only being able to exercise authority over the clergy who had been directly appointed by the government, and even some of these clergy often refused to defer to the bishop unless specifically instructed to do so by the foreign secretary. The creation of the diocese of Gibraltar in 1842 did nothing to improve the situation, even though the bishop's letters patent conferred on him in theory exactly the same powers as were possessed by an English bishop – to appoint officers, to institute and license clergy, and to visit 'with all manner of jurisdiction, power, and coercion ecclesiastical'. The bishop, when he was appointed, was warned by the Foreign Office not to exercise his powers 'so as to excite the jealousies of foreign Governments or People' or to be made the 'source of strife and discord, religious or political'.[20]

When he took up office he did not find much of a welcome amongst the clergy and congregations of his diocese. Some of the clergy in European chaplaincies ignored him, and attempted to secure licences from the bishop of London, in order to circumvent the new bishop's authority. The congregation at the English Church in Rome refused point-blank to accept his authority. They pointed out that they had not received a copy of Lord Aberdeen's announcement about the establishment of the diocese, even though the administrative records showed that it had been sent to them. J.B. Sumner, the new evangelical archbishop of Canterbury, declined to support the bishop. The foreign secretary, Lord Palmerston, who was much influenced in the exercise of his ecclesiastical jurisdiction by his father-in-law, the leading evangelical layman, Lord Shaftesbury, was also unwilling to support the bishop. In 1851 Palmerston confirmed that the bishop of Gibraltar had no jurisdiction over the English Church in Rome, because they had not received the circular announcing the creation of the diocese.

The Foreign Office continued to exercise jurisdiction over chaplains independently of any bishop, and it had the power to retain a chaplain in office indefinitely, even if the bishop had withdrawn his licence. Conversely the Foreign Office could dismiss a chaplain at will, even though the bishop had not withdrawn his licence. In 1845 a dispute broke out between R.T. Lowe, the chaplain appointed by the Foreign Office to Funchal in 1833, and the leading members of the congregation over allegations about Lowe's alleged ritualist practices, but they had been unsuccessful in persuading a foreign secretary to dismiss Lowe until Lord Palmerston took up the case in 1848, and dismissed him. Palmerston pointed out to Blomfield that no ecclesiastical law required a chaplain abroad to have a licence from a bishop, and that in future he would not trouble the bishop to grant licences, and that he would refer any questions concerning overseas chaplaincies to the archbishop of Canterbury. Lowe's case was taken up by the Tory opposition and Anglican High Churchmen, and Palmerston's autocratic and Erastian attitude was attacked. Lowe did not leave Madeira, but continued to minister there from a hired chapel. Blomfield had asked Robert Gray, the newly consecrated bishop of Cape Town to try to achieve a reconciliation, when he called at Madeira on his way to Cape Town. Gray had approved of Lowe and reported 'I fear his opponents are not very respectable'. He also noted that Lowe had the support of Queen Adelaide, who regularly wintered in Madeira. Palmerston's treatment of such matters illustrates the powerlessness of overseas bishops against a minister, if their own powers had not been clearly defined, and if due process of law had not been observed.[21]

It was perhaps a little easier for a bishop to steer a course between existing congregations and the demands of a missionary society or government minister if he were further from Britain. Thus in New Zealand, a traditional High Churchman, with close links with Joshua Watson and the Hackney Phalanx, George Selwyn, had relatively few problems with the settlers, or with governors, and impressed the Maoris because he had taken the trouble to learn their language before he had arrived, and preached in Maori on his first Sunday in the colony. There were, in any case, few clergy in New Zealand, most of the thirty-eight missionaries being laymen, and Selwyn took with him five clergymen and three ordinands, so the men he had taken with him outnumbered the existing clergy. Selwyn was very much a missionary bishop, organizing the Church at a relatively early stage of its existence to proclaim the gospel to the Maoris and to provide spiritual care for the settlers. Initially he got on well with the missionaries, although he caused tensions by distancing himself from the Wesleyan missionaries who were working in New Zealand. The Wesleyans used the Prayer Book for their worship and encouraged their members to attend Anglican communion services, and also welcomed Anglicans to their communion services. Selwyn pointed out that the Wesleyan ministers were schismatics, and forbade Anglicans to participate in Wesleyan communion services. Selwyn also found it hard to establish common ground between the competing interests of the Maoris and the settlers. This in particular contributed to the tensions that developed between Selwyn and the CMS committee in London.

The CMS pointed out to Selwyn that their missionaries should only be employed in work among Maoris, not among Europeans, and as they had done in the West Indies and in India, they claimed the right to station their missionaries. Selwyn, however, insisted on his authority to move missionaries where he wished, and to require them to work with European settlers, as well as with Maoris. He was the bishop, and in his view, he had the right and authority to dispose clergy and lay catechists as he wished. In addition, he was on the spot, and knew the local conditions and needs, and had an overall view of the situation, whereas the CMS committee was on the other side of the world, and had never visited New Zealand and received information which might have been partial, and after much delay. The CMS committee in London proposed as a compromise using with Selwyn the procedures which they had drawn up with Bishop Wilson in India. In effect the compromise meant that the committee would propose where a missionary should be stationed, and the bishop, with his local knowledge, would approve or disapprove the appointment. However, when

Selwyn began to take initiatives in moving the missionaries, the committee in London were resentful. Difficulties also arose because Selwyn had established his base at the CMS station at Waimati, and the local CMS committee suspected him of trying to take over their station, and worse, also suspected that he had 'Romanizing' tendencies. This resulted in a number of complex misunderstandings, and in 1844 the CMS committee refused to renew Selwyn's tenancy at Waimati.

A further dispute broke out during the Maori War of 1844 to 1846, when Selwyn was unwilling to ordain some of the CMS catechists whom the Society had asked him to ordain. He required the five catechists whom he regarded as suitable for ordination to take an oath of canonical obedience to him as bishop, with the implication that there were undertaking to go wherever he directed. Henry Venn as secretary of the CMS protested that this went beyond the precedent set by the agreement with Bishop Wilson. The situation was to a certain extent calmed by the local committee of the CMS offering Selwyn the presidency of the committee, and by Selwyn's acceptance of the offer. However, the Society did withdraw its grant from St John's College, which Selwyn had set up in 1844 when he moved to Auckland, for they disapproved of its churchmanship, and Selwyn was unwilling to permit them, in exchange for their grant, to recruit the staff. Selwyn's aim in establishing the college was to educate Maoris for ordination, but in this too he ran into conflict with Venn. They both wanted an indigenous ministry, but Venn thought that Selwyn was making unnecessary academic demands by requiring knowledge of the Greek New Testament from anyone to be ordained priest. The first Maori candidate was not ordained deacon until 1853, whereas twenty-one European candidates had been ordained from St John's by then, and by 1860 there were still only two Maoris ordained. Venn did not think that this was a very good start to an indigenous ordained ministry.[22]

During the late 1830s and the early 1840s the CMS had suffered a number of attacks from the Tractarians for its failure to place itself under the direction of the English bishops. The increasing emphasis placed on the independent authority of a bishop by the Tractarians, and the Society's difficulties with even a traditional evangelical bishop such as Wilson, caused the CMS committee in London to be even more suspicious of the pretensions of bishops, and led them to restate what they saw as the distinctive position of the United Church of England and Ireland, by law established, in which they claimed that the position of the Church was legitimated and protected from the overweening ambitions of bishops by the legislature, which comprised the godly lay people of the nation. Venn did not regard the Scottish or the American churches as on the same footing as the United Church of England and Ireland, and upon the evidence of their holy communion rites, he doubted whether the United Church ought to regard itself as 'in communion' with them. He resisted what he regarded as the encroachment of Scottish and American bishops. In his view it would be illegal for an American bishop to exercise any spiritual functions in a British colony. He required the CMS missionaries in Shanghai to look to the bishop of Victoria (Hong Kong), rather than to the American bishop consecrated for missionary work on the Yangtse.[23]

The CMS committee was essentially a group of laymen, with the exception of Venn, who had little interest in theologies of the Church and ministry. Their concern was to send people out, whether lay or ordained was irrelevant to them, to preach the gospel, and to spread knowledge of the Bible. The legalistic caution of bishops was deeply frustrating to them. Venn, however, realized the impossibility of missionaries being able to preach throughout the world, which was the aim of the committee, and suggested that the task of mission ought to belong to the local church in each and every place. The task of the missionary in his view was to go where there was no local church in order to establish a 'native' self-governing church. Once a church was established, the missionary should move on. Venn was, in fact, developing a catholic doctrine of the Church for the CMS. However, he still saw the ecclesiastical framework as derived from, and subordinate to, the primary work of evangelism. He came to believe that episcopacy should grow out of a local church, and that it could not be, and should not be the precursor of that church. His adoption of this view was probably in reaction to the view of both the traditional High Churchmen and the Tractarians, that missions should be led by a bishop, going out to create a church, not following once a church had been established.[24] The traditional High Churchmen also envisaged the Church overseas being free of the State, and believed that the English bishops should consecrate bishops to lead missions beyond the bounds of British territories. They saw this as part of a rediscovery of the truth about the primitive Church before the time of Constantine.

These views about the nature of the relationship between the Church and the State became central to thinking about the nature and organization of Anglicanism when, during the 1830s, as we have seen, the British Parliament began to devolve responsibility for administering colonies to local legislatures under a governor appointed by the British crown, and also began to dismantle some of the aspects of a confessional state in England itself, in order to permit greater pluralism of Christian affiliation. This raised questions about the status of the Church of England and its bishops and clergy in the colonies, and about the extent to which English ecclesiastical and civil law applied in self-governing colonies. In the period before the 1830s, as we have seen, all shades of political and theological opinion in England regarded a close relationship between the Church and the State as natural and proper. After the rise of the Tractarians, with the emphasis on the Church as having an authority independent of the State, evangelicals began to see Parliament, or a colonial legislature, with recourse to the civil courts administered by laymen, and with appeal to the Privy Council, as the main line of defence for the doctrines of the established Church from the threat of unbridled episcopacy and clericalism, and from the incipient Romanism which they had come to suspect in the High Church party, and thought they saw realized in Tractarianism. Evangelicals therefore sought to protect the establishment of the Church at home, and to secure the protection of the colonial legislature for the Church overseas.

High Churchmen, in seeking to sever links with the State, argued that the organization of the Church was its own responsibility and that it needed only to take counsel with itself. Samuel Wilberforce had made this point in a sermon commemorating the foundation of the SPCK and the SPG in 1837.[25] This was the policy that Selwyn was determined to implement in New Zealand. His letters patent from the crown authorized him, and not the crown, to appoint archdeacons for his diocese. In 1844 he summoned his nine clergy to a synod 'to frame rules for the better management of the mission, and the general government of the Church', and they passed fifteen canons to effect this.[26]

He had some support for this move from the highest authorities in England. Archbishop Howley, and Gladstone, as secretary of state for the colonies, in 1846, agreed that 'the nearer the internal law of the Church for those colonies could be brought to the footing of voluntary compacts to be enforced upon the principles of the law of contracts the better'. They thus saw the Church in the colonies as a voluntary organization, falling under the general laws of a colony. An important, and long-standing factor in the attitude of successive British governments and the Colonial Office, unless as we will see, they were pursuing their own ecclesiastical ends, was the appointment of Frederick Rogers, subsequently Lord Blachford, as assistant under-secretary at the Colonial Office in 1846. Rogers had been a close friend of Newman, and was associated with R.W. Church and other leading Tractarians in founding the High Church *Guardian* newspaper. From 1860 to 1871 Rogers was under-secretary of state for the colonies, and he did much to persuade successive colonial secretaries that the churches in the colonies should be permitted to organize themselves, and to appoint their own bishops if no State endowments were being provided for the support of the bishop, and that in due course, the form of appointing bishops and creating bishoprics in the colonies by royal letters patent should be abandoned.[27]

Selwyn, on this basis, drew up a constitution for the Church in New Zealand based on the constitution of the PECUSA, providing for a house of deputies of the clergy, elected by the clergy, and a house of laity, elected by adult male members of the Church, and for a house of bishops. Meanwhile, Selwyn also suggested the establishment of a province of the Anglican Church for Australasia. In 1847 Archbishop Howley notified Selwyn that a separate province had been established, with Bishop Broughton, formerly bishop of Australia, now bishop of Sydney, as metropolitan.[28]

Broughton had mixed feelings about this change in his status and such a major expansion of the Church in Australia. In 1836 there had only been one clergyman in Sydney, apart from the bishop, to serve a population of 14,000 people. In 1842 Broughton had been informed that four new dioceses were to be created in Australia – for Tasmania, for South Australia, and at Port Philip and for the Swan River. Broughton welcomed the news, but disliked the locations. When later the Australian quota of new bishoprics was halved, the priority given to Adelaide baffled him, for the arrangement totally ignored population densities, and the geographical considerations which would make for the convenient administration of one area from another. By way of protest Broughton sent the archbishop of Canterbury a map covered with information, for future decisions.[29] The subsequent creation of new dioceses followed the creation of new colonies – Victoria and the diocese of Melbourne in 1847, Queensland and the dioceses of Brisbane in 1859, apart from Sydney where the dioceses of Newcastle, Goulburn and Bathurst were created in New South Wales.

The new bishop of Tasmania, Francis Russell Nixon, was consecrated in 1842, but he almost immediately ran into problems with Lord Stanley, the secretary for the colonies, over his jurisdiction under his letters patent. In the same year Stanley had introduced a scheme for the SPG to recruit laymen, already trained for ordination in England, to go out to Tasmania to be ordained and to work there as 'religious instructors' with the convict gangs. However, Stanley refused to recognize the bishop's jurisdiction over the instructors whom he had ordained, and placed them under the jurisdiction of the comptroller-general of convicts, and the lieutenant-governor of the colony. After the bishop had protested, Stanley, without consulting the bishop, appointed the archdeacon of Hobart as superintendent of convict chaplains, which the bishop regarded as a civil service appointment, and refused to recognize the archdeacon's appointment to such a post. He pointed out that the religious instructors comprised about a third of the clergy in the diocese, over whom he would have no authority. and that the governor would have power to dismiss chaplains without reference to the bishop. Earl Grey, who had succeeded Stanley at the Colonial Office proposed a compromise, based on the analogy of English prison chaplains, by which the bishop would supervise an instructor's conduct and theological opinions, and would be free to discipline clerical offences. In return the bishop would recognize the crown's right to nominate chaplains, but would have the right to grant or withhold licences to the chaplains.[30]

The bishop also discovered difficulties when he attempted to

establish a consistory court. His letters patent gave him jurisdiction to hold a court, but not to summon offenders or swear
witnesses, and it was also unclear whether he could pass sentence of deposition from office on a clergyman who had been
appointed by the crown. When he sought the opinion of the
government law officers in England in 1844, it was agreed that
the government had exceeded its authority in attempting to
introduce, by means of letters patent, the ecclesiastical laws of
England, into a colony where a legislative assembly had been
established by Parliament. This opinion was subsequently confirmed by the case of *Long* v *The Bishop of Cape Town* in 1861.[31]

When it came to funding the additional new dioceses into
which it was proposed that Australia should be divided, Lord
Stanley had thought that a bishop would need an income of
£1,200 a year, which was far more than could be met from the
Colonial Bishoprics Fund. Broughton suggested that £600 a
year would be enough to fund a bishop, and offered £600 a year
towards a bishopric from his own salary. Before any action could
be taken Stanley was succeeded by Gladstone, who secured
royal assent for two new bishoprics in Australia, and from various colonial funds, topped up the amounts offered by the
Colonial Bishoprics Fund and Broughton to amount to £833 a
year, plus a house costing £2,000. Unfortunately, because the
SPG had run short of money in assisting the Colonial
Bishoprics Fund to found other dioceses, it was unable also to
support the additional clergy for whom Broughton was seeking
funds.[32]

By 1846, when the Tory government of which Gladstone had
been a member fell, no appointments had been made to the
two new Australian bishoprics, although Gladstone had already
approached eight candidates. When Earl Grey, in turn, succeeded Gladstone at the Colonial Office he denied that any
'right on the part of the Archbishop of Canterbury to recommend the appointment could be recognised', or that someone
of Broughton's churchmanship should be appointed who might
be expected to work well with him. Grey favoured evangelical
candidates for the bishoprics, and sought the advice of Thornton,
a distinguished evangelical layman, who recommended two
CMS supporters. Howley proposed a compromise, that one
evangelical and one High Churchman should be appointed, and
Grey agreed, and Charles Perry, an evangelical, and William

Tyrrell, vicar of Beaulieu in Hampshire, who though a High Churchman and a close friend of Selwyn, subscribed to the CMS, were nominated.

There were then arguments over the boundaries and names of the dioceses. The Colonial Office wanted Port Philip, but Broughton got his way with Melbourne. Broughton proposed that the other diocese should be centred on Maitland, but the Colonial Office chose Newcastle. The archbishop of Canterbury set up a committee to advise the Colonial Office on revisions to improve on the letters patent drawn up for Broughton for the new bishops, in the light of Bishop Nixon's experience in Hobart, but Grey disbanded the committee, and the letters patent issued for the new bishops were copies of Broughton's. This failure to revise the letters patent for colonial bishops was to have important consequences in the development of the Church in South Africa and the whole Anglican Communion. Unfortunately, when the letters patent for the new bishops were drawn up, and the date of the consecration had been fixed, it was found that the funds which Gladstone had earmarked for the contributions to endow the bishoprics, had now been spent on other Church-related projects in Australia. The SPG, however, managed to raise the additional money, and the two bishops were consecrated in Westminster Abbey on 29 June 1847.

Broughton was also issued with new letters patent, as we have seen, creating him bishop of Sydney and metropolitan of Australasia, with authority to summon the other bishops to meet with him to confer about matters of common concern. He had hoped to call a meeting of the bishops in 1849, but the eruption of a volcano in New Zealand kept Selwyn at home, and Perry declined to leave Port Philip. In 1850 Broughton was spurred on to attempt another meeting by a report in the newspapers of a meeting of the Canadian bishops, and he arranged a meeting for Whitsun 1850. Perry was reluctant to attend. He saw the subdivision of the diocese of Australia as an opportunity for diversity, and seems to have regarded attempts to achieve any unity of action, on the part of Broughton, as unnecessary. He wished for freedom of action in his own diocese, and did not believe in co-operation or consultation, or in informing people of his own plans. However, he did agree to attend the meeting. Broughton wanted the meeting (or at least the subsequent meeting) to be a synod. Perry thought that their letters patent forbade meetings anywhere in British territories to legislate on behalf of the Church. However, since they were not intending to legislate, it was agreed that it should be regarded merely as a meeting which would not therefore run the risk of exceeding their jurisdiction.

The question of authority was a major issue. Selwyn and Broughton both wished for autonomy for the colonial churches. Broughton believed that his letters patent as a metropolitan implied the autonomy of his church, and that Archbishop Howley had intended this, although it was now denied by his successor, J.B. Sumner and Lord Grey. Broughton also believed that his case was supported by the evidence of the practice of the early Church. However, he rejected the model offered by the American Episcopal Church, and claimed that bishops alone had authority in the Church to make decisions. Selwyn and the other Australian bishops opposed this claim, they held that the clergy should be included with the bishops and also the laity, who should sit separately to constitute a provincial synod. A compromise was achieved for a constitution for the province by which the provincial and diocesan synods would consist of bishops and clergy, with which would be associated conventions of laymen. It was proposed that the synods and conventions might deliberate together, but the authority of the laity would be limited to the temporal and the practical. Bishop Tyrrell forwarded copies of the minutes of the meeting to the archbishop of Canterbury, and to all the archbishops and bishops of the United Church of England and Ireland, for their information and comments. Broughton also wrote to the archbishop of Canterbury to secure his co-operation in a plan to secure a constitution for the province.[33]

In 1850 Gladstone had attempted to amend the Australian Colonies Bill to free the bishops, clergy and laity in the colonies to meet, and by mutual consent, to draft rules for the internal government of their own dioceses and to prohibit persons who had consented to those rules appealing against them to English courts. The amendment was overwhelmingly defeated by opposition led by Lord Grey. Meanwhile Archbishop Sumner of Canterbury had replied to Broughton pointing out that synods were an infringement of the royal supremacy, but all the same, inviting Broughton to make a proposal for improving the understanding of their jurisdiction for the consideration of the colonial secretary and the crown law officers. He also offered to sponsor a bill for reforming clergy discipline in the colonies.[34]

Broughton's proposals for a separate episcopal and clerical synod and lay convention failed to find favour with leading lay vestry members in Sydney. Following the Church of England Temporalities Act in New South Wales in 1837, Broughton had been anxious to enlist the support of the lay leaders elected to the new vestries, and he had formed a diocesan committee to raise funds for church extension in the colony. The committee had set up branches in every parish which had undertaken the fund-raising, and had flourished. The diocesan committee, however had languished, with no direct involvement in the fund-raising, and not being consulted about the expenditure of the money raised, or about diocesan decision-making. In secular life its members were major decision-makers, but in the Church they were excluded from decisions. Broughton expected their co-operation in his plans, and was annoyed when they did not always agree with him. The merchants, bankers and politicians (and also some of the clergy) were unhappy about the legal position of the Church in Australia, and especially the jurisdiction of the bishop himself, whom they had come to regard as autocratic and high handed, and whose authoritarianism and ritualism, for he insisted on wearing a surplice to preach, they suspected, smacked of Romanism. He was pilloried in the columns of the *Atlas* as a haughty prelate and a friend of the apostate Newman; alleged English clerical scandals were also widely reported and associated with Broughton. He explained that the substance of the royal supremacy was in its being the expression of the will of the people, but once this substance had ceased to be effective, it was necessary to dispense with this means by which the will of the laity had been expressed, and to replace it with a more practical form of expression. He insisted that the laity ought to share in the conduct of the affairs of the diocese. The principle he enunciated was that 'where ecclesiastical ordinances are to be binding on the laity, they are to be first confirmed by the laity legally represented'. He also saw lay participation as important for discipline in the Church. However, he had not been seen to practise this theory and the bishop's proposal to separate the laity from the bishops and the clergy in the synods and the conventions did not find favour with the meetings of laymen called in each parish in the diocese to discuss the proposed constitution.[35]

The leading laity of other Australian dioceses also objected to the proposed constitution which they saw as excluding them from decision-making in the Church. In Adelaide Anglican lay people wished to be involved in church government in the same way as leading nonconformist lay people were in their churches. Objections also came from Tasmania where Bishop Nixon had a poor record in lay relations. There were also objections from Melbourne, which objected to being subordinated to Sydney. The proposed constitution did not command the support of the whole Church in Australia.

Broughton, in response to Sumner's invitation set out for England to pursue his proposals for self-government for the colonial churches. Perry had meanwhile indicated to Archbishop Sumner that, with colonial ecclesiastical autonomy, 'a system of doctrines and ritual observances might be enforced on a colonial diocese which was totally repugnant to the decisions of the courts at home'. This helped to convince Sumner that the Australian bishops were unfit to exercise the independence they sought. The CMS was also opposed to the independence of colonial churches. Broughton arrived in London in 1852, when talk of the revival of convocation was in the air, but he feared that this might confuse his hopes of colonial ecclesiastical autonomy.

A similar process had been taking place in Canada. In September 1851 the meeting which Broughton had read about, of bishops in the British North American colonies, actually took place in Quebec, chaired by Bishop Mountain. Five of the eight bishops in Canada had attended, and they had recommended that diocesan synods should be formed to work with the bishops at the diocesan level, and that a provincial synod should be established to co-ordinate the dioceses under a Canadian metropolitan. They too had sent the minutes of their meeting to the archbishop of Canterbury, and had also published them.[36]

By 1852 there seems to have been a general agreement among most of the bishops in Australia, Canada, New Zealand and South Africa that the colonial churches needed freedom from English ecclesiastical legislation to hold their own synods, which would include lay participation. In January 1853 Broughton met with Bishop Mountain of Quebec, Bishop Gray of Cape Town and the bishops of Antigua, Newfoundland and Nova Scotia, all of whom were in London for the SPG jubilee celebrations, and put his hopes of a world-wide union of Protestant Episcopal Churches to them, and asked each of them to submit their ideas on the fundamental principles for such a union.[37] The SPG supported the proposal, pointing out that the attorney general appeared to be in agreement with Broughton's view that the Act of Supremacy did not extend to prohibiting synods in the colonies. However it was thought that legislation might be required in the British Parliament to authorize self-government in the colonial churches. The meeting adjourned until the following month, by which time Broughton was dead. However, he had sowed a seed that would in due time germinate.

The movement among the traditional High Church bishops in the colonies for greater autonomy for the Church from the crown and the British government, and for some form of synodical government was also paralleled in England. The constitutional changes in England between 1828 and 1835 were seen as a threat to the established Church in England by many Churchpeople, and the establishment of the Ecclesiastical Commission by Parliament in 1833 to review the finances of the Church was seen as a further threat to the Church. During the 1830s there was much discussion about how the Church might be able to take responsibility for putting its own house in order without the interference of Parliament which was no longer seen by many High Church people as an Anglican body.

The idea of the revival of the convocations was discussed by, and initially attracted the support of, evangelicals as well as High Churchmen. At a meeting for the formal opening of the York convocation in November 1837 there was reported to have been 'a more numerous attendance than has been known for many years' and there was an attempt to move an address to the crown, but the archbishop's commissioner resisted it, and pro-rogued the proceedings. However, those present adjourned to continue informally, and to draw up a petition to the crown on the subject of convocation. From at least 1846 there was an increasing and public agitation for some form of synodical government in the Church of England, and especially for the revival of the Canterbury convocation. The publication of *The Tracts for the Times*, particularly the later numbers, and the aggressive clericalism of their authors was responsible for agitating considerable feelings against clericalism, especially among evangelical and Broad Church lay people, and consequently the restoration of powers to the exclusively clerical convocations came to be viewed by many people with suspicion.

In 1847 in both the provinces of Canterbury and York there had been moves to revive the convocations. In York, however, Archbishop Musgrave, who was a close friend of Earl Grey, was deeply opposed to the revival of the convocation, believing that the Church should rely on the crown to defend it. He was supported by most of the bishops of his province. The furore over the nomination of Renn Hampden, who was suspected of unorthodox theological views by the Tractarians, to the diocese of Hereford in 1848, and the opinion of the law lords that the archbishop of Canterbury ought to resign if he felt unable to consecrate someone nominated by the crown, renewed the demand for the revival of the convocations. The Gorham judgement in 1850 further fuelled the demand among High Churchmen for the revival of the convocations. In this case the Judicial Committee of the Privy Council, a lay court, which had been established as the highest ecclesiastical court, after the abolition of the High Court of Delegates in 1832, but included three bishops as assessors in ecclesiastical cases, on this occasion – the archbishops of Canterbury (Sumner) and York (Musgrave) and the bishop of London (Blomfield) – overturned the judgement of the Exeter consistory court and the Court of Arches on the question of whether Mr Gorham, as an incumbent in the Church of England, was required, when assenting to the Thirty-Nine Articles, to believe in baptismal regeneration. The decision produced protests against the rights of the courts of the crown and Parliament to overturn the ruling of a Church court on what was regarded as a matter of doctrine, and brought a demand among some High Churchmen for a means by which the Church might express itself synodically. This, however alienated some evangelicals, who in the main approved the judgement, from the movement to revive the convocations.

In 1850 the Society for the Revival of Convocation was established, with Henry Hoare, a banker, as its chairman. The clerical leaders of the movement were traditional High Churchmen, such as Samuel Wilberforce, Archdeacon Denison of Taunton,

Bishop Phillpotts of Exeter and Bishop Blomfield of London. The establishment of the Roman Catholic hierarchy in England in 1850 further emphasized for some people the need for some form of independent spiritual authority in the Church of England. However, it exacerbated the fears of some evangelicals and Broad Churchmen who suspected that any attempts to emancipate the Church of England from the State might result in opening doors to Romish influences in the Church of England.

Wilberforce pointed to the successful example of the American Church in governing itself, by means of its general convention, and Bishop Broughton's meeting of Australasian bishops in June 1850 was also quoted as another example (presumably by those who were unaware how relatively unsuccessful it had been). It was argued, however, that the predominance of *ex officio* dignitaries – deans and archdeacons, in particular – in the lower houses of convocations would make them very unrepresentative, and anyway, it was pointed out that there was no provision for the inclusion of the laity. Henry Hoare, optimistically in the event, argued that if the convocations were allowed to meet for business, they would be able to reform themselves.

No royal letters of business had been issued for the consideration of the convocations since the Canterbury convocation had been prorogued in 1717, when it had become entangled in the complex political and constitutional upheavals surrounding the Hanoverian succession, and had been suppressed by the government, for fear that the clergy would undermine the Hanoverian succession, and influence a restoration of the Stuarts. However, the convocations continued to be elected with each new Parliament, and the members assembled, but, having conducted their formal business, including an address to the crown, in the absence of any royal letters of business, the proceedings were prorogued.

In a debate in the House of Lords in 1851 the revival of the convocations was opposed by the leading evangelicals, Lord Shaftesbury and C.R. Sumner, bishop of Winchester. In February 1851 the Canterbury convocation had received a petition for its consideration, which was the first independent action, outside its formal proceedings, which it had taken for many years. More petitions were presented in 1852, and although Archbishop Sumner prorogued the proceedings immediately, the attorney general gave his opinion that the archbishop could only prorogue it with the consent of the majority of the bishops, which made an active Canterbury convocation a much stronger possibility. At the meeting of the Canterbury convocation at the beginning of the new Parliament in 1852, for which some of the seats had been contested, the lower house of the Canterbury convocation took the step of amending the address to the crown, and pointing out that a resumption of the work of the convocation was highly desirable, and requesting permission to draft in outline a clergy discipline bill. After this there was a three-day debate on the desirability of reviving convocation's functions. This initiative demonstrated that legally the convocation, in the absence of royal letters of business, was only prevented from making canons, not from discussing business. In York in 1852 twenty-two proctors and seven archdeacons assembled for the new convocation, and at least seventeen petitions, signed by lay people as well as clergy, supporting the revival of convocations were presented, but the archbishop's commissioner refused to permit any discussion.

The action of the clergy in the convocations in November 1852 excited alarm in Parliament. The convocations were suspected of attempting to rival Parliament, as they had tried to do in the early eighteenth century, and it was also feared that High Church clergy, under Romish influences, were attempting to subvert the Reformation legislation which had brought the convocations of the clergy under the control of the crown and Parliament. The new Prime Minister, Lord Aberdeen, was unenthusiastic about the meetings of the convocations, and tactfully, in response to his feelings, the Canterbury convocation only met for one day in February 1853. However, by January 1854, Samuel Wilberforce had persuaded the Prime Minister that it would not be dangerous for the convocations to meet, if the business required it, on two successive days that month, and that the government should not object to an adjournment to a later date. Archbishop Sumner was also won round to the idea of the Canterbury convocation meeting, and supported the appointment of committees of the convocation, which could meet after the convocation itself had been prorogued. The committees were appointed, and reported to the July meeting of the convocation, when debates took place without acrimony. Sumner was by now won round, and told Lord Aberdeen that, in his view, convocation was a necessity because it transacted business that other institutions would be incapable of handling, for he had realized that the clergy would accept rulings from the convocation that they would not accept from the bishops individually or corporately. In 1855 the Canterbury convocation met 6–9 February, and did a great deal of business, so that even C.R. Sumner, its most able evangelical opponent, was won round. However, it was not until 1861 that the Canterbury convocation received a royal licence authorizing the revision of a canon, and even then it was a long time before the government was willing to advise that the royal assent should be given to a revised canon. The Canterbury convocation also proved hostile to the idea of reforming itself to provide for lay participation in the convocation, and it was not until 1886 that a house of laity, which was a purely advisory body, was set up in Canterbury, and not until 1892 that one was established in York.[38]

Archbishop Musgrave of York had continued to obstruct a meeting of the York convocation until his death in May 1860. He was succeeded by Charles Longley, who was sympathetic to the idea of the convocation meeting, and had favoured the idea of a diocesan conference when he had been bishop of Ripon, but had not called one because he feared that it would be divisive in the new diocese to which he was attempting to give some identity and unity. At the meeting of the convocation in York in August 1860 he allowed the members to present an address, and in February 1861 he permitted the lower house to elect a prolocutor, and both houses then proceeded to business.[39]

The re-establishment of the convocations, even as mere deliberative bodies, was a significant step for the Church of England. While the Church's deliberative assemblies were still clearly subordinate to the crown and Parliament, the Church was now more able to debate its own concerns. However, it is clear that the revival of the convocations only became possible after the real alliance between the Church and the State had begun to decline in importance, and the Church was no longer seen as a threat to Parliament.

The colonial bishops' meetings in the early 1850s prompted a flurry of parliamentary activity concerned with the government of the colonial churches. In 1850 and 1851 Gladstone had raised a question in the House of Commons about the need for self-government for the Church of England in the colonies, in order to put it on the same footing as other churches. In February 1852 he introduced a Colonial Bishoprics bill, and then withdrew it to reintroduce it in a modified form, as a bill for Explaining and Amending the Laws Relating to the Churches in the Colonies, which was an enabling bill, permitting the free exercise of self-government by the colonial churches. It would have permitted and authorized diocesan and provincial synods, and have given lay people the right to be voting members of such synods. The then secretary for the colonies, Sir John Pakington, persuaded Gladstone to withdraw the bill before its second reading, on the grounds that the archbishop of Canterbury and Bishop Broughton were currently discussing the establishment of such synods. However, Pakington also believed that the bill was badly drafted, and he feared that it would be divisive in the Church of England and would result in the destruction of the royal supremacy. Pakington and Gladstone in fact disagreed over the process of how to bring about self-government in the colonial churches. Pakington thought that Parliament ought to grant constitutions to each of the colonial churches, while Gladstone thought that Parliament should pass an enabling act to permit colonial churches to draw up their own constitutions.[40]

Samuel Wilberforce was pursuing a similar approach to Gladstone's, in the House of Lords. He introduced a Missionary Bishops bill into the Lords, which would have allowed the bishops of the Church of England to consecrate bishops to lead missions to the 'heathen' without requiring a commission from the crown. In territories where the crown's writ did not run, Wilberforce argued, the Church should be permitted to act on its own. The bill passed the Lords, but failed in the Commons, where it was opposed by a strong evangelical lobby led by Arthur Kinnaird who used his influence upon behalf of the evangelical leaders to defeat any bills intending to give greater independence to the overseas dioceses. At the same time a Colonial Churches bill, also supported by Wilberforce, was introduced, which would have permitted bishops and laity in colonial dioceses to meet in synods to pass ecclesiastical legislation for their colony, but it too was defeated.

Later in 1852 Archbishop Sumner, after having consulted a number of the colonial bishops then visiting London, introduced into the Lords a permissive Colonial Church Regulation bill, which provided for an elaborate system of church government for any colonial churches which adopted it. It provided for synods, including lay people, but required that any legislation passed by a synod at its first meeting, must be approved by the Queen in Council, thus providing for a minimal establishment. It passed the Lords, but although the government was friendly towards it in the Commons, it was allowed to stand over till the next session, and so failed in the Commons. Although this bill did not pass it was influential in a number of dioceses which later set up their own synods, especially Sydney and Melbourne, whose constitutions were largely modelled on it.

The solicitor general, Sir Richard Bethell, also made an attempt to give the colonial churches the freedom they desired, in line with the generally agreed government policy of colonial self-government. His Colonial Clergy Disabilities bill proposed to empower the metropolitan of any province, or the bishop of any diocese in the colonies, not withstanding any law or usage in England, to meet with their clergy and laity to make resolutions or arrangements for the management or conduct of ecclesiastical affairs in the province or diocese. The bill passed its second reading in the Commons, despite evangelical and nonconformist critics who feared that it might establish a precedent for similar legislation in England. In the committee stage in the Commons, Bethell accepted an amendment safeguarding the royal supremacy and the doctrines of the established Church, but soon after the House was counted out, and this bill too failed.

In March 1854 Lord John Russell and Sir John Pakington introduced another Colonial Clerical Disabilities bill, with only one clause, that no statute currently in operation in England should be construed as in any way impeding the association of colonial bishops, clergy and laity for making laws and governing themselves. This would have safeguarded the royal supremacy, the uniformity of doctrine and the right of appeal to courts in England. This too was opposed by evangelical and nonconformist members, as the previous bill had been, and was withdrawn. The nonconformists, who were rallied by the Liberation Society, which was then energetically campaigning for the disestablishment of the Church of England, regarded these bills as attempts to preserve to the Church of England in the colonies all the privileges it possessed as an established Church in England. In June 1854 Russell announced that the government had decided to abandon any further attempt to pass a Colonial Churches bill, and that the matter would not be raised again that session.[41]

In Canada, New Zealand and South Africa, despite the failure of the British Parliament to pass legislation to grant self-government to Anglican dioceses and provinces, highly important steps for the Anglican Communion were being taken, but not without opposition. In Canada in October 1853 a meeting of Toronto clergy and lay representatives, chaired by their bishop, declared themselves a diocesan synod, and petitioned the Queen for legislation to remove any doubts about the legality of church synods. There was, however, determined opposition from evangelicals in the diocese, who objected to the recommendations by the bishops' meeting, that the three houses should vote separately, for they saw this as giving a bishop a veto on all decisions.

A synod was formed in the diocese of Nova Scotia in 1856, although three parishes opposed it and abstained from membership. The synod was granted incorporation by the Nova Scotia legislature in 1864, after much argument. In 1857 the Canadian legislature passed an Act which gave legal standing to Anglican synods, and also permitted dioceses to subdivide themselves. The diocese of Toronto immediately took advantage of this to create the diocese of Huron. However, royal letters patent were still required for the bishop to be consecrated in England. There was much evangelical opposition to the formation of diocesan synods in Montreal and Quebec, though they were eventually formed in both in 1859, to be followed by Fredericton and Ontario in 1861. In 1860 new letters patent were granted to establish the bishop of Montreal as metropolitan of a province of Canada, and in 1861 he called the first provincial synod. However, the Huron diocesan synod protested vigorously at the wording of the letters patent, and charged their delegates to see that there should be nothing in the constitution of the Anglican Church in the province of Canada which infringed the rights of dioceses. The result of this was that the constitution left each diocese free to make its own canons, and to elect its own bishop, without reference to any other diocese.[42]

In Australia the situation was more complex because there was a sharp churchmanship divide between the evangelical bishops Perry of Melbourne and Barker of Sydney, and the more traditional High Church bishops. During the 1850s after the appointment of Barker to Sydney there was a polarization of churchmanship in Australia, with existing evangelicals tending to move into the diocese of Sydney and a preference on the part of Barker to recruit evangelicals. Following the Australian bishops' meeting in 1850 Bishop Perry of Melbourne set up a committee to plan a conference of clergy and laity, which met in June 1851 and comprised all the clergy in the diocese and fifty communicant laymen, chosen by the church members of the parishes and districts. The conference accepted proposals that a diocesan, but not a provincial, synod should be established; that the current mode of appointing bishops by the crown should be retained, and that the bishop should continue to be subject to the archbishop of Canterbury, not to the local metropolitan; that the clergy should be presented for institution by parish vestries; and that the synod or convention of the clergy and laity should be the court of trial for any clergy, with appeal to the highest ecclesiastical court in England; and that cases of heresy should be adjudicated in England. It was also agreed that the resolutions of the conference should be sent to the archbishop of Canterbury, the metropolitan and the secretary of state for the colonies, and they drafted a petition to the British Parliament for legislation to incorporate this procedure. However, since the Victoria legislature had been established in 1851, the British Parliament declined to receive the petition.

Following this rebuff Perry called a representative conference of clergy and laity to consider a draft bill to be submitted to the Victoria legislature, to give the bishop authority to assemble the Church of England clergy and laity in the colony, and to give the Acts of the assembly the force of law. The bill would require the consent of a majority of the clergy and laity and the assent of the bishop for any Act to be passed. It authorized the appointment of a commission to try any clergyman, with a right of appeal to a court established by the metropolitan, or other superior court. The bill forbade any alteration by the assembly of any of the formularies of the Church of England and provided for the diocese to become a province, and for the crown to nominate bishops. The bill was passed by the Victoria legislature, and received the royal assent in December 1855.[43]

A different approach was taken by the diocese of Adelaide. Bishop Short visited London in 1854 to ascertain from the crown law officers that the Act of Submission of the Clergy did not extend to prohibit or render illegal a diocesan synod in the diocese of Adelaide. On his return in March 1855 he called a synod of his eighteen clergy with twenty-six representative lay people. A constitution was drawn up, and placed before the parochial bodies for their approval, which provided a contract drawn up between the clergy, bishop and lay people, with each bound by mutual consent to the provisions of the constitution. The synod thus constituted met in April 1856, and agreed to seek incorporation from the South Australia legislature, so that it could hold property on behalf of the diocese. A system of clerical discipline was also established. A bill was subsequently drawn up to secure the legislature's approval for the ecclesiastical court, but it was voted out, and the bishop decided to let the enforcement of discipline rest upon the simple contract between the bishop and the clergy who received his licence.[44]

The diocese of Tasmania followed the model of Melbourne. After considerable lay opposition to the establishment of a synod, a constitution was approved in 1856, and an Act modelled on that establishing the constitution in Melbourne was presented to the Tasmanian legislature, but the dangers of this method were illustrated by the action of the governor in amending the bill in the legislature without consulting the bishop or the synod.[45]

When Bishop Broughton of Sydney had died in 1853, the duke of Newcastle, a friend of Gladstone, and a Tractarian was colonial secretary, but he could find no Tractarian or High Churchman who was willing to go to Sydney. When the Crimean War had begun to go badly, Newcastle's portfolio of the colonies and war was divided so as to allow him to concentrate on the War as secretary of state for war, and Sir George Grey became colonial secretary. He looked to Archbishop Sumner for a candidate for the diocese of Sydney, and he suggested Frederic Barker, who had just been appointed the vicar of Baslow in Derbyshire, and had previously been vicar of Edgehill in Liverpool in Sumner's former diocese of Chester. His experience in Ireland and Liverpool had made him a decided evangelical and deeply hostile to Roman Catholics. He was also very suspicious of the High Church clergy he found in his new diocese, and as has been noted, he largely recruited evangelical clergy for his diocese.

It was not until 1858 that Bishop Barker called a meeting

about the establishment of a synod in the diocese, and proposed that a bill should be introduced into the New South Wales legislature to set up a synod. Bishop Tyrrell of Newcastle expressed a wish to join with Barker in the bill, so as to establish a provincial synod for New South Wales. However, when the bill was before the legislature an amendment was proposed to exclude the provision for an episcopal veto in the synod, and the bishops decided to withdraw the bill rather than allow it to be amended. A subsequent election produced a new legislature, which might have been more sympathetic towards the bill, but before the legislature met, the bishops disagreed about the bill. Barker was willing to accept the amendment to exclude the episcopal veto, but Tyrrell was not. The bill was therefore withdrawn again.

When Tyrrell received reports of the judgement in *Long* v *The Bishop of Cape Town*, he decided that no legislation was necessary to set up a synod, but Barker, having consulted the Canadian bishops, thought that an enabling Act was still required. When in 1863 a diocese of Goulburn was created in New South Wales, Tyrrell became further convinced of the need for a provincial synod for the three New South Wales dioceses, but held that legislation would only be required to incorporate the province to permit it to hold property legally. Tyrrell believed that this approach had been confirmed by the Colenso judgement about the Church in South Africa, and that there was nothing to stop them establishing diocesan and provincial synods, which would also be able to elect bishops.

Thus in 1865 the Newcastle diocesan synod requested Bishop Barker, as metropolitan, to call a provincial synod to approve legislation to be put to the New South Wales legislature to permit the diocesan and provincial synods to hold the Church's property. The Sydney synod, however, would only agree to take part in a conference of representatives of the three dioceses to agree a united approach to the legislature, not a synod. When the conference met, the Sydney delegates, supported by the Goulburn delegates, secured the deletion of all references to a provincial synod in the proposed constitution. They thus ensured that all legal power would remain in the hands of the diocesan synods, and even when a provincial synod was achieved in 1872, the Sydney and Goulburn representatives refused to permit it any legislative authority on behalf of the province or the dioceses.The evangelical bishops of Sydney, Bathurst and Goulburn did not want to break the relationship with the British Crown that they thought might be entailed in the establishment of a provincial synod with powers to make canons for the province, nor did the diocese of Sydney wish to put itself at risk from being outvoted by the country dioceses.[46]

Meanwhile, Selwyn had not been idle in New Zealand. In a pastoral letter in April 1852, he set out nine fundamental principles of a Christian constitution for his diocese, based on the recognition of bishops, clergy and lay people as three distinct orders, the consent of all three of which was required for all Acts binding on the Church. He recommended that a draft constitution for the Church in the colony should be submitted to the secretary of state for the colonies, and the archbishop of Canterbury, with a petition to the Queen praying for an Act of Parliament or a royal charter 'to secure to our branch of the English Church the liberty, within certain limits, of framing laws for its own government'. Meetings were held in Auckland, Christchurch, New Plymouth, Wellington and Nelson to seek reactions to these proposals. Having received favourable responses, Selwyn left for England in October 1853 to press for the proposals for the constitution, and for the establishment of four additional dioceses in New Zealand and for the Church in New Zealand to become a separate province.

The proposal for the new bishops was unsuccessful at this stage, because the estimated £40,000 needed to endow the four new bishoprics was not forthcoming. Selwyn sought legal advice from the attorney general and other constitutional experts about the establishment of a synod. They were unanimous that 'a Diocesan Synod is not within the Act of Submission of the Clergy'. He was also advised that a trust deed would enable a synod to hold property on behalf of the Church, with the bishop and any new bishops as *ex officio* trustees, and that such a trust deed could be incorporated by the New Zealand legislature.

Back in New Zealand in May 1857 Selwyn called a conference of leading clergy in the diocese and of members of the New Zealand government to consider a draft trust deed. It was agreed 'that any system which it may be found necessary to establish for the management of the affairs of the Church in New Zealand shall be founded upon the principle of natural compact, but that if legislative enactments be required to give

effect to such system, application be made to the Colonial
Legislature for the necessary legal powers'. It was agreed that a
legislative body of three distinct orders, the general synod, be
established to manage the affairs of the Church. There were
also to be diocesan synods. The nomination of a bishop was to
proceed from a diocesan synod, and if sanctioned by the general synod, was to be recommended by it to the authorities of
the Church and State in England for favourable consideration.
The general synod was to have no power to alter the Authorized
Version of the Bible, the Book of Common Prayer, the Ordinal
or the Thirty-Nine Articles, though it might accept alterations
made by the United Church of England and Ireland, with the
consent of the crown and the convocations. Provision was made
for the separation of the colony from the British Empire, or the
Church from the State in England.

On 2 June 1857 the conference resolved itself into a con-
stituent assembly, and allocated the number of members, clerical
and lay, to be elected by the various dioceses to the general
synod. A bill was subsequently passed through the colonial
legislature empowering the bishop to transfer trust properties
to trustees appointed by the general synod. Selwyn was very
careful to explain that the New Zealand legislature had not been
asked to grant the constitution to the Church, as happened in
Victoria and Tasmania, because if the legislature had passed
the constitution, it could subsequently alter it. In Selwyn's view
the Church was independent of the State, and must reinforce
this by being financially self-supporting. In 1858, New Zealand
was formed into a province, and five additional dioceses were
created.[47]

It took Selwyn thirteen years to achieve the constitution and
assembly for his church, but they were years well-spent, for he
had achieved a process for establishing a church independently
of the State, but with the protection normally afforded by the
State to a voluntary organization, and a decision-making process
for his church, together with a pattern for electing bishops,
which would serve as a pattern for other colonial churches.
Selwyn during these years had taken a very important step
towards creating a federation of interdependent Anglican
provinces. In so doing he had drawn importantly on the example of the PECUSA, and had helped to cement their example

into the Anglican tradition. The constitution of the Anglican Church in New Zealand subsequently provided a model for the constitutions of the Anglican provinces in South Africa, the West Indies, Japan, Canada and China and also had an important influence on the constitution of the Church of Ireland.[48]

CHAPTER 5

The 1860s and the First Lambeth Conference

THE COLENSO CASE

Selwyn's cool, painstaking approach to establishing the position of the Church in a colony is exemplified when it is contrasted with the complications created by a more impetuous, but equally determined bishop. Robert Gray, who was appointed first bishop of Cape Town, by letters patent from the crown in 1848, was another traditional High Churchman, and a close friend of Samuel Wilberforce, who acted as his agent and adviser in England. Gray, like Selwyn, was opposed to the establishment of the Church. He too was determined to establish a synodical assembly to legislate for the diocese, and was determined that the assembly should include lay people. He was also determined not to seek legislative approval for his synod, for what a legislature could make, it could also change or unmake; also in South Africa the legislature might be dominated by Dutch Calvinists.

However his situation was more difficult than Selwyn's. In the very small British settlement in the Cape Colony, which had been ceded to Britain in 1815, at the end of the Napoleonic Wars, the British government had made grants to pay the stipends of clergy of the Church of England and the Dutch Church. In 1832 the Dutch Church with nineteen ministers received £4,200, and the Anglican Church with six clergy received £1,850 a year. In some settlements the government had given land for a church to be built on, and also, in some instances had granted glebe land instead of money for a chaplain's stipend. The SPG made additional grants to upgrade chaplains' stipends, and also from 1821 responded to an offer made by the government, to grant £100 a year to a clergyman for 'native and negro' work, to which the SPG had added £100 a year, and recruited a clergyman for the task.

There were only two Anglican clergy in Cape Town, with a population of 20,000, of whom more than half were white, but mostly Dutch, when Gray arrived. The clergy had been appointed by the Colonial Office, and were evangelicals, and they and their congregations were not enthusiastic about a bishop in their midst. They regarded themselves and their parishes as part of the Church of England, under the jurisdiction of the archbishop of Canterbury. They did not want to be seen as South African, but as British, and they did not want to be part of a South African Church, which might alter their Church of England liturgy, and their ways of doing things.[1]

They were even more unhappy when they observed what they considered the bishop's popish ways, such as wearing a surplice and instituting collections during services in place of pew rents. Gray had taken six new clergy to Cape Town with him. The bishop's presence seems to have been divisive among the Anglicans in the colony. The bishop did not help matters by being critical of the two existing clergy, and noting complaints against them, and by lobbying the governor to grant funds to pay the additional Anglican clergy.

In June 1849 Gray summoned a synod of the sixteen clergy in the colony. They agreed not to seek any church ordinances from the colonial legislature so as not to permit it to interfere with the internal affairs of the Church. Following this meeting there was a widespread protest, which claimed that such a synod would be illegal in England, and that only the crown could summon the legislative assemblies of the Church. A petition was got up which clearly indicated that many people preferred the old ways, by which each congregation was independently in communion with the English Church, rather than being governed by their own bishop. The opinion of the attorney general of South Africa was sought, and he advised, as Selwyn and others had been advised, that there was no English law to prohibit the assembly of a synod in the colony. Gray was thus vindicated in holding a diocesan synod. When he was in London in 1851 Gray tested out on Samuel Wilberforce and Pusey the idea of including lay people in a church convention. Wilberforce agreed that the assent of the laity should be requisite for any Act of the Church, but Pusey opposed the idea of seeking the assent of lay people in matters of doctrine.

In 1853 Gray secured the creation of two new dioceses out of his diocese, and Gray and the two new bishops were all issued with new letters patent. In 1850 a constitutional government had been established in the Cape of Good Hope by the British Parliament, with authority 'to make laws for the peace, welfare and good government' of the colony. The crown had thus ceased to have the power of conferring by letters patent any coercive jurisdiction, ecclesiastical or civil, within the colony, although the new letters patent granted to Gray professed to give him such powers. The lawyers seem not to have taken this into account nor remembered the opinion that was given about the jurisdiction of the bishop of Tasmania, when his new letters patent were granted. The new bishop of Natal was J.W. Colenso, another friend of Wilberforce's, and of Ernest Hawkins, the secretary of the SPG, who was godfather to one of Colenso's sons. His appointment, however, had caused an outcry in England, for he had dedicated a collection of his sermons which he had just published, to F.D. Maurice, who had just been dismissed from his chair at King's College, London for denying the doctrine of eternal punishment.

In 1857 the court of Queen's Bench, in the Eton College case, in which the College had challenged the crown's claim to exercise patronage when an incumbent had been appointed a colonial bishop, had held that the established Church of England could have no legal existence in a colony where there was a separate legislative assembly. As a result of this Sir Robert Phillimore, the leading expert in ecclesiastical law of his day, advised Gray that, in his view, this implied that the courts of South Africa were not part of the system of church courts in England, and that no automatic appeal could be made from any court established by Gray to the archbishop of Canterbury's court, the Court of Arches. In 1858 Lord Carnarvon, the secretary for the colonies, informed Gray that the British government would place no difficulty in the way of his calling a provincial synod. He also indicated that the law officers of the crown held it to be doubtful whether an English bishop could legally consecrate a bishop for a country other than one of Her Majesty's dominions. In view of this the British government would offer no opposition to Gray's taking such a step.[2]

When in 1860 Gray called a second synod, the Revd W. Long, rector of St Peter's Mowbray in Cape Town, refused to attend, on the grounds that the Church in South Africa did not legally exist. He charged the clergy and laity who took part in the synod with having 'seceded from the Church of England'. He published this charge in the *Cape Monitor* and repudiated the bishop's authority. Gray saw Long as a vehicle for evangelical opposition to episcopal authority and synods, and began legal action against Long in his diocesan court, which the first synod had established, and had passed a rule requiring all clergy to attend the synod.

Long had not attended Gray's first synod in 1856 because he denied the bishop's authority to call a synod. He now disputed the legality of the diocesan court, but he was found guilty by Gray of disobeying the synod's legislation, and was sentenced to four weeks' suspension from his living for refusing to publish notice to his vestry to elect a lay representative to the synod and for not attending himself. Long ignored the suspension and then was summoned again by Gray, who, sitting with five senior clergy deprived him of his living for contumacy. Long appealed against his deprivation to the South African Supreme Court, and the chief justice found that Long had bound himself to obey the bishop by accepting a licence from the bishop, and therefore that Gray had jurisdiction over him. Long then appealed to the Privy Council, whose Judicial Committee in 1863 reversed the decision. They held that, because the colonial legislature had been established in South Africa by the crown before Gray's second letters patent were issued, the second letters patent were *ultra vires* because the crown had surrendered the right to exercise certain prerogative powers. They held that the only way that Gray could exercise jurisdiction over the clergy in the diocese was by some sort of contract between him and them.

The first synod had, in effect created a contract of a kind, but Long had never consented to it, and so he could not be compelled to recognize the synod, nor its decisions, and therefore Gray could not punish him for refusing to do so. However, the Committee did recognize Gray's right as a bishop to inhibit Long from exercising his spiritual functions. Gray commented sadly, '... Bishops were sent forth by the Mother Church to found and organise Churches in all parts of the Colonial Empire as best they might, without any code of instructions, without counsel or guide of any kind, without any Board of Mission or recognised authority in any shape, to which they could refer under critical circumstances'.[3]

When the two new dioceses had been created in South Africa, Gray had been consulted, and he had himself nominated Colenso and Armstrong. When Bishop Armstrong of Grahamstown had subsequently resigned, his successor, Cotterill, was nominated by Archbishop Sumner without any consultation with Gray. Gray had been furious and had set his diocesan synod to draw up rules for the election of its future bishop so that the diocese might not have a bishop imposed on it by either crown or archbishop.[4]

Throughout the 1850s Gray was growing nervous of Colenso's opinions, especially his views on the Eucharist, and on revelation and atonement, and his refusal to hold a diocesan synod in Natal, but merely calling a council to which he summoned twice as many lay people as clergy.[5] In 1861 Colenso published *St Paul's Epistle to the Romans; Newly Translated and Explained from a Missionary Point of View* in which he implied that the atonement was an entirely objective event, Christ's saving work needing no personal application to the individual and that both conversion and baptism were, in the last resort, meaningless. The work of the missionary in preaching the gospel, he suggested, was to show 'the heathen' the pattern of Christ, the example of his love, and to assure him that he was already redeemed. Gray regarded the book as offering inadequate teaching on the atonement, conversion, the Church and the sacraments. Bishop Cotterill of Grahamstown urged Gray to ask Colenso to withdraw the book, and as metropolitan, Gray requested Colenso to withdraw it. Colenso refused, and so Gray, not wishing to have two court cases on his hands at once, placed the matter in the hands of the archbishop of Canterbury, and he and Colenso went to England to await Sumner's decision.

In England the Church was already in uproar over the publication of *Essays and Reviews* in 1860, in which Frederick Temple had argued that biblical scholarship must be adult and mature, using fully the gifts of the Spirit and human intelligence; Rowland Williams had described some of the German critics' findings, including the hypothesis that the Pentateuch was not a single literary whole written by Moses; Baden Powell had attempted to reconcile Darwin's evolutionary theories with

Christianity at the cost of dispensing with the miraculous; H.B. Wilson had pleaded for the widest doctrinal latitude in the national Church; and C.W. Goodwin had attempted to show that the picture of the universe as presented in the Bible ought not to be regarded as scientifically inerrant. There had been a public outcry against the book, which was regarded as an invitation to apostasy. Two of the essayists, Wilson and Williams were tried by the highest court in the province of Canterbury, the Court of Arches, and both were suspended from their livings for a year, but the decision was reversed when they appealed to the Judicial Committee of the Privy Council. In February 1861 the book was also condemned at a meeting of the English bishops. Colenso's *Romans*, on this precedent, was therefore referred by the archbishop to a bishop's meeting. Wilberforce suggested to the English bishops that they ask Colenso to withdraw the book, and if he refused to do so, to inform him that they would not permit him to officiate in their dioceses. They did not accept this suggestion. Colenso refused to meet a delegation of the English bishops, which had been agreed as an alternative to Wilberforce's suggestion. Meanwhile, having investigated German critical scholarship further himself, Colenso was working on his own response to *Essays and Reviews* which he eventually published in five parts. The first part was published in London as *The Pentateuch and the Book of Joshua Critically Examined* which was basically a valuable work of biblical criticism, which was condemned out of hand because he went beyond textual analysis, and caused great offence by describing the pseudonymous books of the Old Testament as 'fiction' and 'pious fraud'.

Archbishop Sumner was succeeded by Charles Longley, a traditional High Churchman, who in February 1863 called a meeting of all the English bishops and such Irish and colonial bishops as were available to consider the Colenso affair, in which his book on the Pentateuch had come to assume a greater significance than that on Romans. At a meeting of forty-one bishops an open letter to Colenso was approved, which pointed out that, in their opinion, his book on the Pentateuch could not be reconciled with the promises he had made at his consecration as a bishop, and that in consequence, he ought to resign as a bishop. Having been advised that the English bishops were likely to make this condemnation, Gray had returned to South Africa.

Gray probably assumed that the English bishops had referred the matter back to him to deal with, having expressed their opinion. Meanwhile the dean of Colenso's cathedral in Pietermaritzburg and his archdeacon had formally presented Colenso to Gray for heresy, and the clergy of the diocese had complained of the damage done by his book. The dean of Cape Town cathedral and the archdeacons of Grahamstown and George had also formally petitioned Gray against Colenso. Given this level of protest, Gray felt that he needed to take formal action against Colenso in Cape Town. Gray had sought the advice of Sir Robert Phillimore, the most distinguished ecclesiastical lawyer of his generation, and he had suggested that the judgement in the Long case had strengthened Gray's authority. He thus now summoned the South African bishops, and they agreed to try Colenso on charges relating to his book on Romans. He opened the proceedings against Colenso on 16 November 1863, assisted by the bishops of Grahamstown and the Orange Free State as episcopal assessors, but with no legally qualified assessor, before he had heard the judgement of the Judicial Committee of the Privy Council in the Long case. Colenso, still in England, refused to appear before Gray, and sent as his representative a German who was reputedly 'a known unbeliever', to protest against the proceedings and to deny Gray's authority to try him. Gray, however heard the evidence against Colenso, and in the absence of any defence, deliberated with his episcopal assessors.

On 16 December he declared his judgement, finding Colenso guilty on all counts, and sentenced him to be deposed from his diocese. He was given four months to retract his statements, and advised that he could appeal to the archbishop of Canterbury. This he declined to do, and on the authority of Long's case, and declining even to recognize Gray's jurisdiction to the extent of appealing against it, instead appealed in June 1864 to the Privy Council for an order preventing Gray from interfering in his right to exercise his episcopal office. The Judicial Committee sitting without any bishops present, because in this case the Committee was not acting as an ecclesiastical court, found, in their judgement delivered on 20 March 1865, that Gray had no jurisdiction over Colenso because the crown had not had the power to grant Gray metropolitical status in 1853, when he was granted his second letters patent, because the colony had already been granted its own legislative assembly. Gray bitterly regretted the waste of £10,000 on legal fees involved in obtaining the letters patent. In 1866, disregarding the decision of the Privy Council, Gray excommunicated Colenso.

However, Colenso refused to go and sued the Colonial Bishoprics Fund for the stipend they had declined to pay him since Gray had deposed him, and won. After the Privy Council judgement the Fund had also stopped paying Gray's salary, and had circulated other bishops who had received letters patent at about the same time as Gray, to ask them why they also should not have their salaries withdrawn. In a further case, Colenso sued to gain possession of church property in Natal, and the Privy Council, on appeal, gave him control over all church property in the diocese. In effect between 1858 and 1865 the English courts ruled that

> The Church of England cannot exist outside England; colonial bishops in colonies with independent legislatures are therefore ecclesiastical persons but have no jurisdiction: the Crown cannot any longer create such persons: yet those persons are corporations capable of holding property given to the Church of England elsewhere, and therefore there is a sense in which the Church of England can exist outside England, but perhaps especially in Natal.[6]

THE CREATION OF THE ANGLICAN COMMUNION

The problems highlighted by the Colenso case and subsequent rulings raised large questions about the position of the Church in the colonies. They clarified matters in ways which Gray and Wilberforce welcomed. Gray recognized that these judicial decisions enabled him to create an independent, unestablished province of the Anglican Church in South Africa, with a synodical form of government, its own courts, and an independent workable system of church discipline, which would be based, so far as the civil courts were concerned, on the constitution of a voluntary association.

Although leading bishops had laid very important foundations in establishing independent self-governing provinces in the Anglican Communion, it was Colenso who by accident, and much against his will, for he became a convinced Erastian, was the cause of a major step towards the creation of the modern

Anglican Communion. The judgement in his appeal to the Privy Council clearly established the independence of the Church in colonies where there was a legislative assembly, and by the furore caused by his publications, stimulated a demand for a major meeting of Anglican bishops.

By 1865 forty-five bishoprics had been established in the British colonies and thirty-four bishoprics in the PECUSA, including four overseas bishoprics – Africa, Shanghai and the Valley of the Yangtze River, and a bishop of 'the Dominions and Dependencies of the Sultan of Turkey'. In the twenty-five years since 1840 there had been a proliferation of new Anglican dioceses. The Colonial Bishoprics Fund had enabled a small group of mainly traditional High Church bishops to pursue a policy of establishing a bishopric in each British colony, to provide for the spiritual needs of the colonists, and the SPG and the CMS and other missionary societies had provided assistance for missionary work in these new dioceses, in the areas of some of which, as we have seen, they had been working before the arrival of the bishop.

In PECUSA too there had been a policy of creating a bishopric for each new state, as settlement moved westwards, and as Episcopalian missionaries had gone overseas, so bishoprics had been created for the sphere of their activities. This was likely to lead to overlap of jurisdictions, for example between the English bishop of Jerusalem and the American bishop of the Turkish dependencies and the English bishop of Victoria (Hong Kong) and the American bishop in China. As we have seen, Henry Venn had warned the CMS missionaries in China off the American bishop, because of his doubts about the validity of the authority of a bishop of a church that was not established.

Most of the colonial bishops, whether traditional High Churchmen or evangelicals, believed in involving clergy and laity (who were increasingly being called upon to shoulder the burden of paying for the clergy and their bishops, as government grants were withdrawn) in the government of the Church. The British government's policy of establishing legislative assemblies in colonies from the 1830s onwards, made it necessary for colonial bishops to come to terms with a sharply changed relationship with the State. Few colonial legislatures had the financial resources to pay for bishops and clergy out of their revenues, and in any case they were usually unwilling to continue the establishment of a Church. Whilst some migrants had been concerned to maintain everything much as it had been in the home country, others wished to build a new society, and did not want to be constrained by a requirement to conform to an established Church. Nor could it be expected that colonial legislatures would necessarily be composed of members sympathetic to the Church of England. In the dioceses in the eastern provinces of Canada and in Australia and South Africa, Anglicans were usually in a minority in the population, and although they may have comprised a larger proportion of the governing classes, most commonly sitting in the colonial legislatures and thus might legislate in the interests of their own Church, this was unlikely to be a permanent situation. In a country like South Africa, where English members might not be in a majority in the legislature, bishops and most clergy and lay people were reluctant to seek legislative legitimation for their Church's constitution, for this would permit the legislature to interfere in the Church's ordinances and even doctrine.

Thus, whatever the views of evangelical and Broad Churchmen about the importance of establishment in preserving the true doctrines of the Church of England from interference by unsound clergy and bishops, there was little choice in self-governing colonies, for anything other than a self-governing Church with power to order its own affairs as a voluntary association. This precisely coincided, as we have seen, with the movement for synodical government in the Church of England, and also overseas, where, because the Anglican Church was ceasing to be established, synods were not seen as rivalling the local legislature, and were therefore permitted to develop.

By the mid-1860s a large number of overseas Anglican dioceses, including those in the United States, New Zealand, Canada and South Africa (but not Australia) were effectively independent of the Church of England, having their own procedures for electing bishops, having sufficient bishops of their own to consecrate new bishops, and developing their own patterns of government and discipline. There were also, as we have seen, beginning to be provincial meetings of bishops. The American bishops, of course, met in their general convention, but some of the dioceses in British territories had been grouped in provinces and had been granted metropolitical status and were holding provincial meetings, including lay people and clergy, notably in New Zealand, South Africa and Canada.

Although provision had been made for the election of bishops in New Zealand and in South Africa, the first bishop to be elected by an Anglican diocese had been Benjamin Cronyn as bishop of Huron in 1857. The election was notified to the governor general, asking him to forward the notification to the Queen, with a request that she grant a licence for his consecration, but he had still been consecrated on the authority of royal letters patent and a royal mandate by the archbishop of Canterbury at Lambeth Palace Chapel, in England.

In 1860 the five Canadian dioceses were constituted a province by royal letters patent, and so, when the first bishop of Ottawa was elected by the synod of the diocese in 1862, the governor general was informed, and was again asked to forward the notification to the Queen, with a request that she grant a licence for his consecration, and she issued letters patent and a royal mandate to the archbishop of Canterbury, but he now transmitted them to the metropolitan of the province to consecrate the new bishop in Kingston, Ontario. The following year, when the Quebec diocesan synod elected a successor to Bishop Mountain, the Queen was again notified via the governor general and requested to issue letters patent and a royal mandate, but the law officers of the crown advised that, following the recent Privy Council decisions in *Long* v *The Bishop of Cape Town*, letters patent were no longer deemed to have any force in a self-governing colony. The royal mandate for consecration, however, was issued, but to the metropolitan of the province, not to the archbishop of Canterbury. When in 1866 a coadjutor bishop of Toronto was elected, the diocesan synod petitioned for a royal mandate for the bishop's consecration, but the colonial secretary replied that the crown law officers had advised that there was no longer any means of enforcing such a mandate in a self-governing colony, and pointed out that the provincial synod possessed sufficient powers to proceed without a royal mandate.[7]

Meanwhile, when the first bishops were appointed for missionary dioceses outside the jurisdiction of British rule in 1861, Mackenzie for the Zambezi and Coleridge Patterson for Melanesia, they had been consecrated without letters patent, or a royal mandate, in the provinces where their new missionary dioceses were situated. Subsequently after the Privy Council's judgement in *Long* v *The Bishop of Cape Town*, as we have seen, the Colonial Office ceased to issue letters patent for the consecration of any overseas bishops.

All this might indicate that the various new provinces of the Anglican Church were drifting apart, and establishing their own customs and ways of operating. In fact there was much more coming and going between the Church of England and colonial dioceses than ever before. One of the reasons for this was that transport and communications were improving. Fast sailing ships and then steam ships made it possible for overseas bishops to visit England from time to time. When Bishop Middleton went to Calcutta no provision was made for him to return to England until the end of his fifteen-year term. For the first four bishops of Calcutta their appointment was a sentence of exile as well as a death sentence. By mid-century improved transport facilities made it feasible for the archbishop of Canterbury to invite overseas bishops to take part in the one hundred and fiftieth anniversary celebrations of the SPG in 1851, and bishops came from Scotland, the United States and the colonies. Their appearance in London raised the consciousness of people in the Church of England to the existence of an overseas Anglican Church. The presence of a number of colonial bishops in London in 1851 and 1852 enabled them, as we have seen, to meet and compare notes about matters of common interest.

There had been a slowly growing awareness in England of the colonial Church. Bishops for the colonies initially, like all other bishops, had been consecrated in Lambeth Palace chapel, and had gone off and were seldom seen again. From the 1830s onwards accounts began to be given of their deeds at SPG meetings in dioceses, deaneries and parishes, but from the 1840s seeing them in the flesh and hearing them preach and tell of their work as they travelled round England visiting friends and former parishes must have been a sharp reminder to English clergy and laity that they were part of a growing Church. Even at official levels more began to be made of the consecration of colonial bishops. From 1847 consecrations were held in Westminster Abbey, which allowed for people to attend in large numbers, and of course, the new railway network allowed more friends and relations, former parishioners and supporters to travel to London. On Whit Tuesday 1849 the first bishops for the new dioceses of Rupertsland and Victoria (Hong Kong) were consecrated in Canterbury Cathedral.[8] In 1853 Bishop McIlvaine of Ohio assisted at the consecration of Bishop Jackson of Lincoln,[9] and American bishops began occasionally to be invited to take part in the consecration of English bishops.

In replying to the archbishop of Canterbury's invitation to hold celebrations for the one hundred and fiftieth anniversary of the SPG in every diocese, the moderately High Church Bishop Hopkins of Vermont suggested to the archbishop that he should consider holding a council of bishops in communion with the see of Canterbury. In June 1852 the American bishops were invited by the archbishop of Canterbury to send representatives to the concluding festivities for the SPG anniversary 'to manifest the essential unity of the Sister Churches of America and England'. The bishops of Maryland and New York were nominated to attend and the bishop of Maryland brought a proposal for an 'assemblage of the whole episcopate' to revise the canons of both 'Communions', and in an address in Leeds, Bishop de Lancey of New York proposed an 'Anglican Council of Bishops'.[10] No doubt part of the motivation for these proposals, and much talk among Anglican High Churchmen everywhere about a council of Anglican bishops, was the resurgence of Roman Catholicism in England, North America and Australia. In England the Roman Catholic hierarchy of bishops had been established in 1850 in a blaze of publicity, and many High Church Anglicans were smarting under the attacks of some of their former colleagues as converts, and wished to emphasize the unity of Anglicanism as an episcopal, catholic Church.

Not all American Episcopalians, however, wished for a closer relationship with the Church of England. The American bishops had invited the English bishops to send a delegate to visit the general convention in 1853, and the archbishop of Canterbury commissioned the SPG to arrange a delegation comprising the bishop of Madras, the archdeacon of Middlesex, the secretary of the SPG and Henry Caswall, with a brief to 'strengthen and improve the intimate relations which already happily exist between the Mother and Daughter Churches, and which are the proper fruit of their spiritual unity'. There was also a delegation from the Canadian Church. At the convention it became clear that some Americans were suspicious of the Church of England's close links with the State and feared that the Church of England might attempt to intervene in their affairs. However, the convention did agree to set up a committee to consider relations between the churches, and the presiding bishop was again asked to raise with the archbishop of Canterbury the question of the regular transfer of clergy between the churches, and another committee was appointed to correspond with the archbishop of Canterbury about the jurisdictional conflict which had arisen in China between the American bishop and the bishop of Victoria (Hong Kong).[11]

From the 1840s there had begun to be a sense of the global spread of all Protestant churches, and of the importance of channels of formal co-operation between individual Christians. The Evangelical Alliance had been formed in 1846, and in 1846 and 1854 respectively the YMCA and the YWCA which were both inter-Christian and international organizations had been founded, encouraging an exchange of information about churches in different parts of the world, and visits from representatives of one nation to another. The missionary movement too encouraged the idea of large meetings of representatives of missions from across the world. There were great missionary meetings in New York and London in 1854 and in Liverpool in 1860. All had perhaps been influenced by the success of the Great Exhibition of 1851 in bringing visitors from all over the world to the hub of the British Empire.

The sense of a world-wide network of Anglican dioceses began to grow in the 1850s, and from the time of the SPG jubilee in 1851, and the PECUSA general convention in 1853, the term 'Anglican Communion' began to be used to describe a world-wide Anglican Church.[12] The Church of England was beginning too to develop an identity beyond being the established Church of England. The onslaught of vociferous nonconformists calling, from the mid-1830s onwards, in Parliament and across the country for the disestablishment of the Church of England, and the results of the Religious Census of 1851, had demonstrated that although it might be the established Church, it was not quite the national Church. It had to look elsewhere for its legitimation. For moderate High Churchmen its legitimacy lay in being the ancient Catholic Church in England, truly reformed according to the principles of Scripture and the primitive Church. The criticism and growing numbers of Roman Catholics reinforced their need to assert the apostolicity of their Church, its capacity to be a world-Church and its capacity to teach true Catholic doctrine tested by reference to Scripture and the Fathers of the Eastern and the Western Church. Part of this assertion of identity had been, as we have seen, the campaign to reactivate the convocations, which paralleled the movements to establish synodical government in the colonial churches. By the mid-1860s the convocations of Canterbury and York were operating again, and had begun to give the Church of England a greater sense of its own identity.

THE FIRST LAMBETH CONFERENCE

In order to establish their status as suffragans of the archbishop of Canterbury, Gray and a number of other colonial bishops had attempted to claim seats in the upper house of the convocation of Canterbury when it was revived in 1852. Failing that, Gray began from 1860 to seek the calling of an Anglican synod but he did not envisage that this should include the 'independent' non-English churches in Scotland and the USA. However, largely because of Gray's actions, a number of factors had come much more powerfully into play suggesting the need for some sort of consultative process among the Anglican bishops.

The first and simplest and perhaps the most important reason for calling a meeting of Anglican bishops was a sense of isolation among many of the overseas bishops, and a lack of knowledge about, and the truth of the rumours which they had heard about, other dioceses and provinces. The second cause was the growing confusion over the relationship between the Church in the colonies and the English State, and the varying opinions in the colonies and in England about this relationship. There was a considerable tension between High Churchmen, such as Wilberforce and Longley, who wished to encourage the synodical model so that the dioceses would come together into independent provinces, and Broad Churchmen, such as Tait and evangelicals such as Archbishop Thomson of York, who wished to maintain the link with the English crown and to see colonial bishops continue to be appointed by the crown, and to receive their commission from the archbishop of Canterbury. A third cause was an anxiety among the overseas bishops, including the Irish bishops, that now the Canterbury and York convocations were again deliberating, they might make changes in the Prayer Book and the English Canons and Constitutions of 1604 which would put other churches out of step with the Church of England. Fourth, the bishops in all parts of the world were aware that extraordinary things had been going on in the Anglican Church in other parts of the world, and they wanted to meet and to exchange experiences and ideas. Fifth, the intellectual ferment caused by the publication of Darwin's *Origin of Species* in 1859 and *Essays and Reviews* in 1860 and Colenso's *Pentateuch* in 1862 raised major questions about the nature of inspiration, revelation, creation, salvation and morality, that bishops, and particularly those who were in isolated positions, wanted to get together to talk about, and decide how to define authoritative teaching. Sixth, the question of the authority of a metropolitan over other bishops in his province and his authority to discipline his suffragans and to depose them if necessary, was seen as very important. Related to that, the precise example of Colenso, and whether or not the diocese of Natal was now vacant, was a crucial question for the bishops and the developing Communion.[13]

Longley was the right person in the right place at the right time. As bishop of Ripon at the time of the consecration of Leeds parish church in 1841, he had met Bishop Doane of New Jersey, and during the course of the SPG jubilee celebrations in 1851 and 1852 he had met and got to know more American and colonial bishops. He was, in any case, interested in missions and subscribed to both the SPG and the CMS. At Ripon he had advocated the revival of diocesan synods, but he had not called one himself, because he had thought the diocese was too divided for there to be a constructive meeting, but when he was translated to York, as we have seen, he permitted the York convocation to be revived. He also publicly recognized the Scottish Episcopal Church as in full communion with the Church of England by visiting Inverness to lay the foundation stone of the new cathedral there, and he invited Charles Wordsworth, the bishop of St Andrews to take part in the consecration of an English bishop. He was also unhappy about the jurisdiction of the Judicial Committee of the Privy Council in ecclesiastical cases, and disagreed with the judgements the Committee had given in the Gorham case, as well as in the cases of *Essays and Reviews* and Colenso. He had all the qualities that would make it likely that he would be interested in some sort of pan-Anglican meeting of bishops.

The Colenso case in particular made some colonial bishops feel an urgent need for a pan-Anglican assembly to consider the implications of the decisions. Gray had, with the support of his fellow South African bishops and most of the clergy, excommunicated Colenso. But he wanted the support of the English bishops and clergy before arranging for the election of a new bishop of Natal. This was a major problem for the English bishops, for Colenso had been appointed by the crown, by letters patent, and they were uncertain whether they could in law, or should tactically, treat as deposed a bishop appointed by the crown. And most important, the highest court of the English legal system had ruled that Gray had no authority to try Colenso, and that his excommunication and deposition was illegal. The English bishops were also hesitant as to whether the convocation of Canterbury, which Gray had asked to support him, could be seen as speaking for the Church of England, when the convocation of York had not been asked to consider the matter. Gray had been very disappointed by what he regarded as the faltering voice of the English bishops in convocation in 1864, when they had refused to categorically deny that they were in communion with Colenso, and he had pressed for the calling of a 'national synod' to confirm his sentence on Colenso.[14]

In September 1865 the evangelical Bishop Lewis of Ontario proposed to the Canadian bishops meeting in synod in Montreal that they should ask the archbishop of Canterbury to convene a 'National Synod of the Bishops of the Anglican Church at home and abroad' (which would have excluded the Scottish and the American bishops) to deal with the doctrinal aberrations which, in his view, had been promoted by Bishop Colenso. The bishops and clergy of the Canadian synod endorsed this proposal and dispatched it to Archbishop Longley, who gave a cautious, but encouraging reply in February 1866. The House of Clergy of the Canadian Provincial Synod simultaneously sent a memorial, setting out this proposal to the lower houses of the Canterbury and York convocations. Archdeacon Denison of Taunton and Chancellor Massingberd of Lincoln, both traditional High Churchmen, picked up the memorial and pressed for the calling of an Anglican synod which would include clergy and laity, as well as bishops. However the difficulties of the legality of convening a synod including elected lay people and clergy under the Act of Submission of the Clergy, and Article 21 of the Thirty-Nine Articles were pointed out by Canon Christopher Wordsworth of Westminster Abbey, and the proposal was opposed by the Broad Churchmen in the convocation, but it was agreed to appoint a committee to consider the Canadian synod's proposal.

In a letter he sent to all bishops, deans and archdeacons in the Anglican Communion in October 1866 Bishop Tait of London had sought the views of those to whom he wrote on four questions relating to the structure of the Communion: the desirability, or otherwise, of all bishops in British colonies receiving their mission from the see of Canterbury and taking an oath of canonical obedience to the archbishop; whether it would be desirable that there should be an appeal in 'grave' cases from the judgements of the church courts or decisions of bishops or synods in the colonies to any authority 'at home', and if so, to what authority and under what restrictions; how far the royal supremacy as acknowledged by the Church of England and Ireland could be maintained in the colonial Church; and what might be the best guarantee for maintaining unity of doctrine and discipline between the different churches in the colonies.[15]

There was a further Canadian prod to the proposal when in December 1866 Bishop Francis Fulford of Montreal preached at Christ Church, Oxford, and called for a demonstration of Anglican unity by calling a synod. The sermon was subsequently published as a pamphlet, and in appendices to the sermon Fulford set out an agenda for a synod, and suggested that any decisions of such a synod should not be binding on any province unless they were adopted by a province. He sent the pamphlet to all the English bishops.

At an ensuing debate in the lower house of the Canterbury convocation the proposals for a 'national synod' were bitterly opposed by Broad Churchmen led by Dean Stanley of Westminster. He claimed that such an assembly would be illegal under the Act of Submission of the Clergy, and even if it were to take place, it would be of doubtful value. However the house agreed to set up a committee to consider the question, and, when the committee's report was received and discussed, Christopher Wordsworth carried a motion in favour of a 'national synod' of bishops of the Anglican Church. The York convocation did not discuss the Canadian memorial.

The proposal for a synod was considered at a bishops' meeting in February 1867. A majority of the English bishops were not present and none of the evangelical bishops were there. Bishop Fulford of Montreal and Bishop Whitehouse of Illinois attended the meeting, and spoke strongly for a synod. In reply to a written question from the Broad Church Bishop Tait of London, Archbishop Longley made it clear that there was no intention that such a meeting should enact canons for all or any of the provinces, or make decisions that would be binding on the whole Church. Samuel Wilberforce, the bishop of Oxford, proposed a motion asking the archbishop of Canterbury to call a 'national synod of all the bishops of the Anglican Church, both at home and abroad', and the motion was passed unanimously. Longley accepted the motion as an invitation to go forward with the meeting, even though it was opposed by the powerful Broad Church nexus led by Dean Stanley, and in the knowledge that the majority of the English bishops who were absent from the meeting would probably have opposed the proposal.

The most senior and theologically distinguished bishop in the Canterbury convocation, Connop Thirlwall of St David's was unhappy about the calling of a conference. He believed that the intention of the enthusiasts for the conference was to outvote, with the support of the American and overseas bishops, the more cautious resolutions of the English bishops about Colenso. This view was shared by the archbishop of York, and the bishops of Durham, Carlisle, Ripon, Manchester and Peterborough. Tait however, endorsed Longley's proposal for a conference, and Connop Thirlwall was won over by Longley's private undertaking that the question of Colenso's position would not be discussed.[16]

Longley set up a standing committee to assist in organizing the meeting, which included Tait and Samuel Wilberforce, who became the most influential member. On 22 February 1867 an invitation was sent to all serving Anglican bishops (except Colenso) to attend the meeting 'to pray and deliberate together'. Longley was mindful of the terms of Article 21 stating that 'General Councils may not be gathered together without the commandment and will of princes', and he made it very clear that the invitation was not to a synod, or a council, but to a 'conference' at which the bishops would merely 'pray and deliberate together'.

Because most of the bishops from the province of York had been absent from the bishops' meeting which had endorsed the meeting of Anglican bishops, Longley wrote to the evangelical Archbishop Thomson of York, to ask his consent to invite the bishops in his province to the meeting. Thomson was not happy with the proposal, and was not reassured by Longley's letter. He feared that such a meeting would risk weakening the link between Church and State, and himself declined the invitation. He was supported by the bishops of Durham, Ripon and Carlisle out of the six bishops in his province.[17]

Four English bishops, one Scottish bishop and four American bishops declined the invitation on the grounds of ill-health or their advanced age. Three bishops wrote back saying that they could not afford the expense of the journey. Two American bishops excused themselves on the grounds that the aftermath of the Civil War would not permit them to attend. Seven bishops declined the invitation on the grounds that they had only recently been consecrated and left England for their dioceses. The bishop of Melbourne, perhaps not surprisingly considering his reluctance to attend bishops' meetings in Australia, offered his apologies on the grounds of the length of the journey, Bishop Barker of Sydney also declined the invitation for he disapproved of the conference's implications of separating the Church from the crown. Two American bishops gave no reason. However, with these twenty-four exceptions, the initial response was favourable.

When the agenda and the draft resolutions of the meeting were circulated some bishops withdrew their acceptance. Some evangelical bishops objected to references to the general councils of the Church being placed before Scripture, and to the Reformation being described as 'a return to the primitive and undivided Church' and to the omission of any reference to the Thirty-Nine Articles. Bishops Jeune of Peterborough and Prince Lee of Manchester, who earlier had also opposed the revival of the York convocation, decided at this stage not to accept the invitation to the conference. Bishops Daly of Cashel and Bernard of Tuam also withdrew. There was some pressure from traditional High Churchmen for the bishops of the Church of

Sweden, one of the few other churches of the Reformation that had preserved the episcopal succession, to be invited, but this was opposed by the Tractarians, who pressed for the inclusion of an item on the agenda calling for prayer for union with the churches of Rome and the East.

The signs were that the bishops who attended the conference would be divided on party lines. In general terms the evangelicals and Broad Churchmen were opposed to the idea of the meeting, but some were prepared to attend to make their point, and perhaps move the meeting their way. In general High Churchmen and Tractarians were in favour of the meeting. There were at least six major unofficial items that different groups intended to press on the attention of the meeting. The evangelical bishops, led by Charles Sumner, bishop of Winchester wished to alter the opening phrases of the draft declaration which it was proposed should be issued at the end of the meeting, in order to underline the Protestant nature of the Church of England. Gray of Cape Town and Hopkins of Vermont were also preparing to amend the Declaration in a High Church direction, in accordance with suggestions made by the Tractarian leader Dr Pusey, and to eliminate the passage which described Anglicanism as 'an exemplar for the whole of Christendom'. Bishops Gray and Hopkins were also determined that the meeting should receive information about the sentence Gray had pronounced on Bishop Colenso, and should accept and recognize the sentence. Bishops Tait of London, Connop Thirlwall of St David's, Jackson of Lincoln, Browne of Ely and Sumner of Winchester, representing a spectrum of evangelical, Broad Church and High Church views were equally determined that no action should be taken against Colenso which might be construed as objectionable in the eyes of the State. Tait was also concerned that nothing should be done which might tend to sever the links which bound the colonial Church to the crown. He hoped to win support from the West Indian bishops for this view. Finally some colonial bishops were anxious to set up a 'pan-Anglican synod' which would either act as, or create a final spiritual court. Longley was extremely anxious that the Colenso affair should be kept off the agenda and out of the meeting, because he did not want to give an excuse not to attend the conference to the Broad Church or evangelical bishops who were unwilling to confirm Colenso's deposition against the judgement of the Privy Council. Samuel Wilberforce and Walter Hamilton, the bishop of Salisbury and the only English Tractarian bishop, supported Longley in this, and were prepared to exert pressure on Gray and others not to attempt to persuade the bishops to condemn Colenso. However, it was likely to be a difficult meeting and there was a real risk that it might fall apart.

There was considerable activity in the week before the conference to try to ensure that disputes did not wreck the conference. Wilberforce and Hamilton firmly pointed out to Gray that the question of Colenso's excommunication and the bishops' endorsement of the election of a new bishop in his place could not be considered at the conference because Archbishop Longley had pledged himself that it should not be discussed. They also pointed out that the bishops were not in agreement on the matter and that their division over the issue would add to the scandal. Gray resentfully pointed out that it would be sinful to do nothing, and that the churches of the Anglican Communion must declare that they held no communion with Colenso. Wilberforce and Hamilton tried to persuade Gray to find a suitable priest in South Africa to be elected bishop of Natal, and consecrated by the South African bishops. They pointed out that if the new bishop then came to England, he would be accepted as bishop of Natal by the English bishops. Gray replied that in 1864 the clergy and laity of Natal had resolved not to elect anyone who had been involved in the opposition to Colenso lest it should be said that he had personal objects to serve in his opposition to Colenso. Gray felt badly let down by the American and overseas bishops at a meeting of a large number of English, American and overseas bishops convened by Christopher Wordsworth the day before the conference opened. At the meeting Wordsworth proposed that a committee be set up to consider the Colenso question, and to 'report on the best mode by which the Church might be delivered from the scandal, and the true Faith maintained'. This was endorsed with a request that the archbishop of Canterbury should circulate the report to all the bishops.[18]

In the event seventy-six bishops gathered at Lambeth Palace for a week of meetings on Tuesday, 24 September 1867. It was notable that some areas of the colonial Church were significantly under represented; there was only one bishop from each of Australia and India. The notice for the meeting had in fact been very short. Longley set certain ground rules, which turned out to be very important for the success of the meeting. He reiterated that it was a conference, for the bishops to discuss together and to consult one another, not a synod, nor a council to speak on behalf of the whole Church or even on behalf of the bishops in communion with the archbishop of Canterbury. He also established that it was a private meeting of the bishops, and pointed out that no reference had been made to the British government or the crown in calling the meeting. It had been called by the archbishop of Canterbury entirely on his own initiative, after he had consulted his convocation of Canterbury. Reporters were not permitted to attend any of the meetings, and no record was made of the discussions.

In the discussions about the draft declaration defining the position of the Anglican Church, the evangelical bishops succeeded in making their points, and in amending the declaration, although the majority of the bishops present were High Churchmen. This was probably because, as moderate High Churchmen, they did not share the Tractarian distaste for references to the Reformation and for formularies derived from Reformation statements. They were content that there should be references to the Anglican reformed phrase the 'primitive Church', rather than to the 'undivided Church'. After lengthy debate the bishops also gave their approval to synodical government in the Church at both diocesan and provincial levels. This served to set the tone for the future constitutional development of Anglicanism and indicated the strength of the traditional High Church representation among the bishops.

Bishop Gray continued his intense lobbying for a debate about the Colenso affair. Gray still hoped to secure the support of his fellow bishops in his handling of Colenso. He was supported by Selwyn and also by Hopkins of Vermont, who was now presiding bishop of the PECUSA. Longley pointed out from the chair that the meeting had not been called to discuss the Colenso case, nor was it competent to do so, lacking the information and evidence upon which to make a decision. He also stated firmly that the bishop of Natal had not been invited to the Conference. The fact that no disapproval was voiced was seen by Bishop Eden, the primus of the Scottish Episcopal Church, at least, as the acceptance by the bishops of the *de facto* excommunication of Colenso.[19]

Longley indicated, however, that he would be willing to accept a proposal for a committee to be set up to recommend how the matter of Colenso might be dealt with. Wilberforce, in order not to alienate Gray whom, with Selwyn's support, he was still trying to persuade not to press the issue on to the agenda, proposed a short resolution which accepted the sentence Gray had pronounced on Colenso. This was signed by fifty-six out of a possible seventy-three signatories, which succeeded in demonstrating that Gray had substantial support, but satisfied Longley in keeping the matter off the main agenda. The bishops agreed, however, to set up a committee to investigate the possibilities of a system of courts of appeal for both the home Church and the colonial Church. Longley, with the assistance of Wilberforce, succeeded in avoiding any attempt to officially condemn Colenso, which would have been likely to drive out the English Broad Church bishops and perhaps the evangelical bishops, but he did allow the views of the colonial bishops to be aired, and managed to avoid offending most of them, although Gray felt hurt and let down. On this very tense matter Longley managed most importantly to avoid a public division among the bishops.

At the end of the week committees were set up to report back to the final session of the conference which was adjourned until December, and to deal with the matters on the agenda which had not been dealt with. A revised version of the declaration was agreed, and also an encyclical, for publication, was agreed. In the event only twenty-eight of the bishops were able to remain to reconvene to receive the reports of the committees on 10 December 1867. The reports were merely received, not debated, and it was agreed to recommend all the reports to all the bishops of the Anglican Communion for careful consideration as containing the deliberations of that particular committee of bishops, except the report of the committee on the diocese of Natal.

The committee on synodical government had recommended that wherever a Church was not by law established, there should be diocesan and provincial synods, including clergy and lay people. It also recommended that provincial synods should be superior to diocesan synods, and recommended that provincial synods ought to establish rules and procedures for disciplining clergy and for ordering the Church in the province. The committee recommended that bishops should be elected by the diocese (including both clergy and lay people as electors), and that the election of bishops should be confirmed by the provincial synod. There was no recommendation for a 'higher synod', for it was recognized that the establishment of the Church in some provinces, notably Canterbury and York, would cause difficulties in achieving this. It was also thought that it would be impossible to draw up canons that would be binding on all provinces. The committee appointed to consider the advisability of establishing a voluntary 'spiritual final court of appeal' recommended that such a court should be established, to which each province should elect two representatives. It also recommended that each province should have a court in which all the bishops of the province should sit with the metropolitan as judges, and that two assessors should also sit with them.

The committee appointed to consider the situation in the diocese of Natal recommended that the see should be considered to be spiritually vacant, and that a new bishop should be elected. The encyclical issued at the conclusion of the conference was drafted by Samuel Wilberforce, and was translated into Latin and Greek by Archdeacon Christopher Wordsworth, and also into French, Italian, Spanish, Danish, Bohemian and Armenian. Copies, with accompanying letters, were sent to each of the patriarchs of the Orthodox churches. Henry Manning, now cardinal archbishop of Westminster, described the encyclical as the most important manifesto that had come from the English Church since the Reformation. He claimed that he could find nothing in it with which a Roman Catholic could disagree, not even its strictures about the supremacy of Rome or mariolatry.

Not surprisingly, in view of this, the evangelical press condemned the meeting, and described it as a High Church manoeuvre. This was not, however, the view of the evangelical bishops who had attended the meeting. They spoke positively about it. The Broad Church bishops, however were not won over, although Tait recognized that the meeting had been valuable. The moderate High Churchmen were well-pleased with the result. The other distinctive group there, the American bishops, felt appreciated and that important relationships had been formed.

The successful inclusion of the American bishops was a notable achievement, for they had a strong sense of being outsiders in comparison with the English and colonial bishops.

The colonial bishops came from very similar backgrounds to the English bishops. They had all been educated at Oxford or Cambridge, which in the first half of the nineteenth century were very small worlds, and many of the bishops had been fellows of colleges, or had taught at one of the leading public schools, before perhaps being parish priests for a while, and then being elevated to the episcopate. It was a close-knit world, where a network of patronage was on the lookout for people of promise.[20] These networks had been closely involved, as we have seen, with the Clapham Sect and the Hackney Phalanx, and with the political world.

Also, after the establishment of the Colonial Bishoprics Fund, a small number of energetic bishops became very influential and extensively used their networks of patronage and education in recruiting nominees for oversees bishoprics. There may not have been any translations from overseas bishoprics to English dioceses until Selwyn became bishop of Lichfield in 1868, but there was much common ground between overseas and English bishops, and much correspondence. Even Colenso was part of this network. He had been a fellow of St John's College, Cambridge and had taught maths at Harrow when Longley and Christopher Wordsworth were successively headmasters, and was a close friend of Ernest Hawkins, the secretary of the SPG. To have managed to include the American bishops, who had none of this common background, was no mean achievement.

The conference was perhaps most important for bringing bishops together and, apart from the English Broad Church bishops, establishing a network based on affection and esteem between them, so that they had a sense of being part of the same Church. The conference was also important for establishing a style and pattern of working, that was to become central to Anglican identity. It was a conference where, as Longley had indicated, the bishops would meet to pray and to deliberate together. It was purely a deliberative, consultative and advisory body. It did not attempt to make decisions on behalf of the Church; it merely made recommendations for the consideration of provinces and dioceses. Longley established the role of the archbishop of Canterbury as chairman of the conference, but not as an autocrat over it. He was merely the first among equals. The conference had a degree of informality. It met privately. It worked through committees of the members, thus enabling as many bishops as possible to actively participate, and to have a sense of being involved in the discussions and consultations. At the conclusion an encyclical, not edicts, was issued. The ethos established by Longley at the conference was continued through successive conferences.

The conference provided an important outward expression of Anglican unity. There was no minority report, and no separation off of a dissenting group. Symbolically it was a most important event, for although almost all the bishops were of Anglo-Saxon origins, if not English, they had gathered from all over the world, and it was the first of a series of international gatherings of leaders of particular denominations or communions, including the Council of Roman Catholic bishops held at the Vatican in 1870, and the World Presbyterian Alliance in 1878, the first Methodist Ecumenical Conference in 1881, and the Old Catholic Union of Utrecht formed in 1881.

Despite the tensions over the views expressed in *Essays and Reviews* and in Colenso's publications, as well as over Colenso's appeal to the State to support his position, the bishops did stay together, and most importantly, liberal and critical thought about the Bible and the Christian tradition were not condemned. Also emphasis was placed on the Council of Nicea and the General Councils of the Church, and the attention paid to sending a letter and copies of the encyclical to the ecumenical patriarch and the Orthodox patriarchs as well as the pope, paved the way for future ecumenical developments, as well as restating the traditional Anglican claim to relate to the other churches descended from the 'primitive Church'. Similarly the discussions about the inclusion of the bishops of the Church of Sweden in the conference prepared the way for a closer relationship with the Church of Sweden and in due course with the other Nordic churches.

The conference also confirmed the traditional High Church Anglican concern for synodical government, in which the laity and the clergy should be involved with the bishop in making decisions about the order and the discipline of the Church and its doctrines. The tradition of synodical meetings of clergy and bishops had continued until the early eighteenth century in England and Wales, and still continued in Scotland and the province of Dublin in Ireland, and in theory, until 1832 the English and Irish Parliaments could be seen as assemblies of the laity of the established churches. However, first in New Zealand, and then in Canada and South Africa, the tradition was refocused to provide for the government of dioceses and then provinces of the Church by bishops and representatives of the clergy and laity. This was to be the future pattern in Anglican dioceses and provinces, each of which was seen as autonomous, but in communion with the others, and in interdependence with one another. It was a pattern of relationship which would produce stresses and strains, but also permitted flexibility. This approval of synodical government encouraged the English bishops to continue to establish diocesan 'conferences' to consult representatives of the clergy and laity in their dioceses, and in due course to support the establishment of a Representative Church Council for the Church of England, until legislation could be obtained to establish a Church Assembly, and eventually synodical government jointly for the provinces of Canterbury and York.

Although the atmosphere of some of the debates at the conference had been heated, no one had withdrawn. The Lambeth Conference was very largely a triumph for the traditional High Church group. In addition to the colonial bishops whom we have already noted, a group of English bishops, including Longley, Samuel Wilberforce, Henry Philpotts of Exeter, John Lonsdale of Lichfield, Harold Browne of Ely, Jacobson of Chester, Short of St Asaph, Gilbert of Chichester and Eden of Bath and Wells, supported by Walter Hook, now dean of Chichester, Christopher Wordsworth and Ernest Hawkins, both canons of Westminster, Chancellor Massingberd of Lincoln, and Dean Burgon of Chichester had supported the proposal for a meeting in the Canterbury convocation, and had over many years worked for the revival of convocations in England, and the establishment of lay representation in the councils of the Church of which the Church congresses, which had begun in 1861, were an important part.

The conference also raised the consciousness of the Church of England to the overseas Church and encouraged English Churchpeople to think about mission.

The first Lambeth Conference changed nothing constitutionally in the Anglican Communion. It was merely an informal meeting of bishops with no legislative authority. No doubt they gained much from comparing notes with one another about similar problems over lunch and tea and dinner during the conference and the subsequent committees, but the tensions between some of the English bishops and the colonial bishops over the Colenso affair must have made many conversations difficult. Nor is it surprising that some of the overseas bishops, especially the American bishops, were annoyed that the agenda and proceedings were so dominated by the concerns of the English bishops, and were irritated by the short notice for the conference, given the length of the journeys some of them had to make to attend. No doubt many bishops felt buoyed up by sharing their problems and discovering that other bishops had similar problems, and having re-established old friendships and made new friends.

However, many problems were undiscussed, most notably the complex relationship between Church and State, especially in England, and Ireland and India, but its ramifications reached out into all colonial territories and caused theological and practical problems for most of the bishops in British territories. Nor was there apparently any discussion of the relationships between bishops and the missionary societies, and of the funding of existing work, and the establishment of new dioceses. Mission was strangely missing from the agenda. Guidance had been provided about establishing self-government in dioceses, and for the establishment of provinces, in which a metropolitan might have some authority over diocesan bishops, but no guidance was given about the relationships between provinces, or the position of the many dioceses that were not in a province, and the relationship of any of them to the archbishop of Canterbury. No real consideration was given to questions of doctrine, except in so far as it related to the authority of bishops and the liturgy. In relation to doctrine the conference was more important for what it did not say about the nature and authority of the Bible than for what it said. There was clearly much left for bishops to discuss, but there was no indication at the end of the meeting that they would meet again. They returned to their dioceses to pick up the threads of old problems that would continue to shape the nature of their Church.

The complex relationship between Church and State in England and colonial High Church bishops who wanted to establish a boundary to the State's jurisdiction over the Church was particularly problematic, as we have seen, in relation to establishing bishoprics in areas outside British territory. Although the Jerusalem Bishopric Act permitted bishops to be consecrated to serve in areas outside the jurisdiction of the British crown, the issue of a royal licence for the consecration still caused problems for High Churchmen. When a diocese for Sarawak was set up in 1854, partially funded by the 'White Rajah', Brookes, whose jurisdiction the British government declined to recognize, the title of the see, and the new bishop's authority under the crown was derived from the neighbouring small colony of Labuan.[21]

In 1861 when the king of Hawaii had pressed the Church of England to send him a bishop, Samuel Wilberforce had insisted that should the appointment originate in the British crown such an appointment would be tantamount to territorial usurpation. In the end, a compromise permitted the consecration of Thomas Staley as bishop of Honolulu, the first missionary bishop to be consecrated in England, by means of a royal licence. This solution, however, left Wilberforce unsatisfied. He and his fellow High Churchmen believed that the Church must be allowed free reign to deal with territories beyond the writ of the British government. In Wilberforce's view, to grant the crown a role in such an appointment was to grant the State the power of spiritual as well as temporal authority.[22] Another solution, as we have seen, was for an overseas bishop in a territory where the Church was no longer established, and therefore no longer restricted by the authority of the crown in relation to the Church of England, to consecrate a bishop, as Gray, as bishop of Cape Town, consecrated Mackenzie bishop of the Zambezi.

A different view was taken by Tait, and a number of other English bishops. Tait accepted the advice of the law officers of the crown, when they were consulted following a debate in convocation about the appointment of overseas bishops without royal letters patent, that much as such a 'novel proceeding' was to be 'deprecated and discouraged' they were 'unaware of any statute or rule of common law by virtue of which the Archbishops or their Suffragans would incur any penalty from consecrating in this country or among the heathen'. However, he was very nervous of granting autonomy to colonial churches. He suspected that colonial bishops, left in isolation, might become 'eccentric' in their doctrines, as had Colenso. He was nervous that bishops like Gray might impose a narrow High

Churchmanship on a diocese or province. Tait wished to postpone the loosening of the links which united the colonial dioceses to the Church in England for as long as possible in order
that these churches might have time to settle themselves firmly
upon the lines of the English law, before they should be left to
stand alone. He dreaded and feared an ecclesiastical despotism
separated from the crown such as he suspected Gray of establishing in South Africa.[23]

The whole complex issue of the relationship between the
Church and the State, and the interrelationship between
Anglican provinces and the authority of a metropolitan continued to be particularly pertinent for Gray. Although the bishops
at Lambeth had, by a large majority, given their moral support
to him in his dealings with Colenso, he still had considerable
problems in replacing Colenso. As we have seen, he badly
wanted the support of the Church of England, and he had put
to the convocation of Canterbury three questions for their
consideration for his guidance and reassurance. He had asked
them whether the convocation was in communion with Colenso
or himself and the other South African bishops, whether the
appointment of a new bishop would sever Natal from the
Church of England, and whether, if it were possible to appoint
a new bishop, how it might be done. Wilberforce had piloted
the questions through the convocation on Gray's behalf, but
the answers given were, understandably in the legal context,
cautious. Convocation had confirmed that it remained in communion with Gray, and that it would not regard the appointment
of a new bishop of Natal as severing the connection between
Natal and the Church of England, but it had not said that it
regarded Colenso as excommunicate. It had also said that if the
Church in Natal would draw up a formulary which enshrined
the doctrines and discipline of the Church of England, there
would be, in their opinion, no reason why the archbishop of
Canterbury should not consecrate a new bishop of Natal.[24]

On the strength of this Gray had felt that he might move
to appoint a replacement for Colenso, who by this time had
returned to Natal to resume the hard and expensively won temporalities of his diocese in which he had been confirmed by the
Judicial Committee of the Privy Council. In 1866 there was a
conference of the clergy and communicants in Natal, under the
chairmanship of the dean of the cathedral in Pietermaritzburg,

which only one of the clergy in the diocese had declined to attend. The conference had drawn up a declaration setting out their adherence to the doctrines and disciplines of the Church of England, as suggested by the Canterbury convocation. After a long discussion it had been decided, by the dean's casting vote, to proceed to the election of a bishop. However, three of the clergy had refused to take part in the election. There were two possible candidates, one nominated by the archbishop of Canterbury, who had withdrawn before the conference, and the other W.J. Butler, vicar of Wantage and subsequently dean of Lincoln, a noted Tractarian. When it came to the election, the seven votes in the house of clergy were all for Butler, but the archbishop of Canterbury and Samuel Wilberforce, having satisfied themselves of the canonicity of the election and that Butler would be acceptable to the other bishops in the province and to the Church in England, persuaded him to decline the offer, on the grounds that he was too much an 'extreme man'. However, the principle had been established, that, with the consent of the archbishop of Canterbury, the clergy and laity of the diocese could proceed to elect a new bishop, in spite of Colenso's continuing presence. The Lambeth Conference had also given its tacit approval, but Gray had still to find a candidate.

In January 1867 Gray nominated W.K. Macrorie, vicar of St James's Accrington, to be bishop of Natal. He now ran into a further round of difficulties, and it was another two years before the new bishop was consecrated. If Gray had been content to consecrate Macrorie in Cape Town no difficulty would have arisen. However, he was determined to hold the consecration in England to secure the imprimatur of the English Church upon all that he had done in the Colenso affair. Longley was very doubtful about how to respond to Gray, for this would have been the only consecration that had ever taken place in England without a mandate from the crown, and in the circumstances, it might have serious repercussions. Tait, however, was quite clear that this was not an act with which the English bishops should be associated in view of the delicate legal situation. Sir Roundell Palmer, the attorney general had advised that the consecration of a colonial bishop in England without a royal mandate would be a violation of the Act of Uniformity of 1662. He also wrote to the primus of the Scottish Episcopal Church to warn him that a significant number of the English bishops, while deprecating Colenso's opinions, could not associate themselves with the consecration of a successor to Colenso while the English courts held that his deposition by Gray was illegal.

The secretary for the colonies, the duke of Buckingham, also intervened, and confirmed that Colenso was, in English law, the bishop of Natal and insisted that Macrorie might only minister to members of the 'Church of South Africa' in Natal. He also required that Macrorie should not take his title from Natal or any place in the colony. Gray obeyed this ruling in the letter, though not in the spirit, by nominating Macrorie bishop of Maritzburg (the common abbreviation of Pietermaritzburg). Buckingham thereupon withdrew his objection and invited the archbishop of Canterbury to apply for a royal licence to consecrate the new bishop.

However, on hearing that the new bishop was to be consecrated by royal mandate, the dean of the cathedral at Pietermaritzburg threatened to withdraw from fund-raising for the new diocese, and to meet Macrorie on his arrival in the diocese with a formal protest, for fear that the new bishop, created in this way, would also be immune from the Church courts. When the duke of Buckingham raised further problems about the consecration, Gray losing patience consecrated Macrorie himself on his own authority in Cape Town in January 1869.

Macrorie's consecration in Cape Town on 25 January 1869 illustrates well the enormous difficulty of communications for bishops in colonial provinces, and one of the practical reasons why they seldom met and preferred consecrations of new bishops to take place in England. The bishop of the Orange Free State had to travel 1,800 miles by wagon in 'an African Summer over an African desert' to make up the quorum of three bishops to consecrate Macrorie.

It was necessary to raise money to establish the new diocese, for almost all the property of the diocese of Natal and the church buildings and control of certain reserves for Africans had been vested in Colenso by the Privy Council's decision, although he could not attract clergy or additional funds to maintain them. A large sum of money was collected in England for the new diocese, further reassuring Gray of the implicit support of the English Church. He took the balance of what was needed from a fund he had been accumulating to found a new diocese of George. The SPG also gave Macrorie their financial backing. Seventeen of the twenty clergy in the diocese on his arrival gave their allegiance to Macrorie rather than Colenso. However, the European laity seem to have been fairly evenly divided in their allegiance between the two bishops, and Colenso continued to have a strong following among black Africans. Because he was unable to recruit suitable clergy to work with him, Colenso largely devoted himself to securing political and social justice for Africans.[25]

Colenso died in 1883 and Archbishop Benson tried to persuade Macrorie to resign, on the expectation that he would be elected bishop of Blomfontein, but he declined. The Church council, which Colenso had set up in Natal, as the equivalent of a diocesan synod, elected a bishop and approached Benson with a request to consecrate him as bishop of the diocese of 'the Church of England in Natal'. Benson declined without consulting the bishop of Cape Town, who as metropolitan of the 'Church of the Province of South Africa', felt affronted at the archbishop's appearing to assume superior authority over the province of South Africa.

Eventually, in 1891 Macrorie resigned as bishop of Maritzburg allowing for the appointment of a successor, whom it was hoped would be able to unite in himself the two rival jurisdictions. Because of the importance of securing someone who would be acceptable to the laity of both jurisdictions, the bishop of Cape Town offered to allow the archbishop of Canterbury, whose jurisdiction was acceptable to the 'Church of England in Natal' to nominate a candidate. However, the largely lay Natal Church council refused to accept anyone as their bishop who had already signed, or was willing to sign, the constitution of the Church of the Province of South Africa, which in their view, would be an acknowledgement of the existence of the province, and of the authority of the bishop of Cape Town. The bishops of the province, on the other hand, required that the new bishop should sign the constitution, and so acknowledge the authority of the province. The electoral assembly of the diocese of Maritzburg agreed to the bishop of Cape Town's request to allow the archbishop of Canterbury to nominate their bishop, but insisted that the new bishop should sign the constitution of the province and give an oath of obedience to the bishop of Cape Town as metropolitan. Unfortunately Archbishop Benson did not clear up these difficulties with his nominee Arthur Hamilton Baynes, who had been Benson's domestic chaplain, and had only recently been appointed vicar of Christ Church, Greenwich, and he refused to sign the constitution of the Church council of the diocese of Natal, and to administer that jurisdiction as a separate diocese. Although by this action initially he had alienated the Church council, at length he won over all but one of the parishes of the diocese of Natal to accept his jurisdiction as a bishop of the Church of the Province of South Africa.[26]

The very long, drawn out Colenso affair revealed how uncertain was the precise constitutional position of the Church in South Africa. It was clear that it could not exist as an established Church, but the court rulings had suggested that it was hardly yet an independent organization. No one really knew precisely what the relationship was between an unestablished Church in the colonies and the Church of England 'as by law established'. Until 1861 the relationship between the Church in South Africa and in England was believed to have depended on a legal entity, as well as a vague undefined concept of 'communion' implying a common faith and an agreement on essential matters of worship and doctrine. When the legal entity proved to be illusory, only the concept of 'communion' was left to link Anglicans in South Africa and elsewhere. Until the first Lambeth Conference 'Anglican Communion' was merely a vague sentiment, but the conference had helped to make the concept of 'Anglican Communion' more real in the eyes of the bishops at least, and it had made suggestions about how the provinces of the Anglican Communion outside England might conduct their affairs.

From 1860 the South African bishops had begun to formulate a constitution. The real author of their constitution was the evangelical Henry Cotterill who was bishop of Grahamstown. Step by step he and Gray created the machinery to make the Church in South Africa a voluntary association. The first step was to establish diocesan synods, the first meeting of which sealed a compact between the bishop, clergy and laity of each diocese. The province was then welded into a single association by the bishops meeting together and agreeing to invite the clergy and representatives of the laity to join them. In 1869, in the absence of the formal structure of diocesan, provincial and 'patriarchal' synod, which Gray and Selwyn had wished the Lambeth Conference to institute, the South African bishops met and formally adopted the principles set out in the conference resolution on the government of an independent province, and invited representatives of the clergy and the laity of their dioceses to meet with them as a provincial synod in 1870. The legislation which the provincial synod passed at its first session was designed to create a voluntary association, which recognized and accepted the jurisdiction of the bishops. The legislation also declared that the province could not be bound by the decisions of any legal tribunal other than its own courts or of 'such other tribunal as may be accept by the provincial synod', thus excluding the jurisdiction of the Judicial Committee of the Privy Council. As any new diocese chose to join the association, so it might send representatives of the clergy and laity along with its bishop to take part in the synod. The canons passed by the provincial synod in 1870 were modelled on those which had been adopted by the provincial synods in Canada and New Zealand. The constitution was submitted to Sir Roundell Palmer, before it was finally adopted by the synod.[27]

The disputes within the South African Church over the authority of their bishops and their relationship with the Church of England were still not over. In the 1870s a dispute broke out between the dean of the cathedral in Grahamstown and the bishop of Grahamstown. The dean claimed that, because the cathedral had been constituted as a parish church by an ordinance of the colonial assembly in 1839, before there was a bishop, the bishop had no authority over the cathedral. When the bishop took the case to the South African supreme court, the chief justice ruled that, in law, the province, because it had rejected the authority of the Privy Council, was different from the Church of England and therefore could not claim property that had been given to the Church of England. The bishop then appealed to the Privy Council, as the final court of appeal from the colonial judicature, whose Judicial Committee ruled that the province was legally a different church from the Church of England, because it had excluded appeal to the Privy Council, from its provincial court, which the Committee held was an essential part of the standards of the faith and doctrine of the Church of England. Thus the bishops of the province were still in an uncertain relationship with institutions which predated the formation of the province, if anyone chose to legally contest their authority.[28]

Nor were the problems over the appointment and consecration of bishops at an end. Gray was anxious to create a new diocese for Zululand, which was neither part of South Africa nor a British territory. Miss Mackenzie, the sister of the late bishop of the Zambezi had raised a considerable sum of money in England for a memorial for her brother, and when Gray was in England for the Lambeth Conference in 1867 he had met Miss Mackenzie and discussed with her the possibility of using the money to endow a new diocese for Zululand. She agreed to this and Gray also undertook a preaching tour to raise additional funds. However, there was no recognized procedure for appointing a bishop for a missionary diocese in the province of South Africa. The agreed procedures in the new constitution only applied to an existing diocese, where a bishop must be elected by the clergy and laity, but as yet no diocese existed. Given past experience, it would be unthinkable to seek letters patent from the crown for the consecration, and anyway, Zululand was not British territory. The logical deduction to be made from Gray's scheme for missionary bishops was that the bishops of the province should themselves appoint and consecrate a new bishop. The South African bishops agreed to ask the Colonial Bishoprics Fund to seek a suitable candidate, which would also ensure that most of the leading English bishops associated with the SPG would be involved with the appointment, and Samuel Wilberforce was authorized by the South African bishops to confirm the appointment on their behalf. When the new bishop was chosen the South African bishops then desired that he should be consecrated in England so that Miss Mackenzie and the contributors to the memorial fund might be present, but more importantly for the South African bishops, they would not have to make the very difficult journeys to Cape Town to consecrate him themselves. Little did they realize by this kind gesture what a storm of trouble they were about to unleash.

As we have seen, the colonial Church was going through a period of change which, in most dioceses, involved a process of 'quasi-disestablishment'. As bishops who had been appointed by letters patent issued by the crown died or retired and were succeeded by others who held no such state authority, or new dioceses were created without letters patent Archbishop Tait was aware that care and skill would be necessary to establish new procedures which would both preserve all possible connections with the still established Church of England, and secure for each colonial diocese or province a suitable means of autonomy. Following the ideas he had outlined in his letter to the colonial bishops in 1866, as archbishop of Canterbury Tait planned to pursue a policy during this transition period that would emphasize the existing connection between the Church of England and the colonial churches. He proposed to achieve this by observing an unwritten rule requiring any bishop consecrated in England by the archbishop of Canterbury for a diocese outside the Queen's dominions, to take an oath of canonical obedience to the see of Canterbury, as representing the mother Church from which, in some sense, his mission was derived.

Tait, therefore, required T.E. Wilkinson, who had been nominated bishop of Zululand, to take an oath of obedience, as required by the Prayer Book ordinal, to himself. Gray, with a stern disregard for Tait's attempt to make sense of the anomalies of the situation, made it clear to the bishop-designate and to the archbishop that he would not permit a bishop in his province to owe obedience to the metropolitan of another province. In his view, it would make nonsense of his metropolitical status. Tait responded that he was unable to 'alter at his individual discretion the oath prescribed in the Consecration service', but he would approve any such consecration taking place, if required, in Cape Town or elsewhere, where no such limitations were imposed by law.

Before the matter could be resolved Tait was taken ill and commissioned the bishop of London to consecrate the new bishop in his stead. The archbishop of York, Thomson, now intervened, and insisted that he was the proper person to perform the consecration and to receive the oath in the absence of the archbishop of Canterbury. Thomson was a violent opponent of everything that Gray stood for and had been trying to achieve in South Africa. He had refused to attend the Lambeth Conference in 1867 because he had suspected that Gray and Selwyn might be scheming to weaken the legal position of the established Church in England and the colonies, and to create some new ecclesiastical authority other than the crown.

Thomson thus insisted that Wilkinson should take an oath of obedience to himself as archbishop of York, although he announced that the oath might be transferred to the bishop of Cape Town.

Wilkinson thus arrived in Cape Town as bishop of Zululand and a suffragan of the archbishop of York. Gray, who had not been informed of the subsequent changes in the procedures, was furious. He refused to admit that a bishop who had taken an oath of obedience to one metropolitan could transfer it to another who was not his rightful heir and successor. The hapless Wilkinson thus had to depart for Zululand as a suffragan of the archbishop of York, not the bishop of Cape Town. Gray also refused to allow Wilkinson to be invited to sign the constitution of the province of South Africa, or to attend any meetings of bishops. He was determined that Wilkinson should not in any way be associated with his province. Fortunately, before the next session of the provincial synod Wilkinson resigned, so that no difficult questions were raised as to whether he should be invited to sign the constitution and attend the synod, and Gray's conduct of the matter was thus not called into question.[29]

The whole matter was finally resolved by British parliamentary legislation in 1874, with the Colonial Clergy Act, which provided for the consecration of colonial metropolitans without requiring them to take an oath of canonical obedience, thus releasing metropolitans from any duty of obedience to another metropolitan who had consecrated them, even the archbishop of Canterbury. This gave effective independence from Canterbury to the metropolitans of other provinces. The Act also contained clauses that regularized the position in England of clergy ordained overseas, and permitted them to hold licences to work in the Church of England, which had not previously been legal. These clauses required that any clergy ordained by colonial bishops wishing to officiate or preach in a parish in the Church of England must have the written permission of the archbishop of Canterbury or York and the written consent of the diocesan bishop, and that only after working as a curate for two years might a priest ordained overseas apply to an English bishop for a licence.

While on the one hand the metropolitans of other provinces were granted freedom, on the other hand it was made clear that clergy they ordained might only serve in the Church of England under strict conditions. There in fact seems to have been considerable antipathy towards clergy who had either originated in the colonies, or who had trained specifically for ordination in the colonies. There was a very strong implication that men who had trained at the specifically missionary colleges, such as St Augustine's College, Canterbury, the Dorchester Missionary College or St Peter's College, Burgh le Marsh, had received an inferior training to candidates for ordination in England, and that they were not necessarily suitable for work in English parishes.[30]

Even Tait, with his high view of the relationship between Church and State, could run into difficulties dealing with the British government, as is illustrated over his desire to establish a bishopric in Madagascar. Missionary work had originally begun in Madagascar in 1818 when a group from the London Missionary Society (LMS) began to work there. They were expelled by the ruler in 1833, but when the island was reopened to traders and missionaries in 1861, and the missionaries returned, they found that in their absence Christianity had flourished. The Bishop of Mauritius also visited the island and, after conferring with the missionaries, drew up an informal agreement that while the LMS continued to work in the capital, the CMS might send missionaries to work in the coastal areas under the bishop's supervision. A few years later Samuel Wilberforce and the SPG supported by the bishop of Mauritius, began to campaign for a bishop in Madagascar. The LMS committee, supported by Lord Shaftesbury, lobbied the government against this proposal, and when in 1873 Tait requested a royal licence to consecrate a bishop for Madagascar, the request was refused. Bishop Gray reacted angrily to this, suggesting that it provided good grounds for the disestablishment of the Church of England. Tait, however, interpreted it more calmly, as an instance of the lay element in the Church not endorsing the proposal. However, he did suggest to the SPG that they should approach the Scottish bishops, who proved willing to consecrate Kestell Cornish as a missionary bishop for Madagascar.[31]

The substitution of the practice of appointing bishops by the archbishop of Canterbury by 'Royal warrant under the Sign Manual and Signet' instead of by royal letters patent in British crown colonies also caused problems for newly appointed bishops in those territories. When John Shaw Burdon arrived in

Hong Kong as bishop in 1874, W.H. Baynes the chaplain to the Missions to Seamen at West Point on the island refused to receive the bishop's licence, and denied that the bishop had any authority over him. He claimed that the bishop 'was merely a private person with no jurisdiction, and indeed no connection with any clergyman of the Church of England excepting that of friendly feeling'. The bishop complained to Archbishop Tait, who presumably consulted the British government, for in May 1875 Lord Derby, the foreign secretary wrote to the British consuls in the Treaty Ports in China which were in the diocese of Hong Kong stating that the 'Bishop's superintendence of all Anglican Ministers and Congregations within his Diocese had been ordered: all Consuls were to assist the Bishop by informing all concerned, and they were themselves to show due deference to the Bishop'. In addition Lord Carnarvon, the colonial secretary wrote to the administrator of Hong Kong, in the absence of the governor, expressing the view that the new bishop had not succeeded to the status of the late bishop of Victoria, but he thought that 'the Colonial Chaplain and all the clergy and laity would naturally give recognition due to any holder of the episcopal office', and added that since he could not imagine that there could be any difference of opinion about this, he did not propose to take any special measures to secure the recognition of the bishop. The British Admiralty also ordered all naval chaplains to recognize the authority of the bishop.[32]

THE DISESTABLISHMENT OF THE CHURCH OF IRELAND

In 1869 another dimension was added to the Anglican Communion when the United Church of England and Ireland was divided and the Church of Ireland was disestablished. While in South Africa Bishop Gray had struggled to free his Church from the intricacies of its involvement with the British State, in Ireland the British government intervened to divide the United Church of England and Ireland, and separate the Church of Ireland from the State, against the wills of the bishops, clergy and people of the Church of Ireland, and many in the Church of England. This was a culmination of a policy that British governments had been following since the 1830s, and as has been noted earlier, had already led to the disestablishment of the

Anglican dioceses in Canada and the West Indies. In Ireland, as we have seen, the Reformation had never taken deep roots in the hearts of the majority of the Irish people, largely due to the policies of British governments as well as the clergy and laity of the Church of Ireland, and from the 1830s there had been a major revival of Roman Catholicism in Ireland, which had become increasingly identified with Irish nationalism.

The Churches of England and Ireland had been united in 1801, by the Act of Union of Great Britain and Ireland, as part of an attempt to produce an arrangement that would defuse a possible rebellion in Ireland and make the country more governable by the British during the Napoleonic Wars. Subsequently a major wedge had been driven between the Church and the State in Ireland as well as in England in 1829 by the passage of the Roman Catholic Emancipation Act which had been another attempt to pacify Ireland. Gladstone's immediate reasons for governmental intervention in the Irish Church was again unrest in Ireland. The Fenian outrages in England in 1867, and particularly the attack on Clerkenwell prison in December 1867, in which twelve people were killed and 120 were injured, caused Gladstone to believe that the state of Ireland was a danger to the peace and stability of the England and that the disestablishment of the Church in Ireland would be an important step towards settling Ireland.

Since 1864 Cardinal Cullen, the Roman Catholic archbishop of Armagh, had been campaigning for the disestablishment of the Church of Ireland and had been working closely with the nonconformist British Liberation Society, which wished to secure both the disestablishment and the disendowment of the Churches of Ireland and England. The combined efforts of the two groups had ensured that during the second half of the 1860s the Irish Church question was canvassed throughout the British Isles. By 1868 it was clear to Liberal politicians, and especially Gladstone, that the Irish Church question needed to be resolved with dispatch. Gladstone had arrived at his decision, and his proposal for a solution, however, independently of the agitation, but the agitation did convince the majority of liberal members of the British Parliament, and the majority of the British electorate, that disestablishment in Ireland was essential.

As leader of the Liberal party Gladstone made disestablishment of the Church of Ireland party policy, and attacked the

Conservative government on their Irish policy. This mobilized the nonconformist vote. With the support of the nonconformists and Roman Catholics, boosted in their electoral influence by the extension of the franchise, especially in towns, as a result of the Reform Act of 1868, Gladstone swept the conservatives from power and won the 1868 general election with a majority of 112 seats.[33]

In the early days of the agitation the Irish bishops had confidentially proposed to the British government a bill to abolish seventeen of the thirty Irish cathedrals, and to redistribute their endowments to achieve a minimum stipend of £300 a year for the Irish clergy. Palmerston's government in 1864 had declined to support the bill. Unfortunately, as it turned out, the Irish bishops did not introduce the bill into the House of Lords, so that their willingness to promote reform was never known. In June 1867 the Conservative government had set up a royal commission to consider the position of the Church of Ireland, but its report in July 1869 was too late to influence the new developments following Gladstone's accession to power.

In March 1868 Gladstone had introduced three resolutions into the House of Commons for the disestablishment of the Church of Ireland, and had carried them against Disraeli's government, which subsequently resigned. Gladstone himself largely drafted the parliamentary bill to bring about the disestablishment of the Church in Ireland. He based his draft bill on the Canadian precedent. In 1853 he had been a member of Lord Aberdeen's government which had passed an Act to empower the Canadian legislature to deprive the Anglican Church in Canada of the lands which had been set apart for the support of the clergy, after which, in 1854, the Canadian parliament had passed an act to effect this, reserving a life interest in the land to existing clergy. The Canadian Act had allowed the Anglican clergy to commute their life interests in the land by accepting a lump sum in lieu of their right to an annuity; this they had handed over to the Church authorities, who had taken over the payment of the annuity, while having the capital to invest. At the same time the Canadian Church had been disestablished and had, as we have seen, set up its own synodical system. Gladstone had taken the opportunity of the Canadian bishops' visit to London for the Lambeth Conference in 1867 to talk to them, particularly the bishop of Montreal, about how this had worked.

The Irish bishops held aloof and refused to negotiate with Gladstone over a bill they detested, but there seems to have been little opposition in England compared with the opposition sparked off by Keble in his assize sermon in 1833 opposing the British government's intervention in the Church of Ireland merely to amalgamate a number of dioceses. Perhaps the Fenian atrocities in England had alienated even the High Church supporters who might have been expected to oppose the State's intervention to disendow an Anglican Church. The form of disestablishment and disendowment proposed by Gladstone was total. In this he was following the example of his traditional High Church friends among the colonial bishops, Selwyn and Gray. The Church of Ireland was to be placed in the same position as any religious body in Ireland, but it was given power to reorganize itself.

The Irish bishops had requested permission to convene the Irish convocations in 1861, 1862, 1863 and in 1865. They had been alarmed by the proposals in the revived English convocations to revise canons, which if they had accepted the revisions in Ireland without calling the Irish convocations and seeking their approval, would have been to tacitly surrender the independence of their Church to the Church of England. The British government, however, had ignored their requests. In 1865, however, they received a reply that they were 'mistaken in supposing that the Irish Church had any convocations, [and] that in fact such a body did not exist'. In 1867 an agitation had begun among the Irish clergy, led by William Magee, the dean of Cork, for calling the Irish convocations. The clergy were distrustful of the bishops for not having called a provincial synod, and for not being more active in lobbying the government against disestablishment. They had formed the impression that the bishops were trying to retain power to themselves, and that they were unenthusiastic about holding convocations, and that they wished to let the matter drop.

When Gladstone received a memorial from the Irish bishops in September 1868 requesting a meeting of the convocations, he indicated that he would be happy to advise the cabinet to allow them to be called to discuss the terms of disestablishment, but not if they only wanted to oppose disestablishment. In the absence of any public action by the Irish bishops, Archdeacon Stopford of Kells offered to act as an unofficial representative of the Church of Ireland to the Liberal government. He asked Gladstone to allow a lay and clerical synod to be held in Ireland, on the precedent of those already set up in Canada and Australia, but without power to make legally binding canons. Gladstone consulted the attorney general for Ireland, and then decided not to encourage such a meeting. However, he did decide to use Stopford as his Irish Church agent. It was Stopford who introduced the idea of the commutation of the salaries payable to the existing clergy under the draft legislation, based on his knowledge of the procedures used when government grants were withdrawn from the clergy in the Anglican Church in Canada, and Gladstone, who was also aware of the precedent introduced it into his bill.

Gladstone also sought support from the English bishops. They feared that disestablishment in Ireland would be a precedent for disestablishment in England. Samuel Wilberforce saw the need for compromise in order to secure the best terms, and advised Archbishop Trench of Dublin to that effect. Wilberforce agreed to support Gladstone in the House of Lords, and recruited William Magee, now bishop of Peterborough, and bishops Jacobson of Chester and Connop Thirlwall of St Davids to support the bill.

The purposes of Gladstone's bill were fourfold. First, to sever all official relations between the Irish religious denominations and the State. Second, to create an interim agency to facilitate the transition between the eras of establishment and disestablishment. Third, to create a body to continue the work of the Church of Ireland. Fourth, to sequestrate surplus church funds and to apply them to the general welfare of the Irish people. The English bishops realized that the Liberal majority in the House of Commons was too large for them to ignore, and that the Conservative opposition in the House of Lords was too disunited for the bill to fail there, and that if the bill was defeated by the bishops' votes a constitutional crisis would be risked. In the event the two English archbishops and ten English bishops abstained in the crucial vote after the second reading of the bill in the Lords, and it was passed on 29 July 1869.

The Act set 1 January 1871 as the date of disestablishment of the Church of Ireland and of the dissolution of its union with the Church of England. After that the Irish bishops would be disqualified from sitting in the House of Lords, and the ecclesiastical courts would be abolished as law courts of the realm. The representative body established under the Act would have responsibility for arranging the commutation of the clergy's life interests in the endowments of the Church, for churches, and for arranging the sale of parsonage houses and glebe land. As a result it would become the crucial body for the Church. Otherwise the Church was to be disendowed and all other endowments, including tithe rent charges were to be sold off by three commissioners and used, after 1881, for the benefit of the Irish people to relieve 'unavoidable suffering'.

There were serious tensions within the Church of Ireland over the implications of self-government and over what sort of church it was going to be, and notably over whether the Prayer Book really embodied the doctrines and liturgy the Church would wish to have. The debate on the form of the constitution was therefore conducted in the knowledge that review of the Prayer Book was certain to come before the new central legislative body. The question of what forms of legislation would best promote or obstruct revision was a major preoccupation. The Church started, however, with the advantage that the PECUSA, and the Anglican Churches in Canada and New Zealand had already faced the problem. Their constitutions were available to Irish churchmen in a single volume, published in 1868 by William Sherlock, a County Meath clergyman. He drew attention to the fact that in the PECUSA power, in respect to finance and patronage had been granted to the laity to an extent which was detrimental to the general interests of the Church.

On 6 August 1869 the Irish bishops published a resolution that a general synod, in which clergy and laity should be 'fully and equally represented' should meet as early as possible. They proposed that provincial synods of the clergy, which were in fact the old convocations, should meet to consider the representation of the clergy. The clergy were still suspicious of the bishops' motives, and were also divided among themselves whether dignitaries should be excluded from the clerical representation.

On 18 August, in a letter summoning provincial synods of clergy, the archbishops expressed the hope that the laity would arrange their own representation. A group of leading laymen met later that month, and although there was some demand that they should act alone, they agreed to petition the archbishops to secure the election of lay representatives from each diocese.

The provincial synods met together on 14–16 September in Dublin, and agreed that questions of doctrine should not be limited to discussion by the clergy and that there should be no *ex officio* seats in the synod and also settled on a franchise for the clergy. The lay conference met for three days a month later, also in Dublin, under the presidency of the archbishops. Meetings had previously been held in parishes which had sent representatives to diocesan conferences, and the diocesan conferences had elected representatives to the lay conference. After some sharp disagreements it was agreed that in a synod the clergy and laity might vote separately, but put aside the question of whether bishops should vote separately. They also recommended that there should be two lay representatives to each clergy representative, because, it was alleged, lay people would often be unable to attend synod meetings. A scheme was carried that gave weight to population in the election of the general convention, which would disadvantage the less populous southern and western dioceses. They recommended that the franchise for the convention should be church membership, to be established by declaration of membership by men aged twenty-one and over. The lay conference also proposed that a committee, consisting of all the bishops and two clergy and two laity from each diocese, should be appointed to plan the convention.

The basic problem in setting up a new framework for the Church of Ireland was the merging of the principle of religious democracy and lay power, with apostolic hierarchy and clerical prestige. To satisfy both the clerical and the lay interests, the drafting committee developed an ingenious pyramid of synods and committees, varying from parish vestries to the general synod. On each of these levels considerable power was to be given to the laity, while various *ex officio* and veto powers were to be granted to the clergy and bishops. The ascending arrangement of synods resembled those of dissenting and presbyterian churches, while the arrangements for clergy and bishops remained that of an historic, catholic Church. There was thus an attempt to merge the principles of congregationalism and episcopacy. It was recommended that the general synod should consist of two houses, a house of bishops, and a house of representatives, including representatives of the clergy and the laity, and that normally the two houses should meet together, but that voting should be by orders. Thus the bishops would have an effective veto on all legislation. The general synod, it was recommended, should meet every three years, and have powers over doctrine, discipline and diocesan arrangements. Diocesan synods should reflect the arrangements for the general synod, with voting by houses.

The general convention met on 15 February 1870 to consider the draft. There was a strong, but not dominant anti-episcopal group in the convention who tried to remove the episcopal veto. But the laity did force a compromise by which the house of bishops would be required to have a two-thirds majority before exercising their veto. It was agreed that there should be no modification in the 'articles, doctrines, rites, rubrics, or formularies of the Church' except by two-thirds majorities of each order at two successive meetings of the synod. A representative body, comprising the bishops, and one clergyman and two lay people elected by each diocesan conference, and twelve co-opted members, was agreed which would hold the property of the Church, and be accountable to the general synod.

The proposals for diocesan synods were also agreed and that they should be responsible for electing the bishop, for uniting or dividing parishes, and for appointing a nominating board to help in the choice of parochial clergy. It was agreed that there should be a vestry in each parish, elected by the church members. The laity, however, pressed for more representation in the church courts, so that diocesan courts should consist of the bishop, the chancellor (a legally qualified layman), a clergyman and a layman, and for the court of the general synod to consist of two bishops and three laymen, rather than three bishops and three laymen, as the drafting committee had proposed, thus reducing the bishops' powers over the ecclesiastical courts. It was recommended that the diocese of Armagh should elect a bishop who should then attend a bishops' meeting at which the primate of all Ireland should be elected, and, if the bishop-elect of Armagh were not elected he should become bishop of the diocese vacated by the archbishop-elect. The changes in the draft constitution by the general convention considerably strengthened the popular element in the Church of Ireland, and weakened the power of the bishops. However, the bishops still had considerable power. Providing they could achieve a two-thirds majority among themselves, they possessed an absolute veto, and voting by orders protected the position of the clergy in the diocesan and general synods.

In due course, although the Church lost its tithe rent charges and endowments at disestablishment, the Church of Ireland became self-financing. The Church was fortunate that its laymen included some of the ablest financial names in Ireland, who were willing to serve on the Representative Church Body. Their shrewd investment policies served the Church well. In the course of 1870 the Representative Church Body raised a 'sustenation fund' which attracted £229,754, and by 1889 it had raised £3,733,180 which was very impressive.

However, the members of the Church regarded themselves as having been betrayed by the English bishops in the House of Lords and they deeply resented the attacks made on them by English High Churchmen alleging their extreme Protestantism. This accusation arose from the revision of the canons of the Church of Ireland in 1871, governing public worship, against the wishes of the bishops, which was designed to exclude any possibility of ritualist practices, anxiety about which had arisen from some very moderate ritualist activities in three Dublin parishes in the 1860s, and the revision of the Prayer Book in 1878 in a considerably more Protestant direction. The bishops, recognizing the strength of lay feeling, and the importance of lay funding, achieved a compromise which avoided extreme revision of the Prayer Book, and any confrontation which might have been provoked by the use of their veto. The Irish bishops also lost their regular meetings with the English bishops whom they thought, probably rightly, had no interest in them or in the Irish Church. After disestablishment the Church of Ireland tended to become inward looking and isolated from the rest of the Anglican Communion. From the 1780s the great majority of the Irish bishops and most of the Irish clergy were Irish-born and were also graduates of Trinity College, Dublin, and after 1870 this became almost invariable. Whilst Irish clergy served in other parts of the Anglican Communion, it was unusual for clergy of other provinces to work in Ireland.

The disestablishment of the Church of Ireland was highly significant for the Anglican Communion and the relationships between Church and State. It was the most deliberate breach so far between the Church and the State in a British dominion, and it was to have important implications for the future of other churches, as well as for the long-term political relationship between Ireland and Great Britain. In due course the constitution of the Irish Church provided the model for the Church in Ceylon when it was disestablished. The Church of Ireland was also seen as an object lesson for other churches in the need to identify with the population of a country, and with their culture and institutions. The CMS journal, *The Intelligencer* was edited by Joseph Ridgeway a graduate of Trinity College, Dublin, who regularly quoted the Church of Ireland as an example of a church that had failed in missionary endeavour. He alleged that this was because it had employed English bishops, and had not used the language of the people, and appeared to be the church of the conquerors. What was regarded as the weakness of the Church of Ireland encouraged the CMS in the 1870s to a policy of seeking to integrate the Church fully with the culture of whatever country it found itself in.[34] The working out of that policy is the subject of the next chapter.

CHAPTER 6

Mission and Empire

By the first Lambeth Conference the Anglican Communion may have stretched across the world, but it largely existed to meet the spiritual needs of English settlers overseas. The first sixty years of the nineteenth century had, in fact, seen only a modest amount of missionary activity from Britain. Until 1867, most Anglican overseas dioceses had been established in areas of British emigration. Thirty-two of the dioceses were in Canada, Australia, New Zealand, South Africa and the West Indies; whereas although India was a very significant part of the Empire, it had only three dioceses, and an additional diocese in Ceylon. If Jerusalem and the East, and Gibraltar are discounted, as also catering for the needs of expatriates, there were only eight dioceses by 1867 which could be regarded as in any way 'missionary dioceses' – Victoria (Hong Kong) established in 1848, Sierra Leone in 1852, Mauritius in 1854, Labuan and Sarawak in 1855, the Zambezi (subsequently Zanzibar and East Africa) in 1861, Honolulu in 1861, Melanesia in 1861 and the Niger in 1864. While some attention had been given to missionary work among the indigenous inhabitants in North America, India, New Zealand and, to a lesser extent, South Africa and Australia, and this had been supported by the missionary societies, it was not a major priority in the establishment of dioceses.

The great Christian missionary surge from Western Europe came in the last third of the nineteenth century. By contrast with the earlier period, of the Anglican dioceses established between 1868 and 1900, twenty-one were in missionary areas – six in Africa (apart from South Africa), three in China, three in Japan, three in the Pacific, and one in Korea, and five new dioceses were established in India – while only ten new dioceses were created in areas of considerable British migration – six in Canada and four in Australia. Between 1866 and 1900 the

PECUSA also established four new overseas missionary dioceses (Haiti, Tokyo, Brazil and Kyoto). However, given the very strong preponderance of British settlement represented by the Anglican dioceses, it is perhaps not surprising that by 1900 there had only been two black diocesan bishops (of Haiti and the Niger).

AFRICA

Some explanation is needed as to why, in spite of the attentions of the CMS in West Africa, and the establishment of a diocese of Sierra Leone in 1852 and of the Niger in 1864, and the energies of the South African Church and the CMS, the SPG, and the Universities Mission to Central Africa (UMCA), and the establishment of the diocese of the Zambezi (subsequently Zanzibar and East Africa) in 1861, still relatively few Anglican dioceses had been established in Africa (apart from South Africa) by 1900. In fact the spread of Christianity, and Anglicanism in particular, in Africa was slow.

It is a commonplace of the history of Christian missions in the nineteenth century that the expansion of Christianity during the century is not merely explained by imperialism. Indeed British and Anglican missionaries were often in areas of Africa and elsewhere long before they were annexed to the British crown. Also, not all territories that were annexed to the British crown proved fertile soil in which to plant the Anglican Church; there were, as we have seen, comparatively few Anglicans in India, other than South India, apart from English settlers and Anglo-Indians. Similarly, even after the so-called 'race for Africa' among the European powers after the Congress of Berlin, in 1878, when a very considerable portion of Africa came under British rule, there were comparatively few Anglican dioceses set up in colonial Africa – roughly one for each colony.

Anglican missionary activity had begun in Africa in the mid-eighteenth century, when in 1752 the SPG sent Thomas Thompson who, while working for the Society in New Jersey, volunteered to work as a chaplain at Cape Coast Castle, in what is now Ghana, among black Africans. He made little progress, but did send three boys to England to be educated, one of whom, Philip Quaque, a native of the Gold Coast was ordained by the bishop of London in 1765 as 'Mission School Master and

Catechist to the Negros of the Gold Coast'. He then succeeded Thompson as chaplain to the Castle and continued to work there for fifty years, until his death in 1816. As a missionary he had little success. Nevertheless there came from his small school men who, a generation later, were among the leaders of the struggling coastal church. Two of them, John Martin and Joseph Smith, eventually wrote in 1834 to the Wesleyan Missionary Society to invite them to send missionaries to the Gold Coast.[1] The first major Anglican initiative in Africa was by the CMS in 1804 in Sierra Leone.

In the 1780s Anglican evangelicals began to developing a strategy to fulfil God's will by bringing in the millennium and extending the knowledge of the Christian gospel over all the earth so as to initiate a turning of the nations to Christ in such a way that the kingdoms of this world would become the kingdom of Christ. This strategy emerged from a number of causes, including the rising tide of English evangelicalism which saw the British churches as having a providential role under God, revealed by the success of British colonial expansion, to preach the gospel to all nations; the late eighteenth-century British sense that British culture and institutions provided the yardstick for measuring civilization; and a growing willingness among English merchants to establish overseas bases that might be used for evangelical outreach. Mission was also stimulated by an increasing knowledge of India, as a result of the publicity surrounding the activities of Warren Hastings and Robert Clive, and of the South Seas, as a result of the publication of Captain Cook's *Voyages* with accounts of the Pacific.[2]

In the 1780s Granville Sharp, who in 1772 had been the chief instrument in securing Lord Mansfield's judgement that, 'as soon as any slave sets foot on English soil he becomes free', and was also a member of the evangelical Clapham Sect, had set up the Committee for Relieving the Black Poor to resettle in Sierra Leone an estimated 20,000 or more black slaves who had been freed in Britain, or who had fought for the British in the American War of Independence on the basis of being promised land if they supported the British. On losing the War the British had offered them settlement in Nova Scotia, but there the freed slaves had quickly realized that they were at the end of a long queue of white settlers also hoping for grants of land. They had leaped at the new opportunity that they were offered in Sierra

Leone, where they were seen as a spearhead for Christianizing Africa.

The British government agreed to pay for the passages of the former slaves to Africa. In 1787 a convoy of ships sailed with 351 black and sixty white settlers, accompanied by a chaplain appointed by the SPG. Nearly all the settlers perished from the effects of the climate, or in disputes with the local rulers, with whom the settlement had not been negotiated. In 1791 a new initiative was begun when the Sierra Leone Company was formed, under the direction of another member of the Clapham Sect, Henry Thornton, with the object of substituting legitimate trade for the slave trade. Subsequently Zachary Macauley, another member of the Sect, served as governor of Sierra Leone. In 1792 a further group of freed black slaves who had settled in Nova Scotia were offered land in Sierra Leone. Many of them were Christians, and they too were expected to launch an Anglican mission in Africa. However, they also found the climate difficult, and the local rulers unwilling to grant them good land for cultivating and were rapidly disillusioned and frustrated by their experiences. The difficulties were compounded by the inflation on the cost of goods purchased from Britain caused by the French Wars and the sacking of Freetown by a French fleet in 1794. The black settlers also resented the quit rents imposed on their lands by the Sierra Leone Company, and in 1800 they rebelled, and the rebellion was put down with the help of non-Christian forces. The members of the Clapham Sect involved in the Company were disappointed at what they saw as the ingratitude of the black settlers, and also at the lack of profit produced by the Company.[3]

The CMS, which was founded in 1799, was unable because of the principles upon which it recruited its missionaries, to get any missionaries into the field until 1804, when it sent the first of a series of German Lutheran missionaries to Sierra Leone to reopen the Christian enterprise there. They began by establishing a school. However, this was not a success, because the children only spoke Susa, the local language, the medium of teaching was English, and the teachers were German.

In 1808 Sierra Leone was adopted as a British colony, and the policy was continued of settling freed slaves there, the numbers of whom increased after the abolition of slavery in the British colonies in 1807, and also of settling there slaves liberated from slave ships captured by British naval patrols. The slaves who were liberated from slave ships, had of course, no experience of anything European, nor of Christianity, nor the English language, unlike the freed slaves from the British colonies, and they rapidly outnumbered the Christian black settlers. Nor did it prove that the Christian black settlers were very well-inclined towards Anglicanism. Those who had been settled in Nova Scotia saw it as the religion of the white settlers who had been allocated land, and they were more attracted to the Methodist revivalist preachers whom they had also encountered in Nova Scotia, and it was this brand of Christianity that they brought with them to Sierra Leone.[4]

In 1816 the governor, Sir Charles MacCarthy, attempted a policy of Anglicizing and Christianizing the freed slaves settled from the slave ships. He organized a series of 'recognized villages', and envisaged each as a parish, with a church and a school at the centre of each parish. He invited the CMS to give up their unsuccessful work among the indigenous inhabitants and instead to work in civilizing and Christianizing the freed slaves, so as to turn Sierra Leone into an ordered Anglican society. Edward Bickersteth went out in 1816 on behalf of the CMS, and approved MacCarthy's proposal, and the Society took over the management of the villages. The scheme worked where the few English missionaries who could be recruited were stationed, but in 1824 MacCarthy was killed and the CMS withdrew because the British government had never put up sufficient funds to make the scheme viable.[5]

Although from the point of view of the CMS the scheme in Sierra Leone was a failure, from the point of view of the freed slaves it was a success. It gave them a land in which there was freedom for black Africans, and relative prosperity. It also introduced Christianity, and established a bridgehead for the Church in West Africa. In the 1830s the PECUSA also began missionary work among freed slaves from the USA in Liberia and was relatively successful.[6]

In the late 1830s it was beginning to be suggested that the failure of missionary work in Sierra Leone might be remedied if the obstacle of slavery could be removed. It was clear that an attractive economic alternative would need to be provided to persuade chiefs to abandon the trade and the promotion of legitimate trade with West Africa began to be seen as this alternative. Thomas Fowell Buxton in his *The African Slave Trade and Its Remedy* which was submitted to the British government for consideration for adoption for its colonial anti-slavery policies, before it was published in 1841, recommended that the British government should supplement its naval patrols along the West African coast by sending expeditions through the extensive waterways of the Niger delta and into the interior, in order to make treaties with chiefs, and to demonstrate what opportunities there might be for investing private capital to promote trade, to supersede the slave trade.

Buxton recommended breaking the power of the traditional rulers, who encouraged and supported the slave trade by selling prisoners-of-war into slavery in exchange for European commodities, by encouraging the development of a new commercial and industrial class, reflecting what had happened in Britain through industrialization and the evolution of a class system, which had broken the grasp on power of the *ancien régime* in England. Because the climate was clearly most unhealthy for Europeans, he recommended using Africans from Sierra Leone and the USA who had experienced the benefits of a capitalist society, as their agents. These Africans, however, would be guided by missionaries, who would train some of them as catechists and schoolmasters to preach Christianity, whilst others, as artisans and skilled craftsmen, would provide housing and furniture, to demonstrate the superiority of European and Christian styles of life, and by building roads and bridges, would open up the country for trade, and encourage the cultivation of crops like indigo and cotton, with which Africans might trade with European manufacturers, rather than slaves. Buxton claimed that 'Africa would present the finest field for the labours of Christian missionaries which the world had yet seen'.[7]

Buxton persuaded Lord Melbourne to sponsor a British government expedition to the Niger in 1841. The expedition included two CMS missionaries. It explored part of the Niger delta and established a model cotton plantation. However, it rapidly withdrew, because the climatic conditions were so unconducive to Europeans. Forty-five of the 150 Europeans taking part in the expedition died during the course of it. Although the British government decided not to take any further action, not having any intention at this time of establishing any further colonies in West Africa, the CMS was encouraged to promote missionary work in West Africa, and to attempt to fulfil Buxton's programme under their own auspices. Their aim was to promote a Christian civilization in West Africa. Contemporary British society, with its concern for the fruits of Christian living in successful trade and business ventures, and strong private and public morality, was seen as the example for all people to follow. Civilization and living out the implications of the Christian faith were seen as synonymous. Social customs were regarded as having religious significance, for example English Christian missionaries regarded lack of clothing as indecent and immoral. The CMS missionaries were also concerned to promote trade, believing that, as in England, it would encourage the development of a middle class who would in due course, as in England, promote social reforms. They wished to challenge and to transform African society, but in general, there was little desire for such changes among the inhabitants of the close-knit communal-based societies of the Niger delta and the interior of West Africa.[8]

However, in the 1840s some of the chiefs of the tribes established on the coast of the Niger delta were tolerant and encouraging of the CMS missionaries, most of whom were black, Sierra Leoneans, but included a few German Lutherans and even fewer English men, because they hoped that they would assist in restoring their trade, which had been damaged by the decline in the slave trade. The missionaries also recognized the importance of trade to support themselves and to provide them with transport along the coast. Traders too saw the missionaries as being useful by opening up new areas for trade. Some missionaries wished to involve the British government in this work. Henry Townsend, the leading CMS missionary on the Niger wished to identify the mission work with political influence. He was keen that a British consul should be appointed who would support the missionaries and, as an English Christian, would be a 'secular missionary' forwarding the work of trade and 'civilization'.[9]

The CMS mission to the Niger delta was not a great success. A number of important factors contributed to this. While Sierra Leonean missionaries could be recruited in adequate numbers, English missionaries were more difficult to recruit, and as so often in the past, German Lutheran missionaries from Basle were used, and there could be cultural, linguistic and theological tensions. There was also a tendency on the part of those directing mission strategy not to consolidate their work, but to move the missionaries on to open up new areas, leaving previous work to disintegrate. One reason for this was that the congregations and individuals in England who contributed to collections for the Society's work, expected a rapid return on their contributions in the form of reports of new converts and the opening of new mission stations. There was a pressure for tangible results which militated against real consolidation.

However, perhaps the greatest barrier to the spread of Christianity was the culture clash between the missionaries' understanding of Christianity and the African understanding of religion. For the African, religion permeated every part of existence, there was no separation of the sacred and the secular. Every action had religious connotations, and the organization of life, and the structure of society partook of the sacred. For Africans, identity came from belonging to their village, their tribe, and belonging required participation in social customs, such as initiation rites and marriage, which also had important religious significance. To participate in the life of a village, or town, or tribe required the acceptance of its spiritual and religious presuppositions. Africans had no understanding of the European view that religion and life could be kept in water-tight compartments. Interrelating faith and life had also been the Christian way in Europe before the Enlightenment and the Industrial Revolution placed the emphasis on thinking individuals over against community, asserting themselves out of the local community, which might be seen as evil and sinful, so that the individual became a Christian as a result of a 'conversion experience'. The nineteenth-century Christian emphasis on the individual struggling against the world and its temptations, in which sin could be seen as 'doing what other people do', and the African emphasis on the individual subsumed in the traditions of the community, in which 'sin' was 'not doing what other people do', were dramatically opposed to each other. There was an inevitable culture clash.

Initially the missionaries expected tribal rulers to see the advantages of Christianity and to be converted, and then to conform to the missionaries' expectations of godly rulers, but in West Africa chiefs were seldom converted to Christianity. This immediately posed problems, because it seems to have been a common characteristic of evangelical missionaries, to be opposed to authority and to assume that all government was an evil to be tolerated. The missionaries often resented being subject to pagan chiefs and rulers, and were subversive of their authority, even though the CMS committee advised them to accept such authority. In general missionaries were reluctant to abide by a chief's authority and the laws and customs of the society in which they found themselves, and looked to the higher authority of the British government, or God.

The CMS missionaries in the Niger delta tended to reject most of the African social customs they encountered, because they reflected, in their view, the heathenism that permeated African society and culture. Some customs, such as domestic slavery they found acceptable, because providing the family owning the slaves were baptized, they could be seen as a reflection of the New Testament world and of Victorian family life. Other customs such as polygamy posed major problems for missionaries. Polygamy was a symbol of the communal way of life of African society focused on the family compound. The CMS missionaries, who were looking for a rejection of the old life in conversion, regarded polygamy as a violation of the laws of God, which the convert was required to reject from the start. For the missionaries the outward sign of conversion was the adoption of monogamy.[10] The CMS committee, under the guidance of Henry Venn, their secretary, adopted a more gradualist approach, recommending that polygamous wives might be baptized, for they might have repented of their sin, while having to live with the consequences of it, but forbade the baptism of polygamous men. However, the missionaries refused to baptize the wives of polygamists and were supported by the bishop of Sierra Leone, when he visited the Niger delta in 1857.[11] Potential converts were rapidly reduced in number if all married men were required to abandon all but one wife, and if only one wife might be baptized. From the point of view of Africans this requirement was fundamentally immoral, for it undermined the basis of their society and economy, and would have left the additional wives and their children with no means of support and outside tribal society.

The clash between the CMS missionaries and African culture

over the issue of marriage was merely one example of the culture clash between nineteenth-century Western European Christianity and world-views, and the African religions and their world-view. For the African, religious customs and presuppositions underlay every social transaction. Birth, child-rearing, puberty, marriage, family life, sickness, death, mourning were all governed by customs which presupposed corporate identity with beliefs about the nature of the world around them, and the spirits which guided and directed that world, and needed to be appeased or pleased. The missionaries saw themselves as having little choice but to reject all African social customs as tainted by heathenism. They required from converts a total rejection of their past life, and that they should move into a new world virtually segregated from their old world. The difficulty was that there was not a new community into which to incorporate converts. The missionaries were few and although some were Africans from Sierra Leone, the leaders were Europeans, who were usually too alien in their understanding of the social needs and assumptions of Africans to be able to construct a social model that might be both Christian and attractive to Africans. Islam, moving south, had become more indigenized in sub-Saharan Africa, and more tolerant of African customs, and of course, was often led by Africans, and found it easier to adjust to and convert tribal groups.

A significant dimension of the CMS missionaries' approach was through education. They undertook important work in committing the languages of the Niger delta to writing and in creating grammatical structures and vocabularies for the languages, so that the Bible, the Prayer Book and hymn books could be translated into African languages. They also provided schools to teach children to read, so that they could read the Bible for themselves, and also to learn English, with a view to converting them to Christianity in due course. The chiefs were entirely happy for their children to learn English, because that would give them access to the sources of power and trade that they saw the European missionaries wielding.

Initially Africans, with their unitary view of religion and society assumed that the new learning, the new technology, the new social order were all dependent on accepting the new religion brought by the missionaries. However, they soon discovered the extent to which the new ways disrupted their society and challenged their authority and chiefs did not want their children to be weaned away from the traditional society. The seasonal nature of tribal activities and the requirements that children should assist in work also meant that their attendance at school might be sporadic. In any case, for children, especially boys who were unused to formal education and to being confined in European-style buildings, the education offered by the missionaries was not particularly attractive.

In order to establish a much stronger Christian (and European) context for education the missionaries began to establish boarding schools, which were largely funded by the CMS's supporters in England, for small amounts of money could provide for numerous children. Again parents and chiefs were willing to 'lend' their children to the missionary schools because they wanted their children to learn English, but missionaries sometimes had difficulties in sustaining English 'Christian' standards of personal behaviour. However, in the very long-term these schools did create the middle class whom the Christian missionaries had envisaged would collaborate with them in Christianizing what was to become Nigeria.[12]

For these reasons the spread of Anglicanism, in spite of the high hopes of the CMS, was very slow in West Africa. The first mission station was opened in the Niger delta region in 1845, under an African, Samuel Crowther. As a boy, he had been rescued from slave traders and taken to Sierra Leone, where he had shown sufficient promise to be taken to England to be trained for ordination, and was subsequently ordained to work in Sierra Leone. However, it was not until 1848 that the first three converts were baptized at the new mission station. By 1854 three more CMS mission stations had been opened. By 1861 when Britain established a crown colony in the Niger delta there were still only eight stations in the delta region, including a school for African catechists.

In many ways the Sierra Leoneans were the most effective missionaries in the Niger delta. Their effectiveness lay in the fact that they belonged to two worlds. They came from a tribal background and usually could remember their own language, but had also absorbed much of the European civilizing, Christianizing model. They were the backbone of the missionary outreach, because the few Europeans usually died very quickly in West Africa. After a slow start an African clergy developed quite quickly; by the end of the nineteenth century at least a hundred 'native' clergy, connected with the CMS, had been ordained. Most of them had originated in Sierra Leone, and fifty-five of them had been trained at Fourah Bay College which the CMS had founded in 1827, and eleven had received Durham University degrees, as a result of the College being affiliated to the University in 1879.[13]

This Christian Sierra Leonean culture was predominantly Yoruba. Almost all its principal figures, who returned to the Niger region through Badagry and Lagos as missionaries into the interior were Yorubas who had been captured from slavers and set free in Sierra Leone. They had made Christianity increasingly their own, and were able to promote it so as to appeal to their fellow Yorubas who had not had the Sierra Leone experience. Nowhere else in West Africa did this happen to any considerable extent. Ideally Crowther, who had proved to be a most impressive priest and scholar should have become bishop of Yorubaland. That would have achieved Venn's plan to establish an indigenous leadership and to move the missionaries on to establish new mission stations elsewhere.

However, Venn saw in the Niger an opportunity to provide an example of how his policy of establishing a native church under native ministers and the direction of a native bishop might work in practice, for there was at least the beginnings of an African clergy there.[14] This policy of a locally led and financially self-sufficient church was in part an evangelical response to the realization that British governments were unlikely to continue to support missionary work either financially or politically, and that English missionaries would continue to be difficult to recruit. Shortly after an Englishman, Bishop Vidal was consecrated first bishop of Sierra Leone in 1852, Venn had proposed some 'articles of arrangement' which were designed to make the native church in the Niger delta independent of the CMS, and envisaged a church governed by a bishop assisted by a church council comprising clergy and laity nominated by the bishop, the CMS and the local clergy. This would have transferred real power from the Society to the bishop and the council. The implementation of these articles was delayed by a number of factors, especially the deaths of three bishops of Sierra Leone in rapid succession. Archbishop Sumner, and others, were enthusiastic for the appointment of Samuel Crowther as bishop of Sierra Leone, but Venn resisted this. He may have thought that, with twenty or so European clergy in Sierra Leone, it would not have worked to appoint Crowther bishop. In any case he had other plans for Crowther.[15]

While Venn opposed Wilberforce's proposals for missionary bishops, because he suspected that without a strong laity, bishops might abuse their authority, he was not opposed to the extension of the colonial episcopate, especially if bishops were generally to be guided by 'the laws and constitutions of the Church at home'. He argued from the New Testament that missionary work had taken place in Antioch without an apostolic command, and that Paul had ordained local elders, and that then local bishops had been established. He was supported in these views by Bishop Tait, on the grounds that the claims about missionary bishops in the early Church did not stand up to historical investigation.[16]

By the 1860s Venn was concerned that missionaries had become so involved in 'ministering to the native church' which they had established that they were decreasingly able to 'evangelize the heathen', and so he set out proposals for developing a 'native church' which would work upwards to create the Church, not downwards, by the Society creating a church. He also hoped that by this means churches would become financially self-supporting. He envisaged the development of the 'native Church' in four distinct phases. First, congregations would be founded which would be able to pay for their own teachers; second, native pastorates would be formed out of one or more native congregations under an ordained native pastor, and paid from the 'Native Church Fund' (although, if the Native Church Fund remained under the management of the Society, the pastor should remain under the general superintendence of some of the Society's missionaries); third, where a number of pastorates had emerged, then a district conference could be formed, consisting of clerical and lay representatives of congregations and European missionaries, to administer 'native Church affairs'; fourth, when a sizeable district was provided, there would be no further need of foreign money, and the district would be ready for a native bishop. Venn was opposed to what he regarded as the inappropriateness and harmfulness of the European model for organizing a church, and believed that his proposals would allow structures to develop which would be in keeping with the realities of the local church. These proposals became the CMS strategy for the next thirty years or so.[17]

In 1861 Venn persuaded Bishop Breckles of Sierra Leone to move to the second phase, by permitting a native pastorate to be established, but he objected to Breckles's subsequent attempts to introduce European superintendence to the pastorate. The time was now ripe, in Venn's view, to establish a bishopric of the Niger, for there was a potential African bishop, Samuel Crowther, who had pioneered the CMS mission in the Niger region. He envisaged the diocese as West Africa without Sierra Leone. In 1864, with the financial support of the CMS, the diocese of the Niger was created, and Samuel Crowther was consecrated on 29 June 1864 by the archbishop of Canterbury in Canterbury Cathedral, the first African to become an Anglican bishop. Special trains were run from London and elsewhere to bring people to the service.

Venn expected the Yoruba congregations to throw in their lot with Crowther. He was not surprised nor disappointed when European missionaries declined to accept Crowther's authority, for by the late 1860s Venn had come to recognize a racial divide and he envisaged parallel native and European bishops with independent jurisdictions over their different congregations. He encouraged racial distinctiveness as a means of avoiding paternalistic domination by Europeans.[18]

The whole concept of the diocese, however, was misconceived. In fact, Crowther became a missionary bishop in the Wilberforce mode, rather than according to Venn's plan. His territory was ill-defined, and not many of the existing Yoruba congregations gravitated to his jurisdiction, and he remained dependent on the CMS. Also, while the Niger provided a means of communication, it did not provide a common culture or language between the people who lived in its hinterland. In any case, it was only a means of communication if one had a reliable boat, and Crowther was not given a steamer until 1878, and even then he had to use it to trade, in order to pay its way. It was also unlikely that Africans living on the banks of the Niger would distinguish between mere traders out to exploit them, and Christian missionaries who were supporting themselves by trading. Crowther had difficulty recruiting missionaries to work with him. Africans were as doubtful about working outside their tribal area, as Europeans were reluctant to go to Africa. The range of languages that the diocese covered was vast – Hausa, Nupe, Igpo and Ijo – which meant that even an able linguist like Crowther required an interpreter.[19]

His greatest missionary success was the independent kingdom of Brass on the Niger delta, whose flourishing trade was built on selling alcoholic drink. The king and the great majority of his subjects adopted Christianity in the 1870s, and it was one of the few areas of the diocese where the Church flourished. However, in the 1880s Crowther's position began to be undermined by the Royal Niger Company, which by the end of the decade had established control over trade on the river at the expense of African traders based at centres such as Brass. The Company avoided criticism of its cruelty and rapaciousness by adopting the current English evangelical moral shibboleth of teetotalism, and attacked the trade in drink. This undermined the trade of Brass, causing a recession which the king, understandably, blamed on Christianity, and reverted to 'ju ju'. The most significant achievement of Crowther's twenty-five year episcopate was thus lost.[20]

Meanwhile a new breed of English CMS missionaries had arrived in Nigeria. From the early 1880s the CMS had wished to monitor Crowther and the Niger Mission, for there were criticisms of his lax administration and his generosity to the failings of others. In 1887 the CMS wanted to nominate James Johnson, a black African, as bishop for Yoruba. However, the bishop of Sierra Leone, missionaries, and it would seem, some African clergy all opposed the proposal, perhaps because of tribal tensions and probably they feared that with an African bishop they would lose European financial support. It is clear that as late as 1888 there was no abandonment by the Society of the policy of establishing native leadership in the Church, and there was still a respect form Crowther.

As the leading evangelical missionary society the CMS was influenced by currents within contemporary evangelicalism and contemporary society. This meant imperialism, and the more general ascetic and stringent attitudes developing in British society and in the Anglican evangelical and catholic movements in particular exemplified in evangelicalism by the influence of the Keswick Conventions from 1875 onwards.[21]

The senior members of the Society, however, did not easily abandon their long-standing policy, and were reluctant to recognize the failure of the Niger experiment, and the demand for a renewal of European leadership. They did not, in fact, abandon their aim of independent native churches, they merely saw it as being postponed, for as cautious administrators, they perceived the need for closer control on behalf of the Society.[22]

Young men attracted by the idealism of Hudson Taylor and the China Inland Mission, and influenced by attendance at the Keswick Conventions, and at Cambridge by the encouragement of Handley Moule, the principal of Ridley Hall, an evangelical theological college, were recruited to the CMS, but they were often highly critical of what they regarded as the Society's complacent attitude to preaching the gospel. Those who went to Nigeria were scandalized by the Christians they found in the northern part of Crowther's diocese where they had been sent to work. They were also reacting against what they regarded as the nominal Christianity which they had experienced in England, and were horrified to discover something similar among the African missionaries. They expected evidence of real conversion, and rejected what in their view was superficial and conventional Christianity characterized by the hymn-singing and 'loose living' and gin-selling of the average Christian converts. Although only in their early and mid-twenties, with the rigorous enthusiasm of youth, some of the new recruits to the Society dismissed, on behalf of the CMS, most of the clergy and the archdeacon appointed by Crowther. They were also highly critical of the leadership of Bishop Crowther himself when they returned to the south. While they might claim to respect him as a good and holy man, they were unreserved in their criticism of his family and the position that his son held in the Church. The bishop's wife herself was also criticized for her trading activities. The new missionaries challenged the theory of the mutual interest of Christianity and commerce. The need for it had now, in fact, largely disappeared, for there was no longer an Atlantic slave trade to be counteracted by alternative economic opportunities and so it was no longer a necessary part of mission strategy. The new missionaries also criticized the Sierra Leoneans for their aloofness from native life and for adopting European ways.[23]

In the eyes of the new missionaries the Church as they found it in Nigeria was rotten and needed changing. Wilmot Brooke, an honorary lay missionary, aged twenty-four, whose Anglicanism was very lukewarm, but who was briefly a dominating influence in the CMS's involvement in Nigeria, complained to the CMS London committee about Crowther's missionaries for immorality, illegitimate trading, slave dealing, and other irregularities, and persuaded them to open an investigation. The Society was nervous of these reports from young, inexperienced and idealistic missionaries, but they had also received more balanced reports of Crowther's incompetence over many years. They recognized that part of the problem might be that Crowther was working in a country of which he was not a native. But they also believed that the revived interest in missions and the unprecedented numbers of recruits that they were receiving, especially from Cambridge, must have been providentially destined by God for the new and challenging work, and that the new recruits ought to be given a hearing.

Crowther was therefore invited to London for consultations about his work, and about how the newly recruited missionaries might be deployed under him. During this visit Crowther was personally exonerated from any criticisms, but he was recognized to be something of an overindulgent father, shielding the wrongdoing of his children. On his return Crowther continued to be criticized and interfered with by the CMS missionaries and they tried to suspend the archdeacon, who was Crowther's son. In 1890 Crowther resigned in despair from the CMS Niger Finance Committee, and in effect, from his position of superintendent of the Niger Mission.

The CMS committee had been placed in a difficult position. They were anxious to improve their image in England, which was being tarnished by the widespread reporting of the comments of the new young missionaries, in order to attract new funds and additional recruits. To do this they recognized that they would need to reorganize the Niger Mission which was made more necessary in order resist the southward expansion of Islam, by appointing new European missionaries. However, they did not intend to dismiss Crowther. Brooke and Robinson, the secretary to the Niger Mission who was also young and inexperienced, and had been much influenced by Brooke's views, were not only criticizing Crowther and the Niger Mission, but were also effectively criticizing the whole CMS policy, and its administrative structure, and accusing the committee of a cover-up and of obtaining funds under false pretences. The committee was deeply divided about how to respond to this attack, and ended up criticizing both Crowther and his critics, led by Brooke and Robinson, and proceeded to introduce greater European supervision, thus in effect, caving in to the attacks on their policy of Africanization.[24]

The policy that the Society had pursued under Henry Venn's leadership throughout the middle years of the nineteenth century was in tatters. The idea of the African Church rapidly establishing its own indigenous ministry and episcopate had, in the eyes of the new missionaries, not worked. The indigenous clergy were criticized as badly trained and not up to the intellectual standards of their congregations. Among many of the missionaries there was an antipathy towards educated Africans and an unwillingness by English missionaries to accept the authority of an African bishop and his senior clergy.

Having revealed, to their own satisfaction, the incompetence of Bishop Crowther, the new missionaries reported to the Society their reservations about the capacity of Africans in general to take charge of the Church. From the 1890s most missionary societies abandoned the policy of encouraging the development of an indigenous ministry and leadership in the African churches. Confidence in the progress of civilization was replaced by 'social Darwinism' which posited a racial struggle in which Europeans were clearly superior and therefore ought to lead the inferior African people. Although similar opinions were common among the colonial administrators of the Empire, it did not necessarily mean that the new style English missionaries related closely and well to colonial officials. There were often tensions between missionaries and colonial administrators. The missionaries often adopted the same standards in criticizing the Christian faith and practice of colonial officials as they used for criticizing African leaders, and tended to alienate the colonial administrators (unless they were Anglicans of the same complexion as themselves) by their exclusiveness and rigour. The expansion of Anglican missionary work was not an offshoot of British imperialism, but a parallel and complementary movement.

When the CMS committee proposed J.S. Hill, a European whose whole working life had been as a CMS missionary, first in Lagos, and then in New Zealand, as successor, to Crowther, but for a diocese renamed Western Equatorial Africa, they were resisted by Archbishop Benson, who declined to consecrate Hill. Instead, he requested the CMS to send Hill to Nigeria as bishop-designate, in order to recruit two African priests to be consecrated as assistant bishops to work with him. On his return Hill recommended to Benson and the Society that during the next two or three years the diocese should be divided into three areas under a European bishop, but with two African suffragans. The CMS were deeply opposed to this proposal, for they feared that it would loosen their control over the developing Church. Benson, however, supported Hill's proposal. Hill died in 1894, before any action could be taken, and the CMS nominated Herbert Tugwell to succeed him. He was already a missionary in Yoruba land, and was willing to put Hill's recommendations into practice and to work with two suffragans, only one of whom now would be an African.[25]

The new policies of the CMS, however, while they were detrimental to the development of African leadership in the work of the Society, did encourage some African people to take initiatives. In the 1890s the Niger Delta Pastorate, under Archdeacon Crowther, the bishop's son, separated from the CMS, though not from Anglicanism. In response to this, Bishop Tugwell advocated the appointment of an African bishop to supervise the Niger Delta Pastorate. He was also critical of the behaviour and the attitudes of European missionaries toward black African clergy. The CMS committee were deeply opposed to the idea of a diocese for the Niger delta. Their concern was to maintaining control of the Mission and to resist attempts to establish self-governing churches, for fear that they would stray from evangelical orthodoxy. This reflected the great stress through which Anglican evangelicalism was passing during the late nineteenth century and the early twentieth century, which witnessed battles waged against both Anglo-Catholic rit- ualism and theological modernism, which led to a split in the evangelical movement itself, between liberal and conservative evangelicals.[26] After further consideration, the Society proved willing to accept a new suffragan bishop, working under Tugwell, and a leading African priest, James Johnson was sounded out, as to whether he would accept nomination, but he declined to accept nomination as a suffragan. However, when it emerged that Archbishop Temple supported the CMS in not accepting the need for a new diocese, Johnson agreed to become a suffragan to Tugwell.[27]

By the 1930s, although it had not become a diocese, the Niger Delta Pastorate had established, without European assistance, eleven districts, with an average of sixty churches in each district, with an estimated 13,852 members (compared with 283 members in 1898), which demonstrated the competence of African clergy to lead, administer and organize the local church. Similarly Bishop Johnson opened missions in the Benin area with no support from the CMS, employing African personal, mainly Yoruba-speaking, to run the missions, which expanded rapidly. Fortunately Bishop Tugwell showed himself to be a man of tolerance and wisdom, who was able to maintain these groups within the Anglican fold, who could illustrate Anglican flexibility in the face of the intolerance and incompetence of some over rigorous missionaries.[28]

One of the results of the increasingly negative assessment of African capabilities for leadership by nearly all the missionary societies operating in Africa was the establishment of independent churches. The United Native African Church was dedicated to the evangelization of African society by means of African evangelists under African leadership, as a result of the reaction against the treatment of Bishop Crowther. It altered very little of the teachings it inherited from the Church of England, held its services in Yoruba, allowed polygamy, and introduced African music and chant into the liturgy. The establishment of the African Church (Incorporated) in Lagos in 1891, was also the result of what some Nigerian Anglicans saw as the unjustifiable removal of Bishop Johnson from his post as pastor of St Paul's Breadfruit Church in Lagos. What they seem to have been objecting to was the lack of consultation, the paternalism, and the autocratic manner of the CMS authorities. The only changes they made when they separated were the introduction of services in Yoruba, a new hymn book including African chants, and later, on the matter of polygamy, on the authority of 1 Timothy 3.2 and 3.12, they decided that while clergy should be required to remain monogamous, laymen might take more than one wife. Bishop Johnson had not, in fact, joined the church, for he wished to establish a strict model of Christianity within an Anglican context in Africa, which he believed Europeans would not be able to do.[29]

In East Africa missionary work began half a century later. A similar initiative was undertaken by the CMS to that taken in West Africa. Again the initiative was outside British territory, and well before Britain developed any colonial intentions in the area. In 1857 David Livingstone published his *Missionary Travels and Researches in South Africa* and reopened among English Christians the challenge to Christianize Africa with the renewal of the suggestion that Christian mission should go hand in hand with trade, in order to offer Africans an economic alternative to the slave trade which still continued in East Africa.

Livingstone, like Buxton, believed that commerce and Christianity would free Africans from the threat of slavery. His journeys and writings and carefully organized British lecture tours suggested that Africa was rich in minerals, as well as being fertile for cultivation, and that rivers such as the Zambezi offered highways for trade and commerce into the heart of Africa, along which could be carried the best of European morals, with the opportunity for trade. He gave the impression that new markets were ready and waiting for the booming British industrial economy, which in turn would provide new sources of raw materials for British manufacturers, and that this expansion of trade would promote Christian knowledge and freedom from literal slavery as well as from the slavery of sin and vice and the ignorance of the gospel.

Livingstone was an unusual missionary. He believed in the strength and power of the diffused influence of a white European and Christian civilization as the great Christianizing force in Africa. He saw his role in this as opening the gates for the spread of Christianity by travels, rather than to make converts himself. Unlike other missionaries, he saw his work was not to form new congregations, but to press on and to pave the way for more conventional missionaries to follow in his footsteps. Part, therefore, of his task was to publicize his travels and researches. This he did to tremendous effect. Not only was his book a best seller, combining two favourite Victorian themes, adventure and religion, he was also an attractive and enthusiastic lecturer, who encouraged his audiences to give money to missionary work.

In Oxford and Cambridge, Livingstone aroused the under-graduates to the needs of Africa; and the University of Durham and Trinity College, Dublin accepted invitations to join with Oxford and Cambridge to sponsor a mission to the Zambezi. The mission was to become, as soon as possible, materially self-supporting by teaching Africans to grow cotton, which Livingstone had told the Lancashire cotton manufacturers in his lectures in Manchester, would be growing ready to hand, for export to England. It was proposed that the mission should found an agricultural village where they would show Africans how to grow and export cotton, which would teach them the truth of the Christian religion and the moral consequences thereof, and display in its corporate life the model of a Christian and civilized community, and thus by their presence, their example and their economy, they would begin to destroy slavery.[30] The Manchester cotton manufacturers were much interested in the scheme, for it would provide an alternative source of cotton to the southern United States, and would thus strike a blow at slavery in the United States.[31]

The UMCA was much influenced by High Churchmen who had also enthusiastically linked the development of trade with promoting the gospel. Samuel Wilberforce, in making a substantial donation to its funds, had stipulated that any mission should be led by a bishop. This was intended to be a model missionary enterprise. The previous policy of sending out a bishop after a mission had been established, to supervise the various congregations collected by his forerunners, had led to all sorts of difficulties, as we have seen. In view of Wilberforce's long-held theory it was thought that if a church were properly theologically established, with a bishop at its head, landing in the first boat, then many of the practical problems of establishing episcopal authority would be avoided, for he would be there exercising his godly rule from the beginning. This was to be a new and exemplary beginning for the Church, based on what was claimed to be the model of the early Church. A church was to be planted in its entirety, and would convert, not by preaching and distributing Bibles, but by gathering the heathen into an already existing Christian worshipping community, with its own sacramental life, headed by a successor of the apostles. People's imaginations had been fired by the image of a bishop, like Selwyn sailing among the Melanesian Islands, being the

Church, planting the Church. They envisaged a new bishop sailing up the Zambezi leading the missionaries, as the chief evangelist, as well as the chief pastor.

The man chosen to lead this mission was Charles Mackenzie, who had been a fellow of Gonville and Caius College, Cambridge where he had taught maths, while being curate of a village near Cambridge. He had been inspired by a visit by Selwyn to Cambridge to offer himself for work in the mission field, and had spent a few difficult years as Colenso's archdeacon in Natal. Bishop Gray had intended to make him bishop of one of the new missionaries dioceses he had been planning to create in South Africa. To this end Mackenzie had been in England in 1859 when the promoters of the Central Africa mission were looking for a prospective leader and bishop, and he responded to the invitation to lead the mission. There were problems over his consecration as bishop, for the Zambezi was outside British territory, and therefore royal letters patent could not be issued for his consecration. The problem was solved by Gray offering to consecrate him, whatever the legality of his action in relation to English law, in South Africa, as a 'missionary bishop', to plant the Church in heathen parts. This was the first occasion on which the difficulty of assembling sufficient bishops to consecrate a bishop in the colonies was illustrated. The bishop of St Helena had to make a long sea voyage, but arrived by the agreed date, but the bishop of Grahamstown missed his boat, and failed to arrive, so the consecration had to take place with the canonical minimum of three bishops – Natal, Cape Town and St Helena.[32]

With Livingstone's guidance and advice, a small expedition was set up, and to establish the new Church as an economically viable community, craftsmen and workers were recruited who, it was hoped, would be exemplary Christians, as well as competent craftsmen and agriculturalists. Given the difficulties the missionary societies had always experienced until later in the century in recruiting any English missionaries, it was not easy to find suitable recruits with such a wide range of skills, and there were compromises. More hazards lay ahead. Livingstone had given the impression that the Zambezi would be easy to navigate, and that it would provide an excellent trade route. This was found not to be so when they arrived at the mouth of the river in the paddle steamer they had brought with them. A sand bar made the river difficult of access, and then shallows, rapids, marshes and more sandbanks made it very difficult for inexperienced sailors to navigate the river.

There were also problems for the missionaries in communicating with the Africans they met, for they lacked a knowledge of their languages, and there were no interpreters, or worse, they were unsure of the accuracy and reliability of the interpreters. They discovered that some of the tribes they met were at war with other tribes, and all sides were eager to win the support of the firepower of the Europeans. It was difficult to work out to what extent they were being fed information and manipulated, and for them to know how to react when they discovered that they had been misled. They found that their apparent friends (and enemies, for that matter) did not share their concepts and values relating to freedom, monogamy, compassion, or even truthfulness. There was an absolute clash of cultures. How could they allow themselves to rely on allies who enslaved fellow Africans, had many wives, and looted and stole, and who did not tell the truth? How could they respect and work with such evil authorities? They were even let down by their fellow Europeans, for they found the Portuguese tolerant of, and even engaging in, the slave trade.

There were also tensions among the missionaries. None of them was experienced in the sorts of tasks they had to tackle, and none of them had been chosen for their capacity to work with or lead other people. There were conflicts of authority among the missionaries, and with those to whom they were responsible in London, for the new missionary society did not have the well established procedures of the SPG or the CMS, and, in any case, their lines of communication with London were very stretched and difficult. They had to face new questions, such as whether they should use violence to intervene to free slaves, or whether they should bear weapons in possibly hostile territory. The practical reasons why the British government was averse to encouraging British subjects to undertake missionary work outside territories where the government's writ ran became rapidly obvious. Nor was Livingstone himself much help, he had few gifts of leadership, and was personally unreliable in keeping in touch with the expedition. Also, if he was not guilty of deceit, he was guilty of culpable exaggeration in his descriptions of the Zambezi and its hinterland. He had drawn an ideal picture, which had led Mackenzie and his backers to expect the Zambezi to be like the Thames or Severn, and that the African countryside would be like rural England; so much so that Mackenzie had arranged that his sisters should join him in the following year. Livingstone had failed to make clear the difficulties and perils, and the health hazards for the expedition. He has to be held responsible for the apparent rashness and folly of the missionaries, and for the deaths of Mackenzie, and four other Europeans and three South Africans.[33]

When the chaos of the mission was reported in England there was much disillusion and disappointment at the failure of the brave attempt to pioneer a new approach to mission. However, a new bishop, William Tozer, rector of Burgh le Marsh in Lincolnshire, was appointed to pick up the pieces and to rescue the situation. He recognized the difficulties of maintaining and developing a mission so remote from English lines of communication, and the difficulty of operating within the context of tribal warfare. He, as a realist, rather than a visionary, recognized that discretion would be the better part, and withdrew the mission, ultimately to Zanzibar, off the east coast of Africa, where the diocese was re-established, with good communications to the Cape and, for the future, with the interior. It was also recognized that the policy of linking missionary work with commercial development would not work in East Africa because there was an absence of obvious cash crops, and in any case after the end of the American Civil War Lancashire cotton manufacturers could import cotton from the southern states with a clear conscience.

In 1868 the UMCA began to re-establish its work on the mainland of Africa when it opened a mission station at Mogili, and in 1876 at Masasi, and at Nervala in 1878. The CMS also began to develop missionary work in Central Africa, in response to H.M. Stanley's appeal for missionaries to work in Central Africa. This illustrates the willingness of missionaries to work far beyond the borders of a colony, and undefended by any civil power. However, only one of the party was English, and the only Anglican clergyman in the party was a young Australian. From time to time missionaries were murdered, as was Bishop Hannington on his arrival in Buganda, but there was no demand that the British government should intervene to do something about it. All these missionary institutions in Africa were entirely independent of British colonial development. In fact it was very clearly to uncolonial Africa that the missionaries had gone.[34]

The earliest CMS missionaries had arrived in Buganda in 1878 and began by assimilating themselves to the social structure of the country. When the leading missionaries established a household this looked very much like that of a chief, with African youths given to them as pages, and they were invited to join the chiefs in council. Gradually the missionaries came to resemble the great chiefs of the country in the pattern of their households and their relations with the ruler, the kabaka. Complications were created for the Bugandans by the comings and goings of the missionaries, and by the arrival of the Roman Catholic White Fathers. In a country which took its cue for cultural and political behaviour from its ruler, it was impossible for the two groups of missionaries to agree to a partition of the country between them for missionary purposes. Small groups of Bugandan Christians, however, began to form, and they were much more successful in recruiting Bugandans to Christianity than the European missionaries were.[35] From 1879 the CMS and the White Fathers were competing for converts and the kabaka's court was split into Protestant, Roman Catholic and Muslim factions, each jockeying for power, and each in turn being favoured or persecuted by the kabaka. In 1888 the Muslim faction managed to depose the kabaka and to install his brother in his place, and to expel the Protestant and Roman Catholic members of the court, and a civil war broke out. Subsequently the country was virtually closed to Europeans during the wars. However, Christianity continued to spread rapidly at the initiative of local Christian leaders, as it had a generation earlier in Madgascar.

In 1888 the British government gave a charter to the Imperial British East Africa Company, and encouraged the Company to intervene in Buganda, where the German government had also begun to intervene, and had rallied the White Fathers' Roman Catholic converts to their support. In 1890 an expeditionary force funded by the Company reached Buganda, and succeeded in restoring the deposed kabaka, and won the support of the moderate Roman Catholic converts, and imposed a treaty stating that Buganda was under the protection of the Imperial British East Africa Company, on behalf of the British government.[36]

The aristocratic black converts who led the Anglican and Roman Catholic communities through the years of war and persecution had engendered a movement of mass conversion. However, there were inevitable tensions between these groups in Buganda and the English clerical leaderships of the churches when they returned to the country, for they wished to instil what they saw as order into the Church, and to end the independence. Despite the imposition of the Company's protectorate, the wars and the fighting continued. A.R. Tucker, who was appointed bishop of Eastern Equatorial Africa in 1890, arrived in Buganda at a point when the commander of the expeditionary force had concluded that if the force withdrew the Protestants would be massacred. The Company was reluctant to stay, because they could see no financial advantage to them in remaining in Buganda, and the British government was unwilling to provide money for the force to stay. Bishop Tucker had meanwhile returned to England and, on hearing of the unwillingness of the British government to fund the Company's troops to remain in Buganda, he set out to raise enough money from the CMS's supporters to pay for the Company's forces to remain in Buganda for fifteen months, until the end of 1892.

During the course of 1892 massive evangelical pressure was brought to bear on a Liberal government that was opposed to imperialism and the expansion of the British Empire, to persuade the British government to intervene. Evangelical popular opinion was motivated by opposition to slavery, that continued in East Africa, hostility to Roman Catholics and Muslims, and fear of the French government's imperial ambitions in this part of Africa. It was fear of French expansion in Central Africa which probably motivated the British government to intervene in Buganda, because it did not want the French to control the head waters of the Nile. While the CMS Anglican missionaries emerged as the dominant religious group in Buganda, the missionaries were compromised by the Society's naive involvement with British politics, and their desire to exclude Roman Catholics, and the consequent implications of this for their dealings with the Bugandan leaders.[37]

Bishop Tucker did remain faithful to Venn's tradition in the CMS, and resolved to establish a local clergy. In 1893, among the first six deacons he ordained, were four of the chiefs who had led the church during the persecutions, by which means he respected the spiritual element in the role of chiefs and set out to sanctify the leadership which had emerged in the church, rather than replace it with a new leadership. By 1899 there were twenty-one African clergy in Uganda. However, from the mid-1890s Bishop Tucker and the other missionaries had begun to doubt whether it was appropriate for clerical and secular authority to be concentrated in the same hands, and began to emphasize the authority of the clergy over against the laity. After the British protectorate was established, missionaries also had considerable additional implicit power to impose their views over against the decisions of any of the already established church councils which largely consisted largely of Bugandans. The missionaries began to recruit catechists and ordination candidates from among the Africans in their households, rather than from among the natural leaders. This had two unfortunate consequences. First the missionaries tended to continue to treat African clergy recruited thus as their dependants and servants, and it became difficult to recruit able people with leadership potential to be catechists and clergy. Second, the chiefs, ceasing to have any responsibility for the church, began to fall away from Christian practice. They also resented the imposition of British colonial rule, and came to associate Anglicanism with colonial rule. Thus the goodwill and influence of the natural communal leaders was partially lost to the Anglican Church.[38]

As the Church in Uganda developed in the early 1900s it was Bishop Tucker's intention that the European missionaries should be fully integrated into the local church, and he worked to achieve this when he began to draft a constitution for his diocese, and to make provision for a regular synod. The CMS supported Tucker's proposal for a synod and constitution, but they wished to retain a missionary standing committee to be responsible for stationing and supervising missionaries. The European missionaries, however, resisted Tucker's proposal. They argued that it would be like 'giving school children control of their master', fearing that the proposal would reduce European influence. By 1908 a compromise had been reached which did not give Tucker all that he had hoped for, and conceded a special position to Europeans, by retaining a missionary standing committee appointed by the CMS London committee to station and supervise the missionaries, which in effect created two governing bodies, but it still gave the Church of Uganda a very much stronger position and much more self-government than almost any other African Church had at that time.[39] In practice, however, it left the missionaries largely outside, and therefore above, its control. Nor was there any suggestion of an African bishop for Uganda. This was symbolic of a missionary failure; perhaps basically a racial failure to trust sufficiently a church which had come into existence in so remarkable a way, and with so little effort on the part of European missionaries.[40]

There was of course, a great variety of attitudes among missionaries about 'civilizing' Africans or 'Africanizing' Christianity. Bishop Smithies of Zanzibar, who was supported by the UMCA, wrote in 1892 'What we want is to Christianise them in their own civil and political condition; to help them to develop a Christian civilisation suited to their own climate and their own circumstances. For instance, we do not allow any of the boys in our schools to wear any European clothing; it is not our business to encourage the trade in boots.'[41] The following year the synod of the diocese of Zanzibar resolved to 'strenuously discourage all Europeanisms'.

Few missionaries were racialists. Many of them stressed frequently the intelligence, ability, rationality, and even high moral qualities of the unconverted people amongst whom they worked. However, if they were not racialist, they were paternalists believing in the eventual possibility of the progress of Africans, through education and training, the result was that there were few black African clergy. By 1900 598 men had been ordained into the 'native' ministry, of whom 358 were then serving. Eleven years later in 1911 there were still only 428 indigenous Anglican ministers in Africa, but no bishops.[42] Despite the desire of the first generation of Anglican mission strategists, indigenous leadership was not established in the missionary dioceses in Africa. In fact the policy was effectively reversed, and the stage was set for long-term European leadership of the Church, which ignored the natural patterns of communal and leadership in African societies, and emphasized European leadership and central control, and dependence on external funds to support it. This had a long-term stultifying effect on Anglicanism in Africa.

INDIA AND CEYLON

Similar problems were experienced in India and Ceylon, but here, as we have already seen, the bishops, as government nominees, were less dependent on the missionary societies, so there was greater scope for conflict between the bishops and the societies, but there was still a reluctance, exacerbated by the larger number of expatriates living in India, to give leadership positions to Indians.

When Piers Claughton, bishop of St Helena was translated to Colombo in 1861 he proceeded to emulate Gray in Cape Town, his former metropolitan, and held a synod in Colombo in September 1865, although Ceylon was not a self-governing colony. None of the CMS clerical missionaries attended the synod, on the orders of the CMS London committee on the initiative of Venn, who believed that an attempt to hold a synod of all the clergy, including ordained missionaries, as well as government-paid chaplains, would compromise the CMS's mission work in attempting to create a 'native church' under a native bishop. Claughton was succeeded in 1871 by Reginald Copleston, a bishop of decidedly High Church views who was anxious to divide his diocese into areas equivalent to parishes. He was suspected of expecting government chaplains, who were often young men suspected by the CMS of High Church tendencies, to take charge of more experienced CMS lay missionaries. The CMS therefore claimed that their lay catechists were outside the bishop's jurisdiction.

In 1876 a senior CMS missionary instructed the catechists not even to assemble their congregations in government chaplains' churches. This provoked a major controversy between the bishop and the CMS about the issue of a bishop's jurisdiction over missionaries, whether lay or ordained. The matter was referred to the CMS London committee in 1878, and they agreed to modify the rules that had been drawn up with Bishop Wilson of Calcutta in 1837.[43] They agreed that the Society should apply to bishops for licences for missionaries to work in their dioceses, on the understanding that the bishops would not refuse to grant a licence. The committee had met during the meeting of the Lambeth Conference to consider the question but, because the CMS was adopting a policy of aloofness from the conference, they did not draw the bishops' attention to their decision.

Copleston, on his return from discussing his difficulties with the CMS with his fellow bishops at Lambeth, called another synod which the CMS clergy agreed to attend providing it was understood that the meeting was merely an informal conference, not a synod at which legally binding decisions could be made. Again their ostensible reason was that bringing together a synod including European and native clergy would end in discriminating against the natives. However, they then declined to attend any holy communion service in the cathedral at which there might be ritual to which they objected. The CMS committee in London sympathized with the missionaries, and Copleston agreed to postpone his conference until May 1879 and invited the senior CMS missionary to celebrate the holy communion at the conference to avoid any risk of offending the missionaries. However, at the conclusion of the conference Copleston indicated that he would not license or ordain any new CMS missionary who refused to accept his usual manner of celebrating the holy communion. When they heard of this the CMS London committee asked the archbishop of Canterbury to intervene, but Copleston suggested to the CMS that the matter should be referred either to the metropolitan of India and Ceylon, or to three English bishops or archbishops.

The CMS were unwilling to accept any reference to the metropolitan, for the point they sought to establish was that the Protestant character of the Church of England did not permit unlimited episcopal power in the colonies. Copleston thus again visited London to consult Archbishop Tait who agreed to ask Archbishop Thomson and Bishops Jackson of London, Lightfoot of Durham and Harold Browne of Winchester to consider the matter with him. Neither party would first meet the other, and Copleston was unwilling to admit a right of the archbishop to revise any decision he had made, thinking it proper for him to recognize only the authority of the bishop of Calcutta as his metropolitan. Tait therefore met the parties on neutral territory, in his room in the Houses of Parliament. After protracted negotiations a document was drawn up which all the parties could accept, and which set out a procedure for granting licences for ordained missionaries which would place the Society in the same position as the patron of an English benefice. The missionaries were criticized in the bishops' report for not receiving holy communion from Copleston, and they were advised to attend his synod, on the understanding that at present it was merely a conference. Although the matter had been settled to the general satisfaction of the CMS London committee and of Copleston, the more conservative CMS missionaries in Ceylon continued a sniper warfare against the bishop.[44]

In 1881 the government of Ceylon gave the bishop five years' notice of the withdrawal of their financial support for the diocese and of disestablishing the Church. This opened the way for the Church to manage its own affairs, and to draw up a constitution. However, when Copleston called an assembly for this purpose in July 1881 the CMS missionaries with lay delegates from their congregation attended, but then withdrew in protest against what they considered their underrepresentation. In response a committee was set up, comprising eight clergy, (four evangelicals and four others), with authority to co-opt sixteen laymen, to draft a constitution for the diocese. The constitution they drew up, based on the constitution of the Church of Ireland, because one of the clergy was from the Church of Ireland, was eventually adopted by the Church assembly of the diocese in 1886, under an ordinance of the government of Ceylon which permitted the bishop, clergy and laity of the Church of England in the diocese of Colombo to hold 'Synods, Assemblies or Conventions' to manage their own affairs. The bishopric was also endowed by grants from the Colonial Bishoprics Fund, the SPG and the SPCK to replace the government grants. In the end disestablishment was an important unifying factor in the diocese, for, unlike in Uganda, the evangelicals and the CMS missionaries were drawn into the mainstream of the Church's life. The CMS realized that the danger of compromise might not be too great, given that there were few settlers in Ceylon, and the appointment of a native bishop might not be long delayed, and that compromise would be better than being excluded from the synod and the life of the Church. In the event a Sri Lankan was not appointed as bishop until 1964.[45]

In India from the mid-1850s the SPG had been pressing for additional dioceses. This had been opposed by the CMS, because they feared that the High Church influences in the SPG, unrestrained by the English law, wished to impose an episcopal tyranny on their missionaries and Indian converts. In their view Indians would be too immature as Christians to reject episcopal interference. They also thought, as we have already seen in Africa, that Scripture required evangelists to go first into a new mission field, to create a church in which a bishop might minister. The presence of European bishops, Henry Venn also suspected, would prevent the 'euthanasia' of mission, and the establishment of a 'native church', with an Indian pastorate and Indian bishops. The outbreak of the Indian Mutiny in 1858 also had a sharp impact on the work of missionary societies in India. It prompted evangelical Anglicans to demand that the British government should abandon attempts at neutrality towards Hindu 'idolatry', which was portrayed as the natural cause of the events of the Mutiny, which was thus seen as a judgement on Britain for not having promoted more missionary work. However although English nonconformists were equally opposed to 'idolatry', they were also opposed to any attempts to increase Anglican influence in India, or anywhere else, with the support of government funds. This had repercussions for teaching about Christianity in government schools in India, and also for the creation of new dioceses. While it was recognized that more dioceses were needed, it was feared that parliamentary time would not be available to pass any legislation to set up any new dioceses in India. It was also suspected that the government might be reluctant to include clauses permitting the creation and funding of new dioceses in any legislation for India, for fear of attracting the opposition of both nonconformist and evangelical Members of Parliament.

However, legal advice taken by the bishop of Calcutta suggested that legislation would not be required to establish a diocese in a territory outside the jurisdiction of the former East India Company, and that a diocese could be established outside that jurisdiction without legislation, by letters patent issued by the crown. When a fund of £20,000 had been raised by 1877 to endow the diocese a bishop was appointed to Lahore. A diocese was also established in 1877 in Rangoon, covering Burmese territory which had not been under British rule in 1833. It was endowed with £10,000 raised in the diocese of Winchester, with £5,000 from the SPCK, £2,000 from the SPG and £5,000 from the Colonial Bishoprics Fund.

In 1864, following news of Crowther's appointment as bishop of the Niger, John Thomas, a missionary in Tinnevelly had proposed that an Indian bishop should be appointed there, to have concurrent jurisdiction over Indian clergy and congregations with the European bishop of Madras. Henry Venn had endorsed this proposal, but as an intermediate step, to avoid the necessity of an Act of Parliament, had proposed the appointment of Indian commissaries instead of bishops under the bishop of Madras, to act on his behalf in Indian congregations. Venn saw this appointment of commissaries as a first step towards developing Indian church institutions, rather than establishing Europeanized Indian bishops in South India at this stage. Bishop Cotton of Calcutta was hesitant about this proposal, especially the abandonment of the geographical principle as the basis of a bishop's jurisdiction. As an alternative he proposed the appointment of an Indian coadjutor bishop of Madras. However, the proposal was opposed by the missionaries, and was abandoned. The CMS really did want to establish independent native churches, and a policy to achieve this was pursued by Henry Wright, Venn's successor as secretary of the Society, through native church councils which had been established in South India, where, during the 1870s, pressure was applied to appoint Indian chairmen and vice-chairmen of the councils.

Bishop Gell of Madras in 1871 began to consider the appointment of suffragan bishops for the areas of Tanjore, Tirunevelly and Travancore in South India. The idea was taken up by the SPG and the SPCK, who obtained legal advice that, although no suffragan bishops had been appointed in England since the sixteenth century, there was no legal reason why they might not be appointed in India. However, the legal advice was that any suffragan bishops that were appointed, should be consecrated in England, for there were doubts about the legal rights of the bishops in India to consecrate bishops themselves. The CMS also took up the idea, and proposed that Sargent, one of their missionaries, should become bishop of Tirunevelly. They envisaged that this might be another step towards appointing an Indian as a bishop to be responsible for Indians, and thus fulfil their strategy of the development of a native church, governed by a native bishop. Gell also suggested that, to maintain parity of treatment, the SPG should nominate a bishop for the area of his diocese where their missionaries were working. Nothing came of this, for Bishop Milman of Calcutta did not support the proposal.

However, in 1877 when Bishop Johnson was appointed to Calcutta, he was prepared to implement the proposal for two suffragans for the diocese of Madras, one to be nominated by the CMS and the other by the SPG. The CMS continued to encourage the appointment of Indians to posts of responsibility in the Church in order to prepare them to be bishops. It was indicated to Sargent, the CMS nominee, as soon as he was consecrated that, as soon as possible he ought to begin to arrange the subdivision of his area into further areas, each to be governed by an Indian bishop, and in due course, resign. However, Sargent had doubts about the suitability of Indians to be bishops, and showed little inclination to resign. In 1879 and 1880 the CMS began to press for the appointment of another suffragan in the diocese of Madras for West Tinnevelly, and they indicated that they were prepared to propose what they believed to be an acceptable Indian candidate. However, both Sargent and Gell opposed the proposal, claiming that Indians did not want an Indian bishop, because they thought he would be less influential on behalf of his area, especially in seeking grants from missionary societies, than a European would be.

At a meeting of the bishops working in India in 1888 it was suggested that a new bishop of Travancore and Cochin might be nominated by the clergy and laity of the diocese. The CMS, who provided the stipend for the bishop, however, objected strongly, fearing that such an arrangement would be detrimental to their wish to achieve a 'native church' with its own constitution and clergy.[46]

The bishop of Calcutta also wished to further subdivide his still enormous diocese, and having established a diocesan council, consulted them and obtained their approval for the division, and their support for a proposal that the bishops of the Anglican Church in India ought to have power to form new dioceses, and themselves to consecrate bishops for them. However, when he consulted the British government while he was in London for the Lambeth Conference of 1888 it was made clear that an Act of Parliament would be necessary to permit this, and that it would be impossible to find parliamentary time for such an Act. The bishop ingeniously circumvented this by proposing a consensual compact to the clergy of the district of Chota Nagpur (consisting of three European and fifteen Indian clergy) by which the clergy of the district should take an oath of canonical obedience to an assistant bishop to be appointed for the district, and he as bishop, would promise to give such a bishop as perfect independence as possible, reserving his rights as metropolitan. The clergy accepted this, as did a large meeting of representative lay people, both Indian and European. A suffragan bishop was therefore consecrated on this understanding. Bishop Johnson found that it was easier to carve a diocese of Lucknow out of the diocese of Calcutta, for the kingdom of Oudh and the state of Jhanai, which it was to comprise, had been added to British India in 1856. It was therefore possible for a diocese to be created by letters patent, which was done in 1893.

During the 1880s the CMS missionaries in Bengal, like their colleagues in West Africa, began to criticize the Society's 'native church' policy as racist and unscriptural, and suggested that Indians did not want it and pointed out that the CMS domination of the local church from London was more intense and oppressive than European episcopal domination from Calcutta. Similarly in the late 1880s the Society's missionaries in the Punjab and Sindh also began to assert that the Indian Church was still in its infancy, and that Indians were not fit to lead, except under European direction.

In South India by January 1891 both the suffragans who had been appointed for the diocese of Madras were dead, and Bishop Gell was persuaded to appoint a bishop who was associated with neither of the Societies for Tirunevelly, on the same basis as a bishop had been established in Chota Nagpur, by consensual compact between the diocesan bishop and the clergy and lay people of the district, with an endowment out of which the new bishop would be paid, contributed by the SPCK, the SPG and the Colonial Bishoprics Fund. In 1898 Bishop Johnson of Calcutta also secured the approval of the government of India to divide his diocese still further, by the creation of a diocese of Nagpur.

From the beginning of the twentieth century the synod of Anglican bishops in India began to assume a new significance in the life of the Church in India, and from 1908 it resolved to meet on a regular basis, at least every three years. In 1910 a proposal emerged for a provincial synod for India, which would include the bishops and representatives of the clergy and the lay people. In December 1912 the bishops met with two clerical and two lay assessors from each diocese to consider the proposal for a provincial synod. It was clear that there was enthusiasm for the idea, especially among Indians, and resolutions were drawn up outlining a general scheme for a provincial synod, diocesan representatives on which would be elected by diocesan councils, which would need to be established in every diocese. To a great extent the architect of this development was Bishop Palmer of Bombay. His desire was to develop a new 'Church' spirit in the province and in each diocese, which would overcome any tendency to separate Europeans and Indians, or of developing three separate churches based on the CMS, the SPG, and on the St John's Mission, the three leading Anglian missionary societies working in India. The proposal required each diocese to establish self-government, with each pastorate or district electing lay people to membership of the diocesan council.

From the formation of the Congress Party in the 1880s, there had been a growing desire among Indians for Indian leadership in the Church. The period after 1900 witnessed important advances in support for the Congress Party, and at the same time the YMCA was giving young Indian Christians experience of leadership alongside Europeans. It was from this background that the first Indian bishop came. V.S. Azariah had been secretary of the YMCA for South India since 1896. There he had discovered that Indians and Europeans could work together on terms of equality. In 1903 he had founded the Indian Missionary Society, in which Indians worked amongst Indians in the area of Teluga centred on Dornakal. Bishop Whitehead of Madras encouraged him to consider ordination, and he was ordained deacon in 1909. With the desire to include an Indian in the Church leadership, Azariah was the obvious candidate to become a bishop. Copleston, who was now bishop of Calcutta and metropolitan, however, was insistent that the first Indian to be consecrated an Anglican bishop should not be a suffragan, with the possible implication that he might be regarded as merely ministering to Indians, so it was agreed that a new diocese of Dornakal should be created, and, despite outbursts of protest from many quarters, Azariah was consecrated bishop of Dornakal at the episcopal synod in 1912.[47]

CHINA

China was opened up to European trade and to the activities of European Christian missionaries, including Anglicans, in the

1840s as a result of the 'Opium War', arising from trade disputes and cultural misunderstandings, and the subsequent Treaty of Nanking in 1842; and Hong Kong Island was ceded to the British crown. It was thought by many evangelicals that God had used the 'instrumentality of evils which have arisen through the sin of man and the devices of Satan [the opium trade] for the accomplishment of his benevolent purposes towards China'.[48] A diocese was established in Hong Kong in 1849, and £5,000 of the £10,000 contributed by J.C. Sharpe and Lady Smart for the endowment was intended to provide for a college to train a body of native clergy and Christian teachers 'for the propagation of the Gospel in China according to the principles of the Church of England'. The first bishop, George Smith, had been a CMS missionary in China, and he saw his appointment as an opportunity to extend the Church of England mission in China. In 1853 he came to an understanding with the PECUSA bishop in Shanghai that each would superintend the clergy and congregations of his own church. The second Anglo-Chinese War and the ensuing Treaty of Tientsin in 1858 revived evangelical hopes for the development of trade and mission in China. In 1863 Bishop Smith ordained as deacon a Chinese catechist who had worked in Australia. A second Chinese deacon was ordained in 1868 to work in Foochow and in 1871 Wong Fui Tuk was ordained priest, in an ordination service conducted in Chinese, in Foochow. However the CMS mission to Foochow was hardly a success for although it had been begun in 1849, by 1860 it was reported that there had been no converts.

In the 1860s Henry Venn had sought the division of the diocese of Victoria (Hong Kong), so that the European missionaries would be under the direction of the bishop of Victoria, and the Chinese clergy and congregations under a new bishop of Ningpo, but Archbishop Longley had opposed a racial division and was only willing to accept a geographical division of the diocese. The proposal for a racial division was revived by the CMS in 1869, and Archbishop Tait had proved more sympathetic. However, the proposal was not pursued because the Chinese Church only had 318 communicants and two Chinese deacons, and had no suitable candidate to be nominated as bishop.[49]

Bishop Burdon, who was appointed to Hong Kong in 1874, had been a CMS missionary in China and chaplain at the British

Embassy in Peking. He had learned Mandarin and had translated the Prayer Book and the New Testament into Mandarin. He had strong views about indigenization, and wished to use rice cake and tea as eucharistic elements, because he thought that bread and wine were essentially Western and foreign to the Chinese. This, combined with the doubts about his authority because of his appointment without royal letters patent, led to considerable suspicions of him by the CMS missionaries in Hong Kong.

Japan had become accessible to the Western nations after the treaties of 1854–6 and the northern part of China was opened to European influence after the 'Arrow' War of 1856–8 and the Convention of Peking in 1860. Korea also became accessible to the West as a result of a series of treaties in the 1880s. Following these diplomatic and economic inroads into East Asia, in 1872 a new diocese of North China was created out of the diocese of Hong Kong, without consulting the bishop. In 1880 North China was further subdivided into the dioceses of North China and Mid China. In 1883 Japan, previously part of the still vast diocese of Hong Kong, was created a separate province, and in 1895 West China was carved out of Mid-China. Fukien diocese was established in 1906 and Kwangsi and Hunan became a separate diocese in 1909.

In 1901 the PECUSA had established a second diocese, at Hankow, and it was agreed between the English bishops and Bishop Graves of Shanghai that the Americans should control all Anglican work in the lower Yangtse valley, and the English should be responsible for the Anglican Church in the rest of China. The congregation of the English cathedral in Shanghai, however, objected to being handed over to the American bishop; they were eventually exempted from his authority, and placed under the jurisdiction of the bishop of North China. In the early twentieth century the Anglican Church in Canada had also established a diocese in China. As a result of these piecemeal Anglican initiatives, the Anglican Church in China looked to three different provinces of the Anglican Communion.

Despite the enormous problems of travel in these vast dioceses containing few Anglicans and fewer clergy, the bishops attempted to meet regularly. In 1897 the first conference of Anglican bishops in China and Korea was held in Shanghai, and they met again in 1899 and 1903. In 1906 the clergy of the dioceses of Hong Kong, North China, Shantung, Shanghai and Hankow sent a general letter to their bishops asking for a general Anglican conference to begin to create greater cohesion and unity among themselves, as the necessary prelude to making their influence more widely felt in China. At the subsequent general Anglican conference in 1907 a committee was set up to consider the question of the adaptation of the Church to the local situation. This committee presented a most detailed report dealing with church architecture, teaching, the segregation of men and women in church, marriage rites and burial customs. At the next conference in 1909 there was discussion about setting up a Chinese Anglican Church. This proposal was supported by the CMS, the SPG and the American Episcopal Church mission in China. In 1912 a convention was called, at which all the dioceses in China were represented, and with the support of Archbishop Davidson, the self-governing independent Chung Hua Shen Kung Hui was launched, which was Anglican in creed and form. A provincial synod was set up and synods were established in each diocese.

When the British government had disendowed the cathedral in Hong Kong in 1882 responsibility for its funding and the appointment of the chaplain had been handed over to the 'Church Body'. This body, consisting largely of British settlers had never much liked the missionary emphasis of the bishops of Hong Kong, and when a new bishop was appointed in 1895, they had expressed a preference for someone who had been a parish priest in England, rather than a missionary, and who would pay more attention to the needs of the European community. In spite of this there was considerable expansion of missionary work among the Chinese in the diocese of Hong Kong (which still included a significant part of mainland China, and not merely the British territories), and as a result a separate Chinese 'Church Body' was created in 1902, upon which all the Chinese clergy in the colony, and delegates of the vestries of the various Chinese congregations sat. When a diocesan synod was set up in Hong Kong diocese in 1913, there was a separate Chinese synod to govern the vernacular side of the work in the diocese. The then bishop expressed regret at this division, but acknowledged that it was a matter of language; English residents in the colony did not learn Chinese, and there was thus little community of interest between them and the Chinese Anglicans.[50]

The second half of the nineteenth century witnessed a very considerable expansion of Christian missionary activity into areas of Africa and Asia where the Christian gospel had not previously been preached, and Anglican missionaries played a part in this. Motives for this burst of Christian missionary activity were mixed, and changed during the course of the century. The motives of Buxton and Livingstone in mid-century had been to preach the gospel in Africa to free Africans from slavery by introducing alternative forms of trade with the countries of Western Europe and North and South America. They and their missionary associates, most notably Henry Venn, had envisaged the rapid establishment of local churches; in these churches, after Christianity had been introduced by missionaries, local leadership was expected to emerge, so that quite quickly the churches would become financially independent, and would produce their own candidates for episcopal consecration. In order to achieve this Venn wished to separate native congregations from European congregations and pastors, in order to prevent local churches being overwhelmed by, or merely copying, European models.

By the 1880s, as we have seen, there was a new, more dynamic mood in European and American Christianity driven, in many cases by a motive to preach the gospel in all nations before whatever cataclysmic divine intervention could be expected at the end of the second millennium, popularized in publications such as Henry Grattan Guinness's *The Approaching End of the Age* first published in 1878. New money, new men, and for the first time, women, flooded into the missionary societies and the 'mission fields' in Africa, India, China and the Far East. They saw converts in a new light, as children to be brought up slowly in the gospel, so that they might evolve over several generations to be sufficiently fit to administer and support their own churches. The experiment of a black bishop in Africa, it was thought had been premature, more time, much more time, was needed. In Africa therefore, the encouragement of local leadership was not seen as a priority. In Indian and China these views were less easy to sustain, particularly as an independence movement developed in India in the late nineteenth century and China was never brought under colonial rule. As we have seen, there began to be a slow movement towards creating Indian leadership in the Anglican Church in India, the process in China, however, was much slower.

As has been suggested, the missionary expansion of the Anglican Communion and British imperialism were parallel movements. The missionary expansion did not follow imperial expansion. British rule was established in Africa, Asia and the Pacific during the last twenty years of the nineteenth century largely to protect trade, and to exclude rivals, notably France and Germany. Because formal rule of a country was invariably more expensive than informal influence, colonial rule was less a preference for successive British governments than a last resort. Britain only annexed territories where her existing networks of economic interests were threatened. Because British imperial policy was concerned to be as cheap as possible, the existing Christian missions were used to 'service' the structures of colonial rule by the provision of health care and education, and so were often drawn into a dependent relationship with colonial administrations.[51] However, the development of Christianity, and Anglicanism in particular, in Buganda, Madagascar and China independently of European colonial expansion, illustrates clearly that neither the spread of Christianity nor of its Angli-can manifestation was dependent on British colonial policy.

This chapter has been concerned with the ways in which Anglicanism coped with the expansion of the Church in Africa and Asia, and with the tensions that emerged among Anglican missionary societies, missionaries, British settlers, converts. In some cases new models of the Church and of episcopal organization were developed to promote this expansion, and in India and China, in particular, there began to be pressure for local leadership in the Church, and for account to be taken in the Church of distinctive local cultures. In the next chapter we turn once more to consider the ways in which the expansion in the number of dioceses and the diverse concerns and needs of the local churches, for example, church unity in South India, or local leadership in Africa, were held together in one communion.

CHAPTER 7

The Unity of the Communion: Lambeth Conferences and the Formation of Provinces

When the bishops attending the Lambeth Conference in 1867 dispersed there was no indication that there might be a further meeting of the bishops. However, at the adjourned session of the conference in December 1867, Bishop Selwyn was appointed 'corresponding secretary' of the Anglican Communion. Selwyn took this role seriously, and as part of it he accepted an invitation to attend the general convention of the PECUSA at Baltimore in 1871. In preaching before the convention, Selwyn pointed out that there should be no 'servile uniformity' in the Church, but 'if there be but a recognised authority, which all are willing to obey. The whole of our Church is interested in obtaining this happy combination of elastic freedom with efficient control.' In this he sketched out the essence of the Anglican ideal of authority.

In 1872 the Canadian bishops, meeting in their provincial synod, again invited the convocation of Canterbury to join with them in asking the archbishop of Canterbury to call a second conference of Anglican bishops. Selwyn undertook to introduce the request to the convocation. In the debate in the upper house of convocation he pointed out that, now royal letters patent were no longer required for appointing bishops overseas, overseas bishops had no means of finding out by what laws or principles they were to govern, or on what basis they should negotiate a voluntary compact with representatives of the clergy and laity, and that as bishops were no longer required to take an oath of canonical obedience to the archbishop of Canterbury, the relationship between the archbishop and the overseas bishops had been substantially changed. Selwyn suggested that a confederation of dioceses should be established by voluntary compact, recognizing the archbishop of Canterbury as its head. At the end of a debate the convocation agreed to ask the archbishop of Canterbury to consult the archbishop of York about the possibility of holding a further meeting of Anglican bishops.[1] However, there was no further recorded development.

In 1874 the West Indian bishops invited the convocation of Canterbury to join with them and the Canadian and Australian bishops to request another meeting of Anglican bishops. After discussing the matter, the upper house set up a committee to consider the request.[2] The committee quickly reported and recommended that another conference should be called. The committee did not commend Selwyn's suggestion that the archbishop of Canterbury should assume the title of 'patriarch', which he had thought would emphasis the unity and the coherence of the Communion.[3] Also in 1874 Selwyn attended the Canadian provincial synod followed by another visit to the American general convention. At the general convention there was some feeling among the clergy and laity against another conference if it did not include representatives of clergy and laity, and did not hold discussions in public.[4] Bishop Kersfoot of Pittsburgh was the main enthusiast among the American bishops for another conference, but he encountered significant opposition from his fellow bishops, many of whom were openly distrustful of the proposal. The recently published biography of Bishop Hopkins of Vermont had been highly critical of the arrangements for the 1867 conference, and in particular of Tait's part in it, as being unfriendly to the American episcopate. In the end the American bishops did agree to endorse a request for another conference, but supported the Canadian bishops' request that the 'arrangements for a Conference should be such as to manifest the variety of topics admitted, and the time allowed should be such as would seem to justify a Convocation of our bishops from all over the world'.[5]

At its meeting in February 1875 the convocation of York received a report on these developments and expressed no objection to another conference being called. Tait, who had succeeded Longley as archbishop of Canterbury in 1869, had come to recognize that a conference did fulfil a need and that it was less dangerous for the relationship between Church and State than he had initially feared. He therefore agreed in principle to call a second conference in 1877. In 1876 he wrote to all the Anglican bishops to inquire whether they wished for a conference, and if so, what should be on the agenda. By the end of 1876 ninety bishops had replied, and a majority indicated they would value another conference, although there were some objections. The American bishops wished the conference to be postponed for a year as they had a general convention scheduled for 1877.[6] Recognizing a general wish for another conference, Tait agreed to call one in 1878 and wrote to the bishops,

> We entertain a grateful sense of the advantages of that brotherly intercourse which the last Lambeth Conference tended to encourage and we should look forward with much pleasure to another meeting of the same kind.
>
> [He added] It appears to us that respecting matters of doctrine, no change can be proposed or discussed and that no authoritative explanation of doctrine ought to be taken in hand. Each Church is naturally guided in the interpretation of its formularies by its recognised authorities. Again respecting matters of discipline, each Church has its own appointed courts for the administration of ecclesiastical, with which, of course such a meeting of bishops as is proposed claims no power to interfere.[7]

By making this last point, he emphasized the importance of the bishops not interfering with each other's jurisdictions.

Tait set up an episcopal committee, which included Selwyn, who was now the elder statesman of the Communion, to plan the agenda. It was agreed that it should include discussion about the best mode of maintaining union among the various churches of the Anglican Communion; the establishment of voluntary boards of arbitration for churches to which such arrangements might be applicable; the relations to each other of missionary bishops and of missions from various parts of the Anglican Communion acting in the same country; the numbers of Anglican chaplains and chaplaincies in Europe and elsewhere; modern forms of infidelity and the best means of dealing with them; and the condition and progress and needs of the various churches of the Anglican Communion.[8] The subjects for discussion were, in fact based on the resolutions of the 1867 Conference, for there had been no opportunity then to discuss the reports of the Committees appointed at the conference. In

July 1877 Tait issued invitations to attend a four-week conference at Lambeth in July 1878 to the metropolitans and presiding bishops, to be forwarded to the bishops entitled to receive them in each branch or province of the Church.[9] Retired bishops were not invited (two retired colonial bishops had attended the 1867 conference), and the bishop of Cape Town did not pass on an invitation to Bishop Colenso. Of the 173 diocesan bishops then in the Anglican Communion, 108 accepted the invitation.[10]

In the event 100 bishops attended the conference. The expenses of the conference, so far as they did not devolve upon the archbishop of Canterbury personally for hospitality at Lambeth Palace, were met by the English dioceses, and a committee of laymen was set up to arrange hospitality for the visiting bishops.[11] The archbishop of York, recognizing that the conference posed no threat to the Church of England's relationship with the State, attended and preached the sermon at the opening service. However two English evangelical bishops still declined to attend. It was agreed again that meetings should be private and that no record should be kept or published of meetings. In his opening address Tait emphasized the nature of the English establishment and the variety of the constitutions of the overseas churches and the importance of the bishops tolerating diversity, pointing out, 'This toleration is the same as catholicity'. He reminded the bishops that 'Sects are narrow and intolerant. The Catholic Church of Christ is wide and knows no intolerance. It dwells on the essentials of the Christian faith.'[12]

The conference adopted the procedure of preliminary debates on each agenda subject during the first week of the conference, after which the bishops divided into six committees, one for each agenda item, which then spend two weeks discussing the subject and drafting reports, which were received and discussed in plenary session during the final week of the conference.[13]

This conference set out four principles, contained in the reports of several committees of the conference, to govern relations between the churches of the Communion, which have been repeatedly reaffirmed since 1878. First, that the duly verified action of every self-governing church in the exercise of its own discipline should be respected by all the other churches and their individual members. Second, that no bishop or other minister from one self-governing church should in any sense exercise his ministry in a diocese in any other self-governing church without the permission of the bishop of that diocese. Third, that no bishop should allow a minister coming from another self-governing church to exercise his ministry in his diocese unless the minister brought with him letters testimonial from his previous bishop. Fourth, that no self-governing church should consecrate a bishop as a missionary bishop in any place to which a bishop had already been sent by some other church of the Communion.

It was also recommended that there should not be a central judicial tribunal for the Communion, but that if they wished, individual provinces might make arrangements for appeals to be heard outside the province. The committee on 'Modern Forms of Infidelity and the Best Means of Dealing with Them' announced that they had not found it possible to prepare, in the time allotted for their discussions, a detailed report on so vast a subject.[14] The report at the end of the conference was drawn up by Tait with the assistance of Christopher Wordsworth, bishop of Lincoln and Bishops Fraser of Manchester and Mitchinson of Barbados. Christopher Wordsworth also translated the report into Latin and Greek for transmission to the heads of the Western and Eastern churches.[15]

After the 1878 conference there was no question but that there would be further conferences. There was a sense among the overseas churches that they were not yet strong enough to stand alone and that they needed support and guidance from the archbishop of Canterbury and the English Church until each of them had a strong system of organization and government.[16] E.W. Benson, who succeeded Tait was a distinguished patristic scholar whose life's research was on Cyprian. 'Cyprian and his times', Benson wrote, 'were as innocent of presbyterian and congregational, as they were of papal, catholicity'.[17]

On the basis of his research about the third-century Church Benson was convinced of the importance of the establishment of native churches, and was concerned to maintain the spirit and principles of the early Church in the developing Anglican Communion.[18] Benson took the initiative in calling the third conference for the summer of 1888. The agenda that he drew up for the bishops included, as well as issues relating to the organization of the Communion, social and practical questions that were then concerning the Church, notably, temperance, purity, emigrants, socialism, polygamy and divorce. Of the 211 bishops then serving in the Communion, 147 accepted invitations.[19] Since the previous conference the initiative had been taken in the Church of England to introduce suffragan bishops. By 1888 there were eight suffragan bishops in England, and they and the six retired overseas bishops who held episcopal commissions in England, were also invited.[20] At the opening of the conference Benson reiterated what his predecessors had said, 'that the Conference was in no sense a Synod' and that it was 'not adapted or competent or within its powers if it should attempt to make binding decisions on doctrine or disciplines'.[21]

In 1867 it had been established that although reports of debates should not be published, the reports of committees should be circulated for the information of dioceses. However in 1878 the report of the committee considering 'infidelity' had, as we have seen, not been circulated. This precedent was followed in 1888 with the report of the committee considering the 'definite teaching of the Church', which had been drafted by Bishop Temple of London, and was rejected after what was described as 'a stormy and most unfortunate debate'.[22] The considerable success in 1867 in establishing formulae for the expression of doctrine that would be acceptable to all the bishops present proved more difficult thereafter, as bishops from more varied theological positions felt confident to attend and contribute to the conference.

In addition to the committees on social issues, there were committees on 'Home Reunion', the Scandinavian churches, and the Old Catholic Church and the Eastern Orthodox churches. The conference adopted, with minor modifications, the Chicago Quadrilateral which had been approved by the house of bishops of the PECUSA in 1886, which was intended to form the basis of an invitation to any and all Christian bodies to enter into discussions and negotiations leading to organic union with the Episcopal Church. It set out what were called 'the principles of unity exemplified by the undivided Church during the first ages of its existence'. The four points which formed the basis of the invitation were derived from William Reed Huntingdon's *The Church Idea – A Essay Towards Unity* published in 1876, in which he attempted to define the essential marks of a united Church. They emerged in the report on Home Reunion, with the addition of the Apostles' Creed, as a 'basis on which approach may by God's blessing be made towards Home Reunion', and comprised:

A. The Holy Scriptures of the Old and New Testaments as 'containing all things necessary to salvation being the ultimate rule and standard of faith'.

B. The Apostles' Creed as the Baptismal symbol, and the Nicene Creed as the sufficient statement of the Christian faith.

C. The two sacraments ordained by Christ himself, Baptism and the Supper of the Lord, using Christ's words of institution, and the elements ordained by him.

D. The Historic Episcopate, locally adapted in the methods of its administration to the varying needs of the nations and peoples called of God into the Unity of the Church.[23]

After setting out the Quadrilateral, the bishops rejected a proposal that the orders of a minister of a church which did not episcopally ordain its ministers should be accepted.

This conference was also significant in that it took a step in rehabilitating the Oriental churches of unjustified accusations of heresy, and adding to the initiative taken in 1867, of circulating the conference encyclical to the leaders of the churches, clearly identified the Anglican Communion as a distinctive world-Church, seeking to establish relations with other churches.

On the social questions the committee on polygamy recommended that polygamists should not be baptized, although they accepted that in certain instances the wives of polygamists might be baptized.[24] Their firm line on this was probably helped by the fact that Colenso had produced the best reasoned case in favour of baptizing polygamists and their wives. This resolution, as we have already noted, was immensely significant for the Anglican Church in Africa. It illustrated the weakness of the conference as a deliberative assembly for a world-Church. Of the 147 bishops present only eleven were working in Africa where the issue really applied (and of those, seven were working in South Africa, probably mainly among white settlers). Colenso's arguments were probably rejected out of hand because of what were regarded as his eccentric doctrinal views. There was thus no one to put the case from the African point of view, that polygamy was central to the African social order, and to exclude polygamists from baptism would virtually exclude all adult males from the possibility of being received into the Church, while to require them to reject all but one wife would be dramatically destructive of the existing economic and social order, and would cast vast numbers of women and children into a social vacuum, in which the churches had no capacity to create an alternative society. Coincidentally the first major secession from the Anglican Church in Nigeria was in 1888, and the break-away church permitted the baptism of men and women living in polygamy.[25]

On 'socialism' the bishops were addressed by Henry Scott Holland, then a canon of St Paul's, who became one of the leaders of the Christian Social Union. The committee considering socialism, chaired by Bishop Moorehouse of Manchester, concluded that, if by socialism was meant the union of labour with land and capital and a general concern for the material and moral welfare of the poor, there was no contradiction between socialism and Christianity. The committee set its face against the State ownership of land and capital, but supported the purchase of land by labourers and co-operative societies. They suggested that governments should do more to protect workers from 'the evil effects of unlimited competition', but concluded that 'the best help is self-help'. Clergy, they recommended, should be trained in economics, and should 'enter friendly relations with Socialists', and demonstrate 'how much of what is good and true in socialism is to be found in the precepts of Christ'. The encyclical issued at the end of the conference urged the study 'of what is popularly called Socialism' and the support of any scheme for 'redressing the balance' between people.[26]

The encyclical published at the end of the conference was largely the work of the two very distinguished scholars, J.B. Lightfoot, the New Testament scholar and bishop of Durham and William Stubbs, the church historian and bishop of Oxford; and John Wordsworth, bishop of Salisbury followed his father in translating it into Latin and Greek.

Archbishop Benson had already issued invitations for the next conference to be held in 1897 to coincide with the twelfth centenary of St Augustine's landing in Kent, before he died in 1896 and was succeeded by Frederick Temple. Of the 240 bishops invited, 194 attended the conference in 1897. Benson had tended to draw all things to Lambeth for decision, and had put on the agenda for the 1897 conference, under the heading of the organization of the Anglican Communion, consideration of a 'central consultative body' for the Communion, a 'tribunal of reference', the 'relation of primates and metropolitans in the colonies and elsewhere to the see of Canterbury', and the 'position and functions of the Lambeth Conference'. This aroused the suspicions of the American bishops, and Bishop Doane of Albany wrote to Randall Davidson, the bishop of Winchester, as episcopal secretary to the conference, in February 1897 reporting 'a very decided objection and a strong opposition to any idea of attempting to establish any authoritative relation to the see of Canterbury in America, and I know there is also in the Church of Scotland, it would be absolutely impossible to create anything like a Canterbury Patriarchate to which National Churches would be willing to refer'. He pressed that the item should be dropped from the agenda. Davidson replied that as the South African and Australasian bishops were very keen on the idea of a 'tribunal of reference' it must be discussed.[27]

The committee on the organization of the Anglican Communion gave much time to the consideration of creating a more coherent organization for the Communion. It eventually recommended the establishment of a 'tribunal of reference to which might be referred questions submitted by the bishops of the Church of England and colonial and missionary churches'. The tribunal, they recommended, should be presided over by the archbishops of Canterbury and York, and comprise the bishops of London, Durham and Winchester, and representatives of each province. There was also a hint that the archbishop of Canterbury should assume the title 'patriarch' of the Anglican Communion. However, the American bishops continued their opposition to any idea of a Canterbury patriarchate, and also to the recommendation of the tribunal of reference, which was not adopted. Instead, the recommendation for a Central Consultative Council, as an advisory body, was approved, and Archbishop Temple set it up. The American bishops were suspicious, even of this.[28] They seem to have been determined that the purpose of the conferences should continue to be for talk and consultation, and not for decisions or to exercise authority on behalf of the whole Communion. Despite the somewhat negative part played by the American bishops, Mandell Creighton, the bishop of London, thought the conference 'would have been infinitely poorer if it had not been for the presence of their brethren from the United States . . . [because] . . . they introduce into the discussions a somewhat different element'. He thought that it was a great gain that 'our Church remains the same when it takes its existence among a perfectly independent people. We feel in that a guarantee of its reality, of the fundamental strength of its position, and we feel sure that the great distinctive mark of the Anglican Church throughout the world is that it is the Church and represents the ecclesiastical organisation which is suitable to the life of free men.'[29]

In Canada the metropolitans of the two provinces of Canada and Rupertsland had adopted the title of archbishop in 1894. Benson had disliked this on the grounds that 'archbishop' was not a title that could be conferred by a provincial synod and that the bishops should have been consulted at a Lambeth Conference before such a step was taken. He suspected that in the overseas synods the bishops were acting 'without knowledge of ecclesiastical procedures and a regard for previous obligations and with all due exercise of courtesy'. The committee on the organization of Anglicanism therefore discussed the nomenclature of metropolitans of Anglican provinces, and recommended that henceforward they might adopt the title of archbishop, which was adopted by the conference.[30]

The conference reiterated the points made in the Lambeth Quadrilateral of 1888, and went further in stating that the Anglican Church was not merely an English phenomenon, but the form of the catholic Church for English-speaking Christians, and suggesting that it had a vocation to exemplify Christian unity. There was also, for the first time, a committee on religious communities, which recommended that the bishops should give thanks for their establishment in the Communion, for rendering 'great services to the Church', but it was also noted that they needed 'more regulation'. The committee advised that 'Right relations with the episcopate involve powers of Visitation', a comment that may have reflected Archbishop Benson's experience in 1896, when he had attempted to conduct a visitation of the Community of the Sisters of the Church, but had been seen off by the reverend mother.

It was also recommended that thanks should be given for the revival of the order of deaconesses. The committee recommended that to avoid confusion the title 'deaconess' should be reserved for women who had been 'set apart' by a bishop by 'the laying on of hands'. It also recommended that a standard form for 'setting apart' women as deaconesses should be adopted throughout the Communion, to conform to the common ordinal throughout the Communion, and that there should be uniformity in the licensing of deaconesses, as there was for deacons and priests. The committee on the critical study of Holy Scripture cautiously recommended the practice, which bearing in mind that Archbishop Temple had been one of the contributors to *Essays and Reviews* in 1860, was the least that might be expected.[31]

This conference was also the first that, at least unofficially, was acknowledged by the State. It met in the year of Queen Victoria's Diamond Jubilee and the bishops were invited to Windsor, and the Queen was driven in her carriage along the lines of assembled bishops as they bowed to her, and she stopped and spoke to the archbishop of Canterbury, and a few of the bishops were presented to her by Randall Davidson, the bishop of Winchester (who had been dean of Windsor, and was her closest ecclesiastical adviser).[32]

The encyclical issued at the end of the conference was drafted by the archbishop of Canterbury, without consulting or referring to any other bishop.[33] Temple, in fact, tended to do everything himself, and not to delegate work to his chaplains or advisers. It had, as we have seen, for many years been customary for overseas bishops to consult the archbishop upon points where they needed advice, and the archbishop had usually consulted with the missionary and other societies before replying. Benson had strongly encouraged this, seeing the see of Canterbury as the focus of the Communion. Temple, however, was already aged seventy-five when he became archbishop, and with the best of intentions, he acknowledged most of the letters that he received with a promise that further attention would be given to them when time allowed. Time never allowed, and he seems to have largely abandoned any real correspondence about overseas affairs.[34]

In 1903 Randall Davidson, who had been close to the heart of Church and State and Anglican Communion affairs as chaplain to Archbishop Tait, and then successively dean of Windsor, bishop of Rochester and bishop of Winchester, became archbishop of Canterbury. As Tait's chaplain he had helped to arrange the 1878 conference, and he had been assistant secretary to the conference in 1888, and episcopal secretary in 1898, and had prepared and published a history of the 1867 and 1878 conferences. He was to make a very significant contribution to the Anglican Communion, having already had extensive experience of ecclesiastical politics and diplomacy, and came to the position at a relatively young age, and with an assumption that responsibility for the Communion should be a priority, whereas for most of his predecessors it had been an innovation at an age when they had already become set in their thinking about the Church. Davidson was still young enough to travel, and to take advantage of the much greater speed of communication available in the early twentieth century. He thus accepted, at J. Pierpoint Morgan's persuasion, an invitation to attend the general convention of the PECUSA at Boston in 1904 and combined it with visits to Quebec, Montreal and Toronto. He impressed the Americans he met as someone who was willing to listen, and as 'a democrat'. They were pleased to find that he was utterly opposed to any idea of a Canterbury patriarchate. Davidson also made some important friendships among the American bishops on this visit, especially with Bishop Brent of the Philippines (and from 1917 of Western New York), who was to play an important part in the Anglican Communion and the development of the Ecumenical Movement after the World Missionary Conference in Edinburgh in 1910, which both he and Davidson attended.[35]

As archbishop, Davidson established close links with all parts of the Communion. From his previous experience he already had an extraordinary personal knowledge of the overseas provinces and dioceses, and he took a deep interest in them, and welcomed news about them. His success lay in his desire to know and to help.[36] In 1908 Davidson presided over a pan-Anglican Congress held in London, which was the brainchild of Bishop Henry Montgomery, the secretary of the SPG, who had been bishop of Tasmania. This, for the first time, brought together laity and clergy from across the Anglican Communion, as well as bishops. It was intended to stir the imaginations of the Communion and to give clergy and laity a new sense of unity, besides leading to fresh offers by clergy in England to work in the Church overseas. There was extensive consultation about the agenda, especially with overseas bishops, and preliminary papers on agenda items were prepared by leading scholars and distributed to the participants before they left their homes. The congress was thought to have been an enormous success.[37]

Davidson invited diocesan bishops and bishops holding permanent commissions as suffragans or assistant bishops to the 1908 Lambeth Conference which attracted 242 bishops to London, including twenty-eight English suffragans and fourteen former overseas bishops holding commissions in English dioceses.[38] The committee on the organization of the Anglican Communion considered the role of the Consultative Council which had been set up after the previous conference by Archbishop Temple, and recommended that it should be reconstituted to comprise eighteen members, including a representative from each province, except that Canterbury should be represented by two members and the PECUSA by four. The committee also condemned any suggestions that separate churches should be established for different racial groups, which effectively outlawed the CMS's policy for the establishment of parallel jurisdictions for European and native Anglicans, thus finally obliterating Henry Venn's vision of a native episcopate.[39]

The committee on reunion requested the archbishop of Canterbury to appoint a commission to enter into negotiations on behalf of the Anglican Communion with the Church of Sweden to investigate the possibility of establishing a closer relation between these two national reformed episcopal churches which had retained the episcopal succession at the Reformation. The conference also continued the rehabilitation of the Oriental churches, which had begun at the 1888 conference.[40] However, when the bishops considered a proposal that Presbyterian ordinations should be recognized as regular, Charles Gore, then bishop of Birmingham, a leading Anglo-Catholic, who was convalescing after peritonitis, had himself carried into the meeting on a litter, and threatened to resign if the proposal was passed, and the bishops surrendered.[41]

The committee on marriage problems took seriously the problem of applying a critical study of Scripture to ethical problems, and in view of the theory that Mark's Gospel predated Matthew's Gospel, which traditionally had been considered the earliest Gospel to be written, expressed caution about the Matthean exception, which had generally been considered to permit the remarriage of an 'innocent party' following divorce on the only ground of divorce then permitted, adultery, and expressed hesitation about remarriage even of 'innocent parties'. The committee also condemned the use of artificial means of birth control, on the grounds that it defeated the prime purpose of marriage, as set out in the Book of Common Prayer, and that it discouraged self-control, treated sexual intercourse as an end in itself, and would lead to a declining birthrate, especially among what was described as 'the superior stock'.[42]

While the 1908 conference made an important contribution to the Anglican Church's understanding of its own mission by recalling the Church to the fact that it stood among the people as their servant for Christ and salvation, it made little contribution to the debate about doctrinal development and 'modernism' that was troubling the Roman Catholic Church as well as the Anglican and other churches. It optimistically asserted that 'Men's minds are more and more set towards the spiritual', and went on: 'We are bound by our principles to look with confidence and hope in the progress of thought. But we mark in the present day special reasons for such confidence. Materialism has not for the minds of our generation the strength or the attractiveness that once it had'.[43]

The conference made an important contribution to the development of worship and liturgy in the Communion. For the previous fifty or more years there had been agitation, particularly among Anglo-Catholics in the Church of England, and also in some overseas dioceses, for a revision of the Prayer Book to accommodate more catholic interpretations of the eucharistic liturgy. Arising from this, the conference had appointed a committee to discuss 'Prayer Book adaptation and enrichment' whose members included several of the English bishops concerned with the proposals for the revision of the Prayer Book. The conference approved the seven principles for revision of the Prayer Book recommended by the committee, including the adaptation of rubrics to generally accepted current customs, framing additions to enrich the present services, the provision of alternative forms of public worship, and the provision for 'greater elasticity' in public worship.

The report touched off an explosion of liturgical revision. The Scottish Episcopal Church and the Church of Ireland began work on revision in 1909, and agreed final versions in 1929 and 1926 respectively. The Anglican churches in Canada and South Africa began revision in 1911 and agreed final versions in 1921 and 1954 respectively, and the PECUSA began work in 1913, and approved a final version in 1928. The Church of England had already begun work on drawing up an alternative Prayer Book, but the proposals were rejected by the House of Commons in 1927 and 1928. The very long, drawn out processes allowed the various revising committees to consult each other, and to become acquainted with each other's proposals, so that the influence of the seven principles set out in the 1908 conference report were clearly evident in each of the new liturgies.[44]

It was thought by Gore's biographer that Gore had had a marked influence on the resolutions of the conference, swinging the bishops further towards a Catholic standpoint than they had appeared likely to take, either from the tenor of the preliminary discussions, or from the terms of the committees' reports.[45] Francis Paget, bishop of Oxford, writing to one of his sons, noted '. . . it is very interesting and encouraging; it shows problems in new light, from strange points of view: and it makes one feel very deeply the range and the power of the Anglican Communion. For the speaking on the whole is wonderfully good: sometimes and not seldom, it rises to be quite first rate; and one feels that men are not only saying very ably what they think, but they have thought it very ably before they say it. . .'.[46]

The encyclical issued at the end of the conference was drafted by Davidson himself, assisted by Bishops Paget of Oxford, John Wordsworth of Salisbury and Palmer of Bombay. The 1908 conference was the first of which official cognizance was given by the State, when Edward VII received the bishops at Buckingham Palace.[47]

The Edinburgh Missionary Conference in 1910 focused new issues for the Anglican Communion and other churches. It was realized more clearly that the establishment of indigenous churches raised problems about their relationships with one another, and with the old established communions. The conference made people realize that it was going to be necessary to define what were the real and essential characteristics of the Christian Church.[48] Davidson demonstrated his ecumenical statesmanship over the Kikuyu incident in 1913 when Frank Weston the Anglo-Catholic bishop of Zanzibar, denounced the evangelical bishops of Uganda and Mombasa for heresy for having invited a Church of Scotland minister to preach and nonconformist missionaries to receive holy communion at the end of a meeting of missionaries considering a scheme of federation between the various missionary bodies working in British East Africa. The event had been reported in the *Scotsman* as an example of a means of coalescing episcopacy and presbyterianism. Davidson refused to get overexcited, and summoned the Consultative Body of the Lambeth Conference to consider the issues and to advise him, rather than trying the two bishops for heresy himself, supported by his suffragans, as Weston had melodramatically demanded. He received the advice from the Consultative Body, and delivered his own view, which was basically an expansion of the advice that he had received. He noted that the issue was not one peculiar to East Africa, and that it was the problem of the growing 'native Church', which ought not to 'be hampered in its young life by schisms and divergences whose origin and meaning are due to what may almost be called the accidental happenings of English or Scottish life – political, social and ecclesiastical – 150 or 200 years ago'. He advised that such joint communion services, even held with the best of intentions to demonstrate commitment to unity in the Church, should be abstained from at present, because 'in a world of quick tidings and of ample talk they are shown to be open to the kind of misunderstandings which have arisen', and might be claimed as demonstrations and precedents. He, of course, satisfied neither the Anglo-Catholics nor the evangelicals, but he managed to retain both within the Communion.[49]

He also had to respond to the decision of the British Liberal government in 1911 to include in its legislative programme, without having consulted the bishops, a parliamentary bill to disestablish the four Welsh dioceses. Since the religious census of 1851 it had been common knowledge that the Anglican Church in Wales was a minority church, attracting in 1851 only about 20 per cent of the churchgoing population. The growth of Welsh nationalism during the second half of the nineteenth century was strongly identified with nonconformity and the Liberal party and a determined opposition had been orchestrated against the Church in Wales as an English institution imposed on the Welsh. From 1880 about 90 per cent of the MPs for Welsh constituencies were Liberals and the Liberals also swept to power in the county councils which were established in Wales after 1889 and county councillors had begun to look to the Church's endowments as a source for funding projects to develop Welsh education and culture. However, the Conservative party supported establishment, so while Conservative governments were in power the Welsh dioceses were safe from disestablishment.

In 1906 the Liberal party was swept into power at the general election with a commitment to relieve the alleged disadvantages of nonconformists in England and Wales. In the early 1900s the general lack of popularity of the Anglican Church in Wales had been sharpened by the unrest over funding for Church schools from the local rates, as a result of the 1902 Education Act, and the religious revival in Wales in 1904–1905. However, in the last decade or so of the nineteenth century the Anglican Church in Wales had begun to revive and to grow in strength, while membership of the nonconformist denominations had begun to decline. Easter communicants were growing in numbers in the Welsh dioceses, and after 1870 only Welsh-speaking bishops had been appointed to Welsh dioceses. The Liberal government appointed a Royal Commission on Religion in Wales in 1906 which reported in 1910.

The resulting Welsh Church Disestablishment Bill in 1912 proposed the disendowment of the Welsh dioceses, permitting them to retain endowments producing an income of £102,000 a year, out of a estimated total income of £260,000 from endowments belonging to the Church. The balance was to be divided between the University of Wales, the National Library and the National Museum of Wales, and the various county councils were to receive the parochial endowments in their own counties for use for charitable purposes. The four Welsh bishops were to be removed from the House of Lords and the upper house of the convocation of Canterbury, and the dioceses were required to set up a representative body to hold their property. The bill was rejected three times by the House of Lords, with all the English and Welsh bishops opposing it along with the conservative peers, but under the Parliament Act 1911, the will of the elected representatives in the House of Commons prevailed, and after its passage through the Commons for a third time in

1914, it became law, but because of the European War, its implementation was delayed either for a year, or until the end of the War. The process of disendowment, however, was permitted to begin at once.

In November 1914 the four Welsh bishops, recognizing the inevitable, called a joint meeting of their diocesan conferences to set up a committee to draft a constitution. The committee reported back the following month, and recommended creating a representative body to hold and administer the Church's property and funds, and a governing body to exercise general legislative and administrative authority in the Church. A convention was called at Cardiff in October 1917, upon which the four diocesan conferences had conferred plenary powers, consisting of equal representation from each diocese – the bishop, and thirty-three clergy and sixty-six lay people. They agreed a constitution for the governing body, on which each diocese was to have equal representation. The constitution created a highly centralized system.

Diocesan synods were not established, but diocesan conferences were retained with their main function to elect members to the governing body. Women were allowed to serve as elected members, making this the first Anglican synod to permit the election of women members. The bishops, on whose initiative the whole process had been set up, were given a powerful position. Voting in the new governing body was to be by orders, which would permit any three bishops to veto any matter. When a proposal was made to reduce the power of the bishops, it was rejected by 362 votes to fourteen. The bishops were to be elected by an electoral college representing the whole Church, and consisting of the bishops, and six clergy and six lay electors from the vacant diocese. At its first meeting in 1919 the governing body passed a resolution in favour of forming the four dioceses into a new province, despite the hesitations of the four Welsh bishops, although Archbishop Davidson encouraged them to do this. The archbishop was to be elected by the bishops and the first three clergy and the first three lay people on the list of electors for each diocese. Davidson thereupon, at the request of the governing body, released the Welsh bishops from their oaths of canonical obedience to him, and secured a declaration of the Canterbury convocation that the Welsh bishops were free to form themselves into a province. In 1920 Davidson enthroned the then bishop of St Asaph, who was elected archbishop, as the first archbishop of Wales.[50]

The next Lambeth Conference had been delayed by the European War of 1914–18, and was not held until 1920. The agenda was drawn up by the consultative committee, rather than by the archbishop of Canterbury. There was considerable anxiety about the conference because of the tensions in the Church about theological modernism and also about reunion. There was thought to be a real risk that a minority of Anglo-Catholic bishops would walk out of the conference. Hensley Henson, bishop of Durham, thought that Davidson's friendship with the Anglo-Catholic leaders had enabled them, by threatening to resign, to affect the policy and direction of the conference.[51] Modernism and doctrinal issues were in fact excluded from the agenda. It was the first conference to provide extensive briefings and bibliographies well beforehand, to support the agenda items for the participants. Questionnaires had been issued to 'representative' bishops about the Church's 'relations to non-episcopal churches' and 'marriage questions', and summaries of their answers were laid before the relevant committees. At Davidson's request a number of men and women, clerical and lay, had been invited to write briefing papers on the subjects chosen for discussion at the various committees.[52] The committees were also left free to elect their own chairmen. At previous conferences there had been very few chairmen from overseas dioceses – the bishop of Sydney had chaired one of the committees in 1888, and the bishops of Goulburn and Albany had chaired committees in 1897. However, in the event only three overseas bishops were elected to chair committees in 1920 – Brisbane, Calcutta and Cape Town. It was also notable in that entertainments were laid on for the wives of bishops who accompanied their husbands to London.

There was again a committee on women's work, which expressed the view that the 'setting apart' of deaconesses by the 'laying on of hands' conferred upon them holy orders, and recommended that every diocese ought to have a 'board of women's work'.[53]

The most significant work was that done by the committee on reunion, for by then the main features of Anglicanism as a world-wide fellowship of churches committed to seeking visible unity with all fellow Christians were well-established. After a very hesitant beginning, at the suggestion of Archbishop Lang of York, the chairman, the committee took up the idea of a letter which would constitute an Appeal to All Christian People.[54] It called for a new view of a united, catholic Church, within which existing communions would retain many of their distinctive features. It adopted the Chicago/Lambeth Quadrilateral of 1888, but saw episcopacy as the *plene esse* of the Church, and recommended that churches which did not have episcopacy, should take it into their systems, in order, in due course, to regularize their ministries.[55] The committee was a strong one including Bishops Frank Weston of Zanzibar, Brent of Western New York, Hensley Henson of Durham, Gibson of Gloucester, Palmer of Bombay and Azariah of Dornakal, and it was addressed by a range of theological experts, including Gore and Armitage Robinson, but it was expertly managed by G.K.A. Bell, Davidson's domestic chaplain, and the assistant secretary to the conference. Palmer, assisted by Bell probably wrote the Appeal. The Appeal was much influenced by a memorandum which Davidson had asked A.C. Headlam, then Regius Professor of Divinity at Oxford, to draw up on the relations of the Church of England to other churches.[56] The Appeal set out a new conception of the meaning of reunion, as involving not the absorption of one communion by another, but rather a fellowship of many communions through a 'unity of the whole fulfilled in a diversity of life and devotion'. It asked nobody to repudiate his previous ministry, and offered to non-episcopal churches that Anglican clergy would accept, for example, a Methodist commission, if Methodist clergy would accept an Anglican commission. by episcopal ordination. The Anglican churches were thus recommended to make clear once and for all that they neither expected, nor desired reunion by piece-meal submission.[57]

The Appeal earned the approval of all the bishops, except the most conservative of Anglo-Catholic bishops, and was to be a landmark in the history of the Ecumenical Movement. The influence of the Appeal lay in the catholicity of the experience of the bishops who issued it, and in the circumstances of the moment in history, just after the European War of 1914–18, when there was a seeking for new ways for nations and peoples to coexist, as illustrated in the League of Nations. The bishops agreed to do all they could to bring the Appeal to the notice of people of all denominations in their dioceses, and to do all they could to encourage discussions between representatives of different churches. However, at a practical level, the bishops expressly declared themselves against indiscriminate intercommunion between churches and 'the exchange of pulpits'. The Appeal provided a fresh start for ecumenism, and did much to produce friendly relations between Anglicans and some other churches, but actual reunion was brought no nearer.[58]

Hensley Henson commented at the end of the 1920 Conference

> The bishops themselves impressed me as a body of men intensely earnest, not (with few exceptions) either learned or men of marked intellectual powers, but devoted to their work. They represented an immense variety of experience, endeavour and circumstance ... Some of the missionary bishops are ecclesiastical statesmen of no mean quality... the prevailing spirit of the conference was neo-tractarian, though there were a good many bishops who would call themselves evangelicals.[59]

Part of the impetus for the Appeal to All Christian People had come from the Indian Church, where significant new initiatives were under way. After the Edinburgh Missionary Conference in 1910 there had been movements in South India, where about four fifths of the Indian Christians were to be found, to establish a united, episcopal church. This was given an additional impetus by the Tranquebar Conference in 1919 at which the South Indian bishops (who included Henry Whitehead who had been Superior of the Oxford Mission in Calcutta, and was a convinced Anglo-Catholic) had discussed their vision of a new church which would not be merely other churches joining the Anglican Church. A prime motive was the view that missionary work was hampered by the divisions of the Church which had been imposed from outside. The Lambeth Conference of 1920 encouraged the South Indian bishops, and especially Whitehead to feel that the principle that catholicity involves comprehension, had won the day. However, they were disappointed by the conference's caution on the need for the reordination of non-episcopally ordained ministers.[60]

The committee on the organization of the Anglican Communion had recommended that the conference should encourage the establishment of further provinces, to consist of at least four dioceses, so that each province would have sufficient bishops to consecrate its own bishops under the Canons of Nicea, in order that dioceses should not remain permanently dependent on the see of Canterbury. The continuing complexities of forming a new province were illustrated by the Church in India where, in spite of the establishment of the provincial synod, legal advice proved that the Church in India remained part of the Church of England, and that the synod had no authority to pass any regulations, unless it were authorized to do so by the British Parliament. The growing agitation for Indian independence after the European War had made it more urgent to secure an Indian identity for the Church, including self-government. It was suggested that the Enabling Act of 1919, which had permitted the establishment of a Church Assembly in England with authority to pass measures which merely required to be laid before Parliament, might offer a means of giving the Church in India independence without the necessity of attempting to secure parliamentary time for legislation. However, after lengthy negotiations with the government of India and the secretary of state for India, it was agreed that there would need to be an Act of Parliament as well as a Church Assembly measure. In November 1927 the Indian Church Measure passed the Church Assembly, and in December, the Indian Church Act passed through Parliament.

The Act required that trustees should be appointed to hold property on behalf of the Church and that a constitution should be drawn up. Government funding would also be withdrawn from the bishops of Calcutta, Madras and Bombay when the current incumbents retired or resigned, and endowments would therefore need to be raised to replace this funding for the three dioceses. The government would, however, continue to maintain chaplains to minister to English congregations, but they would be licensed by the Indian bishops. Bishop Palmer of Bombay took the lead in framing the constitution of the new Church of India, Burma and Ceylon as an autonomous province. In drawing up the constitution he emphasized the importance of rules with exceptions to the rules, and had his eye on the possibility of future union schemes.[61]

Following the 1920 conference conversations were initiated with the Ecumenical Patriarch, and the patriarch of Jerusalem and the Church of Cyprus. The way had been additionally paved for these conversations by the contacts which had been established when the Turkish Empire had collapsed at the end of the European War in 1918, and the help and assistance the Church of England had offered to the Serbian Orthodox Church during the War. As a result, at the 1930 conference, there was a delegation from the Orthodox churches led by the patriarch of Alexandria, and including representatives of the four ancient patriarchates and Rumania, Yugoslavia, Greece, Cyprus, Poland and Bulgaria.[62] There was also a delegation from the Old Catholic Church. An additional factor leading to the presence of these delegations was the links that were beginning to be forged between the non-Roman Catholic churches, through the series of ecumenical conferences, beginning with the Life and Work Conference at Uppsala in 1925, which was the first international conference to be attended by a delegation from the Orthodox churches. It would however, be easy to overestimate the significance of the presence of the Orthodox representatives at Lambeth in 1930, for the Orthodox were not united in their attitudes towards Anglicanism, and the patriarch Melitos was much more advanced in his attitudes towards Anglicanism than most of the other delegates.[63]

As a first-fruit of the Appeal to All Christian People the report of the commission which had undertaken discussions with representatives of the Church of Sweden was received, and it was agreed that members of the Church of Sweden should be received into communion in Anglican churches. As a sign of recognition and goodwill Hensley Henson, bishop of Durham and F.T. Woods, bishop of Winchester were asked to go to Uppsala to take part in the consecration of a Swedish bishop. However, the English Free churches declined to send a delegation to the 1930 conference, for they were disappointed at the lack of progress in the discussions that had been initiated after the 1920 Appeal.[64]

There were, however, setbacks to ecumenical dialogue. The non-Catholic, non-Anglican delegates to the 1930 conference were not invited to the opening service of the conference in St Paul's Cathedral, and were not officially welcomed to the conference, whereas the Orthodox received an official welcome. This, following the lack of progress of contacts during the previous decade, left English Free Churchmen feeling hurt. In A.C. Headlam's view, after the 1930 conference most English

Free Church leaders ceased to desire reunion, and merely wished to receive recognition of their ministries, so that they could continue to be separated from the Church of England, which, in any case they suspected, would not take them seriously.[65]

The 1930 conference's most significant contribution to ecumenism was in accepting the report of the committee on unity, which gave approval to the proposals to establish a Church of South India, comprising the Anglican dioceses, the Methodist Church, the Congregational Union and the Presbyterian Church, which was to be achieved by means of the non-episcopal churches taking episcopacy into their systems, as commended at the 1920 conference. In 1927 Palmer, whilst drafting the constitution for the new Church of India, Burma and Ceylon, had begun to see 'union as dying', and that union might be a 'self reducing process' for the Church. He had brought forward a proposal, also in 1927, for an interim period of fifty years during which ministries would be mutually acceptable, if the ministers had assented to the constitution of a new church, and by the end of which all would have been episcopally ordained in the new church. This had paved the way for the 1929 proposal for a United Church of South India. The Anglican bishops, Palmer, Azariah and Western were the principal architects of the scheme, and also had the support and encouragement of Foss Westcott, the bishop of Calcutta and metropolitan of the new Indian church.

Although the proposal went through six revisions between 1929 and 1947, and Palmer retired to England in 1929, he continued to influence its development. Everyone recognized that the scheme must not attempt to produce an Indian copy of the Church of England, but that it must be a local representation of the Catholic Church, comprehending as far as possible all the traditions which were entering the union. In the discussions about the form of the new church in which all the participating churches were taking part, the Anglo-Catholic tradition of Anglicanism was importantly represented by Bishop Western and Bishop Hall of Chota Nagpur, while Bishop Azariah emphasized the Indian context. By 1930 more emphasis was being placed on the catholic tradition of Anglicanism in the South Indian proposals. However, at the Lambeth Conference some violent speeches were made against the scheme, notably by the Bishops of Indiana and Kentucky, but Bishops Palmer of

Bombay and Waller of Madras among the Indian bishops and Bishop Shedder of Nassau in the West Indies, were very successful in bringing the bishops together in their attitudes to the scheme.[66] Bell, now bishop of Chichester, had managed to dissipate the opposition of many of the Anglo-Catholic bishops by stressing that the resultant church would be autonomous and not strictly Anglican, while having a real intercommunion with the churches of the Anglican Communion, although for a time that intercommunion would be limited.[67]

The bishops at the 1930 conference recognized the dispersed nature of authority in the Anglican Communion by allowing for the decision about the South Indian proposals to be left to the Anglican Church in India. This was formally recognized when the conference commended the report of the committee on the Anglican Communion, which had stated that the Anglican Communion is 'bound together not by a central legislative and executive authority, but by mutual loyalty sustained through the common counsel of the bishops in conference'.

The general theme of the 1930 conference, the faith and witness of the Church was considered under six headings – the Christian doctrine of God, the life and witness of the Christian community, the unity of the Church, the Anglican Communion, the ministry and youth and its vocation. The bishops reversed the recommendation of previous conferences in approving the recommendations of the committee on the life and witness of the Christian community, which affirmed that sexual intercourse had a value of its own. A majority of bishops agreed that, while total abstinence was the best means of birth control, for 'morally sound' reasons based on 'Christian principles' other means might be used. There was great tension over this; the now retired Bishop Gore, who had been invited to attend the conference, being a vehement opponent of this concession. The paragraph of the report dealing with this matter was referred back by the full conference for redrafting by the committee, and although the final version was accepted by the conference, it still caused Bishop Carey of Bloemfontein to withdraw from the conference. The bishops also criticized the Anglo-Saxon races for their attitude of racial superiority, and agreed that the continuation of colonies could only be defended if it was intended to share government with the 'subject race'.[68]

The 1930 conference was the first for which financial assistance for the costs of hospitality for the conference at Lambeth was offered to the archbishop, previous conferences having been financed at the archbishop's expense. The English Church Assembly voted two grants of £1,000 each.[69] There were criticisms by almost all the American bishops, and some of the Canadian bishops of the way in which the 1930 conference was handled. They objected to the way in which it was managed by the English bishops. Henson noted

> A striking feature of this Conference to those who know the previous history of the persons concerned is the solidarity created by their academic experience. Lang, Palmer, and Temple are Balliol men, Lang and Headlam, Fellows of All Souls, Headlam Regius Professor of Divinity, Temple Fellow of Queen's [Henson himself had been a Fellow of All Souls, the most academically distinguished graduate society in Oxford]. It is ever the sway of unperceived and unacknowledged personal forces which determines the course of public affairs. These four men – Lang, Temple, Palmer and Headlam – have been the most potent figures in the conference, and the fact is not *solely* due to their official positions and personal ability, though of course these are very considerable. The habit of personal association and the common loyalty to institutions have counted for much.[70]

It must have been difficult for bishops, who had not lived in such company recently, or had perhaps never experienced the cut and thrust of a high table or a senior common room, to feel confident in raising their voices in such company.

In his *Thoughts after Lambeth* T.S. Eliot commented, 'The Church of England washes its dirty linen in public ... In contrast to some other institutions both civil and ecclesiastical the linen does get washed'. Although he disagreed with much that happened at the conference, he added that the conference 'has affirmed, beyond previous Conferences, the Catholicity of the Church'.[71]

After the 1930 conference there were continuing ecumenical developments, with the Orthodox churches, and with the churches of Finland, Latvia and Estonia, and with the Old Catholics, but these were cut short by the rise of National

Socialism in Europe and the German invasions of most of these countries. However, in spite of the severe depredations of the 1939–45 War, a new structure for relations between the non-Roman Catholic churches, the World Council of Churches, was inaugurated in 1948 with the archbishop of Canterbury as one of its presidents.

Although the Lambeth Conference of 1948 welcomed the creation of the WCC, it discovered that it was divided over the first major attempt to form a new church from the Anglican dioceses and English Free churches in South India. The scheme had eventually been commended by the episcopal synod of the Church of India, Burma and Ceylon in 1942, but it had been opposed by the bishop of Colombo, who had rallied the Anglo-Catholic cause and especially the South African bishops and a group of leaders of men's religious communities and some Anglo-Catholic theologians in England. He had requested the metropolitan to refer the scheme to the metropolitans of the Anglican Communion to inquire whether, if the scheme were adopted, they would break off communion with the Church of India, Burma and Ceylon, and also refuse to enter communion with the new Church of South India. Westcott, the metropolitan of India had referred the question to the Consultative Body of the Lambeth Conference.

Meanwhile, there had been a major outburst of agitation against the scheme in England led by Raymond Raynes the Superior of the Community of the Resurrection, who with four of the other five superiors of men's religious communities in the Church of England had threatened secession from the Church if the scheme were adopted. Archbishop Temple declared in response, that the Church of South India would in fact, as had always been recognized, be going out from the Anglican Communion, but that this was not an act of schism. Communicants from the church would continue to be admitted to communion in the Church of England, and episcopally ordained ministers of the church would be permitted to officiate in England under the provisions of the Colonial Clergy Act 1874. Following this furore ten out of eleven of the dioceses of the Church of India, Burma and Ceylon which could vote, voted in favour of the scheme in 1944, and steps were taken to implement it, and the church came into being in 1947.[72] The bishops of the new church, which was no longer part of the Anglican

Communion, were not therefore invited to the 1948 Lambeth Conference.

While the bishops at Lambeth were able to agree that former Anglicans who joined the new church would still be in communion with the archbishop of Canterbury, the Anglo-Catholic bishops in particular were not prepared to grant the non-episcopally ordained ministers of the church any status in the Anglican Communion, and the bishops were divided about the status of those who would subsequently be ordained by the bishops of the Church of South India.

However it was not just the Anglo-Catholic bishops who were hesitant about the processes used in the South India scheme. Kenneth Kirk, the bishop of Oxford, with the support of Dom Gregory Dix, OSB, had helped to modify and focus the issues, so that the bishops indicated that in future they would prefer unity schemes which did not involve a dual ministry, even for an interim period. In one of the rare votes at Lambeth Conferences, 135 bishops held that such ministers should be accepted as true ministers of the Church of Christ, but a substantial minority of ninety-four believed that it was not yet possible to make any decision on the matter. Those in the minority included Archbishops Garbett of York and Gregg of Dublin, and all the Irish bishops. As the total number of bishops attending the conference was 329, it would seem that about a hundred bishops did not vote. This significant number of bishops who voted against, or abstained from voting, illustrates the level of disquiet which the scheme aroused in the Communion.[73] Kirk subsequently worked hard to secure a policy of mutual tolerance in relation to the Church of South India, and Bishop Bell of Chichester secured the approval of the Canterbury convocation in 1950 for a five-year period of limited intercommunion. Subsequently, in 1955 Bell presented a report on the development of the church to the convocations of Canterbury and York, which as a result, voted to accept the ministries of those ordained or consecrated after the inauguration of the church.[74]

The 1948 conference had adopted the agenda of the 1930 conference because of the difficulty of planning and organizing a conference in the immediate post-war period. Eric Mascall, the distinguished Anglo-Catholic theologian had suggested that a group of resident theologians should be appointed to advise the bishops, but Archbishop Fisher refused to accept this suggestion, leaving it to be taken up by Archbishop Ramsey in 1968. Archbishop Fisher's visit to the USA and Canada in 1946 had done much to allay the suspicions of the American bishops, arising from memories the 1930 conference, about the dominance of the conference by the English bishops.[75]

The 1948 conference agreed to reactivate the Anglican Communion Advisory Council on Missionary Strategy which had been set up by the 1878 conference, but had never met. In order to encourage it to meet, the secretary of the Church of England's Church Assembly Missionary Council, canon McLeod Campbell, was appointed secretary of the Advisory Council. However, he was given no funds and no staff to enable him to serve the Advisory Council or to set up the regional officers for liaison and communication which had been agreed by the bishops at the conference. The bishops also agreed to establish a Central College of the Anglican Communion in the premises of the former St Augustine's Missionary College at Canterbury. It was intended that this should function as a staff college, offering scholarships for 'promising indigenous clergy' from overseas dioceses in order to prepare them for leadership in their own provinces. Because the Anglican Communion had no funds or budget to support it, this significant venture, initially under the direction of Kenneth Sansbury, who had extensive experience of work in Japan, was underfunded and underresourced. The conference also recommended that there should be a further pan-Anglican Congress involving lay people and clergy.[76]

The conference once more reaffirmed the indissolubility of marriage, but again avoided any discussion on matters of doctrine, not even referring to the important report 'Doctrine in the Church of England', produced under the chairmanship of William Temple, and published in 1938.

One of the curiosities of the 1948 conference was that of the 326 bishops who attended, only 240 were diocesan bishops, leaving eighty-six who had no jurisdiction. The long-standing custom of including English suffragan bishops, and overseas retired bishops who held commissions in English dioceses had continued, and not having been reviewed, had got out of hand. Sixty-three of those without jurisdiction were from the provinces of Canterbury and York, mostly retired bishops. They in fact outnumbered the bishops from the PECUSA, and even the

English diocesans. The result was that English bishops constituted a third of the total attendance. *Theology* in November 1948 commented on this and criticized the absence of 'inferior' clergy and theologians from the conference as weakening the moral authority of the conference's recommendations, and defeating the Anglican endeavour to commend constitutional episcopacy to the churches. Fisher noted these criticisms and in 1958 retired bishops and suffragans were not invited to the conference.[77]

The early years of the century had seen the continuing development of the African-led Christianity, that we have already noted in Nigeria. In 1914 a group of Anglicans in Uganda had begun a movement of spiritual revival which rejected European medicine and became the Church of the Almighty God or the Bamalaki, and tens of thousands of Christians had joined them, representing a new and populist level of African Christian initiative, quite removed from missionary control. There had been further divisions in the Anglican Church in Nigeria. In 1916 the Christ Army Church separated from the Church of England, in 1923 the Faith Tabernacle, in 1926 the Church of the Lord, and in 1928 the Cherubim and Seraphim Society all separated from the Anglican Church. In the whole of Africa the number of Christians is estimated to have increased fourfold between 1900 and 1930, and to have doubled again between 1930 and 1950. Much of the growth was represented by independent African churches separating from the Anglican and other missionary churches.

The new Independent African churches were not usually challenging the doctrines, theology, or even liturgy of the mission churches, for the most part they tenaciously held on to these traditions. They seem to have been seeking only a mild synthesis with local culture. What they wanted was their own leadership and control over churches.[78]

In the period after the European War of 1914–18 the missionary movement had not flourished. The War had undermined confidence in Christianity amongst many people in Britain and the missionary societies had difficulty raising money and recruiting missionaries. Many of the Anglican missionaries continued to resist the development of indigenous leadership. Many of the second generation of missionaries may have been good people, but they were protective and possessive, and protective love had the effect of damaging where it meant to bless. Catechists and African clergy continued to be recruited from the households of European missionaries, who continued to call them 'boys'. There was a reluctance to hand over authority and power to Africans. Traditional patterns of leadership in African societies were ignored in recruiting and ordaining African clergy. When missionaries did hand over responsibility to Africans, they tended to withdraw power into a higher category in the administrative hierarchy. As the number of European missionaries declined in the second and third decades of the twentieth century, the missionaries tended to be appointed to non-parochial positions, and to withdraw from working alongside African clergy and catechists. Also the increasing emphasis on the provision of specialist services – especially medicine and education, pioneered by American missionary organizations – placed an emphasis on large-scale mission stations offering secondary education and hospital care, that could only be provided by Europeans. This resulted in the withdrawal of European missionaries from villages and from African communities into enclaves of European culture, where Africans were present only as assistants or servants, or as the recipients of the services.[79] The number of missionaries was declining – CMS had 1,385 active missionaries in 1914 and 1,085 in 1939, but this did not mean that Africans were given leadership roles in Anglican or other churches; although, as has been seen, during the period to 1950 the number of Christians in Africa rapidly increased, especially in the independent churches. The policy of Anglican missionaries thus continued to be strongly paternalistic, and under the influence of J.H. Oldham, they believed that the interests of Empire and Church, blacks and whites, settlers and natives, could be harmonized under European direction.[80]

There were some attempts at Africanization, for example in the 1920s Bishop Lucas of Masasi endeavoured to develop a Christian ritual of initiation, incorporating circumcision, which was a predominant practice among his people. In some instances too Anglicans were successful at retaining charismatic leaders within the Church, for example Adam's Preaching Society in the Niger Delta, and a this-worldly holiness group supported by Bishop Agori Iwe of Benin in the 1940s. But many Africans in fact opposed Africanization. Under the influence of the revivalist techniques of some of the evangelical missionaries, they wished to break with their past and to form themselves into a new and purified community. Some also thought that English leadership attracted extra privileges for the Church, and most important, attracted overseas money to support the leadership and new projects. They also recognized that there might well be problems and perhaps tribal tensions within a diocese over establishing indigenous leadership.[81]

There was thus very little attention paid among white Anglicans in Africa to the formation of an African clergy other than parish priests trained to be dependent on the direction and supervision of European missionaries. In comparison with other forms of education which the missionary societies provided, there was remarkably little effort put into theological colleges. Most of the actual mission work of the Church was done by largely untrained lay African catechists. By 1950 no African diocesan bishop had been appointed since the death of Samuel Crowther in 1891. The Anglican Church was providing educational opportunities for Africans, but in the 1950s these were opening opportunities for political leadership, not church leadership. It was most unusual to find an Anglican diocese seriously planning the training of clergy to take over the most senior posts in the dioceses, which were still nearly all held by expatriates. In the 1950s it was the Mothers' Union, rather than African clergy which emerged to provide something not far short of the central core of public Anglican Christian life in Africa. It may well be that the Church's policy of not baptizing men involved in polygamous marriage in a society where polygamy was still strong, had excluded many men who might have been expected to be candidates for leadership.[82]

The revolution in air travel in the 1950s encouraged much more frequent and easy contact between the different dioceses in the Anglican Communion, and enabled Geoffrey Fisher, as archbishop of Canterbury to visit overseas dioceses and provinces, without waiting for bishops to visit him. He travelled extensively, and was able to have an awareness of not just the bishops but the broader situation in Africa, and elsewhere. His major priority in relation to the Anglican Communion was to encourage the formation of autonomous provinces, especially in Africa. His interest in canon law reform in England assisted him in the intricate business of drawing up the legal frameworks for the constitutions of new provinces, and his experience as a headmaster probably made him willing to risk delegating responsibility. He inherited a special committee to advise him on the intricacies of the legal frameworks for new provinces, chaired by Bishop Palmer, formerly of Bombay, who had been instrumental in drawing up the constitution of the Church of India and subsequently the Church of South India, but Fisher enjoyed the work, and largely drew up the constitutions of the provinces of West, Central and East Africa himself. His aim was to establish a uniformity in African Anglicanism independent of the churchmanship of the missionary societies in which most of the dioceses had originated. He used as his model the constitution of the Church in the Province of South Africa, in which the focal point of unity was the metropolitan or arch-bishop who presided over the general synod in which each diocese was represented by clergy and laity as well as bishops. Fisher found that some of the older bishops were reluctant to break the link with Lambeth, and also that it was not always clear, for either geographical or ethnic reasons, into which province a diocese should go.[83]

West Africa was the first new province to be formed. William Temple had asked the West African bishops to consider how a province might be formed before his death in 1944, and by 1948 a draft constitution, based on that of South Africa, had been drawn up. However, there was no obvious common interest between the dioceses of Lagos, Niger and Sierra Leone, where the CMS influence was strong, and Accra, the Gambia and the Rio Pongas, where there was a strong Anglo-Catholic influence. There was also a developing nationalism in these colonies whose boundaries had been drawn by European colonial administra-tors. In 1949 Kwame Nkrumah founded the first truly African nationalist political party, the Convention People's Party, in the Gold Coast. It was feared by the Anglo-Catholic bishops that the formation of a province including 'CMS bishops' might lead to attempts at intercommunion similar to those in which East African bishops had been involved, or attempts at union schemes like that then being developed in South India. The bishop of Accra, who was in his eighties, was particularly opposed to the proposal on the grounds that it might encourage unwise ecumenical schemes, and the bishop of the Niger was also very conservative and hostile to any form of change. The constitu-tion was finally approved by the various dioceses' legislative bodies in 1950, leaving the archbishop of Canterbury as the final court of appeal for the province. The province was formally inaugurated by the archbishop of Canterbury in Freetown, Sierra Leone on 17 April 1951, when the six bishops signed the preamble and the articles of the constitution, after which the archbishop released them from the oaths of canonical obedience to him, and they then elected a metropolitan for the province.[84] However, it was a long time before there was a majority of African bishops in the province. Even in 1956 the diocese of Accra, in which the majority of the clergy were black Africans, specifically requested that their new bishop should be English.[85] The granting of independence to the Anglican dioceses in the British West African colonies took place significantly before they achieved political independence from Britain – Ghana in 1957, Nigeria in 1960 and Sierra Leone in 1961.

The formation of a province in Central Africa, upon which Fisher took the initiative in 1951, was more complex because the dioceses that he was proposing should form the province coincided with the colonies that the British government was proposing to form into the Central African Federation, of Northern Rhodesia (Zambia), Southern Rhodesia (Zimbabwe) and Nyasaland (Malawi). This government proposal was opposed by African political leaders, who saw it as a means of imposing a continuing long-term European rule on the colonies. Fisher, however, believed that the government's proposal was in the long-term interests of the Africans, even though they currently opposed it. The archbishop of Cape Town and the bishops of the dioceses concerned, advised caution on the formation of a province in the current political climate, which Fisher accepted. The province was eventually inaugurated, again with a visit by the archbishop of Canterbury, in Harare in 1955, a year after the ill-fated Central African Federation had been set up.[86] Again the colonies of which these dioceses were part did not achieve their independence until the next decade –Tanzania in 1961, and Malawi and Zambia in 1964.

The province of East Africa, with twelve dioceses, was much longer in gestation, but was brought about in 1960, after the appointment of Trevor Huddleston of the Community of the Resurrection, as bishop of Masasi in 1960. Fisher was also keen to establish Uganda as a separate province, in spite of considerable white opposition, in order to free the Anglican Church in Uganda from Canterbury, and to allow it to develop on its own lines. He had forced the division of the existing diocese into eleven new dioceses, with the suffragans becoming diocesans, and the former diocese becoming a province in 1960.[87] Uganda too, did not gain political independence until 1962 and Kenya in 1963.

The formation of the province of Uganda marked a significant change in the composition of the Anglican episcopate. At the beginning of 1960 there were three black African diocesan bishops. Nearly all the bishops in Africa, including South Africa, were English who had, in some instances, no previous experience of working outside England. By the end of 1960, however, there were seven black African diocesan bishops. In May 1955 Fisher had consecrated four black African suffragan bishops in Namirembe cathedral, and these four became diocesans when Uganda became a province. In Nigeria there were also black African bishops in Ibadan, Ovidu-Benin and Niger Delta. Even in South Africa Alphaeus Zulu was consecrated suffragan bishop of St John's in 1960, and was elected bishop of Zululand in 1966.[88]

Archbishop de Blank of Cape Town was keen to establish an African identity for the Anglican Church in Africa, and had proposed a meeting of the archbishops of the African provinces to coincide with the inauguration of the new province of Uganda in 1960. He saw this as a follow up to the All Africa Bishops' Conference which had been held at St Augustine's College Canterbury in July 1958, in conjunction with the Lambeth Conference. De Blank suggested that there should be a primate for the Anglican Church in Africa. This piece of Anglican triumphalism came to nothing, partly because de Blank had given no thought to how the primacy might be funded. When the African archbishops met in Kampala in 1961, all of them were English. In recognition of this de Blank wished to rapidly accelerate African leadership in the Anglican Church in Africa. However, he and the other archbishops failed to take into account the relative weakness of Anglicanism in Africa, apart perhaps from in Nigeria and Uganda, and its failure to respond to the issues posed by polygamy, urbanization and the expansion of Islam, and the weakness of Anglicanism in relation to other Christian denominations in Africa.[89] However, the archbishops' proposal that a liturgy should be compiled which might be used by Anglican provinces throughout the continent of Africa did come to fruition. *A Liturgy for Africa* was published in 1964, which owing to the influence of Leslie Brown, bishop of Uganda, who had formerly been the convenor of the liturgical committee of the Church of South India, was very similar to the liturgy of that church.[90]

In the Middle East the Jerusalem bishopric which was founded in 1841 was intended to be filled alternately by an Anglican and a Lutheran bishop, but after 1886 the see was maintained by the Anglicans alone. In the early part of the twentieth century the CMS's missionary activities in Palestine had given rise to a substantial number of Arab evangelical Christians who had received from the CMS a constitution which established a Council of the Arab Evangelical Christian Church. By the 1940s there were 8,000 or so Arab Christians governed by this Council, and Archbishop Fisher wanted to bring them into relationship with the bishop in Jerusalem and with the Anglican Communion, and to create a province in the Middle East, which would comprise the dioceses of Egypt, the Sudan and Iran, and give them a focus and an independence from the Church of England. Unfortunately he was a little late in doing this, and by the time he was beginning to set plans in motion a new wave of Arab nationalism had hit the Middle East, and had been focused by President Nasser of Egypt who had nationalized the Suez Canal, to which Britain and France had retaliated with an attempt to reoccupy the Canal Zone. It was no longer the right moment to raise the profile of Anglicanism in the region. Fisher drew back, but as a preliminary step, he established an Anglican archbishopric in Jerusalem to be metropolitan of an episcopal synod of the Middle Eastern bishops. As part of this preliminary reorganization, and in an attempt to indigenize Anglicanism in the region, he also established Jordan as a distinct diocese, with an Arab bishop.[91]

In the Far East, in 1917, a Chinese assistant bishop had been chosen for Chekiang, and it was recognized that there was some urgency to create a means by which he, as a Chinese national, would not be required to take an oath of canonical obedience to the primate of a foreign church, and the process was put in hand to create a constitution for the Chinese dioceses, to form a new province. Following a general synod in 1924, which was also attended by the bishops in Singapore, the Philippines, Sarawak and Labuan to represent the overseas Chinese congregations, this process was completed in 1930, and a new province was inaugurated, and a new metropolitan was elected and consecrated by the bishops in China.[92]

As a result of the Japanese invasion of China and the British territories in the Far East, including Hong Kong, the Chinese Church became very isolated from the rest of the Communion. A by-product of this was the decision of Bishop Hall of Hong Kong, when he was faced with a shortage of priests to minister to his congregations, to ordain a deaconess priest. When Hall informed Archbishop Temple of his action, Temple had expressed the view that Hall should not have taken unilateral action, even in the grave situation in which he found himself, of ordaining a deaconess priest, but that *in extremis* he ought to have licensed her to celebrate the holy communion, which licence could have been withdrawn when normality was restored. After Temple's death in 1944, Fisher endorsed Temple's view, and requested Bishop Hall to suspend the woman, Li Tim Oi from her functions as a priest until the matter had been considered by the house of bishops of the Chinese Church. Fisher also thought it necessary to warn the chairman of the Chinese house of bishops that if they endorsed Hall's action some provinces in the Communion might question whether they could continue in communion with the Church in China. He suggested that the house should recommend that the matter should be referred to the next Lambeth Conference. Hall had refused to suspend Li Tim Oi from her priestly functions, and Fisher recommended to the chairman that the house should recommend that she should be prohibited from the exercise of her priestly ministry by the house.

When the house of bishops of the Anglican Church in China met in March 1946 they agreed to express regret at Bishop Hall's uncanonical action in ordaining a woman as a priest, and requested him to accept the resignation from her priestly ministry, which she had already placed in his hands. The house also passed a motion, to be considered by the forthcoming Lambeth Conference, proposing a canon that would permit deaconesses to be ordained priest for an experimental period of twenty years. Eleven of the members of the house attended the 1948

Lambeth Conference, at which a committee was especially appointed to consider the resolution. The committee subsequently recommended the rejection of the resolution.

With the establishment of the communist regime in China in 1949 the English Anglican bishops in China recognized that the Church would only be able to flourish under Chinese leadership, and in preparation for this, during the first half of 1950, five new Chinese bishops were consecrated. It was also clear to Archbishop Fisher that with the isolation of Hong Kong from mainland China, the diocese of Hong Kong could not remain effectively part of the province of China, and that it ought to return, for the time being at least, to the jurisdiction of Canterbury. Bishop Hall therefore resigned from the house of bishops of the Chinese Church, and a new diocese of South China was created for the territory on the mainland previously within the diocese of Hong Kong, and in recognition of this, the house of bishops and the standing committee of the Chinese Church met in 1951, and severed the diocese of Hong Kong and the territory of Macao from its general synod.[93]

Fisher also wished to bring together the dioceses in South East Asia and the Pacific into provinces. As a first step, after the 1948 Lambeth Conference two councils were set up, one comprising the dioceses of Singapore, Borneo, Hong Kong and Rangoon for South East Asia, and the other comprising the dioceses of New Guinea, Melanesia and Polynesia, for the Pacific. The bishops were expected to meet at least once every two years, and to elect one of their number to chair meetings for a five-year term.[94] The development of a province of South East Asia proved more complicated than Fisher had anticipated. When in 1960 he considered it necessary to appoint an English candidate to the diocese of Singapore to establish a province for the widely differing ethnic groupings of the region, the political independence of Singapore, and a new wave of nationalism, led the Chinese assistant bishop to expect that he should be appointed bishop. Fisher established an uneasy compromise by appointing Kenneth Sansbury, who had been head of St Augustine's College, Canterbury, as bishop of Singapore, and making the Chinese assistant bishop suffragan bishop of Kuala Lumpur in 1961.[95]

Fisher's most difficult challenge in forming a province was

with the Church of England in Australia, the effectiveness of whose general synod was inhibited by its very limited terms of reference, and by the vast distances between the dioceses, and the expense and time involved in travelling for lay people and clergy, before the introduction of cheap air travel. The general synod had no real significance in the life of the dioceses, for any power that it might have achieved had been circumvented by those dioceses or provinces which were apprehensive that their distinctive churchmanship might be threatened. Legal advice had been sought in 1912 which had clearly stated that the dioceses of the Church of England in Australia and Tasmania legally continued to be parts of the Church of England. This meant that the Church in Australia was bound by English laws, and that if the Australian dioceses acted in essential matters in any way independently of the Church of England in England that would mean that, in the eyes of the law, a new church was being created, and that it would be liable to forfeit the property it held in trust as 'the Church of England in Australia'. If therefore, as had happened in the diocese of Natal in the nineteenth century, a group disagreeing with any independent action, tested their claim in the courts to be the 'continuing Church of England in Australia' they would obtain possession of the property of the Church. The inference for some people was that a new constitution was required so that the Church in Australia would no longer be bound by English laws and by the decisions of English courts, as well as being subject to Australian courts in their equitable jurisdiction, and so that if it wished, the Church in Australia might amend or revise the liturgy of the Book of Common Prayer. This, however, was suspected by many Australian Anglicans of all churchmanships as an attempt to break the ties with the home country, and was strongly resisted.[96]

A draft constitution was drawn up for the consideration of the general synod in 1926, but it was opposed by the representatives of the diocese of Sydney. Australian evangelicals were alarmed by the proposals in the Church of England in the 1920s to revise the Prayer Book, and they began to see a need to defend what they regarded as the Reformation principles independently of what happened in England by driving a hard bargain in the constitutional debates in the Anglican Church in Australia. The draft was revised following a campaign by a group of conservative evangelicals from Sydney and the larger (and predominantly evangelical) dioceses were granted a greater representation in the general synod, an unalterable basis of fundamental doctrines was included in the constitution and diocesan autonomy was firmly established. The other dioceses agreed to this, but when legal difficulties arose the opportunity to settle the constitution was lost. When a further revision was considered at a convention in 1932, the Anglo-Catholic representatives were so opposed to it that it was only approved by eighteen of the twenty-five dioceses in Australia. A further draft was prepared for a convention in 1939, but this draft was only approved by seventeen of the dioceses.

The tensions about a constitution for the Australian Church were not merely over churchmanship. The majority of the dioceses were small and rural (and mostly Anglo-Catholic), where it was possible for a bishop to exercise his authority personally, they therefore sought a constitution which would concentrate authority in the hands of the bishop. The dioceses of Sydney and Melbourne were large and urban, and there the bishops needed to work with administrators and in the disputes over the role of an appellate tribunal for the Church in the constitutional debates in the 1920s they accepted the need for laymen and lawyers to play a significant part, which was not accepted by most of the bishops and representatives of the smaller dioceses before the general synod in 1945.[97]

In 1942 parishioners of All Saints, Canowindra complained to Archbishop Mowll of Sydney, as metropolitan of New South Wales about the bishop of Bathurst's authorization of a book called *The Holy Eucharist* or *The Red Book* in place of the Prayer Book. Mowll referred the matter to his conservative evangelical advisers in Sydney, who encouraged a group of twenty-three laymen from various parishes in Bathurst to start a case against the bishop of Bathurst in the Equity Division of the Supreme Court of New South Wales on the ground that only the Prayer Book could be used for public services, and that *The Red Book* contained practices that were unlawful in the Church of England, and thus the use of it was a breach of the trust in which the church buildings were vested. In his judgement, the chief justice in equity for New South Wales, ruled that 'the Church of England came out to New South Wales as part of the established Church of England and nothing has taken place subsequently which has destroyed that relationship'. The bishop appealed to the High Court of Australia, which dismissed his appeal, but limited the injunction on the use of *The Red Book* to the twenty parishes in the diocese whose trust had been proved in the Equity Court. The bishop, on the advice of Archbishop Fisher, who took legal advice on his behalf, waived his right to appeal to the Privy Council in return for the costs that had been awarded against him. This demonstrated the willingness of Sydney churchmen to support laity against bishops of other dioceses who might have authorized similar books, and put the evangelicals in a position of strength in the Australian Church.[98]

Fisher, on a visit to Australia, took soundings in the Church, and formed the opinion that the opponents of the achievement of self-government had been orchestrated by the diocese of Sydney, and that most church people outside Sydney favoured autonomy for the Anglican Church in Australia, based on a constitution for the whole Church in Australia. On the basis of this, Fisher publicly criticized the lack of links between the Australian dioceses and emphasized the unsatisfactoriness of their continuing dependence on the Church of England, if they wished to develop institutions and worship appropriate for a country that was likely to develop differently from England. He suggested that there should be a metropolitan for the whole of the Anglican Church in Australia, and encouraged the Australian Church to begin again to draw up a constitution that would safeguard the special concerns of the diocese of Sydney, and also change the name of the Church to something more appropriate than the 'Church of England in Australia'.

During his return voyage from Australia, Fisher recognizing the great difficulty the Australian dioceses had already experienced during the previous twenty-five or so years in drawing up an acceptable constitution, himself drafted a constitution, providing for a general synod of three houses voting together, except when a separate vote was called for. It also allowed for a diocese to contract out of any canon passed by the general synod. A very large number of amendments were made to it in the draft stage, but in 1955 this constitution was agreed by the general synod. By 1960 all the dioceses in Australia had approved the constitution, and all the state Parliaments had passed enabling legislation to permit the transfer of property to the new body. The draft constitution was supported by the older conservative evangelical leaders, such as Archbishop

Mowll because they realized that as their traditional safeguard, English Church law was in the process of revision, their only possible safeguard against doctrinal change was their own constitution. Younger and even more conservative evangelicals in Sydney wished to amend the draft constitution in such a way as to ensure that there would be no risk of the Church's doctrine ever being changed. Eventually half the members of the Sydney diocesan synod abstained and the constitution was approved by two-thirds of those voting. In 1962 after the constitution had been passed by the other dioceses, and the states and commonwealth of Australia had passed enabling Acts, a general synod was held for the autonomous province, which, at the insistence of the diocese of Sydney, continued to be known as the 'Church of England in Australia'. While the new constitution created an autonomous province for all the Australian dioceses, each diocese was left as the ultimate legislative authority in the province.[99]

Reformed episcopal churches had emerged in Spain and Portugal during the 1860s, when a measure of religious liberty was granted in those countries. Angelo Mora, a Spanish Roman Catholic priest was received into the PECUSA, and became a rallying point for a small number of Portuguese evangelicals who were advocating the formation of a national reformed church. The movement was supported by the Anglican chaplain in Lisbon, a priest of the Church of Ireland. Reaction against the promulgation of the dogma of Papal Infallibility by the First Vatican Council in 1870 caused some Roman Catholics to react against their Church, and to join the reformers. In 1878 the reformed congregations in Spain and Portugal petitioned the Anglican bishops meeting in the Lambeth Conference to consecrate a bishop for them. Their request was coldly received, and it was suggested that the American bishop of Mexico should visit the churches in 1880 to offer 'advice and assistance'. In 1880 the churches drew up their own constitutions, providing for synodical government in each church, and in 1884 compiled their own liturgies.

Their petition was renewed to the Anglican bishops at the 1888 Lambeth Conference, where it was taken up by the archbishop of Dublin, Lord Plunket. He, however, was unable to win the support of his fellow Irish bishops, who refused a petition from the Lusitanian churches to set up a consultative committee of three Irish bishops to supervise their congregations until they had a bishop of their own. Notwithstanding this, Plunket, the same year, ordained a deacon in Portugal. By 1894 he had persuaded the bishops of Clogher and Down to act with him, unless formally forbidden by either the bench of Irish bishops or the general synod of the Church of Ireland, to consecrate a bishop in Madrid for the Spanish Reformed Church. It was perhaps natural that the cause of minority Protestant churches standing, such as the Church of Ireland, in the midst of a predominantly Roman Catholic population, and claiming to restore the primitive doctrine and practice of the Church, should attract the sympathies of the Irish bishops.

However, some of the Irish bishops were very reluctant to support Plunket's desire to 'wander into other dioceses with which their Church had no legal concern'. Bishop Magee of Peterborough warned his Irish friends that their consecration of a bishop for Spain could result in severing relations between the Church of England and the Church of Ireland. Although English Anglo-Catholics, in the middle of the controversy over the validity of Anglican orders in the eyes of the Roman Catholic Church, were very upset by what the *Church Times* described as the 'Spanish scandal', and Lord Halifax, a leading Anglo-Catholic layman, wrote to the archbishop of Toledo to apologize for the presumption of the archbishop of Dublin acting 'without the sanction of your Eminence and of the bishops of your Province of Toledo to consecrate a certain schismatic named Cabrera to the Episcopate', there was little comment in the Church of England. The very small Lusitanian churches remained under the superintendance of a committee of the Irish bishops. In 1956 the bishop of Meath with two American bishops consecrated a second bishop for the Spanish church. In 1963 the Church of Ireland received the Spanish Reformed Church and the Lusitanian Church into full communion, each church then having about ten congregations.[100]

The Anglican Congress in Minneapolis in 1954 was an attempt to draw clergy and lay people into the discussions of the Communion. The Congress comprised the bishops of each diocese accompanied by one priest and one lay delegate. In all 657 delegates attended. One of the difficulties of involving lay people and clergy before the age of relatively cheap air travel was the burden of expense and time placed upon churches or individuals. On this occasion the cost of the Congress in Minneapolis was largely borne by the PECUSA.[101]

In 1958 Fisher also restricted the invitations to the Lambeth Conference, so that only six non-diocesan bishops, all from the provinces of York and Canterbury, were invited, whom it was thought might have important contributions to make. There was also wide ecumenical representation, including the English Baptist Union and Congregational Union, the Lutheran churches, the Orthodox, the Old Catholics, the Scandinavian churches and the Church of Scotland.

There were five committees appointed for the conference – The Bible, Church Unity, Progress in the Anglican Communion, The Reconciling of Conflicts Between Nations, and The Family in Contemporary Society. The 1958 conference, having had time to observe the development of the Church of South India, commended the proposal for a new Church of North India, Burma and Pakistan, largely on the grounds that all clergy would be episcopally ordained from the start. However, there was criticism by some Anglo-Catholics and moderate Catholics (including Archbishop Michael Ramsey of York) that there was inadequate definition of what was being effected by the service of union. On progress in the Anglican Communion it was recognized that the Advisory Council set up in 1948 had failed, and it was proposed to appoint an executive officer, with the task of travelling and keeping in touch with the churches in the Communion. It was thought to be very important that the right person be appointed to this post. It was thought that it needed to be a bishop, who relieved of diocesan responsibilities, could relate closely and on equal terms with other bishops. The most difficult aspect of the job was thought to be to work with an archbishop of Canterbury who after fourteen years, was very familiar with the Communion, and was in such regular touch with the other bishops that it would be difficult for an executive officer to establish his own authority and independence.

Ambrose Reeves, bishop of Johannesburg was approached, but he declined the offer. The real reason for offering him the post was probably to remove him from South Africa where his opposition to apartheid was placing him in a very dangerous position.[102] Subsequently Stephen Bayne, bishop of Olympia in the USA, accepted the post. He had the advantage of not being

English, and of being thus distanced from and independent of Archbishop Fisher. He also possessed the right personality and the humour and tact to carry out the work. However, some of the problems that had prevented the old Advisory Council from working were still unresolved. It took from August 1958 until April 1959 to negotiate the funds to provide a salary for the executive officer, and for money for staff and offices.[103]

In addition to the appointment of the executive officer, perhaps one of the most important products of the 1958 conference was the report *The Family in Contemporary Society*, which frankly admitted the nature of sexuality and its God-given origins, its sacramental character, yet its temptations and possible abuse. Adrian Hastings has suggested that this report was among the ablest to come from any authoritative church body in the twentieth century. In it the bishops demonstrated that they were speaking from both a maturely developed moral theology, and with the benefit of personal experience.[104]

The conference committee on the Bible was chaired by Michael Ramsey, then archbishop of York, who drafted much of the committee's report himself. In the report, which the conference endorsed, the bishops of the Anglican Communion committed themselves decisively to the rightness of modern analytical biblical scholarship, and to the freedom of biblical scholars to probe and explore the biblical texts.[105] The committee on the reconciling of conflicts was unable to reach a common mind, and their difficulties were reflected in the debate on nuclear warfare in the plenary session of the conference, when the bishops agreed to ask governments to abolish nuclear weapons.[106] The conference also sanctioned the ordination of men while they continued in their lay occupations, thus initiating the development of non-stipendiary ministry, and urged the use of trained and qualified women in the service of the Church, thus setting the stage for subsequent debates and developments in the Church's ordained ministry. The conference strongly condemned racialism, and demanded the concern of governments for the plight of refugees.

The 1958 conference also set in motion very important developments in liturgy in the provinces of the Anglican Communion. The 1948 conference had resolved that the Prayer Book 'has been and is, so strong a bond of unity throughout the whole Anglican Communion that great care must be taken to ensure that revisions of the Book shall be in accordance with the doctrine and accepted liturgical worship of the Anglican Communion'. In 1948 the only provinces with rites differing significantly from the Prayer Book were those in Scotland, South Africa and the United States, and in Scotland and South Africa the Prayer Book itself continued in use as an alternative. Furthermore, the ethos of all those rites was very similar – retaining the traditional forms of the Prayer Book, even where the structure had been modified and doctrinal emphases adjusted.

By 1958 the situation had begun to change. Canada, the Church of North India, Pakistan, Burma and Ceylon, and the province of the West Indies all had draft orders for holy communion in use, and stood on the eve of seeking final authorization for these rites. The growing awareness of liturgical revision in the Anglican Communion had become evident at the Anglican Congress at Minneapolis in 1954, which considered worship as one of its four main topics. Important papers by two distinguished Angli-can liturgists, Massey Shepherd, of the PECUSA, and Colin Dunlop, dean of Lincoln, indicated that within unity, variety of forms of worship could exist, and that any revision of forms of worship should be accompanied by controlled experiment and wide consultation. The fruits of the Liturgical Movement were also welcomed, with their emphasis on the Eucharist, and corporate worship. This discussion helped to disseminate awareness of liturgical revision and renewal throughout the Communion.

An immensely significant influence in the development of an awareness of alternative patterns of liturgy was the publication of the eucharistic order of the Church of South India in 1952. This owed much to Dom Gregory Dix's *The Shape of the Liturgy* which had been published in 1945, but it also showed an awareness of Scripture, and awareness of tradition, and an awareness of the spiritual needs of a local community, in a way that no other existing rite had succeeded in doing. Its eucharistic rite demonstrated the Eucharist as a corporate action, and also indicated a new dimension in the concept of flexibility, by a careful blend of elements drawn from existing traditions.

The Liturgical Commission of the Church of England, the Church of North India, Pakistan, Burma and Ceylon, and the Scottish Episcopal Church all wrote reports for the 1958 conference recommending that the bishops should endorse a process of liturgical revision in their provinces. The conference devoted more time to liturgical matters than any previous conference had for the past fifty years. Liturgy was the sole concern of a subcommittee chaired by Archbishop George Simms, then of Dublin, with Leslie Brown, bishop of Uganda, who had previously been convenor of the Church of South India's liturgical committee, as secretary. In view of Leslie Brown's involvement, it is not surprising that the subcommittee's proposals on the Eucharist were a virtual endorsement of the structure of the Church of South India liturgy. The conference endorsed the subcommittee's report, stating 'Loyalty [to the Prayer Book] may easily be overstated . . . Now it seems clear that no Prayer Book . . . can be kept unchanged for ever, as a safeguard of established doctrine'. They went on to state 'Our unity exists because we are a federation of Provinces and Dioceses of the One Holy, Catholic, and Apostolic Church, each being served and governed by a Catholic and Apostolic Ministry, and each believing the Catholic faith. These are the fundamental reasons for our unity.' It was only at a secondary level that the Prayer Book could be said to have given Anglican worship a distinct ecclesiastical culture. What was now needed was a recovery of the worship of the primitive Church, the principle of which Cranmer had endeavoured to follow. These recommendations, endorsed by a conference most of whose members knew little about liturgy beyond the Prayer Book, did however, give an impetus to a movement that was already underway, and would by the next conference be making a considerable impact on the worship and life of most of the provinces of the Communion.[107]

The 1958 conference was the first conference at which there was any significant number of non-European bishops, and affirmed it as an international and interracial Christian fellowship, rather than an almost accidental imperial and missionary prolongation of the established Church of the English nation. Fisher's work in pushing the establishment of new provinces in Africa and encouraging the interaction of dioceses in the Far East was an important contribution to this, and the appointment of an American as executive officer suggested that, in spite of its continuing Englishness, the Communion would find no insuperable difficulty in adjusting to the end of Empire, and the emergence of former colonial dioceses as independent churches in communion with the Church of England and with each other.

In 1963 there followed a second Anglican Congress, on the theme of the Church's mission to the world. This too included lay and clerical delegates from each diocese, as well as archbishops. The discussions at the congress were aimed at achieving a world view of mission on the religious, political and cultural frontiers. The discussions were much influenced by a document which emanated from a conference of the primates and metropolitans of the Communion meeting together with the Advisory Council on Mission Strategy, and the Lambeth Consultative Committee, held in Huron just before the Congress. This document on Mutual Responsibility and Interdependence in the Body of Christ (MRI) challenged Anglicans to a better distribution of resources throughout the whole Communion, and radically altered the understanding of mission in the Communion. It emphasized the interdependence of the provinces of the Communion, and dealt a death blow to the paternalism that had existed towards other provinces by the English and American churches. The MRI document led the delegates to envisage further Anglican provinces joining in new united churches, and thus losing an identifiable Anglican label and provoked much discussion of the meaning of Anglicanism, and its future as a distinct communion.

The 1960s marked a new era in the life of the whole Church. The Second Vatican Council held from 1963 to 1965 introduced new attitudes in the Roman Catholic Church, which opened opportunities for consultations between the two Communions, and a much more relaxed relationship. Relationships with other churches were also changing. While organic union was not achieved between the Church of England and the Methodist Church in Great Britain, there was much greater dialogue between all the churches in England, and the end of a sense of competition between denominations among the churches outside Europe and North America. The new approach to mission inaugurated by the Toronto Anglican Congress in 1963, and the achievement of political independence by most of the nations of Africa and Asia demanded new ways of keeping together the increasing numbers of provinces of the Communion, especially as they began to be led by indigenous bishops.

The 1960s were also a period of theological ferment,

encouraged by easy access to relatively cheap publishing, and radio and television. In England John Robinson's widely publicized *Honest to God* published in 1963, broadened and popularized theological debate. In North America the 'Death of God' theology also raised complex questions about theology and authority in the Episcopal Church. From the mid-1960s indigenous theologies in Africa, Asia and Latin America began to emerge, and focused on the themes of liberating Christianity from its dependence on what was regarded as the 'cultural imperialism' of Western theology, and its compromising association with Western imperial and political expansion. In the late 1960s a more revolutionary Marxism emerged in Africa, which provided a new critique of Christianity for nationalist political leaders. Much of this was focused in the WCC Assembly at Uppsala in Sweden in 1968, when the ecumenical movement was reorientated towards the achievement of liberation and humanitarianism in the world.[108] All this, together with the changing role of women in Western society, brought new issues about the ordination of women to the fore in some provinces of the Communion.

During the 1960s the fruits of several generations of liturgical research, first seen in the liturgy of the Church of South India, began to be seen in Anglican provinces and in most of the other Western churches. As a result the Prayer Book ceased to be the common denominator of worship in the Anglican Communion, and a new shape to liturgy, based on research about the early Church, became the pattern for all churches having their origins in the West.

The 1968 Lambeth Conference also marked a new era in Lambeth conferences. Inevitably, a conference chaired by an archbishop of Canterbury, Michael Ramsey, who was one of the very few theologians to have held that office, would be concerned with new theological issues, in ways in which most of the earlier conferences had not been. It was also a much larger conference, for suffragans and assistant bishops were invited for the first time in their own right, so that the number of bishops attending increased from 300 or so in 1958 to 462 in 1968. Relatively cheap and convenient air travel also meant that most bishops could attend. Closer relations with other churches meant that more observers were invited to attend the conference. The suggestion made in 1948 that theological consultants should be appointed was taken up, and consultants were invited to write introductory discussion papers for each of the thirty-three committees of the conference. Observers and consultants added another hundred or so to the numbers attending the conference. Because of the considerably increased numbers, it was no longer feasible for the bishops to meet in the library at Lambeth Palace, as they had since 1867. The plenary sessions of the conference were held in Church House, Westminster, which also provided facilities to allow the press and public to attend the plenary sessions, to which they were now admitted for the first time. The much increased numbers, the public nature of plenary sessions, the vast agenda, and the much greater variety of backgrounds of bishops from independent provinces which no longer sought their bishops from England, meant that in 1968, and at subsequent conferences, the atmosphere and the method of debates would be different. A new phase was beginning in the Anglican Communion, which to do it justice, will require another book.

Conclusion

The Anglican Communion at a very basic level 'just happened'. It could be seen as the result of initiatives by individuals and groups who, as settlers and traders, took their religious practices with them when they settled or traded in new territories, and employed clergy or provided endowments to pay clergy to minister the Word and sacraments for themselves and their fellow citizens. In addition, associations of individuals, in many instances lay people – in the SPCK, the SPG, the CMS, the UMCA, and numerous other smaller societies – raised money and recruited missionaries, lay and ordained, to preach the gospel in lands where it had not been heard.

At other levels there was, however, strategic thinking based on the traditional Anglican theology derived from Scripture, tradition and reason. For more than a hundred years the establishment of an overseas episcopate for the North American colonies, to provide supervision for the Church and the episcopal sacraments of confirmation and ordination for the Church, was a matter of grave concern for bishops of London and archbishops of Canterbury. Their recognition that without resident bishops, it was difficult for the Church to exist, let alone flourish, illustrates the high view of the nature of the Church and of episcopacy and its apostolic origins which pervaded eighteenth-century Anglicanism. Failing the establishment of a new 'primitive' episcopacy in the American colonies, shorn of the considerable level of 'medieval prelacy' that survived the Reformation in the Church of England, bishops of London took seriously the need to find alternative methods to supervise the clergy and laity in the colonies and appointed commissaries. The politicians who resisted the bishops' initiatives were not in the main godless men. Some of them, such as the duke of Newcastle, were devout Anglicans. They were motivated by political caution, recognizing that in New England at least, there would be strong resistance to the appointment of any bishops, which might unsettle all the colonies, and English dissenters as well.

When the time seemed propitious, after no more damage could be done in the North American colonies, the initiatives of American Anglicans were accepted and their new methods of nominating bishops and governing the Church were approved and episcopacy was rapidly established in the United States and the remaining North American colonies. However, it is important to note that in its transplantation to North America, Anglicanism was changed from being a national communal church to an associational and gathered church. Whether in the United States, or the British colonies, it was one church amongst others, not the church of the state or the colony, and it had to compete with other churches for members, who were required to fund church buildings and the clergy. While the lay element had always been important in the Church of England, expressed through the crown and Parliament, and lay patrons, and the parish vestry, in the United States and the colonies lay people provided the financial means that enabled the gospel to be preached, the sacraments to be administered and pastoral care to be provided. If they provided the means, they naturally wished to ensure that they would have what they considered a good person for the job, whether as a parish priest or as a bishop, and that they should have a voice in the governing and working of the Church. This associational, congregational aspect of Anglicanism has come to pervade the Communion, except in England, and as we have seen, it fitted and fits uncomfortably with hierarchical episcopacy, especially if it is exercised in an autocratic manner.

From at least the late eighteenth century, archbishops of Canterbury have played a key role in the development of the Anglican Communion. From the time of Bishop Inglis's problems in Nova Scotia, overseas bishops have looked to the archbishop for advice, support and comfort. Most archbishops have responded energetically and with considerable skill to this, often unnoticed, part of their role. Some archbishops have made outstanding contributions to the development of the Anglican Communion. Most notable have been Howley, Longley, Tait, Davidson and Fisher. While, as we have seen, no archbishop of

Canterbury has sought the title of patriarch, and whenever it has been proposed it has been strongly resisted, especially by the American bishops, archbishops of Canterbury have been accorded a primacy of honour, and their presidency of the Lambeth Conference has not been questioned. They have thus been *de facto* patriarchs of the Communion. However, any tendency, whether apparent or real, that they have shown to dominate or control the Lambeth Conference or the Communion has been resisted. It has always been clear that the archbishop of Canterbury is only the first among equals, either in the Communion or in his own province of Canterbury or in the Church of England.

The middle years of the nineteenth century were a key period for the development of the Anglican Communion and a group of men of similar theology and outlook, and very considerable administrative and political skills between 1820 or so and 1870, set the framework, as we have seen, for the Anglican Communion as we now know it. They all belonged to the theological tradition which is perhaps best described as 'traditional High Church'. They held a high view of the sacramental nature of the Church and of episcopacy as of the essence of the Church. Many of them were associated with the group known as the Hackney Phalanx, of whom one of the key members was, as we have often noted, a layman, Joshua Watson. Watson is highly significant for the Anglican Communion for he had a gift for friendship and he was able to draw outsiders into what was always an open group and he seldom let people escape from his correspondence. He befriended Bishop Hobart of New York and thereby helped to draw the American bishops into relationship with the English bishops. He kept in touch with members, such as W. G. Broughton and George Selwyn, who were despatched to dioceses in new territories on the other side of the world. As a Member of Parliament, he was on close terms with politicians and with leading Tories from Lord Liverpool onwards. He and his associates were skilled patrons and through their extensive contacts in the small world of nineteenth-century public schools and Oxford and Cambridge, they could spot high-fliers and through the network of patronage, they could test their potential.

Nearly all the significant players in mid-nineteenth century Anglicanism, clergy and laity, knew one another and shared common ground. The network among politicians included Liverpool, Canning, Peel, Gladstone, and among clergy, archbishops Manners-Sutton, Howley, Longley, Benson, and a large number of the leading bishops and clergy, most notably Bishop Blomfield and Samuel Wilberforce, and a slightly younger generation including Christopher Wordsworth, Dean Hook, and among the overseas bishops, Broughton of Sydney, Selwyn of New Zealand, Gray of Cape Town, Tyrrell of Newcastle, New South Wales, and Coleridge of Antigua. Through their dominance of the SPG and of the Colonial Bishoprics Fund and their enthusiasm for synodical government both in the Church of England and in overseas dioceses, and their support for a meeting of Anglican bishops that would include the American and Scottish bishops, and not just those owing allegiance to the British crown, they cast the mould of the Anglican Communion. Also, as biblical and patristic scholars, with a sound knowledge of history, they could envisage a church that was not established nor tied to the State and which shared the characteristics of the undivided Church. They were confident in their convictions that the Church of England and its related churches were part of the Western Catholic tradition, reformed and purified at the Reformation.

The evangelical tradition also contributed notably to the development of the Anglican Communion. The most significant contributor was Henry Venn, secretary of the CMS, but before him, Charles Simeon and the lay members of the Clapham Sect had contributed, particularly to the missionary work in India and Sierra Leone. Here again, their exercise of patronage through the networks established by Simeon and the Milners was of great value in recruiting chaplains and missionaries. Henry Venn's strategic thinking about the mission and the nature of the Church, and the importance of establishing indigenous churches under local leadership in New Zealand, West Africa and India should have been of immense importance for the development of Anglicanism. Lord Shaftsbury's network of contacts also ensured that evangelical clergy were recruited to be bishops of overseas dioceses through the agency of ministers such as Palmerston and Earl Grey.

Unfortunately, as we have seen, there was great risk of misunderstandings between the CMS strategists in London and their missionaries in far-away Africa or India and of three-cornered disputes between bishops, the Society and missionaries. Even after the Society had sought to establish control over their local committees and missionaries by sending out secretaries from London to manage the committees and supervise the missionaries, there was still scope for misunderstanding. The lack of trust and resulting disputes between the CMS and bishops, whether evangelical or High Church, let alone Tractarian and Anglo-Catholic, and between High Church bishops and missionaries over the establishment of synods in Africa, Ceylon and Australia, wasted enormous energy.

The nineteenth-century party divisions in the Church of England were transplanted into overseas dioceses and provinces as a result of the influence of the missionary societies and of partisan bishops. The High Church tradition of the SPG and the evangelical influence of the CMS was mediated in their spheres of influence – for example in West Africa the dioceses in Nigeria and Sierra Leone, under the impact of the CMS, had a succession of evangelical bishops, as did the dioceses in Uganda and Kenya in East Africa, whereas the dioceses in Ghana and Gambia, in West Africa, under the influence of the SPG, had Anglo-Catholic bishops. This could subsequently lead to major tensions over ecumenical consultations, as in East Africa in 1914, and in South India during the 1920s, 1930s and 1940s, and to difficulties in forming provinces. It may have been unhelpful to transplant party divisions which had their origins in England in the eighteenth and nineteenth centuries into new churches, but it did ensure that the creative tensions that have been part of the dynamic of Anglicanism were present in the new churches. There have also been equal criticisms of provinces like South Africa and New South Wales, where as the result of the powerful influence of early bishops, one of the Anglican traditions has come to predominate.

The planning and initiative of the High Church bishops was frustrated not only by misunderstandings with evangelicals, but also with successive colonial secretaries and the staff of the Colonial Office. The struggles over attempts to secure legislation to provide for self-government in colonial churches, so that they could order their own discipline and worship independently of the English Reformation legislation, against the opposition of evangelicals and nonconformists, were time-wasting and frustrating in the extreme. The failure of the draftsmen at the

Colonial Office to take into account the authority granted to legislative assemblies in colonies when drafting letters patent for bishops, created twenty years or so of chaos in the Province of South Africa. Very large sums of money that could have been better spent on salaries for clergy and supporting mission work, were spent on legal fees for the letters patent, and for the legal costs of the subsequent court cases.

Despite the fact that most of the government ministers and judges involved in the constitutional wrangles over the appointment and authority of bishops in overseas dioceses through the middle years of the nineteenth century were themselves devout Anglicans who wished to do their best for the Church, the arrangements for the increase of the number of dioceses were a mess. The CMS, under the influence of Henry Venn, and the SPG and the UMCA under the influence of Samuel Wilberforce, were pursuing similar theological models for the Church. The bishops, however, who were despatched to implement these policies found that the situations which they encountered were so unlike what had been envisaged in England that they had to develop their own models for the Church, and for the relationship between the Church and the State where Anglicans and even Christians might be in a minority. Many bishops must have lamented with Bishop Gray of Cape Town that they had received no advice, instructions or guidelines on how to be a bishop, and how to exercise authority in such new situations.

After the energy expended during the middle years of the century through the SPG and the Colonial Bishoprics Fund, the last third of the nineteenth century was a less fruitful time for raising funds for founding new dioceses. Until the arrival of Bishop Montgomery as secretary at the SPG in 1902, the Society was under cautious and ageing direction. Because the secretary of the Society was also secretary of the Colonial Bishoprics Fund he had little time to put energy into seeking new funds to endow new dioceses or to augment the endowment of existing dioceses. At the end of the Jubilee Meeting of the Fund in 1891, although Gladstone, still one of the treasurers of the Fund, addressed the meeting for just under an hour (which for Gladstone was a fairly short speech), only £800 was contributed, and by 1901 there were only twenty-five subscribers. Also, once autonomous provinces were established in New Zealand, South Africa and the West Indies, they became responsible

for deciding upon the creation of new dioceses in their jurisdictions, and English Anglicans had less sense of responsibility
for finding funds for them. Although the unattached missionary
dioceses were under the jurisdiction of the archbishop of
Canterbury, they were usually thought to be supported by a
missionary society of a particular churchmanship, and they thus
were seen as their responsibility, rather than as the responsibility
of the English Church as a whole. As a result, little effort was
made to increase the resources of the Colonial Bishoprics Fund
after the first Lambeth Conference.[1]

In the last twenty years of the nineteenth century there was,
however, for the first time, no shortage of people wishing to
work in the mission field, especially women, as we have seen,
and West and East Africa began to be spearheaded by missionaries, both evangelical and Anglo-Catholic, who, in most
instances, arrived ahead of the establishment of colonies.
However, in spite of the outstanding examples of Bishop Tucker
in Uganda and Bishop Smithies in Zanzibar, there was a reluctance to take seriously the establishment of local leadership in
the African dioceses. European superiority was emphasized in
Anglican dioceses as well as in British colonies and the long-
standing unwillingness of missionaries to share authority with,
or accept the authority of local leaders became the orthodoxy
of the Church in Africa. India was a slight exception to this,
for alongside the Congress Party's pressure for independence
for India, there was a pressure for Indian leadership in the
Anglican Church in India which, as a result of the determination
of the Anglican bishops, resulted in Bishop Azariah becoming
the first Indian bishop of a new diocese. The Anglican Church
was not alone among the churches in not promoting local
leadership, although the Roman Catholic Church was a little
more advanced than the Anglicans in eventually ordaining local
bishops.[2]

By 1959 most of the bishops of the Anglican Communion
outside the PECUSA were still English and had been educated
in England. Only in the Church of Ireland had all the bishops
been educated locally – to a man, at Trinity College, Dublin. Of
the Canadian bishops, twenty-three had been educated in Canada
and only four in England; in Australia fourteen bishops had
been educated in Australia and twelve in England. In all the

other provinces, English bishops were in the majority, including India where nine bishops were English-educated and six Indian-educated. Even in South Africa only one bishop had been educated in the province. Of the 199 diocesan bishops listed in *Crockford's Clerical Directory 1959–60*,[3] forty-five were graduates of Oxford and forty-one graduates of Cambridge (of whom eighteen of each were English diocesans), and 107 of them had been trained at English theological colleges. In addition, another nineteen English-educated bishops had not attended a theological college. Apart from the American bishops, Lambeth conferences must have been very English affairs. Only four bishops in 1959 were Africans, all from West Africa and six were Indian. One of the major reasons for the small numbers of locally-educated bishops, even from provinces in the 'old dominions', was the failure of Anglicans to become involved in higher education overseas and to assist in the establishment of theology faculties or departments in universities. Apart from the United States and Canada, little energy or money was invested even in building up good theological colleges in the 'old dominions', let alone in Africa. The Church of England in Australia pursued the disastrous policy of nearly every diocese, in spite of their small size and limited funds, establishing its own small college. This long-lasting Englishness of the Anglican churches in the 'old dominions', apart from Canada, probably contributed to the Church's relative lack of impact, as these countries developed independently of Britain in the second half of the twentieth century.

Most of the English leaders of the churches of the Anglican Communion failed to remember or to apply the lessons to be learned from the history of the episcopal churches in Scotland, Ireland and Wales. A study of those churches shows, as we have seen, the importance of propagating the gospel and conducting worship in a language 'understanded of the people'. While considerable effort was taken in translating the Bible and the Prayer Book into local languages, it is not obvious that a knowledge of local languages was a major priority for the missionary societies for the bishops sent out from England. An equally important lesson from the Scottish, Irish and Welsh churches was the importance of local leadership which related to local society, as well as to the local language, and that it should relate to the whole society, and not just to an elite. If the bishops and missionary societies had worked rapidly towards establishing local ministries relating to local patterns of leadership, the Christianizing of Africa and Asia might have produced a much more diverse Church, but one that related closely to the needs of peoples for the experience of hearing the word of God, and receiving the sacraments.

Perhaps as significant as the heavy dependence on the Church of England for theological education of the Church's leaders, was the lack of use of the resources of other churches in the Communion, especially the PECUSA. In 1959, outside North America, one bishop in India was a graduate of Trinity College, Toronto, one West Indian bishop was a graduate of Harvard, and another of the General Theological Seminary in New York, one bishop in Central African had trained at Ridley College, Melbourne and a New Zealand bishop had trained at Moore College, Sydney. A further result of this was that almost the only theological research and writing being undertaken in the Communion was in England, Canada and the United States of America. The heavy dependence of the churches in Africa and Asia on the churches and missionary societies in Britain and North America for funds for paying clergy, especially European missionaries, and for the provision of schools and hospitals created an unhelpful dependence, and discouraged initiatives among local leaders.

It would be hard to deny that in 1959 the most significant element in the cohesion of the Anglican Communion was the Englishness of its bishops. It is not really surprising that the American bishops regarded Lambeth Conferences with suspicion. Given the tendency of English theological colleges to emulate Oxbridge colleges, Lambeth Conferences must have been very upper-middle class, 'high-table' occasions.

Lambeth Conferences were a curious phenomenon. It is tempting to say that they did nothing very much and did it rather well. However, occasionally, they did something important. The large attendance of bishops suggests that the bishops at least valued them. Their willing attendance must be partially accounted for by offering a good reason to return to the 'mother country' to visit family and friends. But it must also have offered a valuable opportunity to talk freely to one's peers and to discuss common problems. As we have seen, before the advent of cheap air travel, being a bishop in Canada, Africa, India, Australia, New Zealand or the West Indies must have been a very lonely experience. However, in spite of the attempts by several archbishops to establish a consultative process for compiling the agendas of conferences, the agendas tended to be dominated by the concerns of the English bishops, and in any case the agendas were dominated by the bishops who could afford the considerable expense of attending, and they did little to meet the needs of the poorest dioceses.

Archbishop Longley achieved considerable success in establishing a format for the Lambeth Conference which has survived, relatively unchanged, for more than a century. Tait increased the length from a week to a month in 1878, but otherwise until 1968, they followed a similar pattern of plenary and committee discussion, always in private and without minutes, and the issue of committee reports and an encyclical of varying degrees of blandness. They have seldom said anything earth-shattering and they have sometimes sunk to optimistic and platitudinous banality, as in 1888 when they discussed 'socialism', and in 1908, 'materialism'. However, occasionally they have said important things, especially on topics they knew something about, notably the nature and organization of the Anglican Communion, as in 1878, and particularly on relations between churches, most notably in 1920 in An Appeal to All Christian People. They have tended to avoid contentious theological issues and as a result, have generally avoided condemning passing fashions, or important new developments. Significantly, they managed to confer their approval on the critical study of Scripture and important developments in moral theology, most notably in the 1958 report on *The Family in Contemporary Society*. The 1958 Conference set an agenda for the Communion on matters such as liturgical revision, and the place of women in the Church, and the nature of Anglicanism, with which it has been preoccupied for forty years. Disappointingly, but understandably, given their Englishness, they have brought few perspectives to bear from the other continents and cultures which the Communion embraced. Although they have always recognized in theory the importance of indigenizing Christianity in other cultures, notably in China, and condemned racism, their pronouncements had little impact on clergy and people outside the conference. In general, apart from on the bishops who attended them it is not obvious that Lambeth Conferences, as private meetings of bishops, had much impact on the churches of the Communion, and particularly the Church of England.

Perhaps that is only to be expected and probably to be welcomed, in a Communion in which authority is dispersed and not centralized and in which a broad range of theological positions is embraced. The range of theological positions held has been such that it could be claimed that the Anglican Communion offered a model for the unity of the whole Church. Individual dioceses of the Communion have been able to engage in some of the few achievements of organic unity between churches, most notably in the Church of South India. However, this development highlighted the tension for many dioceses between a desire to remain part of a world-wide communion, and the possibility of entering into union with other local churches. The Anglican element has obviously been very important in local ecumenical schemes, as in South India. But the separation of the South Indian dioceses was a considerable loss to the Anglican Communion in its ambition to be a world-wide communion.

The familiarity of archbishops of Canterbury and the English bishops who steered the Anglican Communion into existence, from Howley and Blomfield onwards, with patristic theology and the development of the early Church, enabled them to ensure that Anglicanism developed organically and to provide for new dioceses and most importantly, to group dioceses into provinces and to provide local metropolitans as regional points of reference for the Church. Thus, from the meetings of the Australian and Canadian bishops in the early 1850s, there were what were effectively, local councils of the Church, which were also influenced by the Enlightenment model of the constitution of the PECUSA, based on the constitution of the United States. Within provinces there were a wide variety of constitutional arrangements from the strongly centralized constitutions of the Church in the Province of South Africa and the Church in Wales, to the very dispersed pattern in Canada and the West Indies and the deep reluctance of the Church of England in Australia to form anything like a province.

It was this pattern of provincial association that Archbishop Fisher chose to strengthen and develop in the 1940s and 1950s in an attempt to revitalize the Communion. By bullying the bishops of West and East Africa and Australia into forming provinces, he created a context for local leadership, so that local variations in church government and leadership could develop, and the Anglican churches, particularly in Africa, could have the confidence to be less English. This was a far-sighted policy and carried considerable risk that diversity might lead to dissolution. For a variety of reasons there has not been an outflow of churches from the Communion to create local national churches in union with other denominations. Nor has the burst of liturgical experiment and a very general abandonment of the Prayer Book since the 1958 Lambeth Conference led to a breakdown of common prayer and worship in the Communion. There continues to be a family likeness between the liturgies of the churches of the Communion, but the likeness is now shared with nearly all the Western churches.

Alongside this encouragement of greater diversity, Fisher also recognized the importance of establishing minimal central institutions for the Communion, in addition to the modest administrative facilities of Lambeth Palace. His first attempts in 1948 with the Advisory Council on Missionary Strategy and St Augustine's College, Canterbury in 1948 failed through lack of finance. His second attempt in 1958, with the creation of the post of an executive officer and provision for funding other posts and an office and staff, contributed importantly to the future development of the Communion that has ensured that it would be truly multi-racial and with strong indigenous leadership. Under local leadership, as the African independent churches, which broke away from the Anglican dioceses in Africa foreshadowed, the Anglican Communion has grown and flourished in Africa and Asia. Thus by 1988 ten new provinces had been formed in the Communion, and more than half of the dioceses of the Communion were not in the Commonwealth, and the majority of Anglicans were not native English-speakers, or perhaps speakers of English at all.

As we have seen, Anglicanism in its essence has never been merely English, nor has it merely been part of British expansionist policies. There is even an impression that in the areas of the world where there has been extensive British immigration – the USA, Canada, Australia and South Africa, Anglicanism took a long time to take root, and certainly bishops, and even chaplains in any numbers, followed well after settlers had begun to arrive. It is also notable that in these areas Anglicanism has not become a majority church. Where Anglican missionaries preceded colonial rule – in West Africa, Madagascar, and Uganda, for example – it took root rapidly. Interestingly, as Anglican missionaries preceded the establishment of colonies by successive British governments, so Anglican dioceses were formed into provinces and given autonomy before British governments granted 'dominion' status to Canada, Australia and South Africa, and the Lambeth Conference preceded the first Colonial Conference by twenty years. In the twentieth century, as we have seen, Archbishop Fisher was pushing autonomy on to the dioceses in West, Central and East Africa before the countries in those areas were given political independence by Britain.

Since the 1960s the Anglican Communion has continued to develop apace. In the 1950s the Communion was largely Anglo-Saxon, comprising provinces in the 'old dominions' of the British empire. In the 1990s the majority of dioceses are not Anglo-Saxon, and the majority of Anglicans are either non-native speakers of English or non-English speakers. The number of provinces has more than doubled since 1950. More than half the dioceses in the Anglican Communion are not in countries that are members of the Commonwealth, and an increasing number of Anglian churches do not have any association with British history. The fastest growing dioceses are in Africa and New Guinea. 'Anglican' has ceased to mean simply English and has become a term for the particular embodiment of the historic faith, order and worship of the Catholic Church that is the heritage of the Communion.[4]

The embodiment of Anglicanism is still largely Anglo-Saxon. Despite the emphasis of the English Reformation documents on providing a local and national expression of the faith, order and worship of the Catholic Church, many Anglican dioceses have clung to English expressions of their faith long after expatriates have departed. In worship translations of *Hymns Ancient and Modern* with English nineteenth-century tunes have continued in use, and English church structures and titles and robes and vestments are customarily adopted. Much more important for the Communion than issues like the ordination of women as deacons, priests and bishops is the embodiment of the Christian faith in cultures other than Western European cultures.

Indigenous theologies, spiritualties and worship are needed. An incarnational faith must require that people engage with that faith, and work it out in their own contexts.

The Anglican Communion perhaps has a greater potential to achieve this network of dioceses and provinces expressing the Christian faith in forms appropriate to the contexts of the churches, while remaining part of a world-wide Communion, than some other churches with more hierarchical and authoritarian structures.

Like the early Church, the Anglican Church is not a church of fixed structures and systematic theologies. It has maintained that its doctrines are the doctrines of the whole Church, believed by everybody, everywhere and at all times, not the doctrine of a particular tradition. It has avoided endorsing systematic theologies which risk prematurely freezing Christian faith in propositional forms which inhibit further exploration. It derives its teaching, which is proclaimed in its daily liturgy, from Scripture and tradition. Scripture should be accessible to all people, and requires an analytical and critical approach. The traditions of the Church also need to be analytically and critically studied from an historical perspective, to identify what are essentials and what are inessentials in the traditions. Tradition is, of course, embodied in what the people of God do as well as in what theologians and clergy say and write.

The development of tradition may be untidy. The making of the Anglican Communion has certainly been untidy and unsystematic, and deeply frustrating for some of the participants, but it has enabled a number of models of mission and ecclesiology to be explored and tested for the benefit of the whole Church. It also, as this study shows, demonstrates the dynamism of the Christian faith, and its ability to become central to people's lives, especially when it is allowed to speak for itself in worship and life, and in that extraordinarily powerful and flexible expression of order in the life of the Church, the threefold ministry. This pattern of order in the Church, which has been part of its tradition since the apostolic age, has become of the *bene* and *plene esse* of the Church, and consequently of its existence, and a condition of any unions with other churches. However, bishops are not given unfettered authority. The understanding of authority in Anglicanism was classically set out in the Lambeth Conference report of 1948:

Authority as inherited by the Anglican Communion from the undivided Church of the early centuries of the Christian era, is single in that it is derived from a single divine source, and reflects within itself the richness and historicity of the divine Revelation, the authority of the eternal Father, the incarnate Son, and the life-giving Spirit. It is distributed among Scripture, Tradition, Creeds, the Ministry of the Word and Sacraments, the witness of the saints and the *consensus fidelium*, which is the continuing experience of the Holy Spirit through his faithful people in the Church. It is thus a dispersed rather than a centralised authority having many elements which combine, interact and check with each other.[5]

It is a constitutional episcopacy in which the faithful people of God may overrule bishops, as the English Parliament did in 1559, in renouncing the authority of the bishop of Rome over English dioceses and authorizing the use of the Prayer Book, against the wills of the English bishops. Constitutional synods, including lay people as well as bishops and clergy, in every diocese of every province of the Communion, provide a check on the authority of any individual bishop or conference of bishops. Dispersed authority allows for experiment and gradual change, which takes into account the practices and views of all the people of God who owe their allegiance to dioceses in communion with one another and with the see of Canterbury.

The Anglican Communion has studiously avoided the usual ways of maintaining unity in a communion or church, by means of a system of canon law and courts, or a single common liturgy, or a central authority. Instead unity is maintained by each church in the Communion respecting the rights of every other church. This has been strained from time to time, but it has worked, because unity also comes from a common faith consisting of adherence to the Catholic faith as contained in the Scriptures summed up in the Apostles' Creed, as expressed in the sacraments of the gospel and in the rites of the primitive Church, and as safeguarded by the historic threefold ministry. The categories of law and compulsion are superfluous. The various parts of the Communion are held in unity as each grows in charity and in understanding of the common faith. The maintenance of unity thus is a spiritual and moral matter not an issue of rules and law.

Appendix

Provinces

Provinces existing in 1784

Armagh
Canterbury (C)
Dublin
Scotland
York (Y)

Provinces created after 1784

1784 Protestant Episcopal Church in the United States (USA)
1835 India, Burma and Ceylon (IBC); from 1947 India,
Pakistan, Burma and Ceylon (IPBC)
1847 New South Wales (NSW)
1853 South Africa (SA)
1858 New Zealand (NZ)
1862 Canada (Can)
1875 Rupertsland (R)
1883 West Indies (WI)
1887 Japan (J)
1905 Queensland (Q)
Victoria (V)
1912 Ontario (O)
1914 British Columbia (BC)
1914 Western Australia (WAus)
1920 Wales (W)
1930 China (Ch)
1947 Church of South India – withdrew from the Church of

India, Pakistan, Burma and Ceylon and the Anglican
Communion in 1947 (CSI)
1951 West Africa (WA)
1955 Central Africa (CA)
1957 Jerusalem (Jer)
1960 East Africa (EA)
1961 Uganda

Missionary Dioceses under the Jurisdiction of the Archbishop of Canterbury

Africa (MDAf)
Asia (MDAs)
America (MDAm)
Europe (MDE)
Extra Provincial Dioceses in Australia (EPDAus)

Dioceses

Dioceses existing in 1784
ARMAGH (UNIONS AS IN 1834)

Armagh
Clogher
Connor
Derry and Raphoe
Down and Dromore
Kilmore and Elphin and Ardagh
Meath
Tuam, Killala and Achonry

CANTERBURY

Bangor (W)
Bath and Wells
Canterbury
Chichester
Ely
Exeter
Gloucester
Hereford
Lichfield
Lincoln
Llandaff (W)

London
Norwich
Oxford
Peterborough
Rochester
St Asaph (W)
St Davids (W)
Salisbury
Winchester
Worcester

DUBLIN

Cashel and Emly, Waterford and Lismore
Cork, Cloyne and Ross
Dublin and Glendalough and Kilmore
Killaloe, Kilfenora, Clonfert and Kilmacduagh
Limerick, Ardfert and Aghadoe
Ossory, Ferns and Leighlin

SCOTLAND

Aberdeen and Orkney
Argyll and the Isles
Brechin
Edinburgh
Glasgow and Galloway
Moray, Ross and Caithness
St Andrews, Dunblane and Dunkeld

YORK

Carlisle
Chester
Durham
Sodor and Man
York

Dioceses created after 1784

1784 Connecticutt (USA)
1787 New York (USA)
       Pennsylvania (USA)
       Nova Scotia (Can)

1790 Virginia (USA)
        Rhode Island (USA)
1792 Maryland (USA)
1793 Quebec (Can)
1795 South Carolina (USA)
1797 Massachusetts (USA)
1802 New Hampshire (USA)
1811 Vermont (USA)
1814 Calcutta (IBC)
1815 New Jersey (USA)
1817 North Carolina (USA)
1818 Ohio (USA)
1820 Maine (USA)
1823 Georgia (USA)
1824 Barbados (WI)
        Jamaica (WI)
1826 Mississippi (USA)
1829 Kentucky (USA)
        Tennessee (USA)
1832 Michigan (USA)
1835 Chicago (USA)
        Madras (IBC – until 1947, then CSI)
1836 Ripon (C)
        Sydney (NSW)
1837 Bombay (IBC)
1838 Florida (USA)
        Indianopolis (USA)
        Louisiana (USA)
1838 Western New York (USA)
1839 Newfoundland (Can)
        Toronto (Can)
        Missiouri (USA)
1841 Auckland (NZ)
        Delaware (USA)
        Jerusalem (Jer)
1842 Antigua (WI)
        Gibraltar (MDE)
        Guiana (WI)
        Tasmania (EPDAus)
1844 Shanghai (USA)
1845 Colombo (IBC)

Fredericton (Can)
1847 Adelaide (EPDAus)
Cape Town (SA)
Melbourne (V)
Milwaukee (USA)
Newcastle (NSW)
1848 Manchester (Y)
Rupertsland (R)
1849 Hong Kong (Ch until 1949, then MDAs)
1850 California (USA)
Liberia (USA)
1852 Sierra Leone (WA)
Montreal (Can)
1853 Grahamstown (SA)
Iowa (USA)
Natal (SA)
1854 Mauritius (MDAf)
1855 Borneo – formerly Labuan and Sarawak (MDAs)
1856 Christchurch (NZ)
Perth (WAus)
1857 Huron (O)
Minnesota (USA)
1858 Nelson (NZ)
Waiapu (NZ)
Wellington (NZ)
1859 Brisbane (Q)
British Columbia (BC)
Kansas (USA)
1861 Honolulu (USA)
Melanesia (NZ)
Nassau (WI)
St Helena (SA)
The Zambezi – subsequently Zanzibar (MDAf)
1862 Ontario (O)
1863 Blomfontein – formerly Orange Free State (SA)
Goulburn (NSW)
1864 The Niger – subsequently Equatorial West Africa (WAf)
1865 Pittsburgh (USA)
1866 Dunedin (NZ)
1868 Albany (USA)
Easton (USA)

Long Island (USA)
Nebraska (USA)
1869 Bathurst (NSW)
Falkland Islands – subsequently Argentina and Eastern
South America with the Falkland Islands (MDAm)
1870 Zululand (SA)
1871 Arkansas (USA)
1872 Chekiang – formerly North China (Ch)
Moosonee (O)
Trinidad (WI)
1873 Algoma (O)
St John's (SA)
1874 Haiti (USA)
Madagascar (MDAf)
Newark (USA)
Saskatoon (R)
1875 Ballarat (V)
Fond Du Lac (USA)
Niagara (O)
Southern Ohio (USA)
1877 Colorado (USA)
Lahore (IBC)
Quincy (USA)
Rangoon (IBC)
West Virginia (USA)
1878 North Queensland (Q)
Pretoria (SA)
Windward Islands (WI)
1879 Caledonia (BC)
New Westminster (BC)
Travancore and Cochin (IBC – until 1947, then CSI)
1880 Mid China (Ch)
Liverpool (Y)
1882 Newcastle (Y)
1883 British Honduras (WI)
East Carolina (USA)
North Dakota (USA)
South Dakota (USA)
South Tokyo (J)
1884 Eastern Equatorial Africa – subsequently Mombasa
(MDAf)

Mackenzie River (R)
Qu'Appele (R)
Riverina (NSW)
Southwell (Y)
1887 St Albans (C)
Truro (C)
1888 Calgary (R)
Wakefield (Y)
1889 Korea (MDAs)
Oregon (USA)
West Missouri (USA)
1890 Chota Nagpur (IBC)
1891 Mashonaland (CA)
Yukon (BC)
1892 Alaska (USA)
Nyasaland (CA)
Rockhampton (Q)
Southern Virginia (USA)
Spokane (USA)
1893 Lebombo (SA)
1894 Kyushu (J)
Texas (USA)
1895 Dallas (USA)
Lexington (USA)
Los Angeles (USA)
Northern Michigan (USA)
Lucknow (IBC)
Szechwan Western (Ch)
Washington (USA)
1896 Hokkaido (J)
Kobe (J)
Ottawa (O)
Tinnevelly (IBC – until 1947, then CSI)
1897 Uganda (EA)
1898 New Guinea (Q)
1899 Keewatin (R)
1900 Carpentaria (Q)
1901 Bendigo (V)
Cuba (USA)
Gippsland (V)
Hankow (USA)

Philippine Islands (USA)
Puerto Rico (USA)
Salina (USA)
Wangaratta (V)
Western Massachusetts (USA)
1902 Nagpur (IBC)
1903 Shantung (Ch)
1904 Harrisburg (USA)
Bunbury (WAus)
Kootenay (BC)
Mexico (USA)
Montana (USA)
West Texas (USA)
1905 Birmingham (C)
Southwark (C)
1906 Fukien (Ch)
1907 Atlanta (USA)
Eastern Oregon (USA)
Idaho (USA)
Nevada (USA)
Southern Brazil (USA)
Utah (USA)
Wyoming (USA)
1908 Polynesia (NZ)
1909 Accra (WA)
Honan (Ch)
Kwangsi and Hunan (Ch)
Singapore (MDAs)
1910 Anking (USA)
Erie (USA)
Northern Rhodesia (CA)
North West Australia (WAus)
Olympia (USA)
Sacramento (USA)
San Joaquin (USA)
1911 George (SA)
Kimberley and Kuruman (SA)
1912 Dornakal (IBC – until 1947, then CSI)
Iran (Jer)
Mid Japan (J)
1913 Edmonton (R)

Kalgoorlie (WAus)
1914 Armidale (NSW)
Assam (IBC)
Athabasca (R)
Cariboo (BC)
Chelmsford (C)
Grafton (NSW)
Sheffield (Y)
Willochra (EPDAus)
1918 Coventry (C)
1919 Lagos (WA)
Northern Indiana (USA)
Panama Canal Zone (USA)
South Western Virginia (USA)
1920 Bradford (Y)
Egypt and Libya (Jer)
1921 Monmouth (W)
1922 Johannesburg (SA)
South Florida (USA)
Upper South Carolina (USA)
Western North Carolina (USA)
1923 Osaka (J)
Swansea and Brecon (W)
Tokyo (J)
1924 Brandon (R)
Damaraland (SA)
Shensi (Ch)
1925 Bermuda (MDAm)
1926 Blackburn (Y)
Leicester (C)
Masasi (MDAf)
Upper Nile (MDAf)
Waikato (NZ)
1927 Central Tanganyika (MDAf)
Derby (C)
Guildford (C)
Portsmouth (C)
St Arnaud (V)
1928 Nasik (IBC)
1929 Eau Claire (USA)
Rochester (USA)

1932 Saskatchewan (R)
1933 The Arctic (R)
1935 Gambia and the Rio Pongas (WA)
1936 North Africa (MDAf)
      Oklahoma (USA)
1937 Szechuan Eastern (Ch)
1938 Alabama (USA)
1940 Dominican Republic (USA)
      Bhagalpur (IBC)
1945 Sudan (Jer)
1947 Delhi (IPBC)
1949 Central Brazil (USA)
      South Western Brazil (USA)
1950 Basutoland (SA)
      Kurunagala (IPBC)
1952 Ibadan (WA)
      New Mexico and South West Texas (USA)
      Ondo and Benin (WA)
      South West Tanganyika (MDAf)
1953 Amritsar (IPBC)
      Matabeleland (CA)
      Niger Delta (WA)
      Northern Nigeria (WA)
1956 Barrackpore (IPBC)
      East Bengal (IPBC)
1957 Central America (USA)
      Jordan, Lebanon and Syria (Jer)
1958 North West Texas (USA)
1959 Arizona (USA)
      Owerri (WA)

Notes

INTRODUCTION

1. Stephen Neill, *Anglicanism* (Harmondsworth 1958), p. 455.

CHAPTER 1

1. *The Lambeth Conference 1930: Encyclical Letter from the Bishops with Resolutions and Reports* (1930), p. 55.
2. The Book of Common Prayer, see Of Ceremonies – Why Some be Abolished, and Some Retained.
3. For discussions of the implications of the Reformation in England for the Church as an institution, and its relation to the crown and Parliament, see Claire Cross, *The Royal Supremacy and the Elizabethan Church* (1969); Claire Cross, *Church and People 1450–1660* (1976); Paul Avis, *Anglicanism and the Christian Church: Theological Resources in Historical Perspective* (Edinburgh 1989), chapters 2 and 4; W.J. Shiels, *The English Reformation 1530–1570* (Harlow 1989); Diarmad MacCulloch, *The Later Reformation in England 1547–1603* (1990); Susan Doran and Christopher Durstan, *Princes, Pastors and People: The Church and Religion in England 1529–1689* (London 1991); and Christopher Haigh, *English Reformations: Religion, Politics and Society Under the Tudors* (Oxford 1993).
4. For the Reformation in Wales, see Glanmor Williams, *Welsh Reformation Essays* (Cardiff 1967); and Glanmor Williams, *The Reformation in Wales* (Bangor 1991).
5. For the Reformation in Scotland, see Gordon Donaldson, *The Scottish Reformation* (Cambridge 1960); and Ian B. Cowan, *The Scottish Reformation: Church and Society in Sixteenth-Century Scotland* (1982).
6. For the Scottish Church under James VI and Charles I see C.R. Russell, *The Causes of the English Civil War* (Oxford 1990), pp. 109–25.
7. For Tenison's attitude to the Episcopalians in Scotland and the Act of Union see Edward Carpenter, *Thomas Tenison, Archbishop of Canterbury: His Life and Times* (1948), pp. 386–96.
8. For the Scottish Episcopal Church in the eighteenth century, see

Callum G. Brown, *The Social History of Religion in Scotland since 1730* (1987), pp. 23–41; and F.C. Mather, *High Church Prophet: Bishop Samuel Horsley (1733–1806) and the Caroline Tradition in the Later Georgian Church* (Oxford 1992), pp. 116–38.

9. For the Reformation in Ireland see Nicholas Canny, 'Why the Reformation Failed in Ireland: Une Question Mal Posée' (*JEH* 30, 1979), pp. 425–50; K. Bottigheimer, 'The Failure of the Reformation in Ireland: Une Question Bien Posée' (*JEH* 36, 1985), pp. 196–207; Aidan Clarke,'Varieties of Uniformity: The First Century of the Church of Ireland' (*SCH* 25, 1989), pp. 105–22; Steven G. Ellis,'Economic Problems of the Church of Ireland: Why the Reformation Failed in Ireland' (*JEH* 41, 1990), pp. 239–65; and T.C. Barnard, 'Protestants and the Irish Language 1675–1725' (*JEH* 44, 1993), pp. 243–72.

10. Brown, *Social History of Religion in Scotland*, p. 49.

CHAPTER 2

1. H.G.C. Herklots, *Frontiers of the Church: The Making of the Anglican Communion* (1961), p. 15.

2. Quoted in M.E. Gibbs, *The Anglican Church in India 1600–1970* (New Delhi 1972), p. 3.

3. Herklots, *Frontiers of the Church*, p. 75.

4. Herklots, *Frontiers of the Church*, pp. 18–19.

5. Herklots, *Frontiers of the Church*, pp. 26–27.

6. Geoffrey Yeo, 'A Case Without Parallel: The Bishop of London and the Anglican Church Overseas 1660–1748' (*JEH* 44, 1993), p. 452.

7. Quoted in Yeo, 'Case Without Parallel', p. 455.

8. C.F. Pascoe, *Two Hundred Years of SPG: An Historical Account of the Society for the Propagation of the Gospel 1701–1901* (1901), p. 744.

9. Pascoe, *Two Hunded Years*, p. 743.

10. Yeo, 'Case Without Parallel', pp. 458–60.

11. Quoted in Herklots, *Frontiers of the Church*, p. 39.

12. Yeo, 'Case Without Parallel', p. 461.

13. Yeo, 'Case Without Parallel', p. 461; and Herklots, *Frontiers of the Church*, p. 45.

14. For Compton's care of the Church in the North American colonies, see Edward Carpenter, *The Protestant Bishop, Being the Life of Henry Compton 1632–1713, Bishop of London* (1956), chapter 14.

15. For Bray's visit to Maryland see H.P. Thompson, *Thomas Bray* (1954), pp. 45–55.

16. For a brief account of the origins of the SPG, see Hans Cnattingius, *Bishops and Societies: A Study of Anglicanism and Colonial Expansion 1698–1850* (1952), pp. 7–15.

17. Carpenter, *Thomas Tenison*, p. 346.

18. Pascoe, *Two Hundred Years*, p. 744.

19. Pascoe, *Two Hundred Years*, pp. 744–5.
20. Carpenter, *Thomas Tenison*, p. 350.
21. Carpenter, *Thomas Tenison*, p. 352, n. 1.
22. Carpenter, *Thomas Tenison*, p. 348.
23. Yeo, 'Case Without Parallel', p. 468.
24. Norman Sykes, *Edmund Gibson, Bishop of London 1669–1748: A Study in Politics and Religion in the Eighteenth Century* (Oxford 1926), pp. 335–40.
25. Sykes, *Edmund Gibson*, pp. 353–4.
26. Sykes, *Edmund Gibson*, pp. 356–60.
27. H.P. Thompson, *Into All Lands: The History of the Society for the Propagation of the Gospel in Foreign Parts 1701–1950* (1951), p. 102.
28. Sykes, *Edmund Gibson*, pp. 348–50.
29. See G.V. Bennett, *The Tory Crisis in Church and State 1688–1730: The Career of Francis Atterbury, Bishop of Rochester* (Oxford 1975).
30. Sykes, *Edmund Gibson*, pp. 369–70.
31. Sykes, *Edmund Gibson*, p. 374.
32. Stephen Taylor, 'Whig Bishops and America: The Politics of Church Reform in Mid-Eighteenth-Century America' (*The Historical Journal* 36, 1993), pp. 339–40.
33. Taylor, 'Whig Bishops and America', p. 336.
34. Taylor, 'Whig Bishops and America', p. 341.
35. Taylor, 'Whig Bishops and America', pp. 341–2.
36. Edward Carpenter, *Thomas Sherlock 1678–1761* (1936), p. 205.
37. Carpenter, *Thomas Sherlock*, p. 199.
38. Carpenter, *Thomas Sherlock*, pp. 209–10.
39. Carpenter, *Thomas Sherlock*, pp. 211–13.
40. Carpenter, *Thomas Sherlock*, pp. 216–20.
41. Carpenter, *Thomas Sherlock*, pp. 200–2.
42. Carpenter, *Thomas Sherlock*, p. 229.
43. Pascoe, *Two Hundred Years*, p. 743.
44. Taylor, 'Whig Bishops and America', p. 347.
45. Taylor, 'Whig Bishops and America', pp. 351–2.
46. Quoted in Pascoe, *Two Hundred Years*, p. 743.
47. Jack M. Sosin, 'The Proposal in the Pre-Revolutionary Decade for Establishing Anglican Bishops in the Colonies' (*JEH* 13, 1962), p. 77.
48. Sosin, 'Proposal', pp. 78–82.
49. Pascoe, *Two Hundred Years*, p. 746.
50. Thompson, *Into All Lands*, pp. 46–52.
51. For the Church of England in the American colonies, see Frederick W. Mills, Sr, *Bishops by Ballot: An Eighteenth-Century Revolution* (New York 1978), chapters 1–7; and Robert T. Handy, *A History of the Churches in the United States and Canada* (Oxford 1976), chapter 5.

CHAPTER 3

1. Unless otherwise indicated, this account of the establishment of episcopacy in the American states is derived from Mills, *Bishops by Ballot*, chapters 8–12.
2. Pascoe, *Two Hundred Years*, p. 749.
3. Richard P. Heitzenrater, *Wesley and the People Called Methodists* (Nashville 1995), p. 292.
4. Mather, *High Church Prophet*, p. 121.
5. Marion J. Hatchett, 'The Anglican Liturgical Tradition', in *The Anglican Tradition*, ed. Richard Holloway (1984), p. 55.
6. Quoted in Avis, *Anglicanism and the Christian Church*, p. 288.
7. This account of the creation of the diocese of Nova Scotia, and of the episcopate of Charles Inglis is derived from Judith Fingard, *The Anglican Design in Loyalist Nova Scotia 1783–1816* (1972); and Brian Cuthbertson, *The First Bishop: A Biography of Charles Inglis* (Nova Scotia 1987).
8. Cnattingius, *Bishops and Societies*, pp. 28–30.
9. G.W.O. Addleshaw, 'The Law and Constitution of the Church Overseas', in *The Mission of the Anglican Communion*, eds E.R. Morgan and Roger Lloyd (1948), p. 84.
10. Cnattingius, *Bishops and Societies*, pp. 30–6.
11. Peter Burroughs, 'Lord Howick and the Colonial Church Establishment' (*JEH* 25, 1974), pp. 385–6.
12. Cnattingius, *Bishops and Societies*, pp. 69–70. For an account of the Hackney Phalanx see A.B. Webster, *Joshua Watson: The Story of a Layman 1771–1855* (1954).
13. For an account of the ecclesiology of the traditional High Churchmen, see Peter Nockles, *The Oxford Movement in Context: Anglican High Churchmanship 1760–1857* (Cambridge 1994), chapter 3; and for the composition of the Hackney Phalanx, see C. Dewey, *The Passing of Barchester* (1991), pp. 149–68.
14. Burroughs, 'Lord Howick', p. 385.
15. Thompson, *Into All Lands*, p. 109.
16. Webster, *Joshua Watson*, p. 115.
17. Philip Carrington, *The Anglican Church in Canada: A History* (Toronto, 1963), p. 65.
18. Sehon S. Goodridge, *Facing the Challenge of Emancipation: A Study of the Ministry of William Hart Coleridge, First Bishop of Barbados 1824–1842* (Bridgetown, Barbados 1981), pp. 4–12.
19. Cnattingius, *Bishops and Societies*, pp. 148–54.
20. Burroughs, 'Lord Howick', pp. 384–405. For the political and church background in England, see Richard Brent, *Liberal Anglican Politics: Whiggery, Religion, and Reform 1830–1841* (Oxford 1987), pp. 252–300.
21. Carrington, *Anglican Church in Canada*, pp. 82–93; and Thompson, *Into All Lands*, p. 120.
22. Quoted in Pascoe, *Two Hundred Years*, p. 752.
23. Gibbs, *Anglican Church in India*, p. 12.

24. Gibbs, *Anglican Church in India*, p. 10.
25. Norman Sykes, *Old Priest and New Presbyter: The Anglican Attitude to Episcopacy, Presbyterianism and Papacy since the Reformation* (Cambridge 1957), p. 155.
26. Nockles, *Oxford Movement in Context*, p. 156.
27. Gibbs, *Anglican Church in India*, pp. 12–23; and Leonard W. Cowie, *Henry Newman: An American in London 1708–1743* (1956), pp. 104–29.
28. See Peter Stubley, *A House Divided: Evangelicals and the Establishment in Hull* (Hull 1995), pp. 5–10.
29. Gibbs, *Anglican Church in India*, p. 25. For Simeon and the Clapham Sect, see Charles Smyth, *Simeon and Church Order: A Study of the Origins of the Evangelical Revival in Cambridge in the Eighteenth Century*, (Cambridge 1940), pp. 249–312; and Michael Hennell, *John Venn and the Clapham Sect* (1958), pp. 169–25. For the origins of the CMS see Elizabeth Elbourne, 'The Foundation of the Church Missionary Society: The Anglican Missionary Impulse', in *The Church of England c. 1689 – c. 1833: From Toleration to Tractarianism*, eds John Walsh, Colin Haydon and Stephen Taylor (Cambridge 1993).
30. Gibbs *Anglican Church in India*, p. 33.
31. J.D. Bollom, 'English Christianity and the Australian Colonies 1788–1860' (*JEH* 28, 1977), p. 367.
32. Gibbs, *Anglican Church in India*, p. 47.
33. Webster, *Joshua Watson*, pp. 118–19.
34. For Middleton's episcopate see Gibbs, *Anglican Church in India*, pp. 55–74; and Cnattingius, *Bishops and Societies*, pp. 72–101.
35. Quoted in Gibbs, *Anglican Church in India*, p. 87.
36. For Heber's episcopate see Gibbs, *Anglican Church in India*, pp. 82–7; Cnattingius, *Bishops and Societies*, pp. 113–18 and 134; and Derrick Hughes, *Bishop Sahib: A Life of Reginald Heber* (Worthing 1986), pp. 82–180; and Webster, *Joshua Watson*, pp. 159–64.
37. Gibbs, *Anglican Church in India*, p. 122.
38. Manning was a close associate of Samuel Wilberforce, the bishop of Oxford, and a friend of Keble and Newman. He subsequently became archdeacon of Chichester, but in 1851 he became a Roman Catholic, and in due course became a cardinal and archbishop of Westminster.
39. For Wilson's episcopate, see Gibbs, *Anglican Church in India*, pp. 103–32; Cnattingius, *Bishops and Societies*, pp. 159–83, and T.E. Yates, *Venn and Victorian Bishops Abroad: The Missionary Policies of Henry Venn and their Repercussions Upon the Anglican Episcopate of the Colonial Period 1841–1872* (Swedish Institute of Missionary Research, Uppsala, 1978), pp. 26–43.
40. C. Peter Williams, 'British Religion and the Wider World: Mission and Empire 1800–1940', in *A History of Religion in Britain: Practice and Belief from Pre-Roman Times to the Present*, eds Sheridan Gilley and W.J. Shiels (Oxford 1994), p. 389.
41. For the origins of Anglicanism in Australia, see Bollom, 'English

Christianity and the Australian Colonies', pp. 361–71; W.P. Morrell, *The Anglican Church in New Zealand* (Dunedin 1973), p. 3; G.P. Shaw, *Patriarch and Prophet: William Grant Broughton 1786–1853: Colonial Statesman and Ecclesiastic* (Melbourne 1978); Stephen Judd and Kenneth Cable, *Sydney Anglicans: A History of the Diocese* (Sydney 1987); and Stuart Piggin, 'The American and British Contribution to Evangelicalism in Australia', in *Evangelicalism: Comparative Studies of Popular Protestantism in North America, the British Isles and Beyond 1700–1990*, eds Mark A. Noll, David W. Bebbington and George A. Rawlyk (New York 1994).

42. For the first years of the Anglican missionaries in New Zealand see Morrell, *The Anglican Church in New Zealand*, pp. 4–21.

CHAPTER 4

1. A.R. Ashwell, *The Life of the Right Reverend Samuel Wilberforce, DD*, 3 Vols (London 1880), 1: 129.
2. Herklots, *Frontiers of the Church*, p. 103.
3. Ashwell, *Life of Wilberforce*, 1: 111.
4. Robert S. Bosher, *The American Church and the Formation of the Anglican Communion 1823–1853* (Evanston, Illinois 1962), pp. 8–10, and W.R.W. Stephens, *The Life and Letters of Walter Farquhar Hook*, 2 Vols (1878), 1: 30 and 89.
5. Stephens, *Life of Hook*, 1: 198–9.
6. For the part played by Joshua Watson in maintaining links with American and colonial bishops, see Webster, *Joshua Watson*, pp. 134–43.
7. Bosher, *American Church*, p. 13.
8. Yates, *Venn and Victorian Bishops Abroad*, p. 99.
9. Cnattingius, *Bishops and Societies*, p. 200.
10. Herklots, *Frontiers of the Church*, p. 131.
11. Yates, *Venn and Victorian Bishops Abroad*, pp. 77–8.
12. Yates, *Venn and Victorian Bishops Abroad*, pp. 101ff.
13. Nockles, *Oxford Movement in Context*, p. 163.
14. For the Jerusalem bishopric, see P.J. Welsh, 'Anglican Churchmen and the Establishment of the Jerusalem Bishopric' (*JEH* 8, 1957), pp. 193–204.
15. W.F. France, *The Overseas Episcopate: Centenary History of the Colonial Bishoprics Fund 1841–1941* (1941), p. 9.
16. France, *Overseas Episcopate*, pp. 10–12.
17. France, *Overseas Episcopate*, pp. 12–14.
18. France, *Overseas Episcopate*, pp. 15 and 23.
19. France, *Overseas Episcopate*, pp. 15–16.
20. J.E. Pinnington, 'The Consular Chaplaincies and the Foreign Office Under Palmerston, Aberdeen and Malmesbury: Two Case Histories: Rome and Funchal' (*JEH* 27, 1976), pp. 277–84.
21. See also G.I.T. Machin, *Politics and the Churches in Great Britain*

1832–1868 (Oxford, 1977), p. 202; and Charles N. Gray, *Life of Robert Gray, Bishop of Cape Town*, abr. ed. (1883), p. 47.

22. Morrell, *Anglican Church in New Zealand*, pp. 27–47; and John H. Evans, *Churchman Militant: George Augustus Selwyn, Bishop of New Zealand and Lichfield* (1964), pp. 63–115.

23. Yates, *Venn and Victorian Bishops Abroad*, p. 89.

24. C. Peter Williams, *The Ideal of the Self-Governing Church: A Study in Victorian Missionary Strategy* (Leiden 1990), p. 5.

25. Standish Meacham, *Lord Bishop: The Life of Samuel Wilberforce 1805–1873* (Cambridge, Mass. 1970), p. 252.

26. Morrell, *Anglican Church in New Zealand*, p. 48.

27. Herklots, *Frontiers of the Church*, pp. 215–17.

28. Morrell, *Anglican Church in New Zealand*, pp. 49–50.

29. Ross Border, *Church and State in Australia 1788–1872: A Constitutional Study of the Church of England in Australia* (London 1972), pp. 114–23.

30. Border, *Church and State in Australia*, p. 168.

31. Shaw, *Patriarch and Prophet*, p. 244.

32. Shaw, *Patriarch and Prophet*, pp. 234–41.

33. Shaw, *Patriarch and Prophet*, p. 249.

34. Shaw, *Patriarch and Prophet*, p. 254.

35. Border, *Church and State in Australia*, pp. 237–40; and Judd and Cable, *Sydney Anglicans*, pp. 38–41.

36. Carrington, *Anglican Church in Canada*, pp. 11–13.

37. Carrington, *Anglican Church in Canada*, p. 114.

38. For the revival of the Canterbury convocation, see Machin, *Politics and the Churches*, (cf. n.21) pp. 199, 235, 250, 262–3; P.J. Welsh, 'The Revival of an Active Convocation of Canterbury 1852– 1855' (*JEH* 10, 1959), pp. 188–97; and E.W. Kemp, *Counsel and Consent: Aspects of the Government of the Church as Exemplified in the History of the English Provincial Synods* (1961).

39. For the revival of the York convocation, see D.A. Jennings, *The Revival of the Convocation of York* (York 1975).

40. Border, *Church and State in Australia*, pp. 193–7.

41. Morrell, *Anglican Church in New Zealand*, pp. 57–60.

42. Carrington, *Anglican Church in Canada*, pp. 116–19.

43. Border, *Church and State in Australia*, pp. 199–209.

44. Border, *Church and State in Australia*, pp. 214–26.

45. Border, *Church and State in Australia*, pp. 229–33.

46. Border, *Church and State in Australia*, pp. 243–56; Judd and Cable, *Sydney Anglicans*, pp. 68–91; and Paul Struan Robertson *Proclaiming Unsearchable Riches: Newcastle and the Minority Evangelical Anglicans 1788–1900* (Sydney and Leominster 1996), chapter 6.

47. Morrell, *Anglican Church in New Zealand*, pp. 58–65.

48. Evans, *Churchman Militant*, p. 163.

CHAPTER 5

1. For the background to the Anglican Church in South Africa see Peter Hinchliff, *The Anglican Church in South Africa: An Account of the History and Development of the Church of the Province of South Africa* (1963), pp. 10–19; and Gray, *Life of Robert Gray*, pp. 51–98.

2. Gray, *Life of Robert Gray*, pp. 143–7; and Hinchliff, *Anglican Church in South Africa*, pp. 49–52.

3. Gray, *Life of Robert Gray*, pp. 188–213; and Peter Hinchliff, *John William Colenso* (London 1964), pp. 124–5.

4. Hinchliff, *Anglican Church in South Africa*, p. 58.

5. Gray, *Life of Robert Gray*, p. 215.

6. For the Colenso case, see Gray, *Life of Robert Gray*, pp. 215–93; Hinchliff, *Anglican Church in South Africa*; pp. 84–98; and Hinchliff, *Colenso*, pp. 90–163.

7. Robert S.M. Withycombe, 'Mother Church and Colonial Daughters: New Scope for Tensions in Anglican Unity and Diversity' (*SCH* 32, 1996), pp. 434–5.

8. Herklots, *Frontiers of the Church*, p. 191.

9. Bosher, *American Church*, p. 20.

10. Bosher, *American Church*, pp. 19–22.

11. Bosher, *American Church*, pp. 20–22.

12. Bosher, *American Church*, p. 21.

13. Unless otherwise indicated, information about the 1867 Lambeth Conference is derived from Alan M.G. Stephenson, *The First Lambeth Conference 1867* (1967).

14. Gray, *Life of Robert Gray*, p. 329.

15. R.T. Davidson and William Benham, *The Life of Archibald Campbell Tait, Archbishop of Canterbury*, 2 Vols (1891), 1: 370.

16. Davidson and Benham, *Life of Tait*, 1: 374–5.

17. H. Kirk-Smith, *William Thomson, Archbishop of York: His Life and Times 1819–1890* (1958), p. 124.

18. Gray, *Life of Robert Gray*, pp. 362–6.

19. Gray, *Life of Robert Gray*, p. 370.

20. For an example of the operation of such a nineteenth-century ecclesiastical patronage network, see Dewey, *The Passing of Barchester*.

21. Brian Taylor, *The Anglican Church in Borneo 1848–1962* (Bognor Regis 1983), p. 39. The first bishop of Labuan, Francis McDougall, was Colenso's brother-in-law.

22. Meacham, *Lord Bishop*, p. 253.

23. Davidson and Benham, *Life of Tait*, 1: 397.

24. Hinchliff, *Anglican Church in South Africa*, p. 99.

25. Hinchliff, *Anglican Church in South Africa*, pp. 100–3; Gray, *Life of Robert Gray*, pp. 381–424.

26. Hinchliff, *Anglican Church in South Africa*, pp. 106–8; A.C. Benson, *The Life of Edward White Benson, Sometime Archbishop of Canterbury*, 2 Vols (London 1900), 2: 486–500.

27. Hinchliff, *Anglican Church in South Africa*, pp. 111–14; and Gray, *Life of Robert Gray*, p. 424.
28. Hinchliff, *Anglican Church in South Africa*, pp. 124–5.
29. Hinchliff, *Anglican Church in South Africa*, pp. 130–2; Davidson and Benham, *Life of Tait*, 2: 338–9.
30. Kelsey Sterling, 'The Education of the Anglican Clergy', unpublished Leicester University PhD thesis (1982), p. 320.
31. Davidson and Benham, *Life of Tait*, 2: 341–5.
32. George B. Endacott and Dorothy E. She, *The Diocese of Victoria, Hong Kong: A Hundred Years of Church History 1849–1949* (Hong Kong 1949).
33. For accounts of the disestablishment of the Church of Ireland, see P.M.H. Bell, *Disestablishment in Ireland and Wales* (1969), pp. 113–205; Donald Harman Akenson, *The Church of Ireland: Ecclesiastical Reform and Revolution 1832–1868* (New Haven, 1971), pp. 226–72; Machin, *Politics and the Churches in Great Britain, 1832–1868*, pp. 357–71; and R.B. McDowell, *The Church of Ireland 1869–1969* (1975), chapters 2 and 3.
34. C. Peter Williams, '"Too Peculiarly Anglican": The Role of the Established Church in Ireland as a Negative Model in the Development of the Church Missionary Society's Commitment to Native Churches 1856–1872' (*SCH* 25, 1989), pp. 299–310.

CHAPTER 6

1. Adrian Hastings, *The Church in Africa 1450–1950* (Oxford 1994), p. 179; and Thompson, *Into All Lands*, pp. 68–70.
2. Piggin,'American and British Contribution', p. 292; Brian Stanley, 'Commerce and Christianity: Providence Theory, the Missionary Movement and the Imperialism of Free Trade 1842–1860' (*Historical Journal* 26, 1983), pp. 71–94; and Andrew Porter, 'Commerce and Christianity: The Rise and Fall of a Nineteenth Century Missionary Slogan' (*Historical Journal* 28, 1985), pp. 597–621; Brian Stanley, *The Bible and the Flag: Protestant Missions and British Imperialism in the Nineteenth and Twentieth Centuries* (Leicester 1990), p. 58.
3. Peter B. Clarke, *West Africa and Christianity* (1986), pp. 32–6.
4. A.F. Walls, 'A Christian Experiment: The Early Sierra Leone Company' (*SCH* 6, 1970) pp. 110–13.
5. Hastings, *Church in Africa*, pp. 184–6.
6. Clarke, *West Africa and Christianity*, pp. 32–44.
7. J.F.A. Ajayi, *Christian Missions in Nigeria 1841–1941: The Making of a New Elite* (Evanston, Ill. 1969), pp. 10–11; and Porter, 'Commerce and Christianity', p. 613.
8. Ajayi, *Christian Missions in Nigeria*, pp. 12–13.
9. Ajayi, *Christian Missions in Nigeria*, pp. 56–80.
10. Ajayi, *Christian Missions in Nigeria*, pp. 107–8.
11. Ajayi, *Christian Missions in Nigeria*, p. 105.

12. Ajayi, *Christian Missions in Nigeria*, pp. 127–48.
13. Hastings, *Church in Africa*, pp. 339–40.
14. Hastings, *Church in Africa*, pp. 340–1.
15. C.Peter Williams, *The Ideal of the Self-Governing Church: A Study in Victorian Missionary Strategy* (Leiden 1990), pp. 9–10.
16. Williams, *Ideal of the Self-Governing Church*, pp. 15–16.
17. Williams, *Ideal of the Self-Governing Church*, pp. 26–7.
18. Williams, *Ideal of the Self-Governing Church*, p. 40.
19. Hastings, *Church in Africa*, pp. 345–6.
20. Hastings, *Church in Africa*, p. 347.
21. For Keswick conventions and the developments in evangelicalism in the late nineteenth century in England, see D.W. Bebbington, *Evangelicalism in Modern Britain: A History from the 1730s to the 1980s* (1989), pp. 151–80.
22. Williams, *Ideal of the Self-Governing Church*, pp. 100 and 142–5.
23. Hastings, *Church in Africa*, pp. 389–92.
24. Williams, *Ideal of the Self-Governing Church*, pp. 147–79.
25. Williams, *Ideal of the Self-Governing Church*, pp. 189–95.
26. For the tensions in Anglican evangelicalism in the late nineteenth and early twentieth centuries, see Bebbington, *Evangelicalism in Modern Britain*, pp. 181–228.
27. Williams, *Ideal of the Self-Governing Church*, pp. 232–40.
28. Clarke, *West Africa and Christianity*, pp. 99–101.
29. Clarke, *West Africa and Christianity*, pp. 161–2; and Hastings, *Church in Africa*, pp. 494–7.
30. Owen Chadwick, *Mackenzie's Grave* (1959), pp. 15–23.
31. Stanley, 'Commerce and Christianity', p. 82.
32. Gray, *Life of Robert Gray*, p. 184.
33. For a full account of Mackenzie's expedition, see Chadwick, *Mackenzie's Grave*.
34. Hastings, *Church in Africa*, pp. 257–8.
35. John V. Taylor, *The Growth of the Church in Buganda: An Attempt at Understanding* (1958), pp. 59–47.
36. Stanley, *The Bible and the Flag*, pp. 127–8.
37. Stanley, *The Bible and the Flag*, pp. 128–32.
38. Taylor, *Church in Buganda*, pp. 69–83.
39. Taylor, *Church in Buganda*, pp. 87–8.
40. Hastings, *Church in Africa*, pp. 466–70; and Williams, *Ideal of a Self-Governing Church*, pp. 243–53.
41. Hastings, *Church in Africa*, p. 291 quoting C. Wood, *The Life of Charles Alan Smithies* (1898), p. 190.
42. Williams, *Ideal of the Self-Governing Church*, pp. 255–8.
43. See above pp. 96–7.
44. Williams, *Ideal of the Self-Governing Church*, pp. 77–83; Davidson and Benham, *Life of Tait*, 2: 356–8; Gibbs, *Church in India*, pp. 261–77.
45. Williams, *Ideal of the Self-Governing Church*, pp. 103–4.
46. Williams, *Ideal of the Self-Governing Church*, pp. 60–6.
47. Bengt Sundkler, *Church of South India: The Movement Towards*

Union 1900–1947 (1954), pp. 26–35 and 50–63.
48. Stanley, 'Commerce and Christianity', p. 78.
49. Williams, *Ideal of the Self-Governing Church*, p. 42.
50. Endacott and She, *The Diocese of Victoria, Hong Kong*, chapters 1–13.
51. For a more detailed discussion of this, see Stanley, *The Bible and the Flag*, pp. 45–52.

CHAPTER 7

1. Evans, *Churchman Militant*, p. 180.
2. Alan M.G. Stephenson, *Anglicanism and the Lambeth Conferences* (1978), pp. 51–3.
3. Evans, *Churchman Militant*, p. 223.
4. Stephenson, *Anglicanism*, p. 57.
5. Davidson and Benham, *Life of Tait*, 2: 363–4.
6. Stephenson, *Anglicanism*, pp. 57–8.
7. Davidson and Benham, *Life of Tait*, 2: 365.
8. Davidson and Benham, *Life of Tait*, pp. 2: 367–9.
9. *The Six Lambeth Conferences 1867–1920*, compiled by Lord Davidson of Lambeth (1929), pp. 17–19.
10. Stephenson, *Anglicanism*, pp. 61–3.
11. *Six Lambeth Conferences*, p. 25.
12. Davidson and Benham, *Life of Tait*, 2: 372–4.
13. Stephenson, *Anglicanism*, p. 63.
14. *Six Lambeth Conferences*, p. 24.
15. Davidson and Benham, *Life of Tait*, 2: 376.
16. Benson, *Life of Edward White Benson*, 2: 469.
17. Quoted in David L. Edwards, *Leaders of the Church of England 1828–1944* (1971), p. 213.
18. Benson, *Life of Edward White Benson*, 2: 467.
19. Stephenson, *Anglicanism*, p. 75.
20. *Six Lambeth Conferences*, p. 37.
21. Benson, *Life of Edward White Benson*, 2: 214.
22. G.K.A. Bell, *Randall Davidson, Archbishop of Canterbury*, 2 Vols (Oxford 1935), 1: 121.
23. See Oliver Tomkins, 'The Chicago-Quadrilateral and the Ecumenical Movement', in *Communion and Episcopacy: Essays to Mark the Centenary of the Chicago-Lambeth Quadrilateral*, ed. Jonathan Draper (Cuddesdon, Oxford 1988), pp. 5–7.
24. Stephenson, *Anglicanism*, pp. 84–8.
25. Hastings, *Church in Africa*, p. 496.
26. Alan Wilkinson, *The Community of the Resurrection: A Centenary History* (1992), p. 22.
27. Bell, *Randall Davidson*, 1: 300.
28. Stephenson, *Anglicanism*, pp. 100–4.
29. *Life and Letters of Mandell Creighton by His Wife*, 2 Vols (1904), 2: 240–1.
30. Benson, *Life of Edward White Benson*, 2: 474–8.

31. Stephenson, *Anglicanism*, p. 105.
32. Owen Chadwick, 'The Lambeth Conference: An Historical Perspective', in *Lambeth Conferences Past and Present*, ed. Guy Lytle (*Anglican and Episcopal History* 58, 1989), 270.
33. Stephenson, *Anglicanism*, p. 107.
34. Bell, *Randall Davidson*, 1: 291.
35. Bell, *Randall Davidson*, 1: 443, 452, and 562.
36. Bell, *Randall Davidson*, 1: 559.
37. Bell, *Randall Davidson*, 1: 569.
38. *Six Lambeth Conferences*, p. 43.
39. Stephenson, *Anglicanism*, p. 123.
40. Stephenson, *Anglicanism*, p. 123.
41. Wilkinson, *Community of the Resurrection*, p. 149.
42. Stephenson, *Anglicanism*, p. 121.
43. Roger Lloyd, *The Church of England 1900–1965* (London 1966), p. 145.
44. G.J. Cuming, *A History of Anglican Liturgy* (London 1969), pp. 236–43.
45. G.L. Prestige, *The Life of Charles Gore: A Great Englishman* (London 1935), p. 311.
46. Stephen Paget and J.M.C. Crum, *Francis Paget* (London 1912), p. 275.
47. Chadwick, *Lambeth Conferences*, p. 270.
48. Prestige, *Charles Gore*, p. 312.
49. Bell, *Randall Davidson*, 1: 692–708.
50. For the disestablishment of the Church in Wales, see Bell, *Disestablishment in Ireland and Wales*, pp. 226–322; David Walker, 'Disestablishment and Independence', in *A History of the Church in Wales*, ed. David Walker (Penarth 1976), pp. 164–171; and D.T.W. Price, *A History of the Church in Wales in the Twentieth Century* (Penarth 1990), pp. 3–13.
51. Herbert Hensley Henson, *Retrospect of an Unimportant Life*, 3 Vols (Oxford 1943), 2: 4.
52. *Six Lambeth Conferences*, p. 46j.
53. Stephenson, *Anglicanism*, p. 143.
54. J.G. Lockhart, *Cosmo Gordon Lang* (London 1949), p. 248.
55. Stephenson, *Anglicanism*, p. 145.
56. Ronald Jasper, *Arthur Cayley Headlam: Life and Letters of a Bishop* (London 1960), p. 149.
57. Ronald C.D. Jasper, *George Bell, Bishop of Chichester* (Oxford 1967), p. 57.
58. Lloyd, *Church of England*, pp. 405–11.
59. Henson, *Retrospect*, 2: 22.
60. Sundkler, *Church of South India*, pp. 58–63, 115, 131–2.
61. Gibbs, *Anglican Church in India*, pp. 353–8.
62. The leader of the Greek delegates was Athenagoras, who thirty years later was the ecumenical patriarch who received archbishop Ramsey of Canterbury at Constantinople in 1962.
63. Jasper, *Headlam*, p. 209.

64. Lockhart, *Lang*, p. 346.
65. Jasper, *Headlam*, p. 207.
66. Jasper, *Headlam*, pp. 211–12.
67. Sundkler, *Church of South India*, pp. 116–18, 162–85; and Jasper, *Bell*, p. 69.
68. Lockhart, *Lang*, p. 349.
69. Lockhart, *Lang*, p. 344.
70. Henson, *Retrospect*, 2: 276.
71. Quoted in Lockhart, *Lang*, p. 354.
72. Sundkler, *Church of South India*, pp. 328–33.
73. Eric Waldram Kemp, *The Life and Letters of Kenneth Escott Kirk, Bishop of Oxford 1937–1954* (London 1959), pp. 150–86; and George Seaver, *John Allen Fitzgerald Gregg, Archbishop* (London 1963), pp. 259–61.
74. Jasper, *Bell*, pp. 349–50.
75. Edward Carpenter, *Archbishop Fisher – His Life and Times* (Norwich, 1991), pp. 443–7, 454–5.
76. Carpenter, *Archbishop Fisher*, p. 460.
77. Carpenter, *Archbishop Fisher*, pp. 458–9.
78. Clarke, *West Africa and Christianity*, pp. 161–8; and Hastings, *Church in Africa*, pp. 494–532.
79. John V. Taylor, *Church in Buganda*, pp. 85–95; and F.B. Welbourn, *East African Rebels: A Study of Some Independent Churches* (London 1961), pp. 113–34.
80. Hastings, *Church in Africa*, p. 552.
81. Hastings, *Church in Africa*, pp. 587–600.
82. Hastings, *Church in Africa*, pp. 555–6.
83. Carpenter, *Archbishop Fisher*, pp. 500–2.
84. Carpenter, *Archbishop Fisher*, pp. 502–7.
85. John S. Peart-Binns, *Archbishop Joost de Blank: Scourge of Apartheid* (London 1987), p. 138.
86. Carpenter, *Archbishop Fisher*, p. 509.
87. Carpenter, *Archbishop Fisher*, pp. 520 and 543.
88. Adrian Hastings, *A History of African Christianity 1950–1975* (Cambridge 1979), pp. 112–14 and 160.
89. Peart-Binns, *Archbishop Joost de Blank*, pp. 137–9.
90. Cuming, *History of Anglican Liturgy*, p. 262.
91. Carpenter, *Archbishop Fisher*, p. 595.
92. Bell, *Randall Davidson*, 2:1227; and Endaott and She, *The Diocese of Victoria, Hong Kong*, p. 160.
93. Carpenter, *Archbishop Fisher*, pp. 649–65; and Sean Gill, *Women and the Church of England from the Eighteenth Century to the Present* (1994), pp. 242–3.
94. Carpenter, *Archbishop Fisher*, p. 692.
95. Carpenter, *Archbishop Fisher*, pp. 687–92.
96. Border, *Church and State in Australia*, pp. 275–6; and *Francis de Witt Batty: The Bishop, the Leader, the Man: Memoirs and Extracts from His Writings*, ed. Joan Murray (Newcastle, NSW 1996), pp. 66–8.

97. Border, *Church and State in Australia*, pp. 276–9; and Judd and Cable, *Sydney Anglicans*, pp. 210–14.
98. Carpenter, *Archbishop Fisher*, p. 486; and Judd and Cable, *Sydney Anglicans*, pp. 253–4.
99. Carpenter, *Archbishop Fisher*, pp. 488–9; Border, *Church and State in Australia*, pp. 279–80; and Judd and Cable, *Sydney Anglicans*, pp. 255–6.
100. Seaver, *Gregg*, pp. 130–40; and McDowell, *Church of Ireland*, pp. 94–7.
101. Carpenter, *Archbishop Fisher*, p. 460; and John S. Peart-Binns, *Ambrose Reeves: A Biography* (1975), p. 146.
102. Peart-Binns, *Ambrose Reeves*, p. 149.
103. Lloyd, *Church of England*, pp. 580–1.
104. Adrian Hastings, *A History of English Christianity 1920–1985* (1986), p. 449.
105. Owen Chadwick, *Michael Ramsey: A Life* (Oxford 1990), p. 99.
106. Peart-Binns, *Ambrose Reeves*, p. 146.
107. See Lesley Whiteside, *George Otto Simms: A Biography* (Gerrards Cross 1990), pp. 79–80; and for a fuller discussion R.C.D. Jasper, *The Development of Anglican Liturgy 1662–1980* (1989), pp. 190–5, 201–6 and 213–17.
108. For a more detailed discussion of these issues, see Stanley, *The Bible and the Flag*, pp. 16–26.

CONCLUSION

1. France, *Overseas Episcopate*, pp. 17–19.
2. Hastings, *Church in Africa*, p. 555.
3. *Crockford's Clerical Directory 1959–60* (London 1960).
4. John Howe, *Highways and Hedges: Anglicanism and the Universal Church* (1985), p. 81.
5. *The Lambeth Conference 1948* (1948), pp. 84ff.

Bibliography

Addleshaw, G.W.O., 'The Law and the Constitution of the Church Overseas', in *The Mission of the Anglican Communion*, eds E.R. Morgan and Roger Lloyd. SPCK and SPG 1948.

Ajayi, J.F.A., *Christian Missions in Nigeria 1841–1941: The Making of a New Elite*. Evanston, Ill., Northwestern University Press 1969.

Akenson, Donald Harman, *The Church of Ireland: Ecclesiastical Reform and Revolution 1832–1868*. New Haven, Yale University Press 1971.

Ashwell, A.R., *The Life of the Right Reverend Samuel Wilberforce, DD*. 3 Vols, 1880.

Avis, Paul, *Anglicanism and the Christian Church: Theological Resources in Historical Perspective*. Edinburgh, T&T Clark 1989.

Barnard, T.C., 'Protestants and the Irish Language 1675–1725' (*JEH* 44, 1993).

Bebbington, D.W., *Evangelicalism in Modern Britain: A History from the 1730s to the 1980s*. Unwin Hyman 1989.

Bell, G.K.A., *Randall Davidson, Archbishop of Canterbury*. 2 Vols, Oxford, Oxford University Press, 1935.

Bell, P.M.H., *Disestablishment in Ireland and Wales*. SPCK 1969.

Bennett, G.V., *The Tory Crisis in Church and State 1688–1730: The Career of Francis Atterbury, Bishop of Rochester*. Oxford, Clarendon Press 1975.

Benson, A.C., *The Life of Edward White Benson, Sometime Archbishop of Canterbury*. 2 Vols, 1900.

Bollom, J.D., 'English Christianity and the Australian Colonies 1788–1860' (*JEH* 28, 1977).

Border, Ross, *Church and State in Australia 1788–1872: A Constitutional Study of the Church of England in Australia*. SPCK 1972.

Bosher, R.S., *The American Church and the Formation of the Anglican Communion 1823–1853*. Evanston, Ill., Seabury Western Theological Seminary, 1962.

Bottigheimer, K., 'The Failure of the Reformation in Ireland: Une Question Bien Posée' (*JEH* 36, 1985).

Brent, Richard, *Liberal Anglican Politics: Whiggery, Religion, and Reform 1830–1841*. Oxford, Clarendon Press, 1987.

Brown, Callum G., *The Social History of Religion in Scotland since 1730*. Methuen 1987.

Burroughs, Peter, 'Lord Howick and the Colonial Church Establishment' (*JEH* 25, 1974).

Canny, Nicholas, 'Why the Reformation Failed in Ireland: Une Question Mal Posée' (*JEH* 30, 1979).

Carpenter, Edward, *The Protestant Bishop, Being the Life of Henry Compton 1632–1713, Bishop of London*. Longmans 1956.

Carpenter, Edward, *Archbishop Fisher – His Life and Times*. Norwich, Canterbury Press 1991.

Carpenter, Edward, *Thomas Sherlock 1678–1761*. SPCK 1936.

Carpenter, Edward, *Thomas Tenison, Archbishop of Canterbury: His Life and Times*. SPCK 1948.

Carrington, Philip, *The Anglican Church in Canada: A History*. Toronto, Collins, 1963.

Chadwick, Owen, *Mackenzie's Grave*. Hodder and Stoughton 1959.

Chadwick, Owen, 'The Lambeth Conference: An Historical Perspective', in *Lambeth Conferences Past and Present*, ed. Guy Lytle (*Anglican and Episcopal History* 58, 1989).

Chadwick, Owen, *Michael Ramsey: A Life*. Oxford, Oxford University Press, 1990.

Clark, J.C.D., *English Society 1688–1732: Ideology, Social Structure and Political Practice During the Ancien Regime*. Cambridge, Cambridge University Press, 1985.

Clarke, Aidan, 'Varieties of Uniformity: The First Century of the Church of Ireland' (*SCH* 25, 1989).

Clarke, Peter B., *West Africa and Christianity*. Edward Arnold 1986.

Cnattingius, Hans, *Bishops and Societies: A Study of Anglicanism and Colonial Expansion 1698–1850*. SPCK 1952.

Cowan, Ian B., *The Scottish Reformation: Church and Society in Sixteenth-Century Scotland*. Weidenfield and Nicolson 1982.

Cowie, Leonard W., *Henry Newman: An American in London 1708–1743*. SPCK 1956.

Crockford's Clerical Directory 1959–60. Oxford University Press 1960.

Cross, Claire, *The Royal Supremacy and the Elizabethan Church*. George Allen and Unwin 1969.

Cross, Claire, *Church and People 1450–1660*. Fontana 1976.

Cuming, G.J., *A History of Anglican Liturgy*. Macmillan 1969.

Cuthbertson, Brian, *The First Bishop: A Biography of Charles Inglis*. Halifax, Nova Scotia, Waegwoltic Press, 1987.

Davidson of Lambeth, Lord, *The Six Lambeth Conferences 1867–1920*. SPCK 1929.

Davidson, R.T. and William Benham, *The Life of Archibald Campbell Tait, Archbishop of Canterbury*. 2 Vols, 1891.

Dewey, Clive, *The Passing of Barchester: A Real Life Version of Trollope*. Hambledon Press 1991.

Doll, Peter M., 'American High Churchmanship and the Establishment of the First Colonial Episcopate in the Church of England' (*JEH* 43, 1992).

Donaldson, Gordon, *The Scottish Reformation*. Cambridge, Cambridge University Press, 1960.

Doran, Susan and Christopher Durston, *Princes, Pastors and People: The Church and Religion in England 1529–1689*. Routledge 1991.

Edwards, David L., *Leaders of the Church of England 1828-1944*. Oxford University Press 1971.

Elbourne, Elizabeth, 'The Foundation of the Church Missionary Society: The Anglican Missionary Impulse', in *The Church of England c. 1689-c. 1833: From Toleration to Tractarianism*, eds John Walsh, Colin Haydon and Stephen Taylor. Cambridge, Cambridge University Press 1993.

Ellis, Steven G., 'Economic Problems of the Church of Ireland: Why the Reformation Failed in Ireland' (*JEH* 41, 1990).

Endacott, George B., and Dorothy E. She, *The Diocese of Victoria, Hong Kong: A Hundred Years of Church History 1849-1949*. Hong Kong, Kelly and Walsh, 1949.

Evans, G.R. and J.Robert Wright, eds., *The Anglican Tradition*. London and Minneapolis, SPCK/Fortress, 1991.

Evans, John H., *Churchman Militant: George Augustus Selwyn, Bishop of New Zealand and Lichfield*. George Allen and Unwin 1964.

Fingard, Judith, *The Anglican Design in Loyalist Nova Scotia 1783-1816*. SPCK 1972.

Foster, Raymond Samuel, *The Sierra Leone Church: An Independent Anglican Church*. SPCK 1961.

France, W.F., *The Overseas Episcopate: Centenary History of the Colonial Bishoprics Fund*. Colonial Bishoprics Fund 1941.

Gibbs, M.E., *The Anglican Church in India 1600-1970*. New Delhi, ISPCK, 1972.

Gill, Sean, *Women and the Church of England from the Eighteenth Century to the Present*. SPCK 1994.

Goodridge, Sehon S., *Facing the Challenge of Emancipation: A Study of the Ministry of William Hart Coleridge, First Bishop of Barbados 1824-1842*. Bridgetown, Barbados, Cedar Press, 1981.

Gray, Charles N., *Life of Robert Gray, Bishop of Cape Town*. abr. ed., 1883.

Haigh, Christopher, *English Reformations: Religion, Politics and Society Under the Tudors*. Oxford, Clarendon Press, 1993.

Hallett, A.C. Hollis, *Chronicle of a Colonial Church 1612-1826: Bermuda*. Bermuda, Juniperhill Press, 1993.

Handy, Robert T., *A History of the Churches in the United States and Canada*. Oxford, Oxford University Press, 1976.

Hastings, Adrian, *Christian Marriage in Africa*. SPCK 1973.

Hastings, Adrian, *A History of African Christianity 1950-1975*. Cambridge Cambridge University Press, 1979.

Hastings, Adrian, *A History of English Christianity 1920-1985*. Collins 1986.

Hastings, Adrian, *The Church in Africa 1450-1950*. Oxford, Clarendon Press, 1994.

Hatchett, Marion J., 'The Anglican Liturgical Tradition', in *The Anglican Tradition*, ed. Richard Holloway. Mowbrays 1984.

Heitzenrater, Richard P., *Wesley and the People Called Methodists*. Nashville, Abingdon Press, 1995.

Hennell, Michael, *John Venn and the Clapham Sect*. Lutterworth Press 1958.

Henson, Herbert Hensley, *Retrospect of an Unimportant Life*. 3 Vols, Oxford, Oxford University Press, 1942–50.

Herklots, H.G.C., *Frontiers of the Church: The Making of the Anglican Communion*. Ernest Benn 1961.

Hinchliff, Peter, *The Anglican Church in South Africa: An Account of the History and Development of the Church of the Province of South Africa*. Darton, Longman and Todd 1963.

Hinchliff, Peter, *John William Colenso*. Nelson 1964.

Howe, John *Highways and Hedges: Anglicanism and the Universal Church*. CIO Publishing 1985.

Hughes, Derrick, *Bishop Sahib: A Life of Reginald Heber*. Worthing, Churchman Publishing, 1986.

Jasper, R.C.D., *George Bell, Bishop of Chichester*. Oxford, Oxford University Press, 1967.

Jasper, R.C.D., *The Development of Anglican Liturgy 1662–1980*. SPCK 1989.

Jasper, Ronald, *Arthur Cayley Headlam: Life and Letters of a Bishop*. Faith Press 1960.

Jennings, D.A., *The Revival of the Convocation of York*. York, University of York, Borthwick Papers, 1975.

Judd, Stephen and Kenneth Cable, *Sydney Anglicans: A History of the Diocese*. Sydney, Anglican Information Office, 1987.

Kemp, E.W., *Counsel and Consent: Aspects of the Government of the Church as Exemplified in the History of the English Provincial Synods*. SPCK 1961.

Kemp, E.W., *The Life and Letters of Kenneth Escott Kirk, Bishop of Oxford 1937–1954*. Hodder and Stoughton 1959.

Kirk-Smith, H., *William Thomson, Archbishop of York: His Life and Times 1819–1890*. SPCK 1958.

Lambeth Conference 1930: Encyclical Letter from the Bishops with Resolutions and Reports. SPCK 1930.

Lambeth Conference 1948: Encyclical Letter from the Bishops with Resolutions and Reports. SPCK 1948.

Lambeth Conference 1958: Encyclical Letter from the Bishops with Resolutions and Reports. SPCK and Seabury Press 1958.

Life and Letters of Mandell Creighton by His Wife. 2 Vols, 1904.

Lloyd, Roger, *The Church of England 1900–1965*. SCM Press 1966.

Lockhart, J.G., *Cosmo Gordon Lang*. Hodder and Stoughton 1949.

MacCulloch, Diarmad, *The Later Reformation in England 1547–1603*. Macmillan 1990.

Machin, G.I.T., *Politics and the Churches in Great Britain 1832–1868*. Oxford, Clarendon Press, 1977.

Machin, G.I.T., *Politics and the Churches in Great Britain 1869–1921*. Oxford, Clarendon Press, 1987.

Mather, F.C., *High Church Prophet: Bishop Samuel Horsley (1733–1806) and the Caroline Tradition in the Later Georgian Church*. Oxford, Clarendon Press, 1992.

McDowell, R.B., *The Church of Ireland 1869–1969*. Routledge and Kegan Paul 1975.

Meacham, Standish, *Lord Bishop: The Life of Samuel Wilberforce 1805–1873*. Cambridge, Mass., Harvard University Press, 1970.

Mills, Frederick W., Sr, *Bishops by Ballot: An Eighteenth-Century Revolution*. New York, Oxford University Press, 1978.

Minter, R.A., *Episcopacy Without Episcopate: The Church of England in Jamaica before 1824*. Upton upon Severn, Self Publishing Association, 1990.

Morrell, W.P., *The Anglican Church in New Zealand*. Dunedin, Anglican Church of the Province of New Zealand, 1973.

Murray, Joan, ed., *Francis de Witt Batty: The Bishop, the Leader, the Man: Memoirs and Extracts from His Writings*. Newcastle, NSW, Diocese of Newcastle, 1996.

Neill, Stephen, *Anglicanism*. Harmondsworth, Penguin, 1958.

Neill, Stephen, *A History of Christian Missions*. Harmondsworth, Penguin, 1964.

Nockles, Peter, *The Oxford Movement in Context: Anglican High Churchmanship 1760–1857*. Cambridge, Cambridge University Press, 1994.

Paget, Stephen and J.M.C. Crum, *Francis Paget*. 1912.

Pascoe, C.F., *Two Hundred Years of SPG: An Historical Account of the Society for the Propagation of the Gospel 1701–1901*. 1901.

Peart-Binns, John S., *Archbishop Joost de Blank: Scourge of Apartheid*. Muller, Blond and White 1987.

Peart-Binns, John S., *Ambrose Reeves: A Biography*. Victor Gollancz 1975.

Piggin, Stuart, 'Assessing Nineteenth-Century Missionary Motivation' (*SCH* 15, 1978).

Piggin, Stuart, 'The American and British Contribution to Evangelicalism in Australia', in *Evangelicalism: Comparative Studies of Popular Protestantism in North America, the British Isles and Beyond 1700–1990*, eds Mark A. Noll, David W. Bebbington and George A. Rawlyk. New York, Oxford University Press, 1994.

Pinnington, J.E., 'The Consular Chaplaincies and the Foreign Office Under Palmerston, Aberdeen and Malmesbury: Two Case Histories: Rome and Funchal' (*JEH* 27, 1976).

Pobee, John S., 'Newer Dioceses of the Anglican Communion', in *The Study of Anglicanism*, eds Stephen Sykes and John Booty. London and Philadelphia, SPCK/Fortress, 1988.

Porter, Andrew, 'Commerce and Christianity: The Rise and Fall of a Nineteenth Century Religious Slogan' (*Historical Journal* 28, 1985).

Prestige, G.L., *The Life of Charles Gore: A Great Englishman*. Heinemann 1935.

Price D.T.W., *A History of the Church in Wales in the Twentieth Century*. Penarth, Church in Wales Publications, 1990.

Robertson, Paul Struan, *Proclaiming Unsearchable Riches: Newcastle and the Minority Evangelical Anglicans 1788–1900*. Leominster, Gracewing Fowler Wright; Sydney, Centre for the Study of Australian Christianity, 1996.

Russell, C. *The Causes of the English Civil War*. Oxford, Oxford University Press, 1990.

Sachs, William L., *The Transformation of Anglicanism: From State Church* to Global Communion. Cambridge, Cambridge University Press, 1993.

Schenk, Wilbert R., *Henry Venn, Missionary Statesman*. Maryknoll, New York, Orbis Books, 1983.

Scotland, Nigel, *The Life and Work of John Bird Sumner, Evangelical Archbishop*. Leominster, Gracewing Fowler Wright, 1995.

Seaver, George, *John Allen Fitzgerald Gregg, Archbishop*. Faith Press 1963.

Shaw, G.P., *Patriarch and Prophet: William Grant Broughton 1786–1853: Colonial Statesman and Ecclesiastic*. Melbourne, Melbourne University Press, 1978.

Shiels, W.J., *The English Reformation 1530–1570*. Harlow, Longmans,1989.

Smyth, Charles, *Simeon and Church Order: A Study of the Origins of the Evangelical Revival in Cambridge in the Eighteenth Century*. Cambridge, Cambridge University Press, 1940.

Sosin, Jack M., 'The Proposal in the Pre-Revolutionary Decade for Establishing Anglican Bishops in the Colonies' (*JEH* 13, 1962).

Stanley, Brian, *The Bible and The Flag: Protestant Missions and British Imperialism in the Nineteenth and Twentieth Centuries*. Leicester, Apollos, 1990.

Stanley, Brian, 'British Evangelicals and Overseas Concerns 1833–1970', in *Evangelical Faith and Public Zeal: Evangelicals and Society in Britain 1780–1980*, ed. John Wolffe. SPCK 1995.

Stanley, Brian, 'Commerce and Christianity: Providence Theory, the Missionary Movement and the Imperialism of Free Trade 1842–1860' (*Historical Journal* 26, 1983).

Stephens, W.R.W., *The Life and Letters of Walter Farquhar Hook*, 2 Vols, 1878.

Stephenson, Alan M.G., *The First Lambeth Conference 1867*. SPCK 1967.

Stephenson, Alan M.G., *Anglicanism and the Lambeth Conferences*. SPCK 1978.

Stubley, Peter, *A House Divided: Evangelicals and the Establishment in Hull*. Hull, University of Hull Press, 1995.

Sundkler, Bengt, *Church of South India: The Movement Towards Union 1900–1947*. Lutterworth Press 1954.

Sykes, Norman, *Old Priest and New Presbyter: The Anglican Attitude to Episcopacy, Presbyterianism and Papacy since the Reformation*. Cambridge, Cambridge University Press, 1957.

Sykes, Norman, *Edmund Gibson, Bishop of London 1669–1748: A Study in Politics and Religion in the Eighteenth Century*. Oxford, Oxford University Press, 1926.

Sykes, Stephen W., ed., *Authority in the Anglican Communion: Essays Presented to Bishop John Howe*. Toronto, Anglican Book Centre, 1987.

Taylor, Brian, *The Anglican Church in Borneo 1848–1962*. New Horizon, Bognor Regis, 1983.

Taylor, John V., *The Growth of the Church in Buganda: An Attempt at Understanding*. SCM Press 1958.

Taylor, Stephen, 'Whig Bishops and America: The Politics of Church Reform in Mid-Eighteenth-Century America' (*Historical Journal* 36, 1993).

Thompson, H.P., *Into All Lands: The History of the Society for the*

Propagation of the Gospel in Foreign Parts 1701–1950. SPCK 1951.

Thompson, H.P., *Thomas Bray*. SPCK 1954.

Tomkins, Oliver, 'The Chicago-Lambeth Quadrilateral and the Ecumenical Movement', in *Communion and Episcopacy: Essays to Mark the Centenary of the Chicago-Lambeth Quadrilateral*, ed. Jonathan Draper. Oxford, Ripon College Cuddesdon Publications, 1988.

Walker, David, 'Disestablishment and Independence', in *A History of the Church in Wales*, ed. David Walker. Penarth, Church in Wales Publications, 1976.

Walls, A.F., 'A Christian Experiment: The Early Sierra Leone Company' (*SCH* 6, 1970).

Warren, Max, *The Missionary Movement from Britain in Modern History*. SCM Press 1965.

Warren, Max, *Social History and Christian Mission*. SCM Press 1967.

Webster, A.B., *Joshua Watson: The Story of a Layman 1771–1855*. SPCK 1954.

Welbourn, F.B., *East African Rebels: A Study of Some Independent Churches*. SCM Press 1961.

Welsh, P.J., 'The Revival of an Active Convocation of Canterbury 1852–1855' (*JEH* 10, 1959).

Welsh, P.J. 'Anglican Churchmen and the Establishment of the Jerusalem Bishopric' (*JEH* 8, 1957).

Whiteside, Lesley, *George Otto Simms: A Biography*. Gerrards Cross, Colin Smythe, 1990.

Wilkinson, Alan, *The Community of the Resurrection: A Centenary History*. SCM Press 1992.

Williams, C. Peter, '"Too Peculiarly Anglican": The Role of the Established Church in Ireland as a Negative Model in the Development of the Church Missionary Society's Commitment to Native Churches 1856–1872' (*SCH* 25, 1989).

Williams, C. Peter, 'British Religion and the Wider World: Mission and Empire 1800–1940', in *A History of Religion in Britain: Practice and Belief from Pre-Roman Times to the Present*, eds Sheridan Gilley and W.J. Shiels, Oxford, Blackwell, 1994.

Williams, C. Peter, *The Ideal of the Self-Governing Church: A Study in Victorian Missionary Strategy*. Leiden, E.J. Brill, 1990.

Williams, Glanmor, *Welsh Reformation Essays*. Cardiff, University of Wales Press, 1967.

Williams, Glanmor, *The Reformation in Wales*. Bangor, Headstart Press, 1991.

Withycombe, Robert S.M., 'Mother Church and Colonial Daughters: New Scope for Tensions in Anglican Unity and Diversity' (*SCH* 32, 1996).

Yates, T.E., *Venn and Victorian Bishops Abroad: The Missionary Policies of Henry Venn and their Repercussions Upon the Anglican Episcopate of the Colonial Period 1841–1872*. Uppsala, Swedish Institute of Missionary Research, 1978.

Yeo, Geoffrey, 'A Case Without Parallel: The Bishop of London and the Anglican Church Overseas 1660–1748' (*JEH* 44, 1993).

Index